Evolutionary Algorithms
in Theory and Practice

Evolutionary Algorithms in Theory and Practice

Evolution Strategies
Evolutionary Programming
Genetic Algorithms

Dr. Thomas Bäck

Informatik Centrum Dortmund, Germany

New York   Oxford

OXFORD UNIVERSITY PRESS

1996

Oxford University Press

Oxford   New York
Athens Auckland Bangkok Bombay
Calcutta Cape Town Dar es Salaam Delhi
Florence Hong Kong Istanbul Karachi
Kuala Lumpur Madras Madrid Melbourne
Mexico City Nairobi Paris Singapore
Taipei Tokyo Toronto

and associated companies in
Berlin   Ibadan

Published by Oxford University Press, Inc.,
198 Madison Avenue, New York, New York 10016

Oxford is a registered trademark of Oxford University Press

Library of Congress Cataloging-in-Publication Data
Bäck, Thomas, 1963–
Evolutionary algorithms in theory and practice:
evolution strategies, evolutionary programming,
genetic algorithms/ Thomas Bäck.
p. cm. Includes bibliographical references and index.
ISBN 0-19-509971-0 (hard cover)
1. Genetic algorithms.
2. Evolution (Biology)—Mathematical models.
I. Title.
QA402.5.B333 1995 006.3—dc20 95-13506

1 3 5 7 9 8 6 4 2

Printed in the United States of America
on acid-free paper

To Christa
("Du bist das Beste, was mir passieren konnte.")

Abstract

Evolutionary Algorithms (EAs) are a class of direct, probabilistic search and optimization algorithms gleaned from the model of organic evolution. The main representatives of this computational paradigm, Genetic Algorithms (GAs), Evolution Strategies (ESs), and Evolutionary Programming (EP), which were developed independently of each other, are presented in this work as instances of a generalized Evolutionary Algorithm. Based on this generalization and a formal framework for Evolutionary Algorithms, a detailed comparison of these three instances with respect to their operators, working principles, and existing theoretical background is performed. Some new theoretical results concerning recombination in Evolution Strategies, the convergence velocity and selection algorithm of Evolutionary Programming, and convergence properties of Genetic Algorithms are presented.

Besides the algorithmic aspect, the Evolutionary Algorithms are also compared experimentally by running them on a number of artificial parameter optimization problems (sphere model, step function, a generalized function after Ackley, a function after Fletcher and Powell, and a fractal function). On these problems, both concerning convergence velocity and convergence reliability an Evolution Strategy outperforms Evolutionary Programming, which is still slightly better than a Genetic Algorithm.

The second part of the thesis puts special emphasis on analyzing the behavior of simple Genetic Algorithms that work by mutation and (extinctive) selection. For such a $(\mu \overset{+}{,} \lambda)$-GA, a general convergence velocity theory is presented on the basis of order statistics and transition probabilities under mutation for the corresponding Markov chain. Closed expressions for these transition probabilities are presented for a particular objective function called "counting ones". Using these transition probabilities, the convergence velocity and optimal mutation rate for a $(1 \overset{+}{,} \lambda)$-GA are calculated numerically. It turns out that the optimal mutation rate depends mainly on $1/l$ (the reciprocal of the search space dimension) and on the distance to the optimum as well as the selective pressure. As λ increases (i.e., as selective pressure increases), both the optimal mutation rate and convergence velocity increase.

The informal notion of selective pressure admits a quantification by using takeover times (following earlier work by Goldberg) and selection probabilities. This quantification shows that selective pressure grows in the order proportional selection, linear ranking, tournament selection, (μ,λ)-selection, $(\mu+\lambda)$-selection. As clarified by a taxonomy and detailed comparison of selection methods, these five mechanisms represent all principal possibilities to perform selection in an Evolutionary Algorithm.

In addition to the counting ones problem, optimal mutation rates are also analyzed for a $(1+1)$-GA applied to a simple continuous parameter optimization problem. These investigations clearly demonstrate the superiority of a Gray code in comparison to the standard binary code, since the former does not create local optima at the coding level by itself as it is likely to happen when the latter is used. Concerning the

optimal mutation rate, however, both codes yield highly irregular schedules that prevent one from drawing any conclusion towards a heuristic
for an optimal mutation rate control.

The results concerning optimal mutation rates and selective pressure are confirmed by a parallel meta-evolution experiment. The meta-
algorithm, a hybrid of Genetic Algorithm and Evolution Strategy, evolves generalized Genetic Algorithms for an optimal convergence velocity.
The results of this experiment confirm that the optimal mutation rate
and convergence velocity increase as selective pressure increases. On
the other hand, the meta-algorithm clarifies that a combination of techniques from Evolution Strategies and Genetic Algorithms can be used
to develop algorithms for handling nonlinear mixed-integer optimization
problems.

Contents

APPENDICES

Evolutionary Algorithms
in Theory and Practice

Introduction

The conversation between Alice and the Cat gives a perfect characterization of the meandering path full of dead ends, sharp curves and hurdles
one has to follow when doing research. After three and a half years, my
first section of this path through wonderland ends up with the work
presented here. In its final form, it deals with Evolutionary Algorithms
(for parameter optimization purposes) and puts particular emphasis on
extensions and analysis of Genetic Algorithms, a special instance of this
class of algorithms. The structure of this research, however, has grown
over the years and is just slightly related to Classifier Systems, the original starting point of my work. These contain Genetic Algorithms as
a component for rule-discovery, and as Classifier Systems turned out
to lack theoretical understanding almost completely, the concentration
of interest on Genetic Algorithms was a natural step and provided the
basis of this work.

The book is divided into two parts that reflect the emphasis on Genetic Algorithms (part II) and the general framework of Evolutionary
Algorithms that Genetic Algorithms fit into (part I).

Part I concentrates on the development of a general description of
Evolutionary Algorithms, i.e. search algorithms gleaned from organic
evolution. These algorithms were developed more than thirty years ago
in the "ancient" times of computer science, when researchers came up
with the ideas to solve problems by trying to imitate the intelligent capabilities of individual brains and populations. The former approach, emphasizing an individual's intelligence, led to the development of research
topics such as artificial neural networks and knowledge-based symbolic
artificial intelligence. The latter emphasized the collective learning properties exhibited by populations of individuals, which benefit from a high
diversity of their genetic material. Modeling organic evolution provides

1

the basis for a variety of concepts such as genotype, genetic code, phenotype, self-adaptation, etc., which are incorporated into Evolutionary Algorithms.

Consequently, the necessary prerequisites to understand the relations between algorithmic realizations and biological reality are provided in chapter 1. In addition to this, chapter 1 clarifies the relationship between global random search algorithms and Evolutionary Algorithms, Artificial Intelligence and Evolutionary Algorithms, and computational complexity and Evolutionary Algorithms.

Provided with this background, the aim of chapter 2 consists in the presentation of Evolution Strategies, Evolutionary Programming, and Genetic Algorithms as specializations of a unifying formalization of a general Evolutionary Algorithm. This approach allows for a comparison of all components of the algorithms, for an identification of similarities and differences concerning their perception and algorithmic realization, and for the transfer of concepts and sometimes even of theoretical results between the algorithms. In addition to these advantages, chapter 2 may also serve as a detailed overview of the three mainstream representatives of Evolutionary Algorithms for solving parameter optimization problems.

The comparison of these three representatives is also performed in a practical way by running experiments on a number of artificial test functions, which are presented in chapter 3. The basic criteria according to which an assessment of the Evolutionary Algorithms is performed are the speed of the search on the one hand and the reliability of the search (in terms of the chance to get "good" results even if the problem is very complex) on the other hand. These informally stated criteria are clarified in chapters 1 and especially 4, where the experimental results are reported.

Part II focuses the research on Genetic Algorithms and reports on how the transfer of some concepts from Evolution Strategies (and Evolutionary Programming) to Genetic Algorithms was achieved. These concepts are related to the selection and mutation operators, such that chapters 5 and 6 deal with an investigation of the impact of selection operators and the mutation rate on the behavior of Genetic Algorithms. The selection operators are characterized in terms of "selective pressure," which allows for assessing the properties of selection operators in a reliable manner. With respect to mutation, the critical problem turns out to be that of an optimal setting of the mutation rate, considering the actual optimization problem and the influence of selection. This fundamental interaction between mutation and selection is identified to be of more importance than assumed so far, and part II sheds some light on this open question.

The results from chapter 6 are also confirmed by a special experiment reported in chapter 7, where a new kind of Evolutionary Algorithm is presented. This meta-Evolutionary Algorithm performs a search within the space of parameter settings of (generalized, according to chapter 5) Genetic Algorithms and yields results that perfectly come up to expectations derived from the theoretical results reported in chapter 6. In this way, part II clarifies by theoretical as well as experimental investigations that the role of mutation in Genetic Algorithms is generally underestimated and demonstrates how it might be effectively exploited. The work concludes by summarizing some of the important results and pointing toward a number of open questions for further work.

Before releasing the reader to the book's inner world, special thanks are due to all colleagues at the Chair of Systems Analysis for creating a cooperative and stimulating working atmosphere. The basis for this atmosphere is provided by Hans-Paul Schwefel, the head of the chair, to whom I am very grateful for giving me optimal working conditions and for his patience, understanding, and encouragement. Furthermore, I would like to thank Reiner Männer for his kindness to be my second examiner, Ray Paton for his generous help in polishing up my English, and David B. Fogel for his detailed and helpful technical comments. I always enjoyed the discussions with these experts in evolutionary computation.

Finally, a reviewer of the Deutsche Forschungsgemeinschaft (DFG) who recommended my initial project proposal to be worth financial support by DFG deserves my gratitude. Though experiencing a strong cut in research funding in general and basic research funding in particular, I have some hopes raised by receiving this support from DFG that basic research funding will not disappear from the German research scene.

Thomas Bäck
Dortmund, January 1995

Part I

A Comparison of Evolutionary Algorithms

1

Organic Evolution and Problem Solving

Evolutionary Algorithms (EAs), the topic of this work, is an interdisciplinary research field with a relationship to biology, Artificial Intelligence, numerical optimization, and decision support in almost any engineering discipline. Therefore, an attempt to cover at least some of these relations must necessarily result in several introductory pages, always having in mind that it hardly can be complete. This is the reason for a rather voluminous introduction to the fundamentals of Evolutionary Algorithms in section 1.1 without giving any practically useful description of the algorithms now. At the moment, it is sufficient to know that these algorithms are based on models of organic evolution, i.e., nature is the source of inspiration. They model the collective learning process within a *population* of *individuals*, each of which represents not only a search point in the space of potential solutions to a given problem, but also may be a temporal container of current knowledge about the "laws" of the environment. The starting population is initialized by an algorithm-dependent method, and evolves towards successively better regions of the search space by means of (more or less) randomized processes of *recombination, mutation,* and *selection.* The environment delivers a quality information (*fitness* value) for new search points, and the selection process favors those individuals of higher quality to reproduce more often than worse individuals. The recombination mechanism allows for mixing of parental information while passing it to their descendants, and mutation introduces innovation into the population. This process is currently used by three different mainstreams of Evolutionary Algorithms, i.e. *Evolution Strategies* (ESs), *Genetic Algorithms* (GAs), and *Evolutionary Programming* (EP), details of which are presented in chapter 2.

This chapter presents their biological background in order to have

7

the necessary understanding of the basic natural processes (section 1.1). Evolutionary Algorithms are then discussed with respect to their impact on Artificial Intelligence and, at the same time, their interpretation as a technique for machine learning (section 1.2). Furthermore, their interpretation as a global optimization technique and the basic mathematical terminology as well as some convergence results on random search algorithms as far as they are useful for Evolutionary Algorithms are presented in section 1.3. Finally, the chapter is concluded by a (surely incomplete) overview of the history of Evolutionary Algorithms, which now are well over thirty years old and are actually in an impressive period of revival with respect to empirical, theoretical, and application-oriented research.

1.1 Biological Background

Evolutionary Algorithms are based on a model of natural, biological evolution, which was formulated for the first time by Charles Darwin[1]. The *Darwinian theory of evolution* explains the adaptive change of species by the principle of *natural selection*, which favors those species for survival and further evolution that are best adapted to their environmental conditions (the saying "survival of the fittest," however, was coined by one of the protagonists of Darwin, H. Spencer, who wanted to clarify the seemingly tautological nature of Darwin's theory). In addition to selection, the other important factor for evolution recognized by Darwin is the occurrence of small, apparently random and undirected variations between the *phenotypes*, i.e., the manner of response and physical embodiment of parents and their offspring. These *mutations* prevail through selection, if they prove their worth in light of the current environment; otherwise, they perish. The basic driving force for selection is given by the natural phenomenon of production of offspring. Under advantageous environmental conditions, population size grows exponentially, a process which is generally limited by finite resources. When resources are no longer sufficient to support all the individuals of a population, those organisms are at a selective advantage which exploit resources most effectively.

This point of view is presently generally accepted as the correct macroscopic explanation of evolution. However, modern biochemistry and genetics has extended the Darwinian theory by microscopic findings concerning the mechanisms of heredity. The resulting theory is called *synthetic theory of evolution* or, sometimes, *neodarwinism*.

This theory is based on *genes*[2] as transfer units of heredity. Genes are occasionally changed by mutations. Selection acts on the individual (the individual is the *unit of selection*), which expresses in its phenotype the

---

[1]Independently of Darwin, A. R. Wallace came to the same conclusions.

[2]The definition of a gene is postponed here to section 1.1.2.

complex interactions within its *genotype*, i.e., its total genetic information, as well as the interaction of the genotype with the environment in
determining the phenotype. The *evolving unit* is the population which
consists of a common gene pool included in the genotypes of the individuals. The last three sentences characterize this theory in brief form,
but in order to have the basic terminology of genetics available and
to understand similarities and differences between the biological reality
and the algorithmic models, the genetic background will be explained
in more detail. The additional advantage is seen in the possibility to
encounter further natural principles which may be useful but are not
yet incorporated into the algorithms.

In the evolutionary framework, the *fitness* of an individual is measured only indirectly by its growth rate in comparison to others, i.e., its
propensity to survive and reproduce in a particular environment. Furthermore, natural selection is no active driving force, but differential
survival and reproduction within a population makes up selection. Selection is simply a name for the ability of those individuals that have
outlasted the struggle for existence to bring their genetic information
to the next generation. This point of view, however, reflects just our
missing knowledge about the mapping from genotype to phenotype, a
mapping which — if it were known — would allow us to evaluate fitness
in terms of a variety of physical properties.

In a biological context, the term *adaptation*[3] denotes a general advantage in ecological or physiological efficiency of an individual than
achieved by other members of the population, and at the same time it
denotes the process of attaining this state (see [May88], pp. 134–135).
Adaptation is a rather general term that includes nongenetic adaptation of an individual (*somatic adaptation*) as well as the genetic sense of
genotypic changes over many generations. The overall meaning of adaptation is often used synonymously with fitness, i.e., adaptation is the
propensity to grow up (and reproduce) (see [May88], p. 128). Furthermore, the term "adaptation" bears the question "to what?" Basically,
the answer is to any major kind of environment (*adaptive zone*) or, in a
broader sense, an ecological niche (the set of possible environments that
permit survival of a species).

A very popular metaphor for evolutionary change is given by Wright's
model of an *adaptive surface*. Possible biological trait combinations[4]
in a population of individuals define points in a high-dimensional sequence space, where each coordinate axis corresponds to one of these
traits. An additional dimension is used in this model to plot fitness
values for each point in the space, reflecting the selective advantage (or
disadvantage) of the corresponding individuals. In this way, a fitness
landscape or adaptive surface (topography) is defined, which in its sim-

---

[3]From "ad" and "aptare" (to fit on).

[4]Intentionally, a fuzzy terminology is used here. In section 1.1.1 it will become
clear how this space can be understood in terms of nucleotide base sequences.

plified, three-dimensional (two trait dimensions, one fitness-dimension) form looks just like a mountainous region, equiped with valleys, peaks, and ridges (see figure 1.1). When trait combinations in a population change and average fitness increases, the population moves uphill and simultaneously climbs some of the peaks. This way, a natural analogy to the optimization problem emerges by interpreting evolution as a process of fitness maximization in trait space.

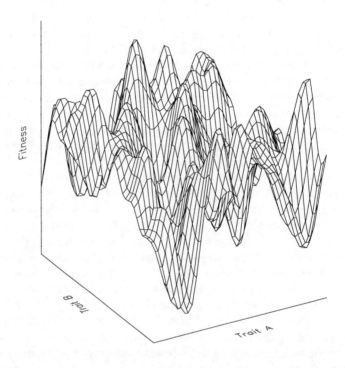

Fig. 1.1: Schematic diagram of an adaptive surface.

However, this is still a picture much too simple to be adequate. It suggests that evolution starts somewhere in the lower regions of sequence space and then steadily and gradually goes uphill, climbing the hill nearest to the starting point[5], indicating the possibility of early stagnation on a hill which is by far not the highest peak. Instead, there are some

---

[5]That is why deterministic optimization strategies following this metaphor are often called *hillclimbing* strategies.

further mechanisms which may allow a population to cross a region of lower fitness between two peaks on the adaptive surface, the most obvious one being environmental changes, which can result in transformation to a completely differently shaped surface. Furthermore, in small populations, fitness decreases can be caused by the phenomenon of *genetic drift*, therefore allowing for a valley-crossing, as Wright points out in the *shifting balance theory* ([Fut90], pp. 196–197). Genetic drift is simply a random decrease or increase of biological trait frequencies, leading to a probability distribution of these frequencies around the equilibrium values when several subpopulations (*demes*) under equal conditions are considered.

It is also worthwhile to mention the view summarized well in the work of Schull, that individuals themselves by means of an adaptation during their development and by trying to cope as best as they can with the situation are also changing the structure of the adaptive surface [Sch91]. On the whole, it is more adequate to think of the adaptive surface as dynamically changing by means of environment-population interactions, a process which is currently not understood completely.

The following excursion to biochemistry and genetics is based on [Got89] and [Küp90], two books (in German), which give excellent introductions even to the reader who is not so experienced with the material. Furthermore, the book by Futuyma [Fut90][6], a complete and instructive textbook on evolutionary biology, provides more information for the interested reader.

1.1.1   Life and Information Processing

Modern molecular genetics led to relatively detailed knowledge about the building plan of living beings, which is encoded in the *deoxyribonucleic acid* (DNA), a double-stranded macromolecule of helical structure (comparable to two intertwined spiral staircases). Both single strands are linear, unbranched nucleic acid molecules built up from alternating desoxyribose (sugar) and phosphate molecules. Each desoxyribose part is coupled to a *nucleotide base*, which is responsible for establishing the connection to the other strand of the DNA. The four nucleotide bases Adenine (A), Thymine (T), Cytosine (C) and Guanine (G) are the alphabet of the genetic information. The sequence of these bases in the DNA molecule determines the building plan of the organism.

The connection between both nucleotide strands is established by hydrogen bonds between the pairs Adenine and Thymine (two hydrogen bonds) and Guanine and Cytosine (three hydrogen bonds). Most importantly, both strands have complementary nucleotide base structures since the nucleotide bases are always arranged such that a *purine* base (Adenine or Guanine) in one strand is connected to a *pyrimidine* base (Thymine or Cytosine) in the other strand and vice versa. This

---

[6]The German translation of [Fut86].

way, the information encoded in the DNA is redundant and allows for a complete *replication* (identical doubling) during cell division. Then, the double helix of the DNA is split up into single strands. Free hydrogen bond places at the nucleotide bases provide positions of chemical reaction where new (complementary) nucleotide bases which stem from cell metabolism can be taken up. Usually only the special pairings (Adenine ↔ Thymine and Guanine ↔ Cytosine) of nucleotide bases are possible during this synthesis step, and under the influence of the enzyme DNA-*polymerase* both single strands are completed to form new copies of the original genetic information.

After having identified the DNA to be the information carrier of life (and evolution), the next important question concerns the mechanism which creates an organism (i.e., the phenotype) from its building plan (i.e., the genotype). On the single cell level, this connection is established by the mechanism of *protein biosynthesis*. Proteins are multiple folded biological macromolecules which consist of a long chain of *amino acids*. The metabolic effects of proteins are mainly caused by their three-dimensional folded structure (*tertiary structure*) as well as their symmetrical structure (*secondary structure*), which results from the amino acid order in the chain (*primary structure*). Typically, a *gene* on the DNA is defined to be a part of the DNA which includes the information for the synthesis of one protein.

The impact of genes on phenotypical features of an organism, however, is far more complicated than simply representing a one-to-one correspondence between genes and features. *Polygeny*, i.e., the combined influence of several genes on a single phenotypical characteristic, and *pleiotropy*, i.e., the influence of a single gene on several phenotypical features, represent the normal rather than the exceptional case (see e.g. [Got89], pp. 149–151, pp. 156–159). Related to these mechanisms, the term *epistasis* is used to denote the impact of one gene — the epistatic one — on the expression of another — the hypostatic — gene (see [Got89], p. 161)[7].

The alphabet of amino acids is finite, consisting of twenty different acids[8]. The process by which a protein (a string from a twenty letter alphabet) is obtained from the corresponding gene (a string from a four letter alphabet) is divided into two physically separated mechanisms called *transcription* and *translation*. In case of eukaryotes, the organisms' building plan is located in the nucleus of each cell, while bio-

---

[7]Davidor transferred the concept of epistasis to Genetic Algorithms as a measure for the nonlinearity and interdependency among the elements representing a genotype. Besides defining a mathematical measure of epistasis for Genetic Algorithms, he also identified the epistasis range for which application of Genetic Algorithms seems recommendable [Dav90, Dav91a].

[8]These are: Alanine (ALA), Arginine (ARG), Aspartic acid (ASP), Cysteine (CYS), Glutamine (GLN), Glutamic acid (GLU), Glycine (GLY), Histidine (HIS), Isoleucine (ILE), Leucine (LEU), Lysine (LYS), Methionine (MET), Phenylanaline (PHE), Proline (PRO), Serine (SER), Threonine (THR), Thryptophane (TRP), Tyrosine (TYR), and Valine (VAL).

synthesis of proteins is performed by the *ribosomes*. The information is transferred from nucleus to ribosome by a *messenger ribonucleic acid* (mRNA) molecule, which is synthesized in the nucleus by means of the transcription process. Similar to nucleic acid, mRNA is a single-stranded molecule which has ribose as its sugar component and carries information by means of the nucleotide bases Adenine, Cytosine, Guanine, and Uracil (U) replacing Thymine. The process of transcription proceeds as follows:

- The enzyme RNA-polymerase loosens the DNA-strand.

- Only one, the so-called *coding strand* of the DNA serves as a matrix for the copy process.

- Recognition regions (*promoters*) on the strands determine the beginning of a gene as well as the coding strand.

- Stop sequences determine the termination point of transcription.

First base	Second base				Third base
	U/T	C	A	G	
RNA: Uracil (U) DNA: Thymine (T)	PHE	SER	TYR	CYS	U/T
	PHE	SER	TYR	CYS	C
	LEU	SER	Stop	Stop	A
	LEU	SER	Stop	TRY	G
Cytosine (C)	LEU	PRO	HIS	ARG	U/T
	LEU	PRO	HIS	ARG	C
	LEU	PRO	GLN	ARG	A
	LEU	PRO	GLN	ARG	G
Adenine (A)	ILE	THR	ASN	SER	U/T
	ILE	THR	ASN	SER	C
	ILE	THR	LYS	ARG	A
	Start/MET	THR	LYS	ARG	G
Guanine (G)	VAL	ALA	ASP	GLY	U/T
	VAL	ALA	ASP	GLY	C
	VAL	ALA	GLU	GLY	A
	VAL	ALA	GLU	GLY	G

Table 1.1. The genetic code.

In this way, transcription creates an mRNA molecule which reflects the structure of the coding strand, except the nucleotide base Thymine is substituted for by Uracil. The mRNA molecules are translocated to the ribosome, where their information is used to synthesize the corresponding protein. The ribosome performs a mapping from triplets of nucleotide bases to amino acids. Each triplet (*codon*) encodes exactly one amino acid or serves as an indicator for starting and stopping the synthesis. The *genetic code*, which is the same for all living beings and has remained unchanged, is given explicitly in table 1.1. Since three positions having four occupation possibilities each are sufficient for encoding $4^3 = 64$ different symbols, the genetic code is redundant. However, only two positions would not suffice to encode twenty amino acids.

Translation from nucleotide base code to amino acid sequence is performed biochemically by adapter-molecules of *transfer*-RNA (tRNA). These molecules are responsible for transport and application of amino acids. At one end, the tRNA-molecules carry an *anticodon* which is complementary to a codon and is bonded to it by hydrogen bonds, such that the codon at the mRNA can be recognized by the tRNA. At the other end, the tRNA molecules carry the amino acid which the codon on the mRNA is mapped to and which is easily passed to the protein chain. For a small segment of DNA the mechanisms of transcription and translation are schematically shown in figure 1.2.

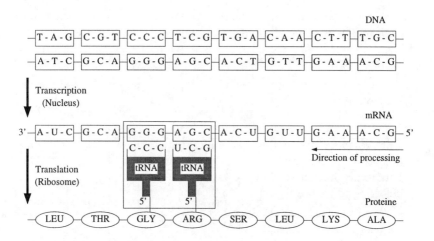

Fig. 1.2: Simplified scheme of protein biosynthesis in living cells.

The processes described so far are basically biochemical information processing mechanisms. They imply the *central dogma* of molecular genetics which states that information is passed from genotype to phenotype, i.e.:

$$DNA \longrightarrow RNA \longrightarrow Protein$$

The dogma implies the proof of the incorrectness of *Lamarckism*, i.e., the theory which states that behaviorally acquired characteristics of an individual can be passed to its offspring. This is impossible, because the phenotype does not change the genotype, there is no information flow backwards[9].

To complete this section on the biochemical background of neodarwinism, the structure of the genetic information contained in the DNA sequence is briefly explained. On the level of single symbols, four different nucleotide bases were identified to form the alphabet of the genetic language. Groups consisting of three nucleotide bases are the units of translation, i.e., symbol groups which encode amino acids or start and stop information for transcription. These groups are called *codons*. A *gene* is a unit which encodes a protein and consists of up to about one thousand codons. However, often not all information of a gene is used for translation, rather the gene subdivides into *exons*, i.e., sequences which are translated, and *introns*, i.e., sequences between exons which do not bear genetic information for the phenotype of the organism[10]. Both the units of transcription (*scriptons*), consisting of up to a few genes each, and the units of replication (*replicons*), consisting of up to several hundred scriptons, are hierarchical organization structures which are mentioned here only for completeness. On the next higher level of organization, the *chromosomes* are structures consisting of some replicons. Chromosomes provide an important logical unit of information transmission to the next generation, as will become clearer in the following section. All genes of an organism, distributed over several chromosomes, are summarized under the term *genome*. Finally, the *genotype* of an organism includes its complete genetic material, i.e., the building plan of the organism. Conceptually, it differs from the genome by a more abstract interpretation, while the term genome is also used to denote the sum of all chromosomes from a cytological[11] point of view.

For providing an overview of the hierarchy discussed so far, table 1.2 summarizes the previous[12]. In chapter 2, the analogies to terminology and information structure in Evolutionary Algorithms will be clarified by referring to this table again.

1.1.2   Meiotic Heredity

The processes discussed in the previous section are in the first place mechanisms responsible for the *ontogenesis* of an organism, i.e., its de-

---

[9]This is true with the exception of some RNA-viruses that show the phenomenon of reverse transcription: The virus-RNA is used as a blueprint for a DNA-molecule, which is then inserted into the host genome (see [Fut90], p. 79).

[10]When the gene includes both exons and introns, by means of transcription a precursor-mRNA containing both introns and exons is created, which is afterwards, by a process called *splicing*, reduced to mRNA, consisting solely of exons.

[11]Cytology: Science of cell and cell division.

[12]The terms *meiosis* and *mitosis* will be explained in section 1.1.2.

Information unit	Function	Number per organism (complexity dependent)
nucleotide base	single symbol	4
codon	unit of translation	64
gene	unit which encodes a protein	several thousand
scripton	unit of transcription	several thousand
replicon	unit of reproduction	some
chromosome	meiotic unit	few
genome	mitotic unit	1
genotype	total information	1

Table 1.2. Hierarchy of the genetic information.

velopment from the fertilized zygote until its death. A fundamental basis of ontogenesis is *mitosis*, the process of cell division by which identical[13] genetic material is distributed to two emerging new cells. After mitosis both nuclei have the same number of chromosomes as the initial cell had. In full-grown organisms, the organs consist of differentiated cells which do not undergo cell divisions. However, most organisms also possess some tissues which continually produce new cell material, e.g., the skin, the bone marrow, and, most importantly for evolution, tissues within the sexual organs. In Evolutionary Algorithms, mitosis is generally neglected because the factor of interest is to model a sequence of generations, i.e., *phylogeny* (evolution) instead of ontogeny. Furthermore, the algorithmic model is based on one set of genetic information per individual, i.e., from a biological point of view unicellular, *haploid* organisms are modeled. In the *diploid* case (e.g., in the case of humans) each body cell includes two sets of chromosomes, such that for each chromosome two *homologous* forms[14] exist. In contrast, haploid organisms possess only one set of chromosomes per body cell. For diploid organisms, corresponding genes in homologous chromosomes are called *alleles*, which make up a much more complicated hereditary situation (summarized by the *Mendelian laws*) than in the haploid case. The details are omitted here, because Evolutionary Algorithms are by far not advanced to a level of development at which complete Mendelian genetics would be benefitted by. However, to see the basic mechanism, the obvious fact that

---

[13]Mutations may occur during mitosis. Later on, when discussing mutations in general, this event will be discussed briefly.

[14]The structure of both sets of chromosomes is identical, but their genetic information content may be different.

alleles of diploid organisms may be identical (*homozygotic*) or different (*heterozygotic*) is worthy of mention here. For the former case, it is at least clear which allele is passed to the offspring. In most cases, only one of two different alleles included in the offspring's genome is phenotypically expressed[15]. This allele is called the *dominant* one in contrast to the other, *recessive* one.

Important for the process of reproduction is not the mitotic but the *meiotic* cell division, which works differently in diploid compared to haploid organisms. First, the diploid mechanism of meiosis is discussed, since although it is more complicated than the haploid case it provides a deeper understanding of the process and can easily be transferred and reduced to the haploid case.

Mainly, meiosis in diploid organisms is the process through which germ cells (*gametes*) are created. In order to form a new diploid zygote by fusion of a gamete from a male and a female parent organism, gametes must be haploid cells. Thus, during meiosis the double genome of a cell is reduced to create two cells containing only one genome each. Practically, four daughter nuclei with a reduced number of chromosomes emerge from the original cell by means of two subsequent cell divisions. What is genetically more important are reordering processes of the genomes as well as reorganization processes of chromosomes during meiosis, which both cause the emergence of gametes consisting of recombined[16] haploid genetic material.

The functional units during the first meiotic *metaphase* and former phases of meiosis are homologous pairs of chromosomes, so-called *bivalents*. The bivalent forms orientate randomly, such that in the following division phase the assignment of chromosomes to one or the other haploid group of chromosomes is stochastic. This completes the first meiotic division, and the second division simply reproduces the new haploid genetic material once again, leading to four haploid cells (*gones*), precursors of the gametes. Before genomes are reordered in the first metaphase, chromosomes undergo reorganization processes in the bivalents during a meiotic stage called *pachytene*. Every chromosome consists of two structurally identical parallel elements, *chromatids*, which are connected in a special region called *centromere*[17]. It is important to see that corresponding regions of chromatids are duplicates of one single allele; different alleles can only occur on different homologous chromosomes. This way, a bivalent really consists of four parallel chromatids. Chromat-

---

[15]An important exception is known as the effect of *incomplete dominance*, where individuals that are heterozygotic for a certain gene can generate a different phenotypic characteristic than either of two alternative homozygotic conditions.

[16]*Recombinants* are organisms having redistributed alleles in some genes when comparing them to their ancestor forms.

[17]The human genome can in this phase best be analyzed, such that usually chromosomes look like an "X" or "Y" when looking at colored microscopic pictures. However, this phase is only obtained by replication processes during the *interphase*, a phase preceding meiosis.

ids at the same chromosome are usually called *sister-chromatids*. Reorganization processes between adjacent non-sister-chromatids occurring in the pachytene phase are called *crossing-over*[18] (or intrachromosomous recombination). Their effect is a segment exchange of chromosome parts. For the diploid case, heterozygotous allele pairs Aa and Bb, and one crossover point the mechanism is shown schematically in figure 1.3.

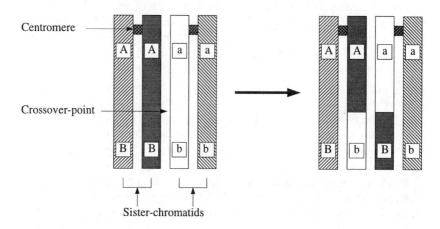

Fig. 1.3: Scheme of one-point crossover between non-sister-chromatides.

The location of the crossover position(s) is completely at random. Furthermore, the number of crossover points depends on the length of the chromosome. In nature, between one and eight crossover points have been observed ([Got89], p. 118).

Caused by these effects, the haploid genetic material of the gametes is usually not identical to any of the two genomes of their parent cell. However, further changes in the genetic material may occur. Before discussing these *mutations*, we return to haploid organisms, where meiosis must necessarily be different from the diploid analogue. In haploid organisms, gametes are of course haploid[19], such that meiosis is a process which follows cell fusion in the zygote and reduces the diploid zygote to a normal haploid cell. Recombination and crossover processes occur in the zygote. Evolutionary Algorithms, as we will see in chapter 2, are generally models of the haploid case.

Concluding this section, table 1.3 summarizes the characteristics of meiosis as discussed above.

---

[18]Crossing-over is often abbreviated as *crossover*, a terminology which will be used from now on.

[19]This implies that gametes are in this case formed by mitosis rather than meiosis.

Occurrence	Diploid organisms: In sexual organs.
	Haploid organisms: In zygotes.
Purpose	Diploid organisms: Formation of gametes.
	Haploid organisms: Recreation of haploid phase.
Development	Two subsequent cell divisions.
	• First Prophase:
	Formation of bivalents.
	Crossover of chromosomes.
	• First Metaphase:
	Reordering of genomes.
	• First Anaphase:
	Halving of the chromosome number.
	Second meiotic division.
Result	Four haploid daughter cells having unequal
	genetic material.

Table 1.3. Characteristics of meiosis.

1.1.3   Mutations

Although DNA-replication is a copying process of overwhelming exactness, it is (fortunately) not perfect. Mutation processes of the genetic material can be caused by a variety of factors, the simplest one being a replication error switching a specific base pair in the original DNA strand to the other possible base pair in the copy. According to data given by Futuyma ([Fut90], pp. 82–83), the bacterium eschericia coli has a genome consisting of $3.8 \cdot 10^6$ base pairs and a probability of spontaneous base pair mutation in the order of $4 \cdot 10^{-10}$. This amounts to a mutation probability per genome and per generation in the order $2 \cdot 10^{-3}$. For the human genome, these values are a factor of one thousand greater. Gottschalk gives a probability of $6 \cdot 10^{-6}$ up to $8 \cdot 10^{-6}$ for the occurrence of a spontaneous mutation of a specific gene ([Got89], p. 197), which is in good agreement with Futuyma's data giving values of 0.5 up to 14.3 mutations per 10^6 cells or gametes, respectively, depending on the specific gene ([Fut90], p. 83).

Such small error rates for the genetic information of mammalian genomes are achieved by providing *repair mechanisms* for DNA, which have emerged during evolution and are also encoded in the DNA (see [Got89], pp. 269–271). Special enzymes are encoded in the DNA, which have been identified as repair enzymes for a variety of damages of the

double strand[20]. In addition to repair enzymes, *mutator genes* that increase the mutation rate of other genes within the genome have also been
identified ([Got89], p. 182). Altogether, the total mutation rate of an
organism is in part regulated by its own genotype (we will return to this
biological fact as a model for algorithmic improvements of Evolutionary
Algorithms in several chapters of the book).

Besides replication errors on a normal level (implicit in the replication process), exogenous factors, so-called *mutagenes*, can drastically
increase mutation probabilities. Examples are radiation (X-ray, ultravi-
olet, cosmic radiation, gamma rays) and some chemical substances.

Mutations can be subdivided according to different criteria. In the
following, a brief look at the classification based on the location of mutations within the organism and a more detailed one at the classification
with respect to the kind (and amount) of mutational deviation are given.

According to the location, *somatic* and *generative* mutations are distuingished. Generative mutations are those which take place in the germ
path or in gametes and are therefore mutations which are passed to the
offspring, while somatic mutations occur in body cells and can therefore
not be passed to the offspring. Somatic mutations may be tragic for
the single individual, e.g. when a carcinogenic *oncogene* is activated by
a single base-pair mutation. However, these mutations do not influence
the development of the species. Therefore, generative mutations are of
main interest in Evolutionary Algorithms[21].

When looking at the kind of mutation, three different deviations of
the copy from the original are usually distinguished:

- *Gene mutations*: A particular gene is changed and may cause a
  deviating effect to the organism.

- *Chromosome mutations*: The gene ordering within a chromosome
  is changed, leading to a new arrangement of genes within the chromosome. Furthermore, the number of genes within the chromosome may be increased or decreased.

- *Genome mutations*: Either the number of genomes or the number
  of chromosomes is increased or decreased.

Gene mutations can be further divided into a number of groups according to the amount of information changed in the gene. *Small mutations* are typically neutral with respect to their selective effect, i.e., they
do not negatively affect the viability of the organism. In contrast, *large
mutations* cause clearly recognizable deviations in the phenotype. They

[20]Some of these mechanisms are e.g. *excision-repairing* (damaged parts are cut
out and substituted by normal ones), *information transfer corrections* (by enzymes
during replication), and *postreplicative repairing*.

[21]With the exception of an early study presented by Schwefel, who tried to model
the process of somatic mutations to apply Evolution Strategies to discrete optimization problems [Sch75a]. More general processes of ontogeny are the subject of
so-called *Haeckel strategies* [BE91].

provide the basis of racial differences, but they are also the cause of defect and lethal mutations. *Progressive (constructive) mutations* are in principle macromutations, which can cause crossings of boundaries between species. Gene mutations in the form of small mutations (especially point mutations) are common models for mutation in Evolutionary Algorithms.

Chromosome mutations can be divided into the following three main groups according to their quantitative or qualitative effect on the genes:

- Losses of chromosome regions (*deficiencies* and *deletions*).

- Doubling of chromosome regions (*duplications*).

- Reorganization of chromosomes (*translocations* and *inversions*).

A necessary prerequisite for chromosome mutations is always the occurrence of breaks in the chromosome. A *deficiency* is a terminal segment loss, caused by the occurrence of one break, while an internal segment loss is called *deletion* and requires the occurrence of two breaks in one chromosome. Both events occur in a single chromosome and are often summarized under the term deficiency. Chromosome mutations can best be investigated (and are sometimes only possible) in the so-called pachyteous phase, between non-sister-chromatides. In the following graphics, however, we restrict attention to as much chromatides or chromosomes as needed for demonstrating the working mechanisms of mutation. Figure 1.4 demonstrates both the effect of a deficiency and a deletion[22].

A *duplication* process requires two homologous starting chromosomes and leads to the doubling of a certain region on one chromosome at the expense of a corresponding deficiency on the other chromosome. After completion of two breaks and restitutional events both resulting chromosomes differ in their structure. Generally, when such an event occurs during meiosis, the deficient gamete is not capable of fertilization. On the contrary, the gamete containing the duplication often shows normal functionality. The schematic mechanism of a duplication event is shown in figure 1.5.

The effects of duplications and deficiencies on the chromosome structure are of a quantitative nature. *Inversion* is a mutation which instead only qualitatively changes the chromosome by rotating an internal segment of the chromosome by 180° and refitting it into the chromosome. A necessary requirement for inversion is the occurrence of two breaks as it is the case for a deletion. When the chromosome is doubly broken, both deletion and inversion have an equal probability of occuring. The principal mechanism of inversion is shown in figure 1.6.

Finally, *translocation* denotes a process by which genetic material is exchanged between *nonhomologous* chromosomes, without any loss of

---

[22]Numbers in the graphics denote chromosomal regions.

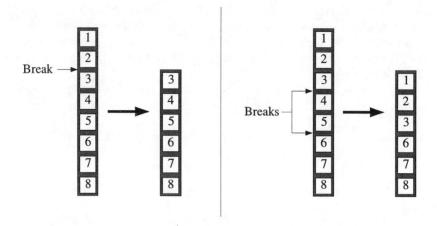

Fig. 1.4: Scheme of terminal (deficiency, left) and internal (deletion, right) segment losses.

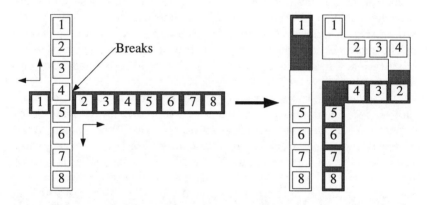

Fig. 1.5: Scheme of a duplication event.

genetic material. Translocation results in two newly combined chromosomes. In principle, with respect to its effect the mechanism is comparable to a one-point crossover, the main difference being that crossover is defined to operate on homologous chromatides. Therefore, we refer to figure 1.3, where the process working on the inner both non-sister-chromatides is schematically identical to the process acting on nonhomologous chromosomes in case of translocation.

We conclude this section by giving some information on genome mutations. Generally, the phenomenon of a change in the number of

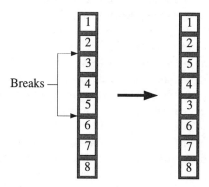

Fig. 1.6: Scheme of an inversion event.

chromosomes is called *polyploidy*, further subdivided into *euploidy* and *aneuploidy*. Euploidy means a change of the genome by complete additional sets of chromosomes, while in the case of aneuploidy a deviation by single chromosomes or chromosome groups is denoted. For aneuploidy, both increases (*hyperploidy*[23]) and decreases (*hypoploidy*[24]) of chromosome number are observed in nature.

So far, genome mutations have not been tested as an extension of evolutionary algorithms. However, some chromosome mutations like duplications, deletions, and inversions were investigated, and we will give some references when discussing the algorithms in chapter 2.

1.1.4   Molecular Darwinism

The complete human genome consists of approximately one billion nucleotide bases (e.g., see [Got89], p. 86). For each position within this information chain one out of four different nucleotide bases can theoretically be placed in the location. This simple consideration leads to a number of $4^{1.000.000.000}$ combinatorial sequence possibilities, a number which is more than huge: It is in fact far beyond any imagination[25]. Even for very much shorter sequences of several hundred nucleotide bases encoding single proteins the probability of creating a special sequence at

---

[23]Important examples of polysomy are trisomics such as those concerning the X-chromosome of human females. Normally, this does not create a striking abnormality ([Got89], p. 334).

[24]A hypoploidy that concerns a sexual chromosome of humans is normally lethal ([Got89], p. 334).

[25]In order to give an impression of the magnitude of this search space, we would like to mention that currently the number 10^{120} is accepted as a kind of universal complexity limit, since it is an upper bound on the number of possible events in the universe up until now. The number results as a product of the 10^{80} stable elementary particles in the universe and the age of the universe, counted by elementary time units, which amounts to about 10^{40}.

random is vanishingly small, such that, from a non-teleological point of
view, the random emergence of self-reproducing units can be called impossible. Throughout this book, we will discuss a more adequate point
of view which is able to explain the efficiency of biological evolution
much better than the pure random search interpretation.

It is thanks to Eigen that the evolution of macromolecules and the
emergence of a unique genetic code are in principle understood, and we
will briefly present an overview of his theory of *molecular Darwinism*,
based on [Eig71, Eig76, Küp90].

At its core, the theory explains the chemical part of evolution starting
from very short and simple molecules capable of replication up to the
first cells. To do so, the idea of Darwinian selection is transferred to any
kind of evolving system in general and macromolecules in particular by
identifying the *necessary* conditions for Darwinian selection:

- *Metabolism*: Any individual species must be built up from energy-
  rich matter which is transformed into energetically lower states,
  i.e., the system must be open and far from equilibrium.

- *Self-reproduction*: Only by means of self-reproduction concurrent
  behavior and selection can emerge.

- *Mutation*: New information can only be generated by a process of
  self-replication with errors.

Considering s different species $i \in \{1, \ldots, s\}$ and their concentrations x_i under the assumptions metabolism, self-reproduction, and mutability Eigen formulated rate equations for the dynamical behavior of
species (see [Eig71], p. 476):

$$\dot{x}_i := \frac{dx_i}{dt} = (A_i Q_i - D_i)x_i + \sum_{k \neq i} \varphi_{ik} x_k + \Phi_0 \frac{x_i}{\sum_{k=1}^s x_k} \quad . \quad (1.1)$$

Here Q_i denotes the *quality factor* and is equal to the fraction of
error-free copies created by replication. A_i is a functional term summarizing concentrations of energy-rich fundamental substances, and the
whole term $A_i Q_i x_i$ is interpreted as the build-up term resulting from
self-replication. On the contrary, D_i denotes a limiting effect on the
lifetime of states, such that the term $-D_i x_i$ incorporates processes of
destruction. Altogether, both terms describe the metabolism, proportionality to x_i includes self-reproduction, and Q_i describes mutability
of the species. Additionally, x_i may grow by errors that occur during
reproduction processes of members of another class $k \neq i$. For all such
classes different from i this effect is summarized in the term $\sum_{k \neq i} \varphi_{ik} x_k$,
where φ_{ik} can be interpreted as transition probability from class k to
class i. Finally, growth and shrinking processes of the total number
of individuals are included in a flow Φ_0, which enters the equation in
proportion to the relative concentration of species i.

Under the assumption of a *constant overall organization* of the system described by the set (1.1) of s differential equations, it can be transformed further. Constant overall organization means buffering the concentrations A_i of energy-rich substances, such that $A_i Q_i = $ const. Furthermore, the total size of the system is limited[26], i.e.:

$$\sum_{k=1}^{s} x_k = c_s = \text{const} \quad . \tag{1.3}$$

Then, in order to remain at a constant population size and defining $E_k := A_k - D_k$, the *excess productivity* $\sum_{k=1}^{s} E_k x_k$ must be compensated by transportation through the flow Φ_0, such that

$$\Phi_0 = -\sum_{k=1}^{s} E_k x_k \quad . \tag{1.4}$$

By defining an *average excess productivity*

$$\bar{E}(t) = \frac{\sum_{k=1}^{s} E_k x_k}{\sum_{k=1}^{s} x_k} \tag{1.5}$$

equations (1.1) can be transferred to

$$\dot{x}_i = (W_i - \bar{E}(t))x_i + \sum_{k \neq i} \varphi_{ik} x_k \quad , \tag{1.6}$$

where $W_i = A_i Q_i - D_i$ characterizes the *selective value* of a species i. The equations (1.6) are inherently nonlinear, since $\bar{E}(t)$ includes the variable x_i. Explicit solutions of (1.6) have been obtained by Eigen under certain conditions, the most important one being constant overall organization. He presented solutions for the case of completely neglected information flow into and out of mutant copies ($\sum_{k \neq i} \varphi_{ik} x_k = 0$) as well as for the case of an approximate consideration of error production, i.e., single-digit defects.

The average productivity $\bar{E}(t)$ provides a self-adjusting threshold value which reflects the self-organization of the system. Only those species having selective values W_i above the threshold $\bar{E}(t)$ will grow, consequently shifting $\bar{E}(t)$ to higher values until an optimum of $\bar{E}(t)$ is

---

[26]This condition also implies a conservation law for the error copies, since any error copy created from one species must enter another species of the system, i.e.:

$$\sum_{i=1}^{s} A_i(1 - Q_i)x_i = \sum_{i=1}^{s} \sum_{k \neq i} \varphi_{ik} x_k \quad . \tag{1.2}$$

reached, representing the maximum selective value of all species. This is characterized as an extremum principle of the form

$$\lim_{t \to \infty} \bar{E}(t) = \lambda_{\max} \quad , \tag{1.7}$$

where $\lambda_{\max}$ denotes the maximum eigenvalue of the $s \times s$-matrix $\mathbf{W} = (\varphi_{ik})$ of transition probabilities between the different classes ($\varphi_{ii} = W_i$)[27].

The largest eigenvalue $\lambda_{\max}$ will in most cases equal the maximum diagonal coefficient $W_{\max}$, up to a second order perturbation term of the form $\sum_{k \neq m} \varphi_{mk}\varphi_{km}/(W_m - W_k)$. The *selection criterion*, which would allow growing of a new species m to become the dominant one, is given by

$$W_m > \bar{E}_{k \neq m} = \frac{\sum_{k \neq m} E_k x_k}{\sum_{k \neq m} x_k} \quad , \tag{1.9}$$

or, including the more exact terms from perturbation theory:

$$W_m > \bar{E}_{k \neq m} - \sum_{k \neq m} \frac{\varphi_{mk}\varphi_{km}}{W_m - W_k} \quad . \tag{1.10}$$

The currently dominant species together with its stationary distribution of mutants emerging from this species are called *quasi-species*. The concentration of the dominant species (*wild-type*) itself may be relatively low, but in combination with the mutant distribution the emergent quasi-species is dominant. Altogether, the dynamical shift of $\bar{E}(t)$ toward the largest eigenvalue allows for coexistence of species as well as growth of new mutants.

An important question concerning the selective creation of information asks for the correlation between parameters of the system and the amount of information which can be created. To investigate this, Eigen assumes a number of l single symbols in the genome and a mean copying accuracy $\bar{q}$ per symbol. Then only a fraction $\bar{q}^l$ of correct copies is produced in each generation, i.e., $Q_m = \bar{q}^l$ for the wild-type. For $Q_m > \sigma_m^{-1}$ as a lower bound, using $|\ln \bar{q}| \approx 1 - \bar{q}$ for $1 - \bar{q} \ll 1$ ($q \approx 1$), one obtains a maximum length $l_{\max}$ such that the information can be preserved by reproduction:

$$l_{\max} = \frac{|\ln \sigma_m|}{1 - \bar{q}} \quad . \tag{1.11}$$

In the simplest case σ_m is the ratio of the wild-type reproduction rate to the average reproduction rate of the rest. The exact form of σ_m can

---

[27]Starting from equation (1.6), a transformation of variables is possible, which yields a new system of equations:

$$\dot{y}_i(t) = (\lambda_i - \bar{E}(t))y_i(t) \quad . \tag{1.8}$$

Here $\bar{E}(t) = c_s \sum_{k=1}^{s} \lambda_k y_k(t)$, $c_s = \sum_{k=1}^{s} x_k = \sum_{k=1}^{s} y_k = \text{const}$, and λ_i denotes the ith eigenvalue of the matrix W.

be calculated from (1.10). Calculation of an approximation from (1.9) yields

$$\sigma_m \;=\; \frac{A_m}{D_m + \bar{E}_{k \neq m}} \;.\qquad(1.12)$$

Equality (1.11) defines an absolute upper bound for the stable reproduction of information and is valid for any kind of information transfer process. Experimental results clearly demonstrated that this form of macromolecular evolution is not able to facilitate the development of self-reproducing entities longer than at the most hundred nucleotide bases. Furthermore, concerning the error rate, Eigen summarized the following observations:

- Error rates too small cause a very small rate of progress of the evolution process.

- Error rates too large cause destruction of information; it "melts" away.

- Optimal evolution conditions are found just below the error rate which causes information to be destroyed.

Up to now we have discussed systems capable of Darwinian selection in its most general case. Self-reproduction implies a rate equation of the principal form[28] $\dot{N} = kN$ and therefore exponential population growth, which in a system of limited population size leads to the emergence of Darwinian selection. Having a sufficiently large selective advantage, any new species created by mutation can in principle grow and become the dominant species at any time[29].

In contrast to this, Eigen's concept of a *hypercycle* leads to a mechanism of selection which is in fact a "winner-take-all" selection. A hypercycle denotes a cyclically coupled arrangement of reproductive units, e.g. a catalytic cycle[30]. Then, population growth follows the rate equation $\dot{N} = kN^2$ and is therefore hyperbolic. Under such circumstances, selection happens only once in case of a limited system. As soon as one species has grown up, *no* growth of new, advantageous mutants is possible. This is not a Darwinian selection, and it does not allow for diversity of species.

Altogether, we can very briefly summarize the statements of the theory concerning the emergence of life starting from biological macromolecules and confirmed by a variety of experiments (see [Eig71], p. 511 ff.) as follows:

---

[28] Here N denotes the number of individuals in the population.

[29] Stable coexistence is possible within a size-limited system if population growth is linear, i.e., $\dot{N} = k$. Under certain conditions, this is compatible with Darwinian selection [Eig76].

[30] A similar catalytic cycle, the so-called *carbon-cycle*, presumably constitutes the driving force of the chemical evolution of stars (see e.g. [Jan84], pp. 135–137).

(1) The first phase is characterized by coexistent evolution of molecular units capable of self-reproduction according to the principle of Darwinian selection. This is limited by the error rates to the emergence of nucleotide segments having lengths below one hundred bases.

(2) Only by means of a hypercyclic composition, the system consisting of self-replicating subunits can be integrated and stabilized as a functional unit. The integrated system is capable of self-replication of molecules which are by large factors longer than the chains of each subunit.

(3) Hypercyclic selection optimizes the system which has emerged first, thereby excluding all alternatives. As a result of non-Darwinian, hypercyclic selection, one universal genetic code is produced.

(4) A compartmentalization process of the hypercycle (i.e., the hypercycle escapes into a system which is saved from any "pollution" caused by unfavorable mutations) allows for the exploitation of genotypic advantages, leading to a joining together of all replicative units the hypercycle consists of. Finally, the first biological cells emerge.

(5) Darwinian evolution leads to the development of the known variety of species.

Though this theory can never explain the precise route of one particular evolution (e.g. our own), it provides insight into the general principles of selection and evolution at the molecular level. Computer experiments were performed by Nowak and Schuster in order to investigate the error threshold above which information dissolves [NS89]. They used a population of strings formed over an alphabet of two symbols instead of the quaternary nucleotide base alphabet, and assigned a fixed replication constant larger than one to the master sequence. Each other possible sequence was assigned a replication rate of one. Under these conditions, which describe a simple single-peak fitness landscape, Nowak and Schuster performed simulations for every value of the copying accuracy q, which was chosen to be identical for both symbols and each location in the sequence (i.e., $\bar{q} = q$). Sequences were grouped into error-classes according to the number of bits in which they differed from the master sequence, and each simulation was run until a stationary state representing the quasi-species was reached. The error threshold can then be identified as a sharp transition (comparable to a phase transition) from a localized quasi-species to a random drift through sequence space, reducing the concentration of the wild-type to its expectation value under the assumption of a uniform random search. Using a birth and death model, they obtained an approximate analytical expression for the dependence of the error threshold on population size c_s, sequence length l, and selective advantage σ_m of the master sequence, which in the limit of large populations amounts to

$$q_{min} \; = \; \sigma_m^{-1}\left(1 + \frac{2\sqrt{\sigma_m - 1}}{l\sqrt{c_s}}\right) \qquad (1.13)$$

This expression is more exact than the lowest order approximation

$$q_{min} \; = \; \sigma_m^{-1/l} \qquad (1.14)$$

already derived by Eigen [Eig71].

As we will see more clearly in chapter 2 when discussing Genetic Algorithms, the findings from Eigen's theory as well as empirical and theoretical results on error thresholds have much in common with Genetic Algorithms. Essentially, the experiment performed by Nowak and Schuster can be interpreted as a Genetic Algorithm without crossover, working on a very simple fitness landscape. Findings on the importance of the error threshold turn out to be valid in principle also in other Evolutionary Algorithms. This can be summarized into the intuitive idea that mutation should not destroy structures more quickly than they reproduce (but if this happens some time, the whole process may be started once again).

1.2   Evolutionary Algorithms and Artificial Intelligence

In Computer Science, *Artificial Intelligence* (AI) has from the very beginning always been one of the most fascinating and, rather quickly, most frustrating research branches. To give a definition of Artificial Intelligence is not as easy as one might expect, but my favorite is still the short sentence by Rich (see [Ric88], p. 1)[31]:

> *Artificial Intelligence is the study of how to make computers do things at which, at the moment, people are better.*

The definition captures the attempt to make computers "intelligent" in a sense coming very close to human intelligence[32]. Rapid progress was expected at the beginning of Artificial Intelligence in about 1950, but the research results did not come up to expectations in many cases.

Nowadays, some researchers in Artificial Intelligence propose to orientate toward imitation of the much more restricted capabilities of less complex animals such as flies or ants. That is why the definition of Artificial Intelligence cited above can today possibly be improved by replacing the word "people" by "living beings." The modern subfield of

---

[31] Reprinted by permission of McGraw-Hill, Inc. from E. Rich and K. Knight: *Artificial Intelligence*, copyright © McGraw-Hill, Inc., 1991.

[32] More specifically, individual intelligence is meant here in contrast to collective intelligence.

Artificial Intelligence which has emerged mainly from such a shift of demands is called *Artificial Life* (AL). Although the term "life" indicates a high-level approach including intelligence, it is essentially a bottom-up approach based upon models of simple living entities. The relation between Evolutionary Algorithms and Artificial Life will be discussed later on.

According to the definition given above, Artificial Intelligence is a many-faceted research field, working on a variety of different tasks such as game playing, theorem proving, forecasting, general problem solving, perception (mainly vision and speech, closely related to natural language understanding), automatic programming, and machine learning in general. The latter topic, machine learning, is one of the most important subfields of Artificial Intelligence. From the beginning of the research on Artificial Intelligence until presently the idea that something which is called "intelligent" should be able to improve its behavior based upon the growing experience it gathers when doing the same (or a similar) action repeatedly and also to develop a concept of what a mistake is and how to avoid it during repeated actions is central to any efforts towards machine learning. The characterization given by Michalski is again only one of several possibilities, but it includes the most important ideas especially when relations between machine learning and Evolutionary Algorithms will be discussed (see [Mic86], p. 10):

> *Learning is constructing or modifying representations of what is being experienced.*

The definition concentrates on an internal representation the learning system (a human being or a computer program) constructs and modifies of its environment (typically, what is experienced by the learning system is the environment or at least a certain part of it). Classical AI research concentrates on the use of symbolic representations based upon a finite number of representation primitives and rules for the manipulation of symbols. Together, representation primitives and manipulation rules are a formal system and therefore provide a universal model of computation. However, the problem of whether or not thinking in general is identical to computation and hence is restricted to partially recursive calculations opens a more philosophical discussion far beyond the scope of this work.

The symbolic period of Artificial Intelligence can be dated approximately from 1962 until 1975, followed by a knowledge-intensive period from 1976 until about 1988 which emphasized on a large amount of knowledge incorporated into the learning systems. However, symbolic representations, e.g. using predicate logic, semantic nets, or frames, were one central characteristic also of this period. Currently, the field of Artificial Intelligence is starting to spread research into a variety of directions and tries to integrate different methods into large-scale systems, thus combining their advantages as far as possible.

But the earliest, so-called subsymbolic period of Artificial Intelligence dates from about 1950 until 1965. This period did not rely on symbolic but on subsymbolic — numerical — representations of knowledge. Evolutionary Algorithms make use of a subsymbolic representation of knowledge encoded in the genotypes of individuals, and in fact some early approaches of Evolutionary Algorithms from the subsymbolic period are known and will be discussed in section 1.4. Here, only the other early subsymbolic knowledge representation example of Artificial Neural Networks (ANN), based upon a simple model of the central nervous systems of higher animals, is mentioned. Knowledge in Neural Networks is distributed over connection weights of the edges between vertices (called *units*) in a graph structure. Units loosely correspond to nerve cells (neurons), edges to dendrites and the axon. Both make up the connections to other nerve cells, and weights can be seen as an analogy to synaptic connection strengths. During learning the weight values are incrementally updated.

The early approaches by Rosenblatt (*Perceptron*, [Ros58]), Selfridge (*Pandemonium*, [Sel59]), and Widrow (*Adelaine*, [Wid62]) are the starting points of the modern research field of Artificial Neural Networks. However, it took a long time to overcome the damage caused by the result of Minsky and Papert [MP69] demonstrating the extremely restricted computational capabilities of simplified perceptron-like network structures. They showed that a perceptron with only one layer of output units and one layer of input units is unable to calculate the logical exclusive-or function. The result stopped research in this field for nearly twenty years, until it was sufficiently well-known that by introduction of an additional layer of units the problem can be solved (the utility of adding additional layers in a neural network was already known in the 1970s). Today, Artificial Neural Networks are subject to many studies and have been applied successfully to a variety of problems in Artificial Intelligence, e.g. pattern recognition, natural language understanding, and data classification. For an overview of applications, the book of Dayhoff [Day90] is instructive.

Returning to the representational difference between subsymbolic and symbolic Artificial Intelligence some remarks on both techniques are important in order to understand why the representation turns out to be a critical choice within programs in Artificial Intelligence. Artificial Intelligence had its main success when the problem domain could be treated as an abstract microworld which is disconnected from the world at large. That is why game-playing has gained much attention from the beginning of research in this field[33]. On the contrary, classical Artificial

---

[33]Samuel's checkers playing program is a famous and successful approach to this task, which was written in the early days of Artificial Intelligence research, i.e. in the subsymbolic period [Sam59]. He used a scoring polynomial for calculating a quality measure for moves and board positions. The scoring function was dynamic insofar as the weight factors within the scoring polynomial were updated in a learning process, based upon success or failure of the moves generated by the program. Of course, assignment of responsibility for a successful game to certain moves is by no means trivial; this *credit assignment problem* is still a critical point. Furthermore, from a set of possible terms in the scoring polynomial only half of the total number was

Intelligence systems suffer from a very narrow application domain and
their brittleness in case of slight modifications of the tasks they are built
for. Examples include the problems with generalization and inductive
inferences in rule-based systems and unforeseen modifications of the environment in case of blocks-world programs. The syntactical details are
important reasons for the brittleness problem, and the representational
bias of symbolic Artificial Intelligence systems cannot be estimated high
enough.

In the field of Artificial Intelligence the concept of adaptation is
closely related and sometimes used synonymously to learning. Remembering the discussion from a biological point of view presented in section 1.1, it can be recognized that adaptation has a more general meaning than learning: Learning refers to a property of individuals that is
experienced during their lifetime, while adaptation can take place both
in individuals when confronted with unknown environments during their
lifetime and with a population of individuals over several generations on
the basis of genotype changes. Furthermore, it is coupled with an improvement of the performance of individuals in their environment, which
is a more ambitious property than some simple forms of learning have
to fulfil.

As an abstraction from biological background, adaptation can be interpreted as a goal-oriented successive progress of improvement of structures in order to give better performance in their environment. This is
well in accord with the fitness interpretation of phenotypic adaptation
(section 1.1) and gives evidence to handle adaptation and optimization
as denoting identical concepts from different disciplines.

To clarify the position of Evolutionary Algorithms within the variety
of machine learning strategies, we use a classification which is directly
based upon the underlying learning strategy and its complexity with respect to the inference process. The classification is essentially a combination of those presented by Michalski, Carbonell, and Mitchell [CMM84]
and the later variant by Michalski [Mic86]:

- *Rote learning*: No inference processes take place. Instead, direct
  implantation of knowledge is performed.

---

in use for evaluation at the same time. In order to test also the inactive terms,
random exchange of scoring terms between the active and the inactive set took place
sometimes. We explained some details here because Samuel's work cannot only be
seen in the light of game playing, but also can be interpreted as an early Evolutionary
Algorithm. Changes in weights and polynomial term structure can be interpreted as
mutation processes, and evaluation of moves on the basis of success or failure within
the total game provides the selection criterion. This way, a scoring polynomial of
high checkers playing fitness is evolved.

However, in a second paper on the checkers playing problem, Samuel no longer
used these "evolutionary" techniques [Sam67]. Instead, he improved performance by
completely relying on tree pruning techniques (*alpha-beta pruning*) and used a "book
learning" procedure (parameter adjustments based on replaying a large number of
games played by checkers masters).

- *Learning by instruction*: This term denotes knowledge acquisition from a teacher or from an organized source and integration with existing knowledge. Mainly selection and reformulation of information are performed.

- *Learning by deduction*: Deductive, truth-preserving inferences and memorization of useful conclusions are summarized by this term.

- *Learning by analogy*: The transformation of existing knowledge that bears strong similarity to the desired new concept into a form effectively useful in the new situation.

- *Learning by induction*: Inductive inferences.

    * *Learning from examples* (*concept acquisition*): Based upon a set of examples and counterexamples, the task is to induce a general concept description explaining all positive examples and excluding all negative examples.

    * *Learning by observation and discovery* (*descriptive generalization, unsupervised learning*): Search for regularities and general rules explaining all or at least most observations in absence of any teacher who provides feedback.

The learning strategies are ordered with respect to an increasing complexity of the inference mechanisms used. The classification includes Evolutionary Algorithms as an example of an unsupervised learning technique, i.e. inductive learning by observation and discovery. The following reasons can be identified for this characterization of Evolutionary Algorithms as learning algorithms:

- No teacher exists who presents examples, counterexamples or even knowledge to the learning system. Instead, the algorithm generates examples on its own.

- The creation of new examples (search points) by the algorithm is an inductive guess on the basis of existing knowledge. If the guess proves its worth, it is kept in the knowledge base (the population), otherwise it is discarded by means of selection.

So far, we have discussed Evolutionary Algorithms with respect to their learning characteristics and therefore related them to Artificial Intelligence as an example of AI programs. Indeed, in many cases Artificial Intelligence tasks can be reduced to the problem of performing a heuristic search within a search space of vast size. The structures within this space can be relatively complex, e.g. permutations, graphs, or game-playing strategies. The search is guided by a heuristic function defined by the researcher who develops the AI program, and by the heuristics that are incorporated into the search algorithm. The purpose of the heuristic function is to determine the desirability of the structures tested by the algorithm and thereby to prune the search tree. It is obvious to see the possibility for using Evolutionary Algorithms as a heuristic search procedure in AI programs. Many such applications of Evolutionary Algorithms have been reported in the literature, searching spaces of different complexity, e.g. production rule spaces (*classifier systems*), game strategy spaces, and program spaces. The clear advantage of Evolutionary Algorithms is their universal applicability to almost any kind of structure space, in contrast to the specificity of classical AI search strategies (e.g. the A*-algorithm, which is essentially a best-first search on graphs).

Finally, concluding this brief survey of the relations between Artificial Intelligence and Evolutionary Algorithms, we return to the modern Artificial Life [Lan89] subfield of AI. Artificial Life research concentrates on computer simulations of simple hypothetical life forms (*life-as-it-could-be* or *synthetical approach*, to use the terminology of Langton) and the problem how to make their behavior adaptive (e.g. adaptability of simple robots to unforeseen situations is desired). Furthermore, self-organizing properties emerging from local interactions within a large number of simple basic agents are investigated. These agents usually at the same time cooperate to solve a problem and compete for a set of limited resources. Basically, the agents' actions can be executed asynchronously, in parallel. Analogies to natural systems can be drawn on a variety of different levels, including particles, cells, organs, individuals, and populations. In many cases the agents are equipped with internal rules or strategies determining their behavior, and an Evolutionary Algorithm is used for evolving these strategies.

Artificial Life research is actually in its starting period, and no clearly defined boundaries can be identified. However, further development of AL will possibly lead to better understanding of the nature of life and emergent, self-organizing behavior in general.

1.3   Evolutionary Algorithms and Global Optimization

Referring again to the adaptive surface metaphor, we can imagine an extremely complex, unknown functional dependence which maps genomes (i.e., a word consisting of letters from the alphabet of nucleotide bases) to fitness measures judging phenotypical expressions of genotypes. During evolution, genotypes producing phenotypes of increasing biological fitness are created by means of the processes mutation and recombination on the genotype and selection on the phenotype. This way, an optimization of fitness takes place, and even if we assume a constant adaptive surface that is not changed according to the positions of individuals themselves, the combination of mutation and recombination allows in principle for leaving a smaller hill of the landscape and therefore prevents evolution from getting stuck on suboptimal hills.

This very simplified point of view provides the basis for the idea to use a simulated evolutionary process for the purpose of solving an *optimization* problem, where the goal is to find a set of parameters (which might be interpreted as a "genotype" as well as a "phenotype") such that a certain quality criterion is maximized or minimized. Problems of this type have an enormous significance in many fields of research and industrial production, e.g. in computer-aided design and construction, biological, chemical, electrical, and medical engineering, production planning, and Artificial Intelligence (see section 1.2)[34].

In a very general form, the main goal of the *global optimization problem* is summarized in the following definition ([TŽ89], p. 1f.):

Definition 1.1 (Global minimum) *Given a function $f : M \subseteq \mathbb{R}^n \to \mathbb{R}$, $M \neq \emptyset$, for $\vec{x}^* \in M$ the value $f^* := f(\vec{x}^*) > -\infty$ is called a* global minimum, *iff*

$$\forall \vec{x} \in M : \quad f(\vec{x}^*) \leq f(\vec{x}) . \tag{1.15}$$

Then, $\vec{x}^*$ is a global minimum point, f is called objective function, *and the set M is called the* feasible region. *The problem of determining a global minimum point is called the* global optimization problem.

Recently, Kursawe has demonstrated that Evolutionary Algorithms can in principle be extended to solve *multiple criteria decision making* (MCDM) problems, where f is of the more general form $f : M \subseteq \mathbb{R}^n \to \mathbb{R}^k$, $M \neq \emptyset$, $k > 1$ [Kur91, Kur92]. For such problems, a set of non-dominated solutions (the *Pareto-set*) exists, such that the quality of a solution can be improved with respect to a single criterion only by becoming worse with respect to at least one other criterion. By incorporating biological concepts like diploidy, dominance, and recessivity into an Evolution Strategy, Kursawe's algorithm is able to generate solutions covering the Pareto set, extending the capabilities of traditional methods which yield just one point of the Pareto set. In the following, we will restrict attention to the single-criterion case, i.e., $k = 1$.

Furthermore, we will concentrate on minimization problems for providing a standardized point of view for algorithmic test runs. This does not restrict generality of the optimization problem, since the identity

$$\max\{f(\vec{x}) \mid \vec{x} \in M\} \quad = \quad -\min\{-f(\vec{x}) \mid \vec{x} \in M\} \tag{1.16}$$

holds. The feasible region M is specified more closely in the next definition ([GMSW89], p. 197):

Definition 1.2 (Constraints) *Let $M := \{\vec{x} \in \mathbb{R}^n \mid g_i(\vec{x}) \geq 0 \ \forall i \in \{1, \ldots, q\} \}$ be the feasible region of the objective function $f : M \to \mathbb{R}$.*

---

[34] An annotated bibliography of applications of Evolutionary Algorithms provides an impressive overview of their potential [BHS92].

The functions $g_i : I\!\!R^n \to I\!\!R$ are called constraints, *and at a point $\vec{x} \in I\!\!R^n$ a constraint g_j is called*

$$
\begin{array}{lll}
\text{satisfied} & :\Leftrightarrow & g_j(\vec{x}) \geq 0 \,, \\
\text{active} & :\Leftrightarrow & g_j(\vec{x}) = 0 \,, \\
\text{inactive} & :\Leftrightarrow & g_j(\vec{x}) > 0 \,, \; and \\
\text{violated} & :\Leftrightarrow & g_j(\vec{x}) < 0 \,.
\end{array}
\tag{1.17}
$$

The global optimization problem is called unconstrained, *iff $M = I\!\!R^n$; otherwise,* constrained.

In section 2.1.5 we will outline that a simple method to handle inequality constraints (it is easy to see that inequality constraints of the form $g_j(\vec{x}) \leq 0$ can be transformed into the form used in definition 1.2) in Evolutionary Algorithms works by repeating the creation of a new solution $\vec{x}$ until all constraints are satisfied. Except a first attempt by Michalewicz and Janikow for linear constraints, general *equality* constraints $g_j(\vec{x}) = 0$ are currently not taken into account by Evolutionary Algorithms [MJ91]. The method indicated for inequality constraints cannot be extended for this case because the new solution will surely be infeasible if it is not generated in a very clever way (which, in general, may require to solve an additional optimization problem per constraint).

In general, the objective function topology shows not only one, but several minima of different depths, divided by higher regions. Most optimization methods, starting by chance in the region of attraction[35] of one of the minima, are able to approach just this minimum, in spite of the fact that it might not be the deepest of all these *local minima*, i.e., a global one. To formalize the notion of a local minimum a *distance measure* or *metrics* is needed for an arbitrary vector space.

Definition 1.3 (Metrics) *Let V be a vector space. A* metrics *on V is a mapping $\rho : V^2 \to I\!\!R_0^+$, such that $\forall \vec{v}, \vec{w}, \vec{x} \in V$:*

$$
\begin{array}{rcl}
\rho(\vec{v}, \vec{w}) & = & 0 \quad \Leftrightarrow \quad \vec{v} = \vec{w} \\
\rho(\vec{v}, \vec{w}) & = & \rho(\vec{w}, \vec{v}) \\
\rho(\vec{v}, \vec{w}) & \leq & \rho(\vec{v}, \vec{x}) + \rho(\vec{x}, \vec{w}) \,.
\end{array}
\tag{1.18}
$$

However, it is also sufficient if instead of a metrics only a *norm* is defined in case of a vector space V on the real numbers (or, more generally, the complex numbers). Informally, the norm of a vector can be seen as a measure of its length.

Definition 1.4 (Norm) *Let V be a vector space on $I\!\!R$. A* norm *on V is a mapping $\| \cdot \| : V \to I\!\!R_0^+$, such that $\forall \vec{v}, \vec{w} \in V$, $r \in I\!\!R$:*

$$
\begin{array}{rcl}
\|\vec{v}\| & = & 0 \quad \Leftrightarrow \quad \vec{v} = \vec{0} \\
\|r\vec{v}\| & = & r\|\vec{v}\| \\
\|\vec{v} + \vec{w}\| & \leq & \|\vec{v}\| + \|\vec{w}\| \,.
\end{array}
\tag{1.19}
$$

---

[35] By which we mean, informally, the set of all points from which a monotonic sequence of down-hill steps leads to the minimum point.

It is easy to verify that any normalized vector space is also a metric space by setting

$$\rho(\vec{v}, \vec{w}) \;=\; \|\vec{v} - \vec{w}\| \;. \tag{1.20}$$

Of course, the inversion of this implication does not hold. Usually, when topologies of the space $I\!\!R^n$ are considered, the *Euclidean norm* is presupposed, i.e., $\forall \vec{x} = (x_1, \ldots, x_n) \in I\!\!R^n$:

$$\|\vec{x}\| \;=\; \sqrt{\sum_{i=1}^{n} |x_i|^2} \;. \tag{1.21}$$

Then, the metrics $\|\vec{x} - \vec{y}\|$ yields the common definition of *Euclidean distance*.

Based on these definitions, the meaning of a local minimum is put in concrete terms as follows:

Definition 1.5 (Local minimum) *For $\hat{\vec{x}} \in M$ the value $\hat{f} := f(\hat{\vec{x}})$ is called a* local minimum*, iff*

$$\exists \varepsilon \in I\!\!R, \varepsilon > 0 : \forall \vec{x} \in M : \quad \|\vec{x} - \hat{\vec{x}}\| < \varepsilon \;\Rightarrow\; \hat{f} \le f(\vec{x}) \,. \tag{1.22}$$

In other words, an ε-*environment* $U_\varepsilon(\hat{\vec{x}}) = \{\vec{x} \in M \mid \|\vec{x} - \hat{\vec{x}}\| < \varepsilon\}$ exists such that $\hat{f}$ is the smallest feasible objective function value within this environment. It is obvious that any global minimum is also a local one. An objective function f is called *unimodal*, if it has exactly one local minimum[36], otherwise it is called *multimodal* ([Sch77], p. 30).

Of course, one is mainly interested in finding a global optimum of a given optimization problem instead of only a local one. Unfortunately, in global optimization no general criterion exists for identification of the global minimum ([TŽ89], p. 2).

Due to the limited exactness of floating-point representations of real numbers by computers, the global optimization problem can be considered as solved if a member of the *level set* $L_{f^*+\varepsilon} = \{\vec{x} \in M \mid f(\vec{x}) \le f(\vec{x}^*) + \varepsilon\}$ has been found by an optimization algorithm. Unfortunately, from a theoretical point of view, the following disappointing theorem holds ([TŽ89], p. 6):

Theorem 1 *The problem to determine a member of the level set $L_{f^*+\varepsilon}$ of an arbitrary global optimization problem with continuous objective function f on a compact feasible region M within a finite number of steps is unsolvable.*

---

[36]This definition demands a connected set of local minimum points, since it takes only the definition of a local minimum by means of its objective function value into account, a practically oriented point of view.

Proof: It is assumed that the objective function has been evaluated at a finite number of points. However, it is still possible that the global minimum of the function differs arbitrarily much from the minimum function value found so far. The statement then holds due to an inductive argument.   Q.E.D.

Practically, however, the demands to a numerical optimization algorithm are weaker. A simple approach which is implicit to any discretized representation of numbers on a computer is a *grid search* ([TŽ89], p. 44; [Zhi92], p. 36ff), which covers the feasible region by an equidistant grid of points and evaluates the objective function at each grid point. The minimum objective function value found this way is declared to be the global minimum, but in general this will not reflect the real global minimum. The error which has to be accepted depends on the resolution of the grid, such that increasing the number k of grid points allowed for each dimension of the search space will generally decrease the error[37]. Conversely, problems arise by the combinatorial explosion of the number of grid points, which is k^n when the dimension of the search space is n. For practical problems exponential growth results in an impossibility to apply a grid search technique including evaluation of the objective function at each point of the grid. Often, the computational effort is prohibitive for even "small" values $n > 5$.

In a very natural way the discussion of global optimization turned from continuous variables to discrete ones by introducing the idea of a grid search technique. Generally, optimization problems with discrete object variables are called *combinatorial optimization problems*. The definition of a global optimum does not of course undergo changes when combinatorial optimization problems are discussed, but for local minima the notion of an ε-environment turns into the concept of *neighborhoods*, based on suitably defined metrics. Both ε-environments and neighborhoods serve to characterize sets of points which are "close" (according to the metrics) in search space to a given point, but the neighborhood is more general. Following Papadimitriou and Steiglitz ([PS82], p. 7), we define a neighborhood as follows:

Definition 1.6 (Neighborhood) *A* neighborhood, *defined on a set S, is a mapping $\mathcal{N} : S \to 2^S$, where 2^S denotes the power set of S.*

Based on neighborhood structures, the definition of a local minimum can now be carried over to discrete spaces.

Definition 1.7 (Local minimum in discrete spaces) *For $\hat{\vec{x}} \in M$, where $M \neq \emptyset$ denotes an arbitrarily defined feasible region, and a neighborhood $\mathcal{N} : M \to 2^M$, the value $\hat{f} := f(\hat{\vec{x}})$ is called a* local minimum *with respect to $\mathcal{N}$, iff*

$$\hat{f} \leq f(\vec{x}) \quad \forall \vec{x} \in \mathcal{N}(\hat{\vec{x}}) . \tag{1.23}$$

---

[37]This is not the case for fractal topologies; see also section 3.5.

In the following, a combinatorial optimization problem class of major interest will be the *pseudoboolean optimization* problem, i.e., the objective function maps vectors of binary object variables to real values. Defining $I\!B = \{0,1\}$ to denote the binary domain of object variables, $f : I\!B^n \to I\!R$ has 2^n possible argument vectors, implying again that complete enumeration of all possible solutions fails to work just for small values of n due to natural restrictions of the available time and resources. A common distance measure for elements of $I\!B^n$, the *Hamming distance*, simply counts the number of positions two binary vectors are differing from one another.

Definition 1.8 (Hamming distance) *For $\vec{a} = (a_1, \ldots, a_n) \in I\!B^n$, $\vec{b} = (b_1, \ldots, b_n) \in I\!B^n$ the metrics defined by*

$$\rho_H(\vec{a}, \vec{b}) = \sum_{i=1}^{n} |a_i - b_i| \tag{1.24}$$

is called Hamming distance.

Using this metrics, neighborhoods $\mathcal{N}_k$ can be defined for all $k \in \{0, \ldots, n\}$ by grouping together all points of identical distance to a given reference point, i.e. [ASS90]:

$$\mathcal{N}_k(\vec{a}) = \{\vec{b} \in I\!B^n \mid \rho_H(\vec{a}, \vec{b}) = k\} \quad . \tag{1.25}$$

Local optima in the binary hypercube are then characterized according to their neighborhood $\mathcal{N}_1$, such that given a function $f : I\!B^n \to I\!R$, $\hat{f} := f(\hat{a})$ is called a local minimum (with respect to $\mathcal{N}_1$) of f, iff $\forall \vec{b} \in \mathcal{N}_1(\vec{a}): \hat{f} \le f(\vec{b})$.

To illustrate some of the topics discussed so far, we mention an example of a pseudoboolean optimization problem which is of some importance in communication engineering and coding theory. The problem is to find binary sequences of high length having minimal autocorrelations, discussed in detail e.g. in [Gol77, Gol82]. It is originally defined on the alphabet $\{-1, +1\}$, where the values indicate radar pulses being in phase or 180° out-of-phase, which $I\!B$ can easily be transformed to by setting $\forall a_i \in I\!B$, $\forall b_i \in \{-1, +1\}: b_i = 2a_i - 1$. The objective function $E : I\!B^n \to I\!R$ ("energy" of a sequence) is defined by

$$E(\vec{a}) = \sum_{k=1}^{n-1} \left(\sum_{i=1}^{n-k} b_i b_{i+k} \right)^2 \quad , \quad b_i = 2a_i - 1 \quad . \tag{1.26}$$

This "energy" value must be minimized or, alternatively, the so-called *merit factor* $F(\vec{a}) = n^2/(2E^2(\vec{a}))$ be maximized. Analytically, there is no way to do so. To give an impression of the highly multimodal character of the search space, figure 1.7 shows the topology of the autocorrelation function for $n = 12$.

The special visualization method used here for creating topological plots of pseudoboolean functions maps binary vectors of length n to an equidistant, diamond-shaped grid with a distance of $1/n$ between neighboring points on an axis parallel to a coordinate axis. Furthermore, rows contain all points having the same number of one bits, and the difference in the number of ones between points on adjacent rows is one. Each of the $n+1$ rows consists of $\binom{n}{i}$ points where i denotes the number of ones (or zeros, equivalently) in the actual row[38].

Evidently, as figure 1.7 shows, the autocorrelation problem is extremely complicated due to the existence of a huge number of local minima of very similar depth. Strings of high order and regularity such as the zero string and the one string have highest autocorrelation, and the deepest minima seem to be located somewhere in the interior of the diamond grid. Nowadays, global minima are known exactly by complete enumeration for sequences up to chain lengths $n \leq 32$. By using the theoretically based hypothesis that *skew-symmetric* sequences of odd length $n = 2k - 1$, defined by

$$\forall a_i \in \{-1, +1\}: \quad a_{k+l} \quad = \quad (-1)^l a_{k-l}, \ \forall l \in \{1, \ldots, k-1\}, \quad (1.28)$$

are good candidates for low autocorrelation values [Gol77], the search space can be reduced to $2^{(n+1)/2}$ elements. Concentrating on skew-symmetric sequences, de Groot, Würtz, and Hoffmann enumerated the search space up to $n = 71$. For longer sequences up to $n = 199$ they used an Evolutionary Algorithm for optimization and obtained reasonable results [dGWH89].

Another important example of combinatorial optimization problems we will discuss here is the *Traveling Salesperson Problem* (TSP), which is informally the problem to find a tour of minimum length for visiting a number of cities in turn, finally returning to the starting city. More formally, given a set $C = \{c_1, \ldots, c_n\}$ of n cities c_i and a distance matrix (ρ_{ij}), where $\rho_{ij} = \rho(c_i, c_j)$ $(i, j \in \{1, \ldots, n\}, \rho_{ij} = \rho_{ji}, \rho_{ii} = 0)$, the

---

[38]Formally, the exact coordinates of each point of the grid are calculated according to the point expression

$$p_{i,j} = \left(\frac{\binom{n}{i} - 1}{2n} - \frac{j}{n}, \frac{i}{n} \right) \quad , i \in \{0, \ldots, n\}, j \in \{0, \ldots, \binom{n}{i} - 1\} \quad (1.27)$$

In this expression i is identical to the number of ones within the bit vector. This way, the outer corners of the diamond grid have coordinates $p_{0,0} = (0, 0)$, $p_{n,0} = (0, 1)$,

$$p_{\lceil n/2 \rceil, 0} \quad = \quad \left(\frac{\binom{n}{\lceil n/2 \rceil} - 1}{2n}, \frac{1}{2} \right) \quad , \text{and}$$

$$p_{\lceil n/2 \rceil, \binom{n}{\lceil n/2 \rceil} - 1} \quad = \quad \left(-\frac{\binom{n}{\lceil n/2 \rceil} - 1}{2n}, \frac{1}{2} \right) \quad .$$

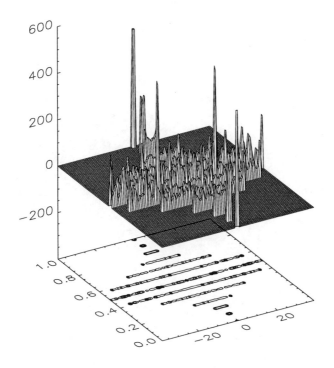

Fig. 1.7: Autocorrelation function of binary sequences ($n = 12$).

task is to find a permutation $\pi \in S_n = \{s : \{1, \ldots, n\} \rightarrow \{1, \ldots, n\}\}$ such that the objective function (the tour length) $f : S_n \rightarrow I\!R$, where

$$f(\pi) = \sum_{i=1}^{n-1} \rho_{\pi(i),\pi(i+1)} + \rho_{\pi(n),\pi(1)} \quad , \tag{1.29}$$

attains its minimum.

Again, the size of the search space grows exponentially depending on n, the number of cities, since there are

$$(n-1)!/2 \approx \frac{1}{2}\sqrt{2\pi(n-1)} \left(\frac{n-1}{e}\right)^{n-1} \tag{1.30}$$

possible tours (the start position is arbitrary, and the tour order may be inverted). Although good approximation algorithms for the TSP

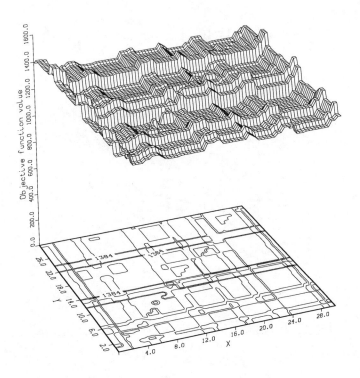

Fig. 1.8: TSP visualization ($n = 30$).

have been developed (see [PS82], p. 410ff.), the problem still offers high attractiveness for applying new algorithms such as evolutionary ones. This is mostly due to the following reasons:

- The problematic of the TSP can be understood easily, since it comes very close to a popular real-world problem[39].

---

[39]This is why David E. Goldberg in his lecture held during the First International

- The TSP serves as the simplest case of a variety of ordering problems which are of enormous relevance to industrial scheduling processes, e.g. flow-shop scheduling and job-shop scheduling.

- Several "standard" TSP data sets are available from literature, e.g. Krolak's 100 city problem [KFM71], such that results are comparable even if the global optimum is not yet known definitely.

- Concerning computational complexity, the TSP as an *NP-complete* problem is known to be a representative for a large class of problems for which — as is widely believed, but not proved until now – no deterministic polynomial-time algorithm exists which solves the problem. This informal notion will be put in concrete terms in section 1.3.2.

Following an idea of Schwefel[40] for mapping permutation problems like the TSP to a continuous representation $\vec{x} \in [u, v]^n$; $u, v \in \mathbb{R}$, the resulting topology of a TSP can be visualized. From $\vec{x} = (x_1, \ldots, x_n) \in [u, v]^n$ a permutation π can be obtained by simply sorting the vector components, which yields a new vector $\vec{x}' = (x_{\pi(1)}, \ldots, x_{\pi(n)})$ such that $x_{\pi(1)} < x_{\pi(2)} < \ldots < x_{\pi(n)}$. The new index order $\pi(1), \pi(2), \ldots, \pi(n)$ is interpreted as the resulting tour permutation. As an example, consider the vector

$$\vec{x} = (-5.8_{(1)}, 1.2_{(2)}, -2.3_{(3)}, 0.5_{(4)}, 3.1_{(5)}, 4.9_{(6)}, -2.9_{(7)}, -0.1_{(8)}),$$

which results in

$$\vec{x}' = (-5.8_{(1)}, -2.9_{(7)}, -2.3_{(3)}, -0.1_{(8)}, 0.5_{(4)}, 1.2_{(2)}, 3.1_{(5)}, 4.9_{(6)})$$

after sorting. The new vector $\vec{x}'$ represents the permutation $\pi = (1, 7, 3, 8, 4, 2, 5, 6)$.

Using a coarse-grained parallel Evolution Strategy, Rudolph reports surprisingly good results for this simple mapping approach on Krolak's 100-city TSP [Rud91]. Here, this mapping is used for visualization purposes starting from a randomly initialized vector $\vec{x}$. To obtain a three-dimensional plot, components $x_3, \ldots, x_n$ are held constant while x_1 and x_2 are varied in the range $[u, v]$. Each such variation yields a valid tour by application of the above mentioned sorting principle. For a 30-city TSP the resulting topology shown in figure 1.8 has characteristic plateaus and many locally optimal tours, indicating the complexity this optimization problem shows also in its "smoothed" version. Of course, the topology changes according to the varying coordinates' index values.

Workshop on Parallel Problem Solving from Nature (PPSN I, Dortmund 1990) called the TSP a "cocktail-party easy" (CP-easy) problem.

[40]Independently, Bean introduced the same method using the term *random keys* to Genetic Algorithms for solving sequencing problems [Bea93, BN93].

Applications of Genetic Algorithms to solve the TSP are relatively frequent, due to the reasons mentioned above. A good overview is given by Goldberg ([Gol89a], pp. 170–175). Different crossover operators for the TSP are compared empirically in [OSH87]. A fine-grained parallel Genetic Algorithm for the TSP is described by Gorges-Schleuter [GS89, GS90]. In [Fog88], Fogel presents application results for Evolutionary Programming on a 50 and 100 city problem.

Finally, to conclude this section with an example from continuous parameter optimization which arises naturally in contrast to the artificial continuous representation for the TSP, we present the global optimization problem caused by the *least square estimation* of model parameters. The problem arises from observed data tuples $\{(x_1, y_1), \ldots, (x_N, y_N)\}$, where x_i are independent variables ("cause") and y_i are dependent variables ("effect"). Assuming the existence of a model or at least a hypothesis $\hat{y}(\vec{a}, \vec{x})$ which describes the dependence between effect y_i and cause x_i, the model parameter vector $\vec{a} \in I\!R^n$ must be estimated by the researcher in order to minimize the sum of squared differences between measured reality and model predictions:

$$f(\vec{a}) \;=\; \sum_{i=1}^{N} (\hat{y}(\vec{a}, x_i) - y_i)^2 \quad . \tag{1.31}$$

Further assuming that the model $\hat{y}(\vec{a}, \vec{x})$ is a twice differentiable, non-linear function of $a_1, \ldots, a_n$, calculation of first and second derivatives yields[41]:

$$\nabla f(\vec{a}) \;=\; 2 \sum_{i=1}^{N} (\hat{y}(\vec{a}, x_i) - y_i) \, \nabla \hat{y}(\vec{a}, x_i)$$

$$\nabla^2 f(\vec{a}) \;=\; 2 \sum_{i=1}^{N} (\hat{y}(\vec{a}, x_i) - y_i) \, \nabla^2 \hat{y}(\vec{a}, x_i) + \tag{1.32}$$

$$2 \sum_{i=1}^{N} \nabla \hat{y}(\vec{a}, x_i) \, (\nabla \hat{y}(\vec{a}, x_i))^T \cdot \mathbf{I} \quad .$$

Since $\nabla \hat{y}(\vec{a}, x_i) \, (\nabla \hat{y}(\vec{a}, x_i))^T \geq 0 \; \forall \vec{a} \in I\!R^n$, the second term of the equation always yields a positive contribution to the Hessian $\nabla^2 f(\vec{a})$.

---

[41]The *gradient*

$$\nabla f(\vec{a}) = (\frac{\partial}{\partial a_1} f(\vec{a}), \ldots, \frac{\partial}{\partial a_n} f(\vec{a}))$$

is the vector of partial derivatives of f (∇ is called *nabla-operator*). The *Hessian*

$$\nabla^2 f(\vec{a}) = \left(\frac{\partial^2 f(\vec{a})}{\partial a_i \partial a_j} \right) \quad \forall i, j \in \{1, \ldots, n\}$$

is a matrix consisting of all second-order partial derivatives. $(\cdot)^T$ denotes matrix transposition, and $\mathbf{I}$ is a unit matrix of appropriate size (here: $n \times n$).

However, the first term may have positive or negative sign, thus in total the entries of the Hessian may be positive, zero, or negative, indicating convex or concave[42] bendings of $f(\vec{a})$. In other words, $f(\vec{a})$ might be multimodal. Only in case of a model linear in a_i, i.e.

$$\hat{y}(\vec{a}, \vec{x}) \;=\; \sum_{i=1}^{n} a_i h_i(\vec{x}) \quad , \tag{1.33}$$

the Hessian is positive, implying a unimodal function $f(\vec{a})$. Then, $\nabla f(\vec{a}) = 0$ is a necessary and sufficient criterion for the optimum. Otherwise, in the more general case, global optimization algorithms are needed. Figure 1.9 shows a representative three-dimensional topology plot of an objective function emerging from a nonlinear parameter estimation problem[43]. The multimodal topology is smooth, reflecting the continuous differentiability of the problem.

Several applications of Evolutionary Algorithms to the parameter estimation problem are reported in literature. Johnson and Husbands applied a Genetic Algorithm to adjust parameters of a model describing the inflow-outflow dependence of a circular water tank with corregated sides [JH91]. Frankhauser used an Evolution Strategy for parameter estimation of a master-equation based nonlinear model of interurban migration processes ([Fra92], p. 39). Fogel demonstrated the application of Evolutionary Programming to system identification problems including parameter estimation and finding a reasonable model as well. The latter requires the incorporation of a measurement for model complexity into the objective function in order to search for the simplest (so-called ARMA) model fitting the data ([Fog91], pp. 157–190).

This brief survey of the many-faceted world of instantiations of global optimization problems was intended to give an impression of the general problem complexity on the one hand and the relevance of global optimization on the other hand. Caused by the existence of a huge number of still unsolved practical problems, researchers have developed a variety of different algorithmic methods to tackle them, Evolutionary Algorithms only being a small group of them. More traditional approaches to global optimization will be a (brief) topic of the next section.

1.3.1   Some Traditional Methods

The large number of existing global optimization methods makes it difficult to classify them adequately. This is clearly demonstrated by Törn

---

[42]Details on quadratic forms, convex and concave functions and positive definiteness (positive semi-definiteness) are omitted, since they are not relevant for the global optimization methods described here and may be found in any textbook of linear algebra.

[43]For reasons of clarity the graphic shows a plot of $-f$, i.e., the objective function has to be maximized then. The location of the global optimum is indicated in figure 1.9 by the broken lines.

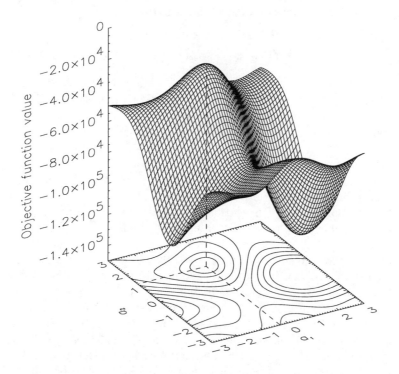

Fig. 1.9: Typical topology of a nonlinear parameter estimation problem ($n = 2$).

and Žilinskas, who discuss six existing classifications before presenting their own (see [TŽ89], pp. 16–19). Of course, neither their classification nor that of Zhigljavsky ([Zhi92], pp. 10–13) is used here. Instead, the following classification, taken from [Rud90], is more appropriate to the properties of Evolutionary Algorithms. The main distinction is made between *volume-oriented* and *path-oriented* methods, the latter group being subdivided further into *prediction* methods and *exploration* methods. Volume-oriented methods are based on the idea that the whole feasible region must be scanned, implying the requirement of a restricted search space of finite volume, while the concept of a path-oriented method is to follow a path in the feasible region, starting from an arbitrary or from the best point known so far. Prediction methods use an explicit internal model of the objective function to predict the steps while exploration methods do not possess an explicit internal model. Usually, the latter test different paths without requiring each trial to be successful, but discard a path if its inappropriateness is confirmed. Some classical representatives of these classes are grid search (see e.g. [Sch77], pp. 32–33), Monte-Carlo strategies (see e.g. [Sch77], pp. 108–110; [Zhi92], pp. 77–80), and cluster algorithms (see e.g. [TŽ89], pp. 95–116) as volume-oriented representatives, tunneling methods (see e.g. [TŽ89], pp. 61–62) as path-oriented prediction methods, and pattern search (see e.g. [Sch77], pp. 54–58) or the method of rotating coordinates (see e.g. [Sch77], pp. 58–63) as path-oriented exploration methods.

As we will see later, Evolutionary Algorithms combine all these features and cannot be assigned specifically to one of the categories given here. They fit best into the group of path-oriented exploration methods, but to a lesser degree they are also predicting as well as volume-oriented methods. The character of the algorithms changes during the course of the optimization process and can also be controlled by exogenous parameters.

To turn over to theoretical results about global optimization methods, a common misunderstanding is discussed first which was previously indiciated at the beginning of the discussion on molecular Darwinism (section 1.1.4). It concerns the *Monte-Carlo* method or *uniform random search*, which is often misinterpreted as an evolutionary method. But evolution has a memory in parent genomes, and offspring are never generated independently from parents, as is the case in uniform random search. To formulate and analyze the algorithm, a volume measure for bodies in n-dimensional Euclidean space is required. The *Lebesgue-measure* provides such a generalized volume concept.

Definition 1.9 (Lebesgue-measure) *Let $A_i \subset I\!\!R^n$ denote a system of pairwise disjunctive subsets of $I\!\!R^n$ ($A_i \cap A_j = \emptyset \; \forall i \neq j$). A measure μ characterizes the Lebesgue-measurable sets of $I\!\!R^n$, iff:*

$$
\begin{aligned}
\mu(A_i) &\geq 0 \\
\mu(A_i \cup A_j) &= \mu(A_i) + \mu(A_j) \\
\mu(\emptyset) &= 0 \\
\mu\left(\bigcup_{i=1}^{\infty} A_i\right) &= \sum_{i=1}^{\infty} \mu(A_i) \quad .
\end{aligned}
\tag{1.34}
$$

The following formulation of a uniform random search algorithm makes use of the probability density function of an n-dimensional uniform probability distribution on the feasible region $M \subseteq I\!\!R^n$, which is simply given by $1/\mu(M)$.

Algorithm 1 (Uniform random search)

```
t := 1;
f₀ := ∞;
while (t < t_max) do
        sample x⃗(t) according to p(x⃗(t)) = 1/μ(M);
        evaluate x⃗(t) : f(x⃗(t));
        if f(x⃗(t)) ≤ f_{t-1} then f_t := f(x⃗(t));
        t := t + 1;
od
```

It is important to note that the probability distribution is constant for each iteration, independent of the actual or previous trials. For this algorithm it can be shown that the sequence $\vec{x}(1), \vec{x}(2), \ldots$ of search points generated asymptotically approaches the global optimum, i.e., the property of *convergence with probability one* holds. The definition is taken from [TŽ89] (p. 78):

Definition 1.10 (Convergence with probability one)
The sequence $\vec{x}(1), \vec{x}(2), \ldots$ *of random vectors* $\vec{x}(i) \in I\!\!R^n$ *converges to* $\vec{x}^*$
with probability one: $\iff$

$$P\{\lim_{i \to \infty} \vec{x}(i) = \vec{x}^*\} = 1 \quad . \tag{1.35}$$

The following convergence theorem for uniform random search, including the proof, is cited from Zhigljavsky's book (see [Zhi92], pp. 78–79).

Theorem 2 *Let* $f : M \subseteq I\!\!R^n \to I\!\!R$ *for a Lebesgue-measurable feasible region* M. *Then, the sequence* $\vec{x}(1), \vec{x}(2), \ldots$ *of random vectors generated by algorithm 1 converges to* $\vec{x}^*$ *with probability one.*

Proof: For arbitrary $\varepsilon > 0$, it is

$$P\{\vec{x}(k) \in U_\varepsilon(\vec{x}^*)\} \quad = \quad 1 - \left(1 - \frac{\mu(U_\varepsilon(\vec{x}^*))}{\mu(M)}\right)^k \quad , \tag{1.36}$$

i.e., $P\{\lim_{k \to \infty} \vec{x}(k) = \vec{x}^*\} = 1.$ Q.E.D.

To put this into a more concrete form, we assume the feasible region M to be a hypersphere of radius R. Furthermore, $U_\varepsilon(\vec{x}^*)$ is a hypersphere of radius ε, centered around $\vec{x}^*$. The Lebesgue-measure of these sets amounts to

$$\mu(M) \quad = \quad \frac{R^n \pi^{n/2}}{\Gamma(\pi/2 + 1)} \tag{1.37}$$

respectively $\mu(U_\varepsilon(\vec{x}^*)) = \varepsilon^n \pi^{n/2}/\Gamma(\pi/2 + 1)$ (where Γ denotes the *Gamma function*[44]), i.e., their volume ratio[45] is

$$\frac{\mu(U_\varepsilon(\vec{x}^*))}{\mu(M)} = \left(\frac{\varepsilon}{R}\right)^n . \tag{1.38}$$

Thus, in order to reach at least a probability p^* to hit $U_\varepsilon(\vec{x}^*)$,

$$p^* = 1 - \left(1 - \left(\frac{\varepsilon}{R}\right)^n\right)^k \tag{1.39}$$

results, or, after solving for the number k of trials:

$$k = \frac{\ln(1 - p^*)}{\ln\left(1 - \left(\frac{\varepsilon}{R}\right)^n\right)} . \tag{1.40}$$

Using the approximation $\ln(1 + x) \approx x$ for $x \ll 1$, we obtain

$$k \approx -\ln(1 - p^*) \left(\frac{R}{\varepsilon}\right)^n , \tag{1.41}$$

which again clearly demonstrates the exponential growth of computation time depending on n. Indeed, it can be shown for $p^* > 0.63$ that the uniform random search performs worse than grid search (see [Sch77], pp. 108–109). This result is only due to not preventing repeatedly sampling the same points.

The main problem with the uniform random search algorithm is given by the restriction to a constant probability distribution. A more general form of the algorithm allows for the construction of a new probability distribution at each iteration. The new distribution may or may not depend on previous trial results generated by the algorithm. This generalized algorithm includes, as we will demonstrate later, certain versions of Evolutionary Algorithms as well as the uniform random search algorithm. Furthermore, it incorporates the random search algorithm by Solis and Wets and provides the basis for the corresponding global convergence result [SW81] and the result presented by Pintér [Pin84]. The description of the global random search algorithm is based again on Zhigljavsky's book ([Zhi92], p. 85).

---

[44]$\Gamma(x) = \int_0^x t^{x-1} \exp(-t) dt.$

[45]Brooks misinterpreted uniform random search by overlooking the fact that the volume ratio depends on n, consequently arriving at the result that the number of search steps is independent of n [Bro58]. This was recognized and corrected by Hooke and Jeeves [HJ58].

Algorithm 2 (Global random search)

$t := 1$;
choose probability distribution p_1 *on* M;
while not *terminate* **do**
         sample $\{\vec{x}_1(t), \ldots, \vec{x}_{N_t}(t)\}$ *from* p_t;
         evaluate $\{\vec{x}_1(t), \ldots, \vec{x}_{N_t}(t)\}$:
                 $\{f(\vec{x}_1(t)), \ldots, f(\vec{x}_{N_t}(t))\}$;
         construct p_{t+1} *according to a fixed rule;*
         $t := t + 1$;
od

Without loss of generality, $\forall t : N_t = 1$ can be assumed. Then, the following convergence theorem taken from [Zhi92] (p. 88) holds[46]:

Theorem 3 *Let f be continuous in the vicinity of $\vec{x}^*$ and assume that*

$$\forall \varepsilon > 0 : \sum_{t=1}^{\infty} q_t(\varepsilon) = \infty \quad , \qquad (1.42)$$

where

$$q_t(\varepsilon) = \inf_{1 \leq i < t} \{\mathcal{P}\{\vec{x}(i) \in U_\varepsilon(\vec{x}^*)\}\} \quad . \qquad (1.43)$$

Then for any $\delta > 0$ the sequence of random vectors $\vec{x}(1), \vec{x}(2), \ldots$ generated by algorithm 2 with $\forall t : N_t = 1$ falls infinitely often into the set $L_{f^*+\delta}$ with probability one.

Proof: Fix $\delta > 0$ and find $\varepsilon = \varepsilon(\delta) > 0$ such that $U_\varepsilon(\vec{x}^*) \subset L_{f^*+\delta}$. Determine the sequence of independent random variables $\{\chi_t\}$ on the two point set $\{0, 1\}$ such that

$$\mathcal{P}\{\chi_t = 1\} = 1 - \mathcal{P}\{\chi_t = 0\} = q_t(\varepsilon) \quad . \qquad (1.44)$$

Then, $\mathcal{P}\{\vec{x}(t) \in U_\varepsilon(\vec{x}^*)\} \geq \mathcal{P}\{\chi_t = 1\}$, and the theorem is proved if one can show that $\{\chi_t\}$ infinitely often takes value one. The latter follows from equation (1.42) and Borel's zero-one law (see [Rén77], pp. 326–328, p. 342), which completes the proof.   Q.E.D.

Theorem 3 does *not* in general imply global convergence with probability one according to definition 1.10. Although the set $L_{f^*+\delta}$ is sampled infinitely often, the global minimum is also "lost" again by the algorithm as long as no countermeasure to prevent such losses is added. The simplest countermeasure is to accept $\vec{x}(t)$ only if it improves the objective function value monotonously (i.e., $f(\vec{x}(t)) \leq f(\vec{x}(t-1))$),

---

[46]The notation used by Zhigljavsky in his book in English language is not always clear. It is more useful sometimes to have a look at the mathematical notation used in a book written by Zhigljavsky and Žilinskas, although the book is in Russian language [ZŽ91]. For the theorem discussed here, p. 124 of the latter book was very helpful.

but more complicated methods are possible. Nevertheless, theorem 3 is useful and will be referred to in chapter 2, as it provides the basis of some known proofs of global convergence with probability one. Due to its generality, the theorem does no longer allow for an estimation of the computational complexity of the algorithm as uniform random search did. In general, we have to assume exponential complexity in n.

These algorithms together with their convergence theorems conclude this section on global optimization and its mathematical background as far as related to Evolutionary Algorithms. Disregarding the emphasis on a similarity to the biological model, Evolutionary Algorithms can be interpreted as global random search techniques and therefore may be categorized as an instance within a variety of techniques proposed and analyzed by researchers. Overviews of these techniques are given in both books extensively referenced in this section, i.e., [TŽ89] and [Zhi92]. But the reverse interpretation does not hold; there is no reason to agree with Törn and Žilinskas who reduce Evolutionary Algorithms to nothing more than a notational convention, writing (see [TŽ89], p. 74)[47]:

> *Even the simplest random search algorithm may be inter-*
> *preted in terms of biological evolution. Generating a random*
> *trial point is analogous to mutation and the step towards the*
> *minimum after a successful trial is a selection.*

Evolutionary Algorithms, in contrary, try to benefit from looking at nature and modeling concepts gleaned from biological evolution as these obviously have proven to be useful, but this depends somehow on one's "world model." It is this interpretation from life surrounding us which helps to develop better stochastic search algorithms which are widely applicable and at the same time relatively efficient. Those who interpret uniform random search in terms of biological evolution do wrong by nature in assuming her to use disproportionately silly mechanisms.

1.3.2 Computational Complexity of Global Optimization

Within this section some important results on the computational complexity of global optimization problems will be summarized. These results will be helpful as they allow estimation of the limits of what can be achieved by trying to solve global optimization problems using a random search technique or, more specifically, an Evolutionary Algorithm. For a more formal treatment of an algorithm, the concept of a *Turing machine* is used. A Turing machine is the abstract machine capable of computing any function $f : A^* \rightarrow A^*$ for which an algorithmic description can be given. The *alphabet* A is a finite set of symbols, and A^* denotes the set of all finite strings of symbols from A, including the empty string.

---

[47]Reprinted by permission of Springer-Verlag and the authors from A. Törn, A. Žilinskas: *Global Optimization*, Lecture Notes in Computer Science 350, p. 74, copyright © Springer-Verlag Berlin Heidelberg 1989.

This equivalence of Turing machines (and, consequently, a number of different formal systems which are known to be computationally equivalent with Turing machines) and algorithms, known as *Church's thesis*, is the basis of modern theoretical computer science. A Turing machine is surprisingly simple, shown schematically in figure 1.10. It consists of a *two-way infinite tape*, made up of tape squares each of which is allowed to contain just one of a finite set T of *tape symbols* and which are labeled by integer numbers. A *read-write head* is able to look up and manipulate the tape, one tape square at each time step. The read-write head is controlled by the "program" of the Turing machine, the *finite state control*, which is defined by a transition function ϑ.

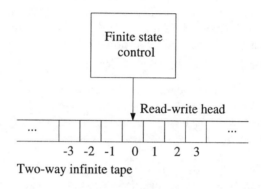

Fig. 1.10: Schematic diagram of a Turing machine.

Definition 1.11 (Deterministic Turing machine) *A* deterministic Turing machine *(DTM) is an eight-tuple*

$$DTM = (T, A, b_T, Q, q_0, q_Y, q_N, \vartheta) \qquad (1.45)$$

where T is a finite set of tape symbols, $A \subset T$ *is a subset of* input symbols, $b_T \in T - A$ *is a distuingished* blank symbol, Q *denotes a finite set of* states, *including a* start-state $q_0 \in Q$ *and two different* halt-states $q_Y \in Q$ *and* $q_N \in Q$.

$$\vartheta : (Q - \{q_Y, q_N\}) \times T \to Q \times T \times \{-1, +1\} \qquad (1.46)$$

is the transition function.

Informally, the DTM works as follows: The machine receives an input string $s \in A^*$ on certain subsequent fields of the tape, say fields $1, \ldots, |s|$, the rest of the tape containing blank symbols. The computation starts in state q_0 having the read-write head placed on field number 1. A state transition of the form

$$\vartheta(q, s_1) \quad = \quad (q', s_2, \Delta) \tag{1.47}$$

indicates that, being in state q and reading symbol $s_1 \in T$ with its read-write head, the machine operates by overwriting s_1 by $s_2 \in T$, moving the read-write head one field to the left (right), if $\Delta = -1$ ($\Delta = +1$), and going into state $q' \in Q$. If the new state $q' = q_Y$ or $q' = q_N$, computation ends, the answer being "yes" in the first, "no" in the second case. Usually being notated in the form of a transition table, ϑ provides the finite control ("program") of the machine.

Based on this working mechanism, all input strings $s \in A^*$ to a deterministic Turing machine can be classified according to the acceptance criterion provided by the distuingished halt-state q_Y.

Definition 1.12 (Recognized language of a DTM)
A DTM D with input alphabet A accepts $s \in A^*$ iff D halts in state q_Y when applied to s. The language L_D recognized by D is

$$L_D \quad = \quad \{s \in A^* \mid D \text{ accepts } s\} \quad . \tag{1.48}$$

Most critical to assessing the efficiency of an algorithm is its running time needed for performing the calculation. Very naturally, the basic time unit of a Turing machine is one execution step (1.47) of the transition function. Then, an informal notion of the time complexity of a Turing machine is as follows:

Definition 1.13 (Time complexity function of a DTM)
For a DTM D that halts for all inputs $s \in A^*$, the time complexity function $\tau_D : \mathbf{Z}^+ \to \mathbf{Z}^+$ *is:*

$$\tau_D(n) \quad = \quad \max\{m \mid \exists s \in A^* , \; |s| = n : \\ \text{the time to accept } s \text{ by } D \text{ is } m\} \quad . \tag{1.49}$$

D is called a polynomial time *DTM iff there exists a polynomial p such that $\forall n \in \mathbf{Z}^+ : \tau_D(n) \leq p(n)$.*

The basic idea is to distinguish between algorithms requiring at most polynomial computation time and those requiring more than polynomial (i.e., exponential) time. While the former are generally interpreted to be treatable, a problem is interpreted as intractable if all deterministic algorithms to solve it are of at least exponential time complexity[48]. Therefore, the class P of languages formally captures the idea of polynomial time algorithms or tractable problems.

---

[48]But bear in mind that for small problem sizes (i.e., small values of n), an exponential time bounded algorithm can be more efficient than a polynomial one.

Definition 1.14 (P)

$$P \; = \; \{L \mid \text{\textit{There is a polynomial time DTM }} D \; : \; L = L_D\} \quad .(1.50)$$

In contrast to a deterministic Turing machine, a *nondeterministic* one (NDTM) captures the intractable problems in the sense explained above. A NDTM is almost identical to a DTM, except that the transition function now allows for an arbitrary choice out of a set of possible transitions from a current state and input symbol.

Definition 1.15 (Nondeterministic Turing machine)
A nondeterministic Turing machine *(NDTM) is an eight-tuple*

$$NDTM = (T, A, b_T, Q, q_0, q_Y, q_N, \vartheta) \tag{1.51}$$

where T, A, b_T, Q, q_0, q_Y, q_N *are defined as in the deterministic case and*

$$\vartheta : (Q - \{q_Y, q_N\}) \times T \rightarrow 2^{Q \times T \times \{-1,+1\}} \tag{1.52}$$

maps a state / symbol pair to a set of possible actions.

An alternative but completely equivalent formulation of the idea is presented in [GJ79] (p. 28–31): A NDTM is a DTM which is extended by a "guessing" module, which writes a string $s \in A^*$ to the tape in an arbitrary, nondeterministic manner, possibly never halting. Then, the normal DTM part runs on the guessed string, either accepting it or not accepting it (i.e., performing a check whether the guess was right). This way, whenever a solution to the problem is guessed, it is assured that the NDTM can check the solution in polynomial time.

Definition 1.16 (Recognized language of a NDTM)
A NDTM D *with input alphabet* A *accepts* $s \in A^*$ *iff at least one of the infinite number of possible computations of* D *on* s *halts in state* q_Y. *The language* L_D *recognized by* D *is*

$$L_D \; = \; \{s \in A^* \mid D \text{ \textit{accepts} } s\} \quad . \tag{1.53}$$

Now, when there may be several distinct computations of D on input s leading to acceptance, the *time to accept* s is defined as the minimum time over all accepting computations of D on s.

Definition 1.17 (Time complexity function of a NDTM)
The time complexity function $\tau_D : \mathbb{Z}^+ \rightarrow \mathbb{Z}^+$ *of a NDTM* D *is given by*

$$\begin{aligned} \tau_D(n) \; = \; \max\{&m \mid \exists s \in L_D \, , \; |s| = n \; : \\ &\text{\textit{the time to accept }} s \text{ \textit{ by } } D \text{ \textit{ is } } m\} \quad . \end{aligned} \tag{1.54}$$

Finally, the class NP is defined as

Definition 1.18 (NP)

$$NP = \{L \mid There\ is\ a\ polynomial\ time\ NDTM\ D\ :\ L = L_D\}\ (1.55)$$

It is obvious from the definitions that any decision problem solvable by a deterministic polynomial time algorithm is also solvable by a non-deterministic polynomial time algorithm, i.e., $P \subseteq NP$. Furthermore, it is widely believed, but not proved, that $P \neq NP$, because nobody has been able to find a deterministic polynomial time algorithm for a problem in NP.

What is still needed is to establish the connection between optimization problems, decision problems, and accepted languages. Rather than going too much into details about the second connection, it is sufficient to recognize that an encoding of a problem instance as a word taken from a finite alphabet is always possible (see [GJ79], pp. 18–21, for further details). Concerning the formulation of optimization problems as decision problems, the pseudoboolean optimization problem $f : \mathbb{B}^n \to \mathbb{Z}$ (restricting here the possible range of values to $\mathbb{Z}$) is cited here from the work of Hart and Belew as a decision problem [HB91]:

Definition 1.19 (Pseudoboolean optimization problem)
Given a string encoding integers n and c and a DTM D_f which computes a function $f : \mathbb{B}^n \to \mathbb{Z}$ in polynomial time, the decision problem of pseudoboolean optimization is: Does there exist an $\vec{x} \in \mathbb{B}^n$ such that $f(\vec{x}) > c$?

In any case, a decision problem can be no harder to solve than the corresponding optimization problem. Hart and Belew also show the *NP-completeness* of this decision problem, a term which, to express it informally, denotes the hardest problems in NP. If only one NP-complete problem could be solved in polynomial time, then all problems in NP could be solved in polynomial time. The reason is that for an NP-complete problem $L \in NP$ all other problems in NP can be mapped to L by a *polynomial transformation*.

Definition 1.20 (Polynomial transformation)
A polynomial transformation from a language $L_1 \subseteq A_1^*$ to language $L_2 \subseteq A_2^*$ is a function $h : A_1^* \to A_2^*$ such that:

(1) There is a polynomial time DTM program that computes h.

(2) $\forall s_1 \in A_1^*: s_1 \in L_1 \Leftrightarrow h(s_1) \in L_2$.

The notation $L_1 \bowtie L_2$ denotes the existence of a polynomial transformation from L_1 to L_2.

Definition 1.21 (NP-completeness) *A language L is NP-complete iff $L \in NP$ and:*

$$\forall L' \in NP\ :\ L' \bowtie L\ .\ \ \ \ \ \ \ \ \ \ (1.56)$$

Polynomial transformation is a transitive relation, such that for demonstrating that a language L_2 is NP-complete it suffices to show $L_2 \in NP$ and to find a polynomial transformation from a known NP-complete language $L_1 \in NP$ to L_2. Of course, there must exist a first NP-complete problem for which NP-completeness has to be shown explicitly. This is the satisfiability problem for boolean expressions, and its NP-completeness is the subject of Cook's theorem (e.g. [AHU74], pp. 379–383).

According to the exponential growth of the search space as discussed in section 1.3.1, it is not surprising that the decision problem to check whether a given feasible solution of a smooth, nonconvex nonlinear optimization problem is not a local minimum is also NP-complete. The result implies that any global optimization problem that goes beyond a very low complexity is an NP-complete problem [MK87].

In addition to NP, Hart and Belew need the class RP for deriving their results. RP is a class of languages almost identically defined as NP, but with the exception that for acceptance of $s \in A^*$ at least half of all computations halt in state q_Y (compare definition 1.16). It is known that $RP \subseteq NP$ and $P \cap RP \neq \emptyset$, and it is widely believed that $RP \neq NP$. The main result presented by Hart and Belew states that no single nondeterministic algorithm exists which is able to approach the global optimum of arbitrary functions $f : \mathbb{B}^n \to \mathbb{Z}$ to a certain accuracy ε in an efficient way, i.e., in a time polynomial in n [HB91]:

Theorem 4 *If $RP \neq NP$, then no nondeterministic polynomial time algorithm $\mathcal{A}$ can guarantee that $\forall f : \mathbb{B}^n \to \mathbb{Z}$:*

$$f^* - \mathcal{A}(f) \;\leq\; \varepsilon \qquad\qquad (1.57)$$

for a constant $\varepsilon \in \mathbb{R}$, $\varepsilon > 0$. Here $\mathcal{A}(f)$ is used to denote the result algorithm $\mathcal{A}$ yields when applied to problem f.

Practically, this is a big disappointment. Though it was known in advance that there does not exist a deterministic polynomial time algorithm capable of exactly solving arbitrary pseudoboolean optimization problems, there was some hope that nondeterministic efficient algorithms might exist to do so, e.g. Evolutionary Algorithms. This is not the case, however. Even worse, no efficient nondeterministic *approximation* algorithm for arbitrary pseudoboolean optimization problems exists!

Intuitively, such a result can be explained by considering an objective function that consists of a flat plateau that contains a very sharp hole where the minimum is located (e.g. a pseudoboolean function that yields identical function values for all but one argument vector which is sought after). Assuming such a flat plateau, no other method than those requiring exponential time is able to locate the minimum. Since theorem 4 in principle also includes problems of this kind, the result is quite understandable. In realistic applications, however, it is a reasonable assumption that the structure of the optimization problem provides more useful topological information for the algorithm and that we are not interested in locating solutions that are sharply isolated in flat regions ("needle in a haystack").

1.4 Early Approaches

More than thirty years ago, during the subsymbolic period of Artificial Intelligence, some researchers presented first attempts to model natural evolution as a method for searching for good solutions of problems defined on vast search spaces. These spaces are clearly too large for complete enumeration, particularly as only very restricted computer power was available at that time. The approaches reported in the literature are briefly discussed here, because the application domains of automatic programming, sequence prediction, numerical optimization, and optimal control are even more interesting currently than at that time. Additionally, the basic algorithmic concepts used thirty years ago are still the basic techniques used in the modern algorithms (though currently extended by many other useful techniques and confirmed by some theoretical results).

The term *automatic programming* denotes the task of finding a program which calculates a certain input-output function. However, this task has to be performed by a computer program, i.e. an artificially intelligent program which is able to "write" and test computer programs. We will not discuss here all problems related to automatic programming, but an attempt towards evolving computer programs as performed by Friedberg et al. in 1958 was surely much too early for having real success [Fri58, FDN59] (due to the restricted performance of the computers available at that time). The computer program to be evolved by Friedberg's Evolutionary Algorithm was binary encoded and was modified by instruction interchange and random changes of instructions. To perform these random changes, whenever a mutation occurred, a complete new instruction was chosen to substitute the mutated one. The simple program generation tasks were to find, starting from a random program, the identical mapping and the complement mapping on a single bit, a program calculating the sum of two input bits, and a program having an internal counter where the output should depend on the number of program executions. Since the modification methods of instruction interchange and random instruction changes were undirected[49] Friedberg introduced a "success number" for instructions. The success numbers indicated how well the instructions had served over thousands of previous trials, and the mutation rate depended on the success numbers of the instructions. This way, instructions which were successful in previous trials

---

[49] As we will see later on, such an evaluation scheme as used by Friedberg will nowadays be called a (1,1)-strategy.

were less often mutated than worse instructions. Not surprisingly, the success numbers proved to be useful for the evolution process. However, the complete evolution mechanism was found to perform worse than a pure random search, which was mainly due to the absence of an effective selection mechanism. The success numbers could not provide sufficient selective pressure because they needed many trials before representing the instructions' usefulness at least approximately correct. Furthermore, the approach measured quality of the program by combining the binary feedback information from execution of the program (output bit is correct or is incorrect) and the local quality information associated with each instruction. This is a questionable method for judging the quality of the program, since the fitness function is extremely discontinuous[50]: Small changes in program syntax usually cause large changes in the input-output behaviour of the program.

Concerning selective pressure, Friedberg proposed to use a mechanism to test several different programs created by random instruction changes and instruction interchanges from the actual one and to choose the best of the new programs as the next starting point. Such a selection mechanism comes close to the modern ones discussed in chapter 2, where it will be denoted a $(1,\lambda)$-strategy (assuming λ descendants are created from the ancestor). Friedberg could not implement it due to memory restrictions of the IBM 704 computer he used for the experiments.

Bremermann's work was more oriented towards optimization [Bre62]. He used discrete as well as continuous object variables and a discrete mutation mechanism also for continuous variables, since the work was at the beginning closely oriented to the knowledge about the discrete nature of the genetic code. Since he knew about Friedberg's disappointing results, Bremermann assumed the necessity of choosing relatively simple optimization problems and restricted the experiments to linear and convex programming. For binary object variables he correctly argued that multiple mutations — extremely unlikely events — are necessary to overcome "points of stagnation". Furthermore, he presented an estimation of the optimal mutation probability, which was the value $1/l$ (l being the number of bits an individual consisted of) [BRS65]. This value is still in use as a general heuristic, although most people who use it are not aware of its originator. In order to overcome the problem of stagnation points, Bremermann invented the idea of creating a number of descendants from an ancestor by means of mutation and then to reduce a subset of these descendants to a new, single ancestor of the next generation by mating techniques. The subset consists of the best solutions occurring among the descendants. In particular, he used an averaging process in case of continuous object variables, but he also tried exchanges of information between individuals in more complicated forms of the algorithm. However, most of the results were disappointing, and the algorithms had to incorporate additional heuristics to converge

---

[50]Every programmer will confirm the statement from personal experience.

toward a solution. From lots of practical experience with applications of Evolutionary Algorithms it can be concluded that Bremermann's application to linear and convex programming used a much too simple problem domain, where Evolutionary Algorithms can not compete with the variety of specialized optimization techniques.

While both approaches presented so far have — due to reasons indicated in the discussion given above — failed to provide an efficient instrument for solving a problem from the actual domain chosen by the author, Fogel presented successful results from another approach to evolutionary computation in 1964 [Fog64, FOW66]. This approach is called *Evolutionary Programming*.

In contrast to Bremermann, they used a more complicated application domain, and in contrast to Friedberg they provided a real selective pressure as well as a reasonably graded quality function, which was able to reward small improvements of the quality of the evolving objects. For measuring the quality of an individual in the framework of a sequence prediction problem, the sequence generated by the individual was compared to a target sequence and the percentage of correct letters determined the individual's fitness. An individual was a symbolic representation of the transition table of a finite-state-machine (FSM), and by means of mutation the single offspring individual could differ from its ancestor either by an output symbol, a state transition, the number of states, or the initial state. After testing the performance of the offspring FSM, the better individual of both ancestor and offspring became the ancestor of the next step. The worse one was discarded[51]. Similar to Bremermann, Fogel, Owens, and Walsh argued that such a search mechanism might become trapped in a local optimum. Therefore, they used a population in order to solve this problem, and they realized a population-based algorithm that created an offspring population from a parent population of the same size by mutating each individual. Selection then determined the best half of parents and offspring to form the next parent population[52]. In addition, they also mentioned the ideas to permit multiple mutations and to use recombination as well as mutation.

Although their work avoided the mistakes made by Friedberg and Bremermann, it did not find a suitable acknowledgement in the following years. Instead, the idea of Evolutionary Algorithms received small attention until the beginning of the seventies, when *Genetic Algorithms* in the United States and *Evolution Strategies* in Germany were fully developed independently of each other. An overview of the history of these modern Evolutionary Algorithms will be presented in chapter 2.

It seems natural to assume that the disappointing results by Friedberg and Bremermann in combination with insufficient hardware power (which made planning and execution of programming projects a difficult task) caused both the ignorance of the work of Fogel, Owens, and

---

[51] Such a selection scheme would presently be called a $(1+1)$-strategy.

[52] This can be denoted a $(\mu+\mu)$-strategy, where μ is the population size.

Walsh and the stagnation of development in the field of Evolutionary Algorithms. Goldberg presents a misjudgement, when he gives his opinion on the work of Fogel, Owens, and Walsh (see [Gol89a], p. 106)[53]:

> *The evolutionary programming of Fogel, Owens, and Walsh with its random alteration of a finite-state-machine and save-the-best selection was insufficiently powerful to search other than small problem spaces quickly.*

He strongly emphasizes the importance of recombination over mutation, and especially the interaction of both operators and the selection technique will be one of the major topics to be discussed and analyzed in the remaining chapters of this book.

Finally, we mention the *Evolutionary Operation* (EVOP) approach as presented by Box for the first time in the late fifties [Box57, BD69]. Though this method emphasized on the natural model of organic evolution by performing a mutation-selection process in the sense of a $(1+\lambda)$-strategy (where $\lambda = 4$ or $\lambda = 8$, the so-called 2^2 and 2^3 *factorial design* method, respectively), it was basically intended to serve as an industrial management technique. This management technique provided a systematic way to test alternative production processes that result from small modifications of the standard parameter settings, this way leading to its stepwise improvement. The method was not intended to be realized as a computer algorithm, but if it were realized, it would probably resemble a $(1+\lambda)$-Evolution Strategy without a step-size adaptation mechanism (see section 2.1).

1.5 Summary

Within this first, introductory chapter we have discussed Evolutionary Algorithms from a wide range of different points of view, thus reflecting the enormous degree of interdisciplinarity related to this fascinating field of research. Four important aspects of Evolutionary Algorithms were discussed in detail: The biological background (section 1.1), the relation to Artificial Intelligence (section 1.2), the relation to global optimization (section 1.3) and the computational complexity of the global optimization problem (section 1.3.2). A lot of background information and theoretical results collected together highlights the basic design of Evolutionary Algorithms and some of their general limitations imposed by the global optimization problem per se.

The connection between optimization and evolution turned out to be established by the adaptive landscape metaphor relating fitness to trait combinations. Though we did not discuss the biological background in full detail, the basic processes of transcription and translation, the

---

[53]David E. Goldberg, GENETIC ALGORITHMS IN SEARCH, OPTIMIZATION, AND MACHINE LEARNING (pg. 106), ©1989 by Addison-Wesley Publishing Company, Inc. Reprinted by permission of the publisher.

genetic code and the hierarchical structure of the genetic information were explained in section 1.1.1. In connection to meiotic heredity, the crossover mechanism occurring during the formation of gametes as well as the various forms of mutation events observable in organic evolution were presented in sections 1.1.2 and 1.1.3, thereby introducing the mechanisms responsible for genetic variation.

Section 1.1.4 served as an excursion to evolution processes on the lower level of biological macromolecules, explaining the existence of a unique genetic code for all forms of life on earth by the concept of hypercycles. Identifying mutation, self-reproduction, and metabolism as necessary conditions for selection to occur, Eigen's mathematical model yields important insights into the nature of the evolution process and the optimal error rate, which is just below the critical value that prevents stable reproduction of information. A transfer of these results to simplified instances of Genetic Algorithms will become obvious in subsequent chapters.

Historically, Artificial Intelligence was the research field in which the first efforts towards problem solving with Evolutionary Algorithms were dealt with, i.e. automatic programming and sequence prediction. The impact of Evolutionary Algorithms to this important field of computer science was discussed in section 1.2. Evolutionary Algorithms are inductive learning algorithms that can serve as a powerful search method in many fields of Artificial Intelligence research, including Neural Networks, Classifier Systems, game playing, and Artificial Life.

In section 1.3 Evolutionary Algorithms were approached from the global optimization point of view, i.e. emphasizing the application problem and traditional methods for its solution. Three examples of global optimization problems representing different search spaces were presented in order to clarify the complexity and generality of the global optimization problem: The autocorrelation of binary sequences, the traveling salesman problem, and the general nonlinear parameter estimation problem. Besides introducing the basic terminology from global optimization, the uniform random search algorithm and a general global random search algorithm were discussed. While global convergence with probability one holds for both these algorithms, the former suffers from exponential time complexity. The latter is too general for time complexity analysis, but allows the transfer of the global convergence property to special variants of Evolutionary Algorithms.

Closely related, but from a computer science point of view, section 1.3.2 summarized some results on computational complexity of global optimization problems. In general, global optimization is NP-complete, which is surely not surprising. More disappointing is a result for pseudoboolean problems indicating that even at least an efficient (i.e. polynomial time) approximation algorithm for such problems does not exist. This may exclude only pathological problems from efficient approximation, but actually there is no theory available that supports such a classification of problems. Empirical results, however, confirm the assumption that practical applications allow for good approximations to be located by domain-dependent, specialized Evolutionary Algorithms.

Section 1.4 concludes the first chapter by mentioning the early approaches to use algorithms gleaned from the model of organic evolution for problem solving, pointing at the difficulties and mistakes that led to a relatively long period of stagnating research in this field.

2

Specific Evolutionary Algorithms

In this chapter, an outline of an Evolutionary Algorithm is formulated that is sufficiently general to cover at least the three different main stream algorithms mentioned before, namely, Evolution Strategies, Genetic Algorithms, and Evolutionary Programming. As in the previous chapter, algorithms are formulated in a language obtained by mixing pseudocode and mathematical notations, thus allowing for a high-level description which concentrates on the main components. These are: A population of individuals which is manipulated by genetic operators — especially mutation and recombination, but others may also be incorporated — and undergoes a fitness-based selection process, where fitness of an individual depends on its quality with respect to the optimization task. This is captured by the following definition:

Definition 2.1 (General Evolutionary Algorithm) *An* Evolutionary Algorithm *(EA) is defined as an 8-tuple*

$$\text{EA} = (I, \Phi, \Omega, \Psi, s, \iota, \mu, \lambda) \tag{2.1}$$

where $I = A_x \times A_s$ *is the space of individuals, and* A_x, A_s *denote arbitrary sets.* $\Phi : I \to \mathbb{R}$ *denotes a fitness function assigning real values to individuals.*

$$\Omega = \{\omega_{\Theta_1}, \ldots, \omega_{\Theta_z} \mid \omega_{\Theta_i} : I^\lambda \to I^\lambda\} \cup \{\omega_{\Theta_0} : I^\mu \to I^\lambda\} \tag{2.2}$$

is a set of probabilistic genetic operators ω_{Θ_i}, *each of which is controlled by specific parameters summarized in the sets* $\Theta_i \subset \mathbb{R}$.

$$s_{\Theta_s} : (I^\lambda \cup I^{\mu+\lambda}) \to I^\mu \tag{2.3}$$

denotes the selection operator, which may change the number of individuals from λ *or* $\lambda + \mu$ *to* μ, *where* μ, $\lambda \in \mathbb{N}$ *and* $\mu = \lambda$ *is permitted.*

*An additional set Θ_s of parameters may be used by the selection oper-
ator. μ is the number of parent individuals, while λ denotes the number
of offspring individuals. Finally, $\iota : I^\mu \to \{true, false\}$ is a termination
criterion for the EA, and the generation transition function $\Psi : I^\mu \to I^\mu$
describes the complete process of transforming a population P into a subsequent one by applying genetic operators and selection:*

$$
\begin{aligned}
\Psi &= s \circ \omega_{\Theta_{i_1}} \circ \ldots \circ \omega_{\Theta_{i_j}} \circ \omega_{\Theta_0} \\
\Psi(P) &= s_{\Theta_s}(Q \cup \omega_{\Theta_{i_1}}(\ldots(\omega_{\Theta_{i_j}}(\omega_{\Theta_0}(P)))\ldots))
\end{aligned}
\tag{2.4}
$$

Here $\{i_1, \ldots, i_j\} \subseteq \{1, \ldots, z\}$, and $Q \in \{\emptyset, P\}$.

The space of individuals may be arbitrarily complex, i.e. there are
no restrictions on the structure of the sets A_x and A_s, though they will
usually be relatively simple in the following. Even the fitness function Φ
may include some intermediate calculation steps, one of those always being evaluation of the objective function value which provides the basis
of the fitness value. Whenever $\mu \neq \lambda$, the operator set Ω includes a distinguished operator $\omega_0 : I^\mu \to I^\lambda$ which serves to change population size
forming λ offspring individuals from μ parents. This change is taken back
by selection, which performs a fitness-based change of population size
to μ individuals. While genetic operators are always probabilistic, selection may be probabilistic or completely deterministic. Both selection
and genetic operators may be controlled by some exogenous parameters. The termination criterion ι may range from arbitrarily complicated
criteria — e.g. genotypic or phenotypic diversity of the population, relative improvement of the best objective function value over subsequent
generations — to rather simple ones, e.g. testing whether a prespecified
number of generations is completed. A complete generation step, i.e. the
transition from the actual parent population to the subsequent one, consists of application of the genetic operators in a defined order, followed
by selection. This is captured in the generation transition function Ψ,
iterated application of which generates a *population sequence*:

Definition 2.2 (Population sequence) *Given an Evolutionary Algorithm with generation transition function $\Psi : I^\mu \to I^\mu$ and an initial
population $P(0) \in I^\mu$, the sequence $P(0), P(1), P(2), \ldots$ is called a population sequence or evolution of $P(0)$:* $\iff$

$$
\forall t \geq 0 \quad : \quad P(t+1) = \Psi(P(t)) \quad .
\tag{2.5}
$$

Creation of the initial population $P(0)$ is discussed later in connection
with the explanation of particular instances of Evolutionary Algorithms.
Usually, $P(0)$ is initialized at random, but it may also be generated
from one (known) starting point. The stopping criterion ι characterizes
the end of this artificial evolution process, and the result of a run of
an Evolutionary Algorithm is in most cases the individual of minimal
objective function value encountered during the complete evolution[1].

---

[1]This is typical for problem solving applications where emphasis is put on finding
best solutions.

This individual is not necessarily identical to the best one contained in the final population. The following definition summarizes this informal description of the running time and result of an Evolutionary Algorithm:

Definition 2.3 *Given an initial population $P(0) \in I^\mu$ for an Evolutionary Algorithm with generation transition function Ψ, the running time τ_{EA} is given by*

$$\tau_{EA} = \min\{t \in I\!N \mid \iota(\Psi^t(P(0))) = true\} \quad . \tag{2.6}$$

An individual

$$\vec{a} \in \bigcup_{t=0}^{\tau_{EA}} \Psi^t(P(0)) \tag{2.7}$$

is called the result *of an Evolutionary Algorithm when applied to the initial population $P(0)$, iff*

$$f(\vec{a}) = \min\{f(\vec{a}') \mid \vec{a}' \in \bigcup_{t=0}^{\tau_{EA}} \Psi^t(P(0))\} \quad . \tag{2.8}$$

The genetic operators are characterized here as macro-operators that transform a complete population into another complete population. This high-level description is put into more concrete terms by specifying the mechanisms which lead to the creation of a new individual from one or more ancestors. Basically, the high-level operators are reduced to a description by low-level operators as indicated in the following definition:

Definition 2.4 (Asexual, sexual, panmictic genetic operators)
A genetic operator $\omega_\Theta : I^p \to I^q$ is called

asexual   :⇔ $\exists \omega'_\Theta : I \to I$:
$$\omega_\Theta(\vec{a}_1, \ldots, \vec{a}_p) = (\omega'_\Theta(\vec{a}_1), \ldots, \omega'_\Theta(\vec{a}_p)) \wedge p = q \; ,$$

sexual   :⇔ $\exists \omega'_\Theta : I^2 \to I$:
$$\omega_\Theta(\vec{a}_1, \ldots, \vec{a}_p) = (\omega'_\Theta(\vec{a}_{i_1}, \vec{a}_{j_1}), \ldots, \omega'_\Theta(\vec{a}_{i_q}, \vec{a}_{j_q}))$$
where $\forall k \in \{1, \ldots, q\} \; i_k, j_k \in \{1, \ldots, p\}$ (2.9)
are chosen at random,

panmictic :⇔ $\exists \omega'_\Theta : I^p \to I$:
$$\omega_\Theta(\vec{a}_1, \ldots, \vec{a}_p) = (\underbrace{\omega'_\Theta(\vec{a}_1, \ldots, \vec{a}_p), \ldots, \omega'_\Theta(\vec{a}_1, \ldots, \vec{a}_p)}_{q})$$

The definition characterizes the essential number of individuals taken into account by the operators. Mutation is an example of an asexual operator, while recombination is typically sexual (i.e., it involves two parent individuals), but may also be extended in some variants of Evolutionary

Algorithms to a panmictic form (without any biological basis, see section 1.1.2). In the following, the symbols m and r are used to denote the high-level description of mutation and recombination, respectively, while m' and r' denote their asexual, sexual, or panmictic form.

The description given so far can be directly translated into a general algorithmic outline of an Evolutionary Algorithm. In algorithm 3, t denotes the generation counter, $P(t) = \{\vec{a}_1(t), \ldots, \vec{a}_\mu(t)\}$ is the population at generation t, consisting of individuals $\vec{a}_i \in I$, and μ denotes the parent population size. $Q \in \{\emptyset, P(t)\}$ denotes an additional set of individuals (e.g. the parent population) that may be taken into account by selection.

Algorithm 3 (Outline of an Evolutionary Algorithm)

$$t := 0;$$
$$\textit{initialize } P(0) := \{\vec{a}_1(0), \ldots, \vec{a}_\mu(0)\} \in I^\mu;$$
$$\textit{evaluate } P(0): \{\Phi(\vec{a}_1(0)), \ldots, \Phi(\vec{a}_\mu(0))\};$$
$$\textbf{while } (\iota(P(t)) \neq \textbf{true}) \textbf{ do}$$
$$\qquad \textit{recombine: } P'(t) := r_{\Theta_r}(P(t));$$
$$\qquad \textit{mutate: } P''(t) := m_{\Theta_m}(P'(t));$$
$$\qquad \textit{evaluate } P''(t): \{\Phi(\vec{a}_1''(t)), \ldots, \Phi(\vec{a}_\lambda''(t))\};$$
$$\qquad \textit{select: } P(t+1) := s_{\Theta_s}(P''(t) \cup Q);$$
$$\qquad t := t + 1;$$
$$\textbf{od}$$

In the following sections, Evolution Strategies, Evolutionary Programming, and Genetic Algorithms are presented within the general framework introduced so far. Since a unified notation has been introduced, similarities and differences of the algorithms can easily be identified. After giving a short overview of the history of each of these algorithms, their mechanisms of initialization, fitness evaluation, mutation, recombination, and selection are described. Furthermore, the basic theoretical results are summarized, stressing such results which are important in subsequent chapters. The chapter is concluded by a summarizing comparison of the algorithms with respect to their similarities and differences as well as their relation to the underlying model of organic evolution.

2.1 Evolution Strategies

Evolution Strategies are a joint development of Bienert, Rechenberg and Schwefel, who did preliminary work in this area in the 1960s at the Technical University of Berlin (TUB) in Germany. First applications were experimental and dealt with hydrodynamical problems like shape optimization of a bended pipe [Lic65], drag minimization of a joint plate [Rec65], and structure optimization of a two-phase flashing nozzle [Sch68][2]. Due to the impossibility to describe and solve such optimization problems analytically or by using traditional methods, a simple algorithmic method based on random changes of experimental setups was developed. In these experiments, adjustments were possible in discrete steps only, in the first two cases (pipe and plate) by changing certain joint positions and in the latter case (nozzle) by exchanging, adding or deleting nozzle segments. Following observations from nature that smaller mutations occur more often than larger ones, the discrete changes were sampled from a binomial distribution with prefixed variance. The basic working mechanism of the experiments was to create a mutation, adjust the joints or nozzle segments accordingly, perform the experiment and measure the quality criterion of the adjusted construction. If the new construction happened to be better than its predecessor, it served as basis for the next trial. Otherwise, it was discarded and the predecessor was retained. No information about the amount of improvements or deteriorations was necessary. This experimental strategy led to unexpectedly good results both for the bended pipe and the nozzle.

Schwefel was the first who simulated different versions of the strategy on the first available computer at TUB, a Zuse Z23 [Sch65], later on followed by several others who applied the simple Evolution Strategy to solve numerical optimization problems. Due to the theoretical results of Schwefel's diploma thesis, the discrete mutation mechanism was substituted by normally distributed mutations with expectation zero and given variance [Sch65]. The resulting *two membered* ES works by creating one n-dimensional real-valued vector of object variables from its parent by applying mutation with identical standard deviations to each object variable. The resulting individual is evaluated and compared to its parent, and the better of both individuals survives to become parent of the next generation, while the other one is discarded. This simple selection mechanism is fully characterized by the term $(1+1)$-selection.

For this algorithm, Rechenberg developed a convergence rate theory for $n \gg 1$ for two characteristic model functions, and he proposed a theoretically confirmed rule for changing the standard deviation of mutations (the *1/5-success rule*) [Rec73]. This strategy and the corresponding theory are discussed in section 2.1.7.

Obviously, the $(1+1)$-ES did not incorporate the principle of a population. A first *multimembered* Evolution Strategy or $(\mu+1)$-ES having $\mu > 1$ was also designed by Rechenberg to introduce a population concept. In a $(\mu+1)$-ES μ parent individuals recombine to form one offspring, which after being mutated eventually replaces the worst parent individual — if it is better (extinction of the worst). Mutation and adjustment of the standard deviation was realized as in a $(1+1)$-ES, and the recombination mechanisms will be explained in section 2.1.3. This

---

[2]This experiment is one of the first known examples of using operators like gene deletion and gene duplication, i.e. the number of segments the nozzle consisted of was allowed to vary during optimization.

strategy, discussed in more detail in [BHS91], was never widely used but provided the basis to facilitate the transition to the $(\mu+\lambda)$–ES and (μ,λ)–ES as introduced by Schwefel[3] [Sch75b, Sch77, Sch81a]. Again the notation characterizes the selection mechanism, in the first case indicating that the best μ individuals out of the union of parents and offspring survive while in the latter case only the best μ offspring individuals form the next parent generation (consequently, $\lambda > \mu$ is necessary). Currently, the (μ,λ)–ES characterizes the state-of-the-art in Evolution Strategy research and is therefore the strategy of our main interest to be explained in the following. As an introductory remark it should be noted that the major quality of this strategy is seen in its ability to incorporate the most important parameters of the strategy (standard deviations and correlation coefficients of normally distributed mutations) into the search process, such that optimization not only takes place on object variables, but also on strategy parameters according to the actual local topology of the objective function. This capability is termed *self-adaptation* by Schwefel [Sch87] and will be a major point of interest in discussing the Evolution Strategy.

2.1.1   Representation and Fitness Evaluation

As indicated previously, search points in Evolution Strategies are n-dimensional object parameter vectors $\vec{x} \in I\!R^n$ so that application to optimization problems as introduced in definition 1.1 of section 1.3 is an easy task. Given the objective function $f : I\!R^n \to I\!R$, the fitness function Φ is in principle identical to f, i.e. given an individual $\vec{a} \in I$, we have

$$\Phi(\vec{a}) \;=\; f(\vec{x}) \;\; . \tag{2.10}$$

Here $\vec{x}$ is the object variable component[4] of $\vec{a} = (\vec{x},\vec{\sigma},\vec{\alpha}) \in I = I\!R^n \times A_s$, where

$$
\begin{aligned}
A_s &= I\!R_+^{n_\sigma} \times [-\pi,\pi]^{n_\alpha} \\
n_\sigma &\in \{1,\dots,n\} \\
n_\alpha &\in \{0, (2n-n_\sigma)(n_\sigma-1)/2\} \;\; .
\end{aligned}
\tag{2.11}
$$

Besides representing the object variable vector $\vec{x}$, each individual may additionally include one up to n different standard deviations σ_i as well as up to $n \cdot (n-1)/2$ (namely, when $n_\sigma = n$) rotation angles $\alpha_{ij} \in [-\pi,\pi]$

---

[3]The material presented here is based on [Sch81a] and a number of research articles, but in the meantime an updated and extended edition of Schwefel's book was published (i.e., [Sch95]).

[4]We could be even more formal here by defining projections which yield different components of $\vec{a}$. However, this would unnecessarily complicate notations and is omitted here, because the meaning of components can be identified by the symbols used for notation, i.e. $\vec{x}$, $\vec{\sigma}$, $\vec{\alpha}$.

$(i \in \{1, \ldots, n-1\}, j \in \{i+1, \ldots, n\})^5$, such that the maximum number of strategy parameters amounts to $w = n \cdot (n + 1)/2$. For the case $1 < n_\sigma < n$, the standard deviations $\sigma_1, \ldots, \sigma_{n_\sigma-1}$ are coupled with object variables $x_1, \ldots, x_{n_\sigma-1}$ and σ_{n_σ} is used for the remaining variables $x_{n_\sigma}, \ldots, x_n$.

The number n_α of rotation angles depends directly on n_σ, the number of standard deviations, and n, but it can also explictly be set to zero, indicating that this strategy parameter part of individuals is not used[6]. The set of strategy parameters consisting of standard deviations and rotation angles provides a complete description of the generalized n-dimensional normal distribution with expectation value vector $\vec{0}$, having probability density function

$$p(\vec{z}) = \frac{\exp\left(-\frac{1}{2}\vec{z}^T \mathbf{C}^{-1} \vec{z}\right)}{\sqrt{(2\pi)^n \cdot \det \mathbf{C}}} \quad . \tag{2.12}$$

Here $\mathbf{C}^{-1} = (c_{ij})$ is the covariance matrix with diagonal elements $c_{ii} = \sigma_i^2$, i.e. the variances. Schwefel clarifies that the axes of the mutation ellipsoids (surfaces of equal probability density to place an offspring by mutation) are parallel to the coordinate axes only if $\mathbf{C}$ is a diagonal matrix ([Sch81a], p. 239f.). In the more general case of covariances which do not vanish, the mutation ellipsoids may have arbitrary orientation in the search space, and mutations of object variables are linearly correlated. In this way, the individuals may adapt to any advantageous direction of search, which is useful for example in case of narrow valleys where an orientation of mutation ellipsoids along the valley is most appropriate.

Figure 2.1 illustrates the most commonly occurring case for $n = 2$. Five individuals and their corresponding mutation hyperellipsoids are shown on a hypothetical objective function topology characterized by lines of equal objective function value. The left part of the figure shows the mutation ellipsoids (which are spheres in this case) for $n_\sigma = 1$, i.e., identical standard deviations along both coordinate axes. For $n_\sigma = 2$ (middle graphic) two different standard deviations allow for the deformation of spheres to ellipsoids in such a way that a preference direction may be found. This is even easier if, as shown in the right part of the figure, a linear correlation is introduced ($n_\sigma = 2$, $n_\alpha = 1$) such that the ellipsoids may rotate towards a direction of preference different from the coordinate axes. The three individuals located close to the upper left, upper right and lower right corner are now able to achieve larger steps towards the optimum than in the uncorrelated case.

---

[5]In the following we will switch between a vector interpretation and a matrix interpretation for $\vec{\alpha}$ just as it is most convenient. The underlying simple index transformation from $(i, j) \in \{1, \ldots, n-1\} \times \{i+1, \ldots, n\}$ to $\{1, \ldots, n \cdot (n-1)/2\}$ is given by the mapping $(i, j) \mapsto \frac{1}{2}(2n - i)(i + 1) - 2n + j$ [Rud90].

[6]This case is different from that which arises from setting $n_\sigma = 1$. When the user chooses $n_\alpha = 0$, he disables this feature of the algorithm completely, however having full choice of $n_\sigma \in \{1, \ldots, n\}$.

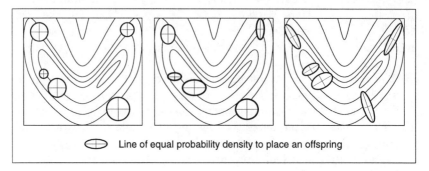

Line of equal probability density to place an offspring

Fig. 2.1: Illustration of mutation hyperellipsoids in case of simple mutations with $n_\sigma = 1$ (left), simple mutations with $n_\sigma = 2$ (middle), and correlated mutations with $n_\sigma = 2$, $n_\alpha = 1$ (right). In each graphic five individuals and their ellipsoids of equal probability density to place an offspring are shown on a hypothetical topology which is represented by lines of equal objective function value.

However, it is not advisable to incorporate the covariances directly into the representation and apply mutations to them, because it is difficult to guarantee that the coordinate system remains orthogonal or, equivalently, the covariance matrix remains positive definite. This is why the rotation angles α_{ij} are used for performing the rotation alignments of the mutation ellipsoids. These angles are related to covariances and variances by equation 2.13:

$$\tan(2\alpha_{ij}) \;=\; \frac{2c_{ij}}{\sigma_i^2 - \sigma_j^2} \;. \tag{2.13}$$

In the following, we will use the notation $\vec{N}(\vec{0}, \mathbf{C})$ to denote a realization of a random vector distributed according to the generalized n-dimensional normal distribution with expectation $\vec{0}$ and covariance matrix $\mathbf{C}^{-1} = \mathbf{C}^{-1}(\vec{\sigma}, \vec{\alpha})$, represented by a vector $\vec{\sigma}$ of standard deviations and $\vec{\alpha}$ of rotation angles. Algorithmically, the generation of a correlated realization $\vec{\sigma}_c$ from an uncorrelated one[7] $\sigma_u = \vec{N}(\vec{0}, \vec{\sigma})$ can be performed by multiplication of σ_u by n_α rotation matrices $\mathbf{R}(\alpha_{ij}) = (r_{kl})$. The form of these matrices is given by a unit matrix except that for the following entries holds: $r_{ii} = r_{jj} = \cos\alpha_{ij}$, $r_{ij} = -r_{ji} = -\sin\alpha_{ij}$ (see [Sch81a], p. 241; [Rud90], p. 51), i.e., the trigonometric expressions are located in columns and rows i and j, each.

Multiplication by such a matrix performs a coordinate transformation with respect to axes number i and j and angle α_{ij}. Since n_α

---

[7] $\vec{\sigma}_u$ is a vector of realizations of $N(0, \sigma_i)$-distributed random variables ($i \in \{1, \ldots, n_\sigma\}$).

rotations are needed to represent all correlations, the complete relation between $\vec{\sigma}_c$ and $\vec{\sigma}_u$ results as

$$\vec{\sigma}_c = \left(\prod_{i=1}^{n-1} \prod_{j=i+1}^{n} \mathbf{R}(\alpha_{ij}) \right) \cdot \vec{\sigma}_u \quad . \tag{2.14}$$

Only a few lines of code are sufficient to perform these calculations [Sch80], though equation (2.14) acts as a deterrant. Recent investigations by Rudolph confirm the validity of this mechanism, since he was able to show that it guarantees creation of orthogonal transformations and at the same time allows for creation of any possible orthogonal transformation, i.e. using rotation angles does not restrict the generality of mutations [Rud92a].

2.1.2   Mutation

After presenting so much information about the underlying representation for mutations, the remaining explanations for this operator are brief. A most general mechanism is discussed here, i.e. an individual space $I = \mathbb{R}^n \times \mathbb{R}^n \times \mathbb{R}^{n \cdot (n-1)/2}$ is assumed. Mutation $m_{\{\tau,\tau',\beta\}}$: $I^\lambda \to I^\lambda$ is an asexual operator, hence it suffices to present its reduced form $m'_{\{\tau,\tau',\beta\}} : I \to I$ which yields a triple $(\vec{x}', \vec{\sigma}', \vec{\alpha}')$ when applied to a particular individual $(\vec{x}, \vec{\sigma}, \vec{\alpha})$. The notation $N(0,1)$ is used here to denote a realization of a normally distributed one-dimensional random variable having expectation zero and standard deviation one, while $N_i(0,1)$ indicates that the random variable is sampled anew for each possible value of the counter i. Using this notation, mutation is formalized as follows ($\forall i \in \{1,\ldots,n\}$, $\forall j \in \{1,\ldots,n \cdot (n-1)/2\}$):

$$
\begin{aligned}
\sigma'_i &= \sigma_i \cdot \exp(\tau' \cdot N(0,1) + \tau \cdot N_i(0,1)) \\
\alpha'_j &= \alpha_j + \beta \cdot N_j(0,1) \\
\vec{x}' &= \vec{x} + \vec{N}(\vec{0}, \mathbf{C}(\vec{\sigma}', \vec{\alpha}')) \quad .
\end{aligned}
\tag{2.15}
$$

First, the standard deviations and rotation angles are mutated using a multiplicative, logarithmic normally distributed process in case of the standard deviations and an additive, normally distributed variation in case of the rotation angles. Finally, for mutation of the object variable vector $\vec{x}$ the resulting vectors $\vec{\sigma}'$ and $\vec{\alpha}'$ are used to create the random vector for modifying $\vec{x}$. The global factor $\exp(\tau' \cdot N(0,1))$ allows for an overall change of the mutability and guarantees the preservation of all degrees of freedom[8], whereas $\exp(\tau \cdot N_i(0,1))$ allows for individual

---

[8]Notice that for $\tau' = 0$ and $n \gg 1$ the total step size

$$\sigma = \left(\sum_{i=1}^{n} \sigma_i^2 \right)^{1/2}$$

would have almost no chance to undergo substantial changes.

changes of the "mean step sizes" σ_i. A logarithmic normal distribution for the variations of standard deviations σ_i is motivated as follows[9] (see [Sch77], p. 168):

- A multiplicative modification process for σ_i guarantees positive values of standard deviations.

- The median (1/2-quantile) of a multiplicative modification must be one (this implies the next condition to be fulfilled).

- To guarantee an average neutrality of the process in absence of selective pressure, a multiplication by a certain value must occur with the same probability as multiplication by the reciprocal value.

- Smaller modifications must occur more often than larger ones.

The factors τ, τ', and β in equation (2.15) are rather robust parameters, which Schwefel suggests to set as follows (see [Sch77], p. 167–168):

$$
\begin{aligned}
\tau &\propto \left(\sqrt{2\sqrt{n}}\right)^{-1} \\
\tau' &\propto \left(\sqrt{2n}\right)^{-1} \\
\beta &\approx 0.0873 \ .
\end{aligned}
\tag{2.18}
$$

Usually, the proportionality constants for τ and τ' have the value one, and the value suggested for β (in radians) equals 5°. τ and τ' can be interpreted in the sense of "learning rates" as in artificial neural networks, and preliminary experiments with different proportionality factors indicate that the search process can be tuned for particular objective functions by modifying these factors.

However, it is still possible for the standard deviations to become practically zero by the multiplicative process and for the rotation angles to leave the range $[-\pi, \pi]$ of feasible values. To prevent both events, the algorithm in the first case forces all standard deviations to remain larger than a minimal value[10] ε_σ, and in the second case angles are circularly

---

[9]In case $n_\alpha = 0$, equations (2.15) reduce to the mutation rule

$$
\begin{aligned}
\sigma_i' &= \sigma_i \cdot \exp(\tau' \cdot N(0,1) + \tau \cdot N_i(0,1)) \\
x_i' &= x_i + \sigma_i' \cdot N_i(0,1) \ ,
\end{aligned}
\tag{2.16}
$$

which can also be applied if $1 < n_\sigma < n$. For $n_\sigma = 1$, however, the global and the individual factor for the modification of σ_i merge into one common factor where $\tau_0 \propto 1/\sqrt{n}$:

$$
\begin{aligned}
\sigma' &= \sigma \cdot \exp(\tau_0 \cdot N(0,1)) \\
x_i' &= x_i + \sigma' \cdot N_i(0,1) \ .
\end{aligned}
\tag{2.17}
$$

[10]In addition, Schwefel requires $\sigma_i \geq \varepsilon_\sigma' |x_i|$ where $1 + \varepsilon_\sigma' > 1$ in order to assure that σ_i remains sufficiently large to cause a modification of x_i (see [Sch77], p. 132).

mapped to the feasible range, i.e. whenever an angle would become an amount c_α larger (smaller) than π $(-\pi)$, it is mapped to $-\pi + c_\alpha$ $(\pi - c_\alpha)$:

$$
\begin{aligned}
|\alpha_j'| > \pi &\implies \alpha_j' := \alpha_j' - 2\pi \cdot \text{sign}(\alpha_j') \\
\sigma_i' < \varepsilon_\sigma &\implies \sigma_i' := \varepsilon_\sigma \quad .
\end{aligned}
\tag{2.19}
$$

Altogether, this special mutation mechanism enables an Evolution Strategy to evolve its own strategy parameters, i.e. standard deviations and covariances (represented by rotation angles) during the search, exploiting an implicit link between appropriate internal model and good fitness values. The resulting evolution and adaptation of strategy parameters according to the topological requirements has been termed collective *self-adaptation* by Schwefel [Sch87]. See also [HB92] for a demonstration of the self-adaptation mechanism in case of a simple, time-varying objective function.

2.1.3   Recombination

A variety of different recombination mechanisms are currently used in Evolution Strategies, and the operators are sexual as well as panmictic. In the sexual form, recombination operators act on two individuals randomly chosen from the parent population, where choosing the same individual twice for creation of one offspring individual is not suppressed (but this could be introduced easily)[11]. Conversely, for the panmictic variants of recombination one parent is randomly chosen and held fixed while for each component of its vectors the second parent is randomly chosen anew from the complete population. In other words, the creation of a single offspring individual may involve up to all parent individuals (this method for recombination emphasizes the point of view that the parent population as a whole forms a gene pool from which new individuals are constructed).

Recombination is always used in Evolution Strategies for the creation of all offspring individuals, when $\mu > 1$. Furthermore, not only the object variables but also strategy parameters are subject to recombination, and the recombination operator may be different for object variables, standard deviations, and rotation angles. This implies that recombination of these groups of information proceeds independently of each other, i.e. there is no restriction for strategy parameters to originate from the same parent as object variables do. The utilization of independent recombination on object variables and strategy parameters (standard deviations and rotation angles) is justified by experimental observations concerning the performance of the resulting variants of Evolution Strategies. Theoretical investigations of this topic are still an open field of research.

---

[11]As an aside, it is a characteristic property of all recombination operators that incest can never create anything new, i.e. $\forall \vec{a} \in I : r'(\vec{a}, \vec{a}) = \vec{a}$.

The different traditional recombination operators of Evolution Strategies are called *discrete recombination* and *intermediate recombination*, both existing in sexual and panmictic form. In case of discrete recombination, for each component of the vectors it is decided at random from which of both parents (in the sexual case) the component is copied to the offspring individual. The panmictic variant chooses for each component a new parent individual from the whole parent population. Intermediate recombination indicates that the offspring's components are obtained by calculating the arithmetic mean of the corresponding components of both parents. For the panmictic variant one parent is selected at random and held fixed while for each component the second mating partner is chosen anew from the population. Recently, Schwefel proposed to generalize intermediate recombination by allowing arbitrary weight factors from the interval $[0,1]$ besides the value 0.5 and furthermore by choosing the weight factor anew for each component in case of panmictic intermediate recombination. Though this generalization, which will be referred to as *generalized intermediate recombination* in the following, promises to be useful, it has not yet been extensively tested.

In order to formalize what has been explained so far, sexual and panmictic forms are summarized here for recombination creating an individual $\vec{a}' = (\vec{x}', \vec{\sigma}', \vec{\alpha}')$ from a population $P(t) \in I^{\mu}$, i.e. $r' : I^{\mu} \to I$. We implicitly assume the sexual form $r' : I^2 \to I$ to act on two randomly selected parents without formally distinguishing it, and present the rules representatively only for the object variables ($\forall i \in \{1, \ldots, n\}$):

$$
x_i' = \begin{cases}
x_{S,i} & \text{no recombination} & r'_- \\
x_{S,i} \text{ or } x_{T,i} & \text{discrete} & r'_d \\
x_{S,i} \text{ or } x_{T_i,i} & \text{panmictic discrete} & r'_D \\
x_{S,i} + (x_{T,i} - x_{S,i})/2 & \text{intermediate} & r'_i \\
x_{S,i} + (x_{T_i,i} - x_{S,i})/2 & \text{panmictic intermediate} & r'_I \\
x_{S,i} + \chi \cdot (x_{T,i} - x_{S,i}) & \text{generalized intermediate} & r'_g \\
x_{S,i} + \chi_i \cdot (x_{T_i,i} - x_{S,i}) & \text{panmictic generalized} & r'_G \\
& \text{intermediate}
\end{cases}
$$

The indices S and T denote two parent individuals selected at random from the population (the index i in T_i indicates T to be sampled anew for each value of i), $\chi \in [0,1]$ is a uniform random variable, sampled anew for each possible value of the counter i when used in the form χ_i and sampled only once per creation of one offspring individual when it is not indexed, and "or" denotes a decision by a fair random coin toss. Fixing $\chi = 1/2$ and $\chi_i = 1/2 \ \forall i \in \{1, \ldots, n\}$, respectively, generalized intermediate recombination reduces to intermediate recombination. Since the complete recombination operator results from combining component-wise operators (for object variables, standard deviations, and rotation angles), a recombination operator is in the following denoted by $r_{r_x r_\sigma r_\alpha}$, where r_x, r_σ, $r_\alpha \in \{-, d, D, i, I, g, G\}$ (according to the "code" defined in the last column of 2.20) indicate recombination mechanisms used on the three different components of individuals. This results in $7^3 = 343$ different operators. For the two-dimensional case the different recombination result possibilities are schematically shown in figure 2.2.

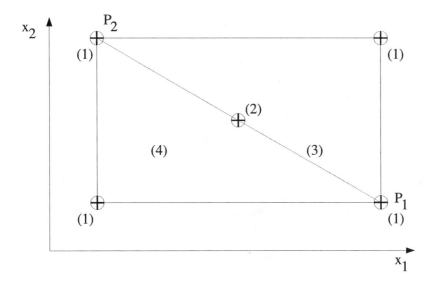

Fig. 2.2: 2-dimensional schema of different recombination mechanisms.

Here P_1 and P_2 indicate the object variable points represented by two parent individuals. Only the corners (indicated (1) in the figure) of the rectangle defined by P_1 and P_2 can be reached by means of discrete recombination. Intermediate recombination yields the center (2) of the rectangles' diagonal lines. Generalized intermediate recombination allows for a result located anywhere on the diagonal line (3) connecting P_1 and P_2, and finally panmictic generalized intermediate recombination allows for creation of an arbitrary point located somewhere within the rectangle (4), where parents are still restricted to P_1 and P_2. However, it is important to note that by means of recombination the n-dimensional hyperbody formed by the parent population can never be left by any offspring individual, i.e. recombination causes more or less volume reduction.

Schwefel reports a remarkable acceleration of the search process by introducing recombination ([Sch77], p. 171) and identifies recombination of strategy parameters as a necessary prerequisite to facilitate self-adaptation of strategy parameters [Sch87]. Following his suggestions, discrete recombination on object variables and (panmictic) intermediate recombination of strategy parameters should be preferred, i.e. r_{dII}. In order to explain the accelerating effect of recombination of object variables, Schwefel counted the number of possible recombination results in case of discrete and panmictic discrete recombination, which is stated here from ([Sch77], p. 171) in the following theorem, completed by the number of recombination results for (panmictic) intermediate recombination.

Theorem 5 (Number of possible recombination results)
Given a parent population of μ individuals with different n-dimensional object variables each, the combinatorially possible number of different recombination results of object variables is

$$\mu + \binom{\mu}{2}(2^n - 2) \qquad \textit{for discrete recombination,}$$

$$\mu^n \qquad\qquad\qquad \textit{for panmictic discrete recombination,} \qquad (2.20)$$

$$\mu \cdot (\mu + 1)/2 \qquad\quad \textit{for intermediate recombination, and}$$

$$(\mu \cdot (\mu + 1)/2)^n \qquad \textit{for panmictic intermediate recombination.}$$

Proof: The first two cases are subject of theorem 6. For intermediate recombination, the order in which both individuals are chosen from the population is unimportant. Assuming individuals $\vec{a}_1, \ldots, \vec{a}_\mu$, for $\vec{a}_1$ there are μ possible mating partners, for $\vec{a}_2$ there are $\mu - 1$, and so on, leading to a total of $\sum_{i=1}^{\mu} i = \mu \cdot (\mu + 1)/2$ mating possibilities, each of which creates one offspring individual. By applying the same argument to n individually created components, the result for panmictic intermediate recombination is obtained.   Q.E.D.

However, Schwefel's results for discrete recombination can be generalized by giving an expression for the possible number of results when an arbitrary number ϱ of individuals $(1 \leq \varrho \leq \mu)$ may be taken into account by discrete recombination, this way capturing all cases between sexual and panmictic discrete recombination.

Theorem 6 (Generalized discrete recombination)
Given a parent population of μ individuals having component-wise different n-dimensional object variable vectors each, and assuming that $1 \leq \varrho \leq \mu$ individuals may be chosen for producing one offspring by means of discrete recombination, the number $R(\mu, \varrho, n)$ of combinatorially possible recombination results is given by

$$R(\mu, \varrho, n) = \sum_{i=1}^{\varrho} \binom{\mu}{i} i! \cdot S(n, i) \quad , \qquad (2.21)$$

where

$$S(n, i) = \frac{1}{i!} \sum_{j=0}^{i} (-1)^j \binom{i}{j} (i - j)^n \qquad (2.22)$$

denotes the 2nd kind Stirling numbers.

Proof: A certain choice of a parent may repeat up to $\varrho-1$ times during selection of the ϱ parents, since there is no guarantee to choose different parents. Hence, for $i \in \{1,\ldots,\varrho\}$ each possibility to select i parents out of μ possible ones must be taken into account. The order does not play any role, such that this number is $\binom{\mu}{i}$. For each of these choices the number of possibilities to choose n positions out of i elements such that each of the i elements occurs in the result *at least once* must be counted, since just these are combinations that introduce *new* offspring possibilities. This number is identical to the number of n-permutations of i elements with repetitions such that each element occurs at least once, which is given by $\sum_{j=0}^{i}(-1)^j \binom{i}{j}(i-j)^n$ (see e.g. [Dör77], p. 364). The result follows from combining both expressions. Q.E.D.

Using the expression from theorem 6, the results stated in theorem 5 can be derived as follows:

$$
\begin{aligned}
R(\mu, 2, n) &= \sum_{i=1}^{2}\left[\binom{\mu}{i} \cdot \sum_{j=0}^{i}(-1)^j \binom{i}{j}(i-j)^n\right] \\
&= \mu + \binom{\mu}{2} \cdot \sum_{j=0}^{2}(-1)^j \binom{2}{j}(2-j)^n \\
&= \mu + \binom{\mu}{2}(2^n - 2) \\
R(\mu, \mu, n) &= \sum_{i=1}^{\mu}\binom{\mu}{i}i! \cdot S(n,i) \\
&= \sum_{i=1}^{\mu}\frac{\mu!}{(\mu-i)!}S(n,i) \\
&= \sum_{i=0}^{\mu}\mu(\mu-1)\ldots(\mu-i+1)S(n,i) \\
&= \mu^n
\end{aligned}
$$

For the last simplification, see e.g. [GKP89] (p. 248).

It is interesting to look at plots of the function $R(\mu, \varrho, n)$ in order to get an impression of the size of the virtual enlargement of the population provided by recombination. Figure 2.3 shows plots of $R(10, \varrho, n)$ for $n \in \{5, 10, 15, 20\}$ and ϱ varying over the range $\{1,\ldots,10\}$.

Even for two recombination partners the number of possible results is very large ($R(10, 2, 5) = 1,36 \cdot 10^3$, $R(10, 2, 20) = 4,718 \cdot 10^7$) and in fact larger than most practically usable population sizes, such that only a small fraction of the available offspring can be tested. Recombination of more than two parents is therefore not expected to be much more effective than sexual recombination in the case of the object variables.

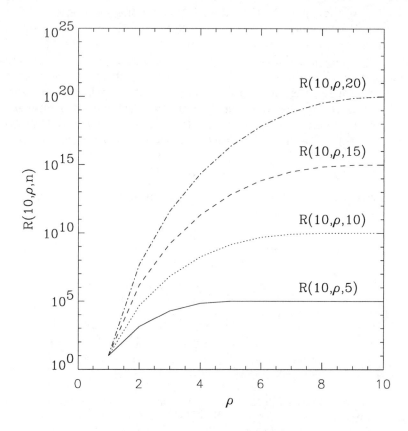

Fig. 2.3: Recombination result numbers $R(\mu, \varrho, n)$ for discrete recombination (number of parent individuals $\mu = 10$, number of recombinants $\varrho \in \{1, \ldots, 10\}$, $n \in \{5, 10, 15, 20\}$).

2.1.4   Selection

The selection operators used in Evolution Strategies are completely deterministic. Schwefel ([Sch77], p. 140) introduced an elegant notation for selection mechanisms in Evolution Strategies, characterizing the basic method and the numbers of parent and offspring individuals, respectively. He distinguishes between a $(\mu+\lambda)$-selection $s_{(\mu+\lambda)} : I^{\mu+\lambda} \rightarrow I^{\mu}$ and a (μ,λ)-selection $s_{(\mu,\lambda)} : I^{\lambda} \rightarrow I^{\mu}$. The former selects the μ best individuals out of the union of parents and offspring to form the next parent generation, while the latter selects the μ best individuals out of the offspring only[12]. More formally, this can be expressed as follows:

---

[12]Practically, for (μ,λ)-selection $\mu < \lambda$ is required, because the extreme case $\mu = \lambda$ leads to a random walk behavior of the algorithm, i.e., no selection takes place.

$$s_{(\mu+\lambda)}(P) \;=\; P' \quad \text{such that:}$$
$$\not\exists \vec{a}_k \in P - P' : (\exists \vec{a}_i \in P' : f(\vec{x}_k) < f(\vec{x}'_i)) \qquad (2.23)$$

(the case $s_{(\mu,\lambda)}$ is identical, except that P consists of the offspring population only).

At first glance, the $(\mu+\lambda)$-selection with its guaranteed survival of the best individuals seems to be more effective, because a monotonous course of evolution is achieved this way. However, this selection mechanism has several disadvantages when compared to (μ,λ)-selection, which restricts lifetimes of individuals to one generation[13]:

- In case of changing environments the $(\mu+\lambda)$-selection preserves (outdated) solutions and is not able to follow the moving optimum. (Of course, a possibility to circumvent this problem is to reevaluate the parent population also, but this is not part of the original Evolution Strategy algorithm and would introduce an overhead of μ evaluations per generation in contrast to the (μ,λ)-strategy.)

- The capability of a (μ,λ)-selection to forget good solutions in principle allows for leaving (small) local optima and is therefore advantageous in case of multimodal topologies.

- $(\mu+\lambda)$-selection hinders the self-adaptation mechanism with respect to strategy parameters to work effectively, because misadapted strategy parameters may survive for a relatively large number of generations when they cause a fitness improvement by chance.

Therefore, the (μ,λ)-selection is recommended, investigations from a particular objective function (the sphere model, see section 2.1.7) indicating a ratio of $\mu/\lambda \approx 1/7$ being optimal concerning the accelerating effect of self-adaptation (but μ has to be chosen clearly larger than one, e.g. $\mu = 15$) [Sch87]. Summarizing the conditions for a successful self-adaptation of strategy parameters, the following list is obtained:

- A (μ,λ)-strategy is required in order to facilitate extinction of maladapted individuals.

- Selective pressure may not become too strong, i.e., μ is required to be clearly larger than one.

- Recombination on strategy parameters is necessary (usually, intermediate recombination gives best results).

Finally, anticipating a closer discussion of the importance of selection in Evolutionary Algorithms, we mention the fact that the ratio μ/λ provides the basic parameterization instrument for controlling the character of the search. Decreasing μ emphasizes on path-oriented search

---

[13]In [SB92], Schwefel indicates the generalization of lifetimes to allow for any number of generations between the limits one $((\mu,\lambda)$-selection) and infinity $((\mu+\lambda)$-selection) as a further interesting research topic.

and convergence velocity, while increasing μ leads to a more volume-oriented search (cf. the discussion of optimization method classification in section 1.3.1).

2.1.5 Other Components

Still missing in this discussion of Evolution Strategies are explanations of the initialization process, the termination criterion, and constraint handling. These are briefly summarized here.

In the original implementation, Schwefel provided the possibility of creating a complete initial population $P(0) = \{\vec{a}_1(0), \ldots, \vec{a}_\mu(0)\}$ from a single initial starting point by means of mutation. This was done in order to achieve comparability with traditional optimization methods (see [Sch81a]). The starting point may be defined by the user of the algorithm, if this is intended, or can be chosen from the feasible region according to a uniform, n-dimensional probability distribution (if the feasible region is explicitly constrained).

Concerning the initialization of standard deviations $\sigma_i(0)$, Schwefel recommended a choice $\sigma_i(0) \approx \Delta x_i / \sqrt{n}$, where Δx_i denotes the estimated distance between starting point and optimum ([Sch77], p. 138). Practical experience, however, suggests that the choice of initial standard deviations should be a bit smaller, and throughout the experiments described in chapter 4 $\sigma_i(0) = 3.0$ was a useful setting. We explicitly mention this rule to choose small initial standard deviations because, depending on the topology of the objective function, a combination of a too large $\sigma_i(0)$ and weak selective pressure (a too large value of μ) may cause the algorithm to diverge. Practically, this behaviour is observed only in few applications and is easily controllable by the indicated measures. Whenever initial standard deviations are not too large, however, the self-adaptation process quickly scales them into the appropriate range.

Furthermore, Schwefel's original algorithm is able to handle inequality constraints g_i (definition 1.2) by simply repeating the creation of an individual (by means of recombination and mutation) and evaluation of the new individual as long as the individual violates one or more of the constraints or, expressed in biological terms, is a *lethal* mutant. However, since we will not treat constrained problems with an Evolution Strategy in the following discussion and formulation of the generation-based form of the algorithm is considerably complicated by introducing constraint handling, it is omitted here. Following the mechanism indicated above, the reader should have no problems with extending the basic algorithm accordingly.

Finally, termination is tested by comparing worst and best fitness value of the parent population, either absolute or relative (see [Sch77], pp. 169–170):

$$\iota(\{\vec{a}_1(t), \ldots, \vec{a}_\mu(t)\} =$$
$$\begin{cases} \text{true }, \max\{\Phi(\vec{a}_i(t))\} - \min\{\Phi(\vec{a}_i(t))\} \le c(P(t)) & (2.24) \\ \text{false }, \text{otherwise.} \end{cases}$$

Here,

$$c(P(t)) \quad = \quad \varepsilon_{\Phi,1} > 0 \qquad\qquad (2.25)$$

in case of the absolute measure, and

$$c(P(t)) \quad = \quad \frac{\varepsilon_{\Phi,2}}{\mu} \cdot \left| \sum_{i=1}^{\mu} \Phi(\vec{a}_i(t)) \right| \qquad (2.26)$$

in case of the relative measure, where $\varepsilon_{\Phi,1} > 0$ and $\varepsilon_{\Phi,2} > 0$ denote constants. Our experiments, however, will usually be based on the much simpler criterion $t \le t_{\max}$, where $t_{\max}$ denotes an externally given maximum running time.

2.1.6   Conceptual Standard Algorithm

Combining the topics discussed in the previous sections, the following conceptual algorithm of a $(\mu+\lambda)$–ES and a (μ,λ)–ES, respectively, results:

Algorithm 4 (Outline of an Evolution Strategy)

> $t := 0;$
> *initialize* $P(0) := \{\vec{a}_1(0), \ldots, \vec{a}_\mu(0)\} \in I^\mu$
>   **where** $I = \mathbb{R}^n \times \mathbb{R}_+^{n_\sigma} \times [-\pi, \pi]^{n_\alpha}$
>   **and** $\vec{a}_k = (x_i, \sigma_j, \alpha_{j'})$, $i \in \{1, \ldots, n\}$
> $j \in \{1, \ldots, n_\sigma\}$, $j' \in \{1, \ldots, n_\alpha\}$;
>   **or** $\vec{a}_k = (x_i, \sigma_j)$, $i \in \{1, \ldots, n\}$, $j \in \{1, \ldots, n_\sigma\}$;
> *evaluate* $P(0) :$ $\{\Phi(\vec{a}_1(0)), \ldots, \Phi(\vec{a}_\mu(0))\}$
>   **where** $\Phi(\vec{a}_k(0)) = f(\vec{x}_k(0));$
> **while** $(\iota(P(t)) \ne \textbf{true})$ **do**
>   *recombine:* $\vec{a}_k'(t) := r'(P(t)) \; \forall k \in \{1, \ldots, \lambda\};$
>   *mutate:* $\vec{a}_k''(t) := m'_{\{\tau, \tau', \beta\}}(\vec{a}_k'(t)) \; \forall k \in \{1, \ldots, \lambda\};$
>   *evaluate:* $P''(t) := \{\vec{a}_1''(t), \ldots, \vec{a}_\lambda''(t)\} :$
> $\{\Phi(\vec{a}_1''(t)), \ldots, \Phi(\vec{a}_\lambda''(t))\}$
>   **where** $\Phi(\vec{a}_k''(t)) = f(\vec{x}_k''(t));$
>   *select:* $P(t+1) :=$ **if** (μ, λ)-*selection*
>   **then** $s_{(\mu,\lambda)}(P''(t));$
>   **else** $s_{(\mu+\lambda)}(P(t) \cup P''(t));$
> $t := t + 1;$
> **od**

Using the framework for an Evolutionary Algorithm given in definition 2.1, an Evolution Strategy is now summarized as follows:

Definition 2.5 (Evolution Strategy) *An Evolutionary Algorithm*

$$\text{EA} = (I, \Phi, \Omega, \Psi, s, \iota, \mu, \lambda)$$

is called Evolution Strategy: $\Longleftrightarrow$

(1) $I = \mathbb{R}^n \times \mathbb{R}_+^{n_\sigma} \times [-\pi, \pi]^{n_\alpha}$, *where* $n_\sigma \in \{1, \ldots, n\}$ *and* $n_\alpha \in \{0, (2n - n_\sigma)(n_\sigma - 1)/2\}$,

(2) $\Phi = f$,

(3) $\Omega = \{m_{\{\tau, \tau', \beta\}} : I^\lambda \rightarrow I^\lambda\} \cup \{r_{r_x r_\sigma r_\alpha} : I^\mu \rightarrow I^\lambda\}$ *where the operators are defined as in (2.15) and (2.20),*

(4) $\Psi(P) = s(Q \cup m_{\{\tau, \tau', \beta\}}(r_{r_x r_\sigma r_\alpha}(P)))$ *where* $Q = \emptyset$ *in case of* (μ,λ)-selection *and* $Q = P$ *in case of* (μ+λ)-selection,

(5) $s \in \{s_{(\mu+\lambda)}, s_{(\mu,\lambda)}\}$, *the selection operator, is defined as in (2.23),*

(6) *the termination criterion* ι *is given e.g. by (2.24), and*

(7) *if* $s = s_{(\mu,\lambda)}$, *then* $1 \le \mu \le \lambda$ *is required (otherwise, there are no special restrictions on the relation between* μ *and* λ*).*

This definition does not incorporate early variants of the strategy such as the (1+1)–ES and (μ+1)–ES, but it summarizes all strategies that self-adapt at least one strategy parameter. Simpler strategies use a completely different mutation operator and are therefore not discussed here (but the (1+1)–ES is presented in section 2.1.7).

To conclude the presentation of the algorithm underlying an Evolution Strategy and to give the necessary details to those who wish to implement it, in table 2.1 we formalize a standard Evolution Strategy by identifying the critical exogenous parameters and defining default values for them.

Whenever no different parameterization is explicitly mentioned, a standard Evolution Strategy according to this description is assumed in the following. If an exact description of an Evolution Strategy deviating from the standard is required, it will be written in the format $ES(n_\sigma, n_\alpha, r_{r_x r_\sigma r_\alpha}, s \in \{s_{(\mu,\lambda)}, s_{(\mu+\lambda)}\})$. For example, the notation $ES(n, 0, r_{dI}, s_{(15,100)})$ denotes the standard Evolution Strategy.

From the point of view of a practician, who is confronted with an optimization problem of completely unknown topological characteristics, it is advisable to perform experiments which follow a kind of "default hierarchy" from simple towards increasingly complex algorithms. Such a hierarchy of Evolution Strategies is given by

(1) $ES(1, 0, r_{dI}, s_{(15,100)})$,

---

[14]The setting of $\sigma_i(0)$ depends on the particular objective function. $\sigma_i(0) = 3.0$, however, turns out to be a reasonable choice even if nothing is known about the objective function.

Parameter	Default
Number of standard deviations n_σ	$n_\sigma = n$
Initial standard deviations[14] $\sigma_i(0)$	$\sigma_i(0) \approx 3.0$
Number of rotation angles n_α	$n_\alpha = 0$
Recombination operator r	$r = r_{dI}$
Selection operator s	$s = s_{(\mu,\lambda)}$
Parent population size μ	$\mu = 15$
Offspring population size λ	$\lambda = 100$

Table 2.1. Default settings of exogenous parameters of a standard Evolution Strategy.

(2) $ES(n, 0, r_{dI}, s_{(15,100)})$,

(3) $ES(2, 1, r_{dII}, s_{(15,100)})$,

(4) $ES(n, n \cdot (n-1)/2, r_{dII}, s_{(15,100)})$,

and it provides a possibility to improve results by trying more complex strategies at the cost of additional computing time. The suggestion of case (3) requires some additional explanation. Its utilization is justified by the idea that two standard deviations allow for the adjustment of a preferred direction of search where the standard deviation is relatively large in comparison to the $n-1$ remaining directions of constant standard deviation. The single rotation angle then allows for an arbitrary orientation of this preferred direction. Such a strategy might be very useful for a topology where the search can proceed along a valley with relatively flat bottom and steep walls.

2.1.7   Theory

In his book of 1973, Rechenberg laid the foundations of the theory of Evolution Strategies by calculating the convergence rates of the simple (1+1)–ES for two basic objective functions [Rec73]. Using the convergence rate expressions, he derived the optimal value of the single standard deviation of the mutation operator in a (1+1)–ES as well as the corresponding maximal convergence rates and optimal probabilities for a successful mutation. Finally, these results allowed for the formulation of a theoretically based rule for a deterministic adjustment of the standard deviation during evolution. This rule is called 1/5-*success rule*, reflecting the theoretical result that, on average, one out of five mutations should cause an improvement with respect to objective function values to achieve best convergence rates (after [Rec73], p. 123):

The ratio of successful mutations to all mutations should be
1/5. If it is greater than 1/5, increase the standard deviation,
if it is smaller, decrease the standard deviation.

The algorithm these results refer to uses only one individual which
is modified by means of mutation, based on one standard deviation $\sigma(t)$
determining modification values for all components of the object variable
vector. Neither recombination nor self-adaptation are involved by this
algorithm, which is presented here in the now habitual notation:

Algorithm 5 ((1+1)-Evolution Strategy)

$t := 0$;
initialize $P(0) := \{\vec{x}(0)\} \in I$ **where** $I = I\!R^n$ **and** $\vec{x} = (x_1, \ldots, x_n)$;
evaluate $P(0) : \{\Phi(\vec{x}(0))\}$ **where** $\Phi = f$;
while $(\iota(P(t)) \neq$ **true**) **do**
    mutate: $\vec{x}'(t) := m(\vec{x}(t))$
        where $x'_i := x_i + \sigma(t) \cdot N_i(0,1) \; \forall i \in \{1, \ldots, n\}$
    evaluate: $P'(t) := \{\vec{x}'(t)\}$:
        $\{\Phi(\vec{x}'(t))\}$ **where** $\Phi = f$;
    select: $P(t+1) := s_{(1+1)}(P(t) \cup P'(t))$;
    $t := t + 1$;
    if $(t \bmod n = 0)$ **then**
$$\sigma(t) := \begin{cases} \sigma(t-n)/c & \text{, \textbf{if} } p_s > 1/5 \\ \sigma(t-n) \cdot c & \text{, \textbf{if} } p_s < 1/5 \\ \sigma(t-n) & \text{, \textbf{if} } p_s = 1/5 \end{cases}$$
        where p_s *is the relative frequency of successful*
                      mutations, measured over intervals of,
                      say, $10 \cdot n$ *trials;*
        and $0.817 \leq c \leq 1$;
    else
        $\sigma(t) := \sigma(t-1)$;
    fi
od

Only the realization of the 1/5-success rule deserves a deeper explanation; all other components of the algorithm should be immediately clear
from the $(\mu+\lambda)$–ES. Adjustment of $\sigma(t)$ is performed every n mutations
in this algorithm, where the number of mutations and the number of
generations are identical[15]. In order to apply the 1/5-success rule the
algorithm keeps track of the observed ratio of successful mutations to
the total number of mutations, measured over intervals of $10 \cdot n$ trials.
According to this ratio, the standard deviation is increased, decreased,
or remains constant ([Rec73], p. 123). The choice of $c = 0.817$ was
theoretically derived by Schwefel[16] (see [Sch77], p. 130-131).

[15]In [SB92], Schwefel indicates the alternative possibility to adjust $\sigma(t)$ at each
generation, which works by substituting the constant c by $c^{1/n}$.

[16]In implementations, the slightly corrected form $c = 0.85$ is used since the sphere
model (for which the results were derived) is likely to require the fastest adaptation
of the step size.

Rechenberg derived his convergence rate results for the model functions

$$f_1(\vec{x}) \quad = \quad F(x_1) = c_0 + c_1 \cdot x_1 \tag{2.27}$$

where $\forall i \in \{2, \ldots, n\}: -b/2 \le x_i \le b/2$, and

$$f_2(\vec{x}) \quad = \quad c_0 + c_1 \cdot \sum_{i=1}^{n} (x_i - x_i^*)^2 \quad = \quad c_0 + c_1 \cdot r^2 \quad . \tag{2.28}$$

f_1, the *corridor model*, represents a corridor of width b, where improvements are accomplished only by moving along the x_1 axis. f_2, the *sphere model*, represents the simplest kind of nonlinear function, where $(x_1^*, \ldots, x_n^*) = \vec{x}^*$ denotes the minimum and r is the actual Euclidean distance between $\vec{x}$ and $\vec{x}^*$. Both for f_1 and f_2, c_0 and $c_1 \ne 0$ denote arbitrary constants. The *convergence rate* φ is defined as the expectation of the distance k' covered by mutation, i.e.

$$\varphi \quad = \quad \int p(k') \cdot k' \, dk' \quad , \tag{2.29}$$

where $p(k')$ denotes the probability for a mutation to cover a distance k' towards the optimum (see [Sch77], p. 142). The limits of integration depend on the particular objective function.

Without presenting their derivation, we summarize only the resulting expectation values φ_1, φ_2 for the rates of convergence, expressed in terms of dimensionless, normalized variables $\sigma_1' = \sigma_1 n/b$, $\varphi_1' = \varphi_1 n/b$, $\sigma_2' = \sigma_2 n/r$, and $\varphi_2' = \varphi_2 n/r$ (both equations are valid for $n \gg 1$):

$$
\begin{aligned}
\varphi_1' &= \frac{\sigma_1'}{\sqrt{2\pi}} \left(1 - \sqrt{\frac{2}{\pi}} \frac{\sigma_1'}{n} \right)^{n-1} \approx \frac{\sigma_1'}{\sqrt{2\pi}} \exp\left(-\sqrt{\frac{2}{\pi}} \sigma_1' \right) \\
\varphi_2' &= \frac{\sigma_2'}{\sqrt{2\pi}} \exp\left(-\frac{\sigma_2'^2}{8} \right) - \frac{\sigma_2'^2}{4} \left(1 - \mathrm{erf}\left(\frac{\sigma_2'}{\sqrt{8}} \right) \right)
\end{aligned}
\tag{2.30}
$$

where erf denotes the error function[17].

These results are obtained by Rechenberg by integrating the product of the useful distance covered by a mutation and the probability of occurrence of such an improvement over the complete success area available for mutations (see equation (2.29)). Similarly, by integrating only the probabilities of improvement occurrences over the success area, he derived expectation values of the corresponding success probabilities $p_i = \mathcal{P}\{f_i(m(\vec{x})) \le f_i(\vec{x})\}$ $(i \in \{1, 2\}; n \gg 1)$:

$$
\begin{aligned}
p_1 &= \frac{1}{2} \left(1 - \sqrt{\frac{2}{\pi}} \frac{\sigma_1'}{n} \right)^{n-1} \approx \frac{1}{2} \exp\left(-\sqrt{\frac{2}{\pi}} \sigma_1' \right) \\
p_2 &= \frac{1}{2} \left(1 - \mathrm{erf}\left(\frac{\sigma_2'}{\sqrt{8}} \right) \right)
\end{aligned}
\tag{2.31}
$$

---

[17]$\mathrm{erf}(x) = \frac{2}{\sqrt{\pi}} \int_0^x \exp(-t^2) \, dt$ (see [Rec73], p. 108).

By setting $\left.\dfrac{\mathrm{d}\varphi'_i}{\mathrm{d}\sigma'_i}\right|_{\sigma'^*_i} = 0$ it is possible to determine the optimal standard deviations σ'^*_i ($i \in \{1,2\}$) that maximize the convergence rates φ'_i and to determine the maximum values $\varphi'^*_i = \varphi'_i(\sigma'^*_i)$ of convergence rates. Furthermore, substituting σ'^*_i in the expressions (2.31) yields the optimal success probabilities p^*_i. The results are summarized in the following survey:

$$
\begin{array}{llll lll}
\sigma'^*_1 & = & \sqrt{\frac{\pi}{2}} & \approx & 1.253 & \sigma'^*_2 & \approx & 1.224 \\
\varphi'^*_1 & = & \frac{1}{2e} & \approx & 0.184 & \varphi'^*_2 & \approx & 0.2025 \\
p^*_1 & = & \frac{1}{2e} & \approx & 0.184 & p^*_2 & \approx & 0.270
\end{array}
\qquad (2.32)
$$

The optimal success probabilities p^*_1 and p^*_2 are both close to the value $1/5$, such that Rechenberg derived the $1/5$-success rule from these results. A retransformation of variables clearly demonstrates that the optimal standard deviation as well as the maximum convergence rates are *inversely proportional* to the number n of variables and proportional to a general topology parameter characterizing local objective function topologies, i.e. b and r.

In figure 2.4 standardized convergence rates (i.e. the ratio φ_i/φ^*_i, upper graphic) and success probabilities (p_i, lower graphic) are plotted over standardized standard deviations (σ_i/σ^*_i) for both objective functions. The standardization implies direct comparability of the curves. Looking at the indicated range of standard deviation ratios in the upper graphic that yield a convergence rate larger than half the maximum one, one realizes that this ratio may vary within one order of magnitude without hindering reasonable convergence rates. This indicates a high robustness of the algorithm concerning the choice of σ. The indicated order of magnitude within which reasonable performance is observed is sometimes called the *evolution window* (see [Rec73], p. 140). The lower graphic marks the optimal values of success probabilities[18] by dotted lines, corresponding to the location of maxima in the upper graphic. Optimal values are near 0.2, this way giving a graphical visualization of the $1/5$-success rule.

Figure 2.4 also provides a hint to a problem that may arise when using the $1/5$-success rule: Whenever the topological situation does not lead to success rates larger than $1/5$, the search stagnates prematurely due to the deterministic decrease of step sizes towards zero. This often happens along active constraints, or in case of corners of level sets $f = $ const if f is not continuously differentiable or discontinuous. Furthermore, the $1/5$-success rule gives no hint how to handle σ_i individually

---

[18] By the way, "optimal" means maximizing convergence rates, *not* maximizing success probabilities. The latter would imply stagnation of the search, because for $\sigma \to 0$ any local topology degenerates, having straight lines of equal objective function value in the close vicinity of any point. Then, the probability to improve is one half, but the convergence rate is zero.

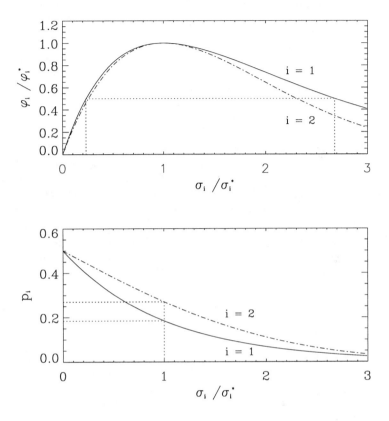

Fig. 2.4: The evolution window.

and therefore it does not enable a suitable scaling of mutation step sizes along different axes of the coordinate system.

Though Rechenberg (see [Rec73], p. 93) presented an intuitive argumentation, Born was the first who derived the result of global convergence with probability one for this algorithm in a mathematically sound way, under the condition of a positive standard deviation $\sigma \geq \varepsilon_\sigma > 0$ [Bor78]. Recently, Rudolph recognized the close correspondence of a (1+1)–ES and the general algorithm of global random search (algorithm 2) and derived the analogue of theorem 3 [Rud92b]:

Theorem 7 *Let $f^* > -\infty$ and*

$$\forall \varepsilon > 0 : \sum_{t=1}^{\infty} q_t(\varepsilon) = \infty \quad , \tag{2.33}$$

where $q_t(\varepsilon) = \mathcal{P}\{\vec{x}(t) \in L_{f^*+\varepsilon}\}$. If $\mu(L_{f^*+\varepsilon}) > 0$ and the probability density function used for mutations is stepwise continuous, then algorithm 5 will reach the region $L_{f^*+\varepsilon}$ with probability one as t increases:

$$\mathcal{P}\{\lim_{t\to\infty} \vec{x}(t) \in L_{f^*+\varepsilon}\} = 1 \quad. \tag{2.34}$$

Proof: See [Rud92b] and theorem 3.   Q.E.D.

To extend the convergence rate theory to cover the case of a $(1,\lambda)$-strategy with a single standard deviation that is not undergoing self-adaptation and without recombination, Schwefel derived an approximation theory for the corridor and sphere model, using an approach that is sufficiently general to cover (μ,λ)–ES and $(\mu+\lambda)$–ES. It is summarized here from [Sch77] (pp. 142–145). The basic idea is to concentrate on the progress of the average of the μ best individuals that form the next generation, where each offspring covers a certain distance k. Using $p_\nu(k')$ to denote the probability describing the event that the νth-best offspring covers distance k', the corresponding probability of the average of the μ best is

$$p(k') = \frac{1}{\mu}\sum_{\nu=1}^{\mu} p_\nu(k') \quad. \tag{2.35}$$

By definition of expectation value, the convergence rate results by integrating the product of the probability to cover a distance and the corresponding distance over all distances, i.e.:

$$\varphi = \int_{k'=k_{\min}}^{\infty} p(k') \cdot k' \, dk' \quad. \tag{2.36}$$

For the restricted case of one single standard deviation and absolute coordinates of object variables rather than relative ones (which would make φ independent of start configurations), Schwefel presented a combinatorial expression for $p_\nu(k')$:

$$p_\nu(k') = \lambda\binom{\lambda-1}{\nu-1} \cdot p_{k_j=k'} \cdot p_{k_j<k'}^{\lambda-\nu} \cdot p_{k_j>k'}^{\nu-1} \quad. \tag{2.37}$$

This expression includes the probability $p_{k_j=k'}$ $(j \in \{1,\ldots,\lambda\})$ that a certain offspring individual numbered j covers the improvement distance k' exactly, a smaller distance $(p_{k_j<k'})$, or a larger one $(p_{k_j>k'})$, respectively. Since $p_\nu(k')$ characterizes the νth-best individual, $\nu - 1$ individuals must be better and $\lambda - \nu$ must be worse. The combinatorial factor reflects the possible choices of the νth-best (λ choices) and the $\nu - 1$ better individuals ($\binom{\lambda-1}{\nu-1}$ choices).

Expression (2.37) is well known from the theory of *order statistics* which deals with ordered sequences of jointly distributed random variables $X_1, \ldots, X_\lambda$. Arranging the X_i in nondecreasing order, the reordering $X_{1:\lambda} \leq X_{2:\lambda} \leq \ldots \leq X_{\lambda:\lambda}$ is called the order statistics of $X_1, \ldots, X_\lambda$, and (2.37) is just the probability density function of $X_{\nu:\lambda}$ (see e.g. [ABN92], p. 10). Notice that by introducing $p_\nu(k')$ to characterize the ν-th best individual a minimization task is assumed because the order statistics is always nondecreasing.

Theorem 8 combines equations (2.36) and (2.37) to yield the convergence velocity of a $(\mu \overset{+}{,} \lambda)$-ES in case of a minimization task.

Theorem 8 (Convergence velocity of $(\mu \overset{+}{,} \lambda)$-ES)
Let $\varphi_{(\mu \overset{+}{,} \lambda)}$ denote the expectation of the progress rate of the population average for a $(\mu \overset{+}{,} \lambda)$-ES using one single standard deviation and no recombination or self-adaptation. Assuming a minimization task, $\varphi_{(\mu \overset{+}{,} \lambda)}$ can be calculated according to

$$
\varphi_{(\mu \overset{+}{,} \lambda)} = \frac{\lambda}{\mu} \int_{k'=k_{\min}}^{\infty} k' \cdot \sum_{\nu=1}^{\mu} \binom{\lambda-1}{\nu-1} \cdot
$$
$$
\cdot p_{k_j=k'} \cdot p_{k_j<k'}^{\lambda-\nu} \cdot (1 - p_{k_j<k'})^{\nu-1} \, dk' \quad ,
$$

(2.38)

where $k_{\min} = 0$ for a $(\mu+\lambda)$–ES and $k_{\min} = -\infty$ for a (μ,λ)–ES.

Proof: In addition to the derivation given in the text, the identity $p_{k_j<k'} + p_{k_j>k'} = 1$ is used here. Since a $(\mu+\lambda)$–ES accepts only improvements for the μ best, distances smaller than $k' = 0$ are not allowed in contrast to the (μ,λ)–ES.   Q.E.D.

The outermost integration cannot be performed even for a $(1,\lambda)$–ES for the corridor and sphere model, such that Schwefel had to rely on an additional assumption in order to arrive at approximate results. In case of a symmetric and unimodal function $p(k')$ the expectation value φ would be identical to the optimum point k'^* where $p(k')$ attains its maximum. Indeed, for an inclined plane as objective function a comparison of the result obtained by using this assumption of a symmetric and unimodal $p(k')$ to numerically calculated values of the exact theory showed close correspondence.

As result of lenghty calculations for a $(1,\lambda)$–ES, Schwefel arrived at the following equations determining the interrelations between normalized standard deviation, normalized progress rate, and offspring number for the corridor and sphere model, where notational conventions are as in equations (2.30) (see [Sch77], pp. 150-164 for the complete derivation):

$$\lambda_1 \approx 1 + \sqrt{\pi} \frac{\tilde{\varphi}_1}{\sigma_1' \sqrt{2}} \exp\left(\left(\frac{\tilde{\varphi}_1}{\sigma_1' \sqrt{2}}\right)^2\right) \cdot$$

$$\cdot \left(\operatorname{erf}\left(\frac{\tilde{\varphi}_1}{\sigma_1' \sqrt{2}}\right) + 2\exp\left(\frac{\sigma_1'}{\sqrt{2\pi}}\right) - 1\right) \quad , \quad \text{where}$$

$$\tilde{\varphi}_1 = \frac{\varphi_1'}{1 - \left(1 - \exp\left(-\frac{\sigma_1'}{\sqrt{2\pi}}\right)\right)^{\lambda}} \tag{2.39}$$

$$\lambda_2 \approx 1 + \sqrt{\pi}\left(\frac{\varphi_2'}{\sigma_2' \sqrt{2}} + \frac{\sigma_2'}{\sqrt{8}}\right) \cdot \exp\left(\left(\frac{\varphi_2'}{\sigma_2' \sqrt{2}} + \frac{\sigma_2'}{\sqrt{8}}\right)^2\right) \cdot$$

$$\cdot \left(1 + \operatorname{erf}\left(\frac{\sigma_2'}{\sqrt{8}}\right)\right)$$

Figure 2.5 shows the numerical evaluation of the sphere model curves, displaying normalized convergence velocity φ_2' over the normalized standard deviation σ_2' for $(1,\lambda)$-ESs with $\lambda \in \{1, 2, 5, 10, 100\}$ and $(1+\lambda)$-ESs with $\lambda \in \{1, 2, 5, 10\}$ (adapted from [Sch77], p. 154). First, one observes the fact that convergence velocity may become negative for a $(1,\lambda)$-ES in case of σ_2' becoming too large (or for the random walk $(1,1)$-ES), while the $(1+\lambda)$-strategy guarantees positive convergence velocity. Second, as the number of offspring is increased the maximal convergence velocity and the corresponding optimal normalized standard deviation are also increasing. The speedup of a $(1,\lambda)$-ES when compared to a $(1+1)$-ES turns out to be of order $\mathcal{O}(\ln \lambda)$, an asymptotic bound which can not be improved by a $(1+\lambda)$-ES (see [BRS93]). The locations of the maxima of the curves in figure 2.5 can be calculated by numerical methods from equations (2.39), and for the sphere model the result is indicated by the dotted curve in figure 2.5.

Since the speedup is just logarithmic and no unlimited computing resources can be presupposed, the location of the maximum of the function $\varphi_i'^*/\lambda_i$ is even more interesting. The resulting optimal offspring number λ_i^* yields the most reasonable compromise between computational effort to be invested and progress rate gained[19]. Only by relying on numerical iteration methods[20] for solving the equations, Schwefel obtained the results $\lambda_1^* = 6$ and $\lambda_2^* = 4.7 \approx 5$, thus recommending a $(1,5)$-ES or $(1,6)$-ES to be used. This ratio of μ/λ is usually extrapolated to larger populations by multiplying both μ and λ by the same integer, though equation (2.38) indicates that φ depends on the absolute values of μ and λ rather than merely their ratio. However, numerical integration of equation (2.38) indeed demonstrates that for sufficiently large values of $\mu \gg 1$ just the ratio μ/λ determines the convergence rate. Theoretical results concerning the relation of self-adaptation, convergence rate, and ratio of parent to offspring number have not been

---

[19]For massively parallel computers, however, the argument does not hold since offspring can be produced and evaluated in parallel.

[20]In fact, Schwefel used an Evolution Strategy for this purpose.

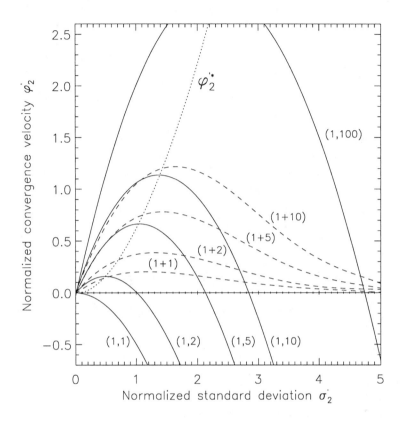

Fig. 2.5: Normalized convergence velocity φ_2' over the normalized standard deviation σ_2' for the sphere model, $(1+\lambda)$-ESs with $\lambda \in \{1, 2, 5, 10\}$, and $(1,\lambda)$-ESs with $\lambda \in \{1, 2, 5, 10, 100\}$. The dotted curve indicates the location of the maxima of the curves.

obtained yet.

2.2 Evolutionary Programming

The original Evolutionary Programming method as discussed in section 1.4 used uniform random mutations on discrete underlying alphabets and, in its most elaborated form, a $(\mu+\mu)$-selection mechanism. Following on from the initial work of L. J. Fogel [Fog62, FOW66] this approach remained greatly underused for approximately thirty years. Then, in the late 1980s D. B. Fogel (his son) extended Evolutionary Programming for applications involving continuous parameter optimization problems. Evolutionary Programming for continuous parameter optimization has many similarities with Evolution Strategies: mutations are normally distributed and, what is more interesting, the more elaborated versions of Evolutionary Programming incorporate variances of mutations into the genotype, thus facilitating the self-adaptation of these parameters. When reviewing Fogel's book [Fog91] and thesis [Fog92b], five different variants of Evolutionary Programming can be identified:

- *Standard* EP, which is characterized by the absence of any self-adaptation mechanism ([Fog92b], pp. 140–142; [Fog91], p. 45–46),

- *continuous standard* EP, where the term "continuous" indicates that in contrast to the generation-based working mechanism a newly created individual is immediately evaluated and inserted into the population ([Fog92b], pp. 152–153),

- *meta*-EP, which incorporates variances into the genotype in order to allow for their self-adaptation ([FFA91]; [Fog92b], pp. 155–158),

- *continuous meta*-EP, ([Fog92a], p. 158), and

- *Rmeta*-EP, which in addition to standard deviations also incorporates covariances (which are represented by correlation coefficients) into the genotype for self-adaptation ([FFAF92]; [Fog92a], pp. 287–289).

The last method (extension of which to the continuous variant is obvious) was implemented and tested by Fogel only for the two-dimensional case. For reasons of comparability to the generation-based algorithms, the continuous variants will not be discussed in the following. Furthermore, Rmeta-EP must be interpreted as an algorithm that is proposed rather than being completely elaborated (questions similar to those discussed in section 2.1.1 arise automatically, but the extension to the case $n > 2$ is certainly doable). The state-of-the-art may therefore, for our purposes, be given by meta-EP, and for reasons of completeness the presentation is based on the simpler underlying standard Evolutionary Programming algorithm.

It should also be noted that, though Evolution Strategies and Evolutionary Programming turn out to be surprisingly similar, their development proceeded independently of each other. It was only in 1992 that first contacts of a few researchers in the field of Evolution Strategies to the EP-community were established (contacts between researchers in Genetic Algorithms and the EP-community were made for the first time in 1990). This was largely due to the dissemination of information about the "First Annual Conference on Evolutionary Programming" that took place in early 1992 in San Diego [FA92].

2.2.1   Representation and Fitness Evaluation

In general, according to its definition, Evolutionary Programming for continuous parameter optimization assumes the existence of a restricted

subspace $\times_{i=1}^{n}[u_i, v_i] \subset I\!\!R^n$ ($u_i < v_i$) of $I\!\!R^n$ as the domain of optimization, thus seemingly implying the existence of $2n$ inequality constraints
$g_j(\vec{x}) = x_j - u_j \geq 0$ for $j \in \{1, \ldots, n\}$ and $g_j(\vec{x}) = v_{j-n} - x_{j-n} \geq 0$ for
$j \in \{n+1, \ldots, 2n\}$. However, these constraints are taken into account
by the algorithm *only during initialization* for setting up the start population, but the operators do not obey them, such that the search space
is principally unconstrained, i.e. $A_x = I\!\!R^n$.

The same holds for variances $\vec{v}$ in meta-EP, which are for initialization required to be generated in a range $[0, c]$, $c > 0$ denoting an exogenous parameter. During optimization, they may vary in the range of positive real numbers $I\!\!R_+$. The number of variances in case of meta-EP is
required to be n, i.e. there is no degree of freedom for the user to choose
between $1 \leq n_\sigma \leq n$ standard deviations as in Evolution Strategies.
This way, individuals are of the form $\vec{a} = (\vec{x}, \vec{v}) \in I = A_x \times A_s$,
where $A_x = I\!\!R^n$ and $A_s = \emptyset$ (standard Evolutionary Programming)
or $A_s = I\!\!R_+^n$ (meta-EP), respectively[21].

Fitness values $\Phi(\vec{a})$ are obtained from objective function values $f(\vec{x})$
by possibly imposing some random alteration κ and then *scaling* them
to positive values (but notice that scaling is not necessarily required —
it is mentioned here in order to present the most general description
of the algorithm). In order to meet the requirement of a useful scaling
function δ, it is assumed to be of the general form $\delta : I\!\!R \times \Theta_\delta \to I\!\!R_+$
where, as usual, Θ_δ denotes an additional set of parameters involved in
the process. Altogether, the fitness function takes the form

$$\Phi(\vec{a}) \quad = \quad \delta(f(\vec{x}), \kappa) \quad . \tag{2.40}$$

This transformation is intended to generalize fitness evaluation and
can also be used in the form $\Phi = f$ without causing serious technical
problems.

2.2.2   Mutation

In the case of standard Evolutionary Programming ($I = I\!\!R^n$), the Gaus-
sian mutation operator $m_{\{\beta_1, \ldots, \beta_n, \gamma_1, \ldots, \gamma_n\}} : I^\lambda \to I^\lambda$ is an asexual operator, such that again only the reduced form $m'_{\{\beta_1, \ldots, \beta_n, \gamma_1, \ldots, \gamma_n\}} : I \to I$,
$m'(\vec{x}) = \vec{x}'$ is presented here. The operator works with a standard devi-
ation that is obtained for each component x_i of the object variable vector
as the square root of a linear transformation of the fitness value $\Phi(\vec{x})$,
i.e. ($\forall i \in \{1, \ldots, n\}$) (see [Fog92b], p. 141):

---

[21]In case of Rmeta-EP, $A_s = I\!\!R_+^n \times [-1, 1]^{n \cdot (n-1)/2}$ includes also the complete
vector of *correlation coefficients*

$$\rho_{ij} \quad = \quad \frac{c_{ij}}{\sqrt{\sigma_i \sigma_j}} \in [-1, 1]$$

($i \in \{1, \ldots, n-1\}$, $j \in \{i+1, \ldots, n\}$) representing the covariance matrix $\mathbf{C}^{-1}$.

$$x_i' = x_i + \sqrt{\beta_i \cdot \Phi(\vec{x}) + \gamma_i} \cdot N_i(0,1) \quad . \tag{2.41}$$

The proportionality constants β_i and offset values γ_i are $2n$ exogenous parameters that must be tuned for a particular task. Often, however, β_i and γ_i are set to one and zero, respectively, such that $x_i' = x_i + \sqrt{\Phi(\vec{x})} \cdot N_i(0,1)$. Some problems of this approach are obvious (see also [BRS93]):

- If the global minimum's fitness value is different from zero, exact approachment of the global minimum point is not possible.

- If fitness values are very large, almost random walk behavior of the search is expected and any decrease of standard deviations is likely to be reverted by still large mutations.

- Appropriate tuning of either the linear transformation between fitness and variance or the scaling function is just impossible, if the user of the standard Evolutionary Programming algorithm does not know about the approximate location of the global minimum point.

To overcome the indicated tuning difficulties, meta-EP self-adapts n variances per individual in a manner quite similar to Evolution Strategies. Mutation $m_{\{\zeta\}}'$ applied to an individual $\vec{a} = (\vec{x}, \vec{\nu})$ produces a result $(\vec{x}', \vec{\nu}')$ as follows ($\forall i \in \{1, \ldots, n\}$) (see [Fog92b], p. 157)[22]:

$$
\begin{aligned}
x_i' &= x_i + \sqrt{\nu_i} \cdot N_i(0,1) \\
\nu_i' &= \nu_i + \sqrt{\zeta \nu_i} \cdot N_i(0,1) \quad .
\end{aligned}
\tag{2.42}
$$

Here, ζ denotes an exogenous parameter to assure that ν_i tends to remain positive. In [FFAF92], it is indicated to divide standard deviations by the control parameter rather than multiplying, but our presentation orientates to the thesis of Fogel [Fog92b]. Both methods are equivalent but the problem arises when comparing results according to the setting of ζ.

---

[22] Again, description of Rmeta-EP is devoted to a footnote. An individual $\vec{a} = (\vec{x}, \vec{\nu}, \vec{\rho})$ consisting of object variables, variances, and correlation coefficients ρ_j ($j \in \{1, \ldots, n \cdot (n-1)/2\}$) undergoes mutation $m_{\{\zeta, \varpi\}}'$ to yield $(\vec{x}', \vec{\nu}', \vec{\rho}')$ according to (see [Fog92b], p. 288):

$$
\begin{aligned}
\vec{x}' &= \vec{x} + \vec{N}(\vec{0}, \mathbf{C}(\vec{\sigma}, \vec{\rho})) \\
\nu_i' &= \nu + \sqrt{\zeta \nu_i} \cdot N_i(0,1) \\
\rho_j' &= \rho_j + \sqrt{\varpi \rho_j} \cdot N_j(0,1)
\end{aligned}
$$

where $|\rho_j'| > 1 \implies \rho_j' := \text{sign}(\rho_j')$ guarantees correlation coefficients to remain within the feasible range.

Fogel defines an analogue rule to (2.19) for guaranteeing positive variances, i.e.

$$\nu_i' \leq 0 \quad \Longrightarrow \quad \nu_i' := \varepsilon_\sigma > 0 \quad , \tag{2.43}$$

however allowing variances to become arbitrarily close to zero might in the extreme case cause an arbitrarily slow convergence behavior.

Though the basic idea to have the algorithm adapting its parameter setting on-line during the search is the same as in Evolution Strategies, some differences can be identified:

- Evolution Strategies use the mutated strategy parameters for modification of object variables, while Evolutionary Programming first modifies object variables and mutates strategy parameters in the second step, leading to a delayed effect of strategy parameter changes. Until now, both modification orders have not been compared to each other, but in principle the order should not make any difference.

- More importantly, the log-normally distributed alterations in Evolution Strategies automatically guarantee positivity of σ_i as well as no drift in case of zero selection pressure, whereas fluctuations in the meta-EP approach are neither neutral nor do they guarantee positive ν_i-values.

Just this short comparison hints to a large number of open research questions which by far cannot be discussed here. Instead, we continue by turning to the recombination philosophy of Evolutionary Programming.

2.2.3   Recombination

A brief approach to this issue would be to mention that Evolutionary Programming does not use any kind of recombination operator at all but instead relies on the power of mutation alone. However, it is advisable to go beyond this assessment and to look for reasons given in literature (if we are not satisfied with historical arguments — the first Evolutionary Programming algorithm was mainly criticized for its lack of recombination; see section 1.4).

Fogel and Atmar [FA90] presented empirical evidence that Gaussian mutation alone is a more effective search operator than a one-point crossover operator and even more effective than the combination of crossover and mutation, when comparing performance in case of a pleiotropic optimization problem for certain systems of linear equations. But empirical results can be generalized only with reservations, and certainly problems can be defined such that crossover is especially appropriate[23].

More instructive are arguments based on evolutionary biology. Fogel correctly argues that defining evolution primarily by the mechanisms of genetic change rather than by their phenotypic effects is inappropriate (see [Fog92b], pp. 477–481), thus indicating that the role of crossover is often overemphasized. Atmar characterizes crossover as being no more than a second- or third-order component of evolution and claims that, in contrast, an evolutionary advantage of sex has to be seen in the possibility of segregating defects out of the germline rather than enhancing evolutionary optimization by recombining good variants, which is the main point of view from researchers in the field of Genetic Algorithms [Atm92].

Polygeny and pleiotropy in most circumstances hinder the latter possibility from working, since the classic "one gene-one trait" assumption is recognized to be invalid in organic evolution [Fog92b, FA90]. Atmar notes that the evolutionary purpose of crossover is currently still unclear [Atm92].

2.2.4 Selection

Since no recombination is used in Evolutionary Programming, it is clear from the asexual property of mutation that the offspring population is size-identical to the parent population, i.e. $\lambda = \mu$. Then, a probabilistic selection method operates on the union of parents and offspring to reduce the total number of individuals from 2μ to μ. This way, the selection mechanism can be interpreted as a kind of probabilistic $(\mu+\mu)$-selection. Selection is controlled by an additional parameter $q \in I\!N$ ($q \geq 1$), determining the number of individuals to which each individual $\vec{a}_k \in P(t) \cup P'(t)$ is compared (selection based on such pairwise comparisons is often called *tournament selection*, q denoting the tournament size). For each individual $\vec{a}_k$ ($k \in \{1, \ldots, 2\mu\}$), q individuals are chosen at random from $P(t) \cup P'(t)$ and compared to $\vec{a}_k$ with respect to fitness values, counting how many of the q individuals are worse than $\vec{a}_k$, resulting in a score $w_k \in \{0, \ldots, q\}$. After doing so for all 2μ individuals, they are ranked in descending order of the score values w_i, and the μ individuals having highest score are selected to form the next population. More formally, $s_{\{q\}} : I^{2\mu} \rightarrow I^{\mu}$, $s_{\{q\}}(P(t) \cup P'(t)) = P(t+1)$, $q \in I\!N$ is based on w_i as follows ($\forall i \in \{1, \ldots, 2\mu\}$):

$$w_i = \sum_{j=1}^{q} \begin{cases} 1 \text{ , if } \Phi(\vec{a}_i) \leq \Phi(\vec{a}_{\chi_j}) \\ 0 \text{ , otherwise} \end{cases} . \tag{2.44}$$

---

[23] In the field of Genetic Algorithms, Eshelman and Schaffer investigated the niche of crossover (two-point and uniform; see section 2.3) in contrast to mutation and devised a problem where crossover has a competitive advantage over mutation [ES93]. They indicate, however, that the niche for pair-wise mating is much smaller than most researchers in that field believe.

$\chi_j \in \{1, \ldots, 2\mu\}$ denotes a uniform integer random variable that is sampled anew for each comparison. The best individual is assigned a guaranteed maximum fitness score q, such that its survival under selection is always guaranteed[24].

In order to formalize the intuitive feeling that this kind of selection turns into $(\mu+\mu)$-selection as q increases, without loss of generality, we assume that parent and offspring individuals $\vec{a}_1, \ldots, \vec{a}_\mu, \vec{a}'_1, \ldots, \vec{a}'_\mu$ are ordered according to fitness and sequentially renumbered, i.e., $\vec{a}_1, \ldots, \vec{a}_\mu$ $\vec{a}_{\mu+1}, \ldots, \vec{a}_{2\mu}$ such that $\Phi(\vec{a}_i) \leq \Phi(\vec{a}_{i+1})\ \forall i \in \{1, \ldots, 2\mu-1\}$. Looking at a particular individual $\vec{a}_j$ $(j \in \{1, \ldots, 2\mu\})$, we use $\mathcal{B} = (\Phi(\vec{a}_j) \leq \Phi(\vec{a}_\chi))$ to denote the event that a randomly sampled individual $\vec{a}_\chi$ is at least as worse as $\vec{a}_j$ with respect to fitness, and $\bar{\mathcal{B}} = (\Phi(\vec{a}_j) > \Phi(\vec{a}_\chi))$ to denote the complementary event. For one trial, the probability of $\mathcal{B}$ to occur is just

$$p := \mathcal{P}\{\mathcal{B}\} \quad = \quad \frac{2\mu - j + 1}{2\mu} \quad , \tag{2.45}$$

and $\mathcal{P}\{\bar{\mathcal{B}}\} = 1 - p$. Performing q independent trials as in our case, the resulting distributions of fitness scores w_{jq} $(j \in \{1, \ldots, 2\mu\})$ are binomial distributions, i.e. for each value of j:

$$\mathcal{P}\{w_{jq} = k\} \quad = \quad \binom{q}{k} p^k (1-p)^{q-k} \quad . \tag{2.46}$$

The expression reflects that in order to obtain a score $w_{jq} = k$, event $\mathcal{B}$ must occur k times and event $\bar{\mathcal{B}}$ therefore occurs $q - k$ times, repeated sampling of individuals being allowed.   Furthermore, the absolute frequency $H_{jq}(\mathcal{B})$ of $\mathcal{B}$ within q trials is also a random variable, following a binomial distribution with parameters q and $\mathcal{P}\{\mathcal{B}\}$ (see [Dör78], p. 351), and the same is true for the relative frequency $h_{jq}(\mathcal{B}) = H_{jq}(\mathcal{B})/q$, having expectation

$$E(h_{jq}(\mathcal{B})) \quad = \quad p \tag{2.47}$$

and variance

$$V^2(h_{jq}(\mathcal{B})) \quad = \quad \frac{1}{q} \cdot p \cdot (1 - p) \tag{2.48}$$

(see [Dör78], p. 351). Now, by noting that $\forall j \in \{1, \ldots, 2\mu\}$

$$\lim_{q \to \infty} V^2(h_{jq}(\mathcal{B})) \quad = \quad 0 \quad , \tag{2.49}$$

we realize that for increasing q any deviation from the expectation value becomes arbitrarily small, i.e. almost surely the expectation values of the

---

[24]This general property of a selection mechanism is usually called *elitist*, a terminology originally introduced by K. De Jong in the field of Genetic Algorithms (see [DeJ75], p. 101f.). Of course, normal $(\mu+\lambda)$-selection in Evolution Strategies is also elitist.

relative frequencies are exactly realized for large q. Since $E(h_{1q}(\mathcal{B})) = 1 > \ldots > E(h_{\mu q}(\mathcal{B})) = \frac{\mu+1}{2\mu}$ are the μ largest expectation values, for $q \to \infty$ exactly the μ best individuals are selected this way. Thus, the following theorem can be formulated:

Theorem 9 (Selection in Evolutionary Programming)
Let $s_q : I^{2\mu} \to I$ denote the selection mechanism of Evolutionary Programming and $s_{(\mu+\lambda)} : I^{\mu+\lambda} \to I^\mu$ denote the $(\mu+\lambda)$-selection of Evolution Strategies. Then, for any $P \in I^{2\mu}$,

$$\lim_{q \to \infty} \mathcal{P}\{s_{\{q\}}(P) = s_{(\mu+\mu)}(P)\} = 1 \quad , \qquad (2.50)$$

i.e. for q increasing towards infinity the effect of Evolutionary Programming selection becomes almost surely identical to the effect of $(\mu+\mu)$-selection.

Proof: The proof steps have been explained in detail in the text section preceding the theorem.   Q.E.D.

To get a feeling for the selection mechanism, relative frequencies $h_{jq}(\mathcal{B})$ resulting from a numerical simulation are plotted over j for $\mu = 50$ (i.e. $j \in \{1, \ldots, 100\}$) and values $q = 10$ (left) and $q = 100$ (right) in figure 2.6.

While expectation values p are located on the diagonal line from the upper left to the lower right corner (dotted diagonal), standard deviations $\sigma_{h_{jq}(\mathcal{B})} = \sqrt{V^2(h_{jq}(\mathcal{B}))}$ are indicated by the dashed curves located at the bottom of both figures. A simple calculation leading to the result that $V^2(h_{jq}(\mathcal{B}))$ attains its maximum $1/(2q)$ for $j = \mu - 1$ confirms the immediate observation that deviations from the expectation value are maximal for individuals of average quality. For $q = 10$, some individuals will be selected though they range on places around eighty according to quality ordering. Conversely, for $q = 100$ the difference to $(\mu+\mu)$-selection has vanished almost completely.

After the formalized treatment of probabilistic selection in Evolutionary Programming, this section concludes by summarizing the main reasons for researchers in this field insisting on probabilistic selection. Of course, as Fogel also points out ([Fog92b], p. 477), selection in nature is probabilistic. Furthermore, he refers to the work performed by Galar ([Fog92b], p. 111–112), who discusses the so-called "saddle-crossing problem" of a population located on a suboptimal peak that has to cross a valley in order to climb a better peak in the neighborhood. Galar presents empirical evidence that a "soft" selection mechanism assigning nonzero selection probabilities to even the worst individuals enables Evolutionary Algorithms to cross such saddles [Gal89]. Furthermore, in [Gal91] the empirical result of recombination being an obstruction to the saddle-crossing capability of large populations is obtained. Galar claims the unambigous identification of "handicapped individuals," i.e. those of average fitness, to be fundamental for the process of

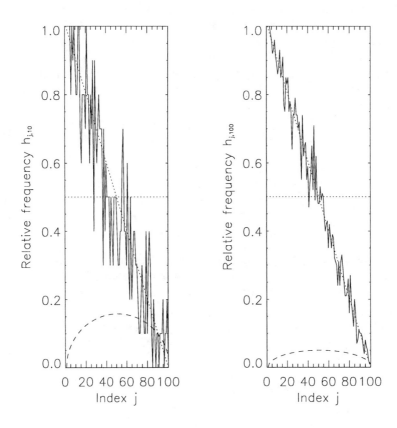

Fig. 2.6: Relative frequencies h_{jq} of the event $\mathcal{B}$, resulting from a numerical simulation for $q = 10$ (left) and $q = 100$ (right). The dashed curves at the bottom of the figures are plots of the standard deviation $\sigma_{h_{jq}}(\mathcal{B})$.

escaping evolutionary traps [Gal85]. His empirical results confirm the main design choices of Evolutionary Programming, i.e. renunciation of recombination and emphasis on probabilistic selection.

2.2.5   Other Components

This section is intended to give some information on initialization, constraint handling, and termination of the algorithm. As it was already indicated in section 2.2.1, Evolutionary Programming generates a start population $P(0)$ by uniform random sampling of each component x_i of the object variable vectors from constrained ranges $[u_i, v_i] \subset \mathbb{R}$ $(u_i < v_i)$. For meta-EP, variances $\nu_i \in [0, c]$ $(c > 0)$ are also sampled according to a uniform distribution[25]. However, the boundaries u_i, v_i do not restrict the feasible region during optimization, and even obedience of the upper bound c of variances is not controlled by Evolutionary Programming, such that these bounds are just quantities influencing initialization. Handling inequality constraints has so far not been incorporated into Evolutionary Programming in general, but the method used in Evolution Strategies (see section 2.1.5) can directly be transferred to Evolutionary Programming.

Termination of an Evolutionary Programming algorithm is usually controlled by specifying a maximum number of generations $t_{\max}$ for the running time, i.e.

$$\iota(P(t)) \;=\; \begin{cases} \text{true , if } t > t_{\max} \\ \text{false , otherwise} \end{cases} \qquad (2.51)$$

2.2.6 Conceptual Standard Algorithm

As indicated repeatedly in the previous expositions, meta-EP is understood as the standard instance of an Evolutionary Programming algorithm, such that it is presented here in its algorithmic formulation:

Algorithm 6 (Outline of meta-EP algorithm)

$t := 0;$
$initialize\ P(0) := \{\vec{a}_1(0), \ldots, \vec{a}_\mu(0)\} \in I^\mu$
      where $I = I\!R^n \times I\!R^n_+$
      and $\vec{a}_k = (x_i, \nu_i, \forall i \in \{1, \ldots, n\});$
$evaluate\ P(0):\ \{\Phi(\vec{a}_1(0)), \ldots, \Phi(\vec{a}_\mu(0))\}$
      where $\Phi(\vec{a}_k(0)) = \delta(f(\vec{x}_k(0)), \kappa_k);$
while $(\iota(P(t)) \neq$ **true**$)$ **do**
    $mutate:\ \vec{a}'_k(t) := m'_{\{\varsigma\}}(\vec{a}_k(t))\ \forall k \in \{1, \ldots, \mu\};$
    $evaluate:\ P'(t) := \{\vec{a}'_1(t), \ldots, \vec{a}'_\mu(t)\}:$
        $\{\Phi(\vec{a}'_1(t)), \ldots, \Phi(\vec{a}'_\mu(t))\}$
        where $\Phi(\vec{a}'_k(t)) = \delta(f(\vec{x}'_k(t)), \kappa_k);$
    $select:\ P(t+1) := s_{\{q\}}(P(t) \cup P'(t));$
    $t := t + 1;$
od

The meta-EP algorithm is formulated in the framework provided by definition 2.1 as follows:

Definition 2.6 (Meta-Evolutionary Programming)

An Evolutionary Algorithm

$$\mathrm{EA} = (I, \Phi, \Omega, \Psi, s, \iota, \mu, \lambda)$$

is called meta-Evolutionary Programming *algorithm:* $\Longleftrightarrow$

---

[25] Correlation coefficients $\rho_j \in [-1, 1]$ for Rmeta-EP are initialized analogously.

(1) $I = I\!\!R^n \times I\!\!R^n_+$,

(2) $\forall \vec{a} = (\vec{x}, \vec{\sigma}) \in I$: $\Phi(\vec{a}) = \delta(f(\vec{x}), \kappa)$, where $\delta : I\!\!R \times \Theta_\delta \to I\!\!R_+$ denotes a scaling function as in (2.40) and κ is a random noise term (that may even not be used by δ),

(3) $\Omega = \{m_{\{\varsigma\}} : I^\mu \to I^\mu\}$ where $m_{\{\varsigma\}}$ is defined as in (2.42),

(4) $\Psi(P) = s_{\{q\}}(P \cup m_{\{\varsigma\}}(P))$ where $q \in I\!\!N$ denotes the tournament size for selection,

(5) $s_{\{q\}} : I^{2\mu} \to I^\mu$, the selection operator, is defined as in (2.44),

(6) the termination criterion ι is given by (2.51), and

(7) $\lambda = \mu$.

A simplification of that definition to standard Evolutionary Programming is obvious (reduce I to $I\!\!R^n$ and exchange mutation as in (2.42) by (2.41)).

Finally, again in order to complete the description from a practical point of view to facilitate implementation and application of the algorithm, an attempt was performed to identify default values for the most important exogenous parameters of standard-EPand meta-EP[26]. The collection of values presented in table 2.2 is compiled from Fogel's thesis[27] (see [Fog92b], p. 168, p. 173, p. 292).

Standard parameterizations refer, if not explicitly stated differently, to this table. In the following, the notation $EP(\beta_i, \gamma_i, q, \mu)$ is used to denote an instance of standard Evolutionary Programming, while $mEP(\zeta, c, q, \mu)$ characterizes a meta-EP algorithm (range bounds are omitted due to their indicated unimportance to the optimization process itself). The default meta-EP algorithm is therefore denoted by $mEP(6, 25, 10, 200)$.

2.2.7 Theory

The standard Evolutionary Programming algorithm was analyzed by Fogel (see [Fog92a] and [Fog92b], pp. 142–151), who investigated the case $\Phi(\vec{x}) = f(\vec{x})$ for $EP(1, 0, q, \mu)$, resulting in a modification rule

$$x_i' = x_i + \sqrt{f(\vec{x})} \cdot N_i(0, 1) \qquad (2.52)$$

for mutations. His analysis aims at giving a proof of convergence with probability one for the resulting algorithm. Furthermore, an analysis of the special case $EP(1, 0, q, 1)$ is also performed. With a population size

---

[26]For Rmeta-EP, a default value $\varpi = 6$ for the scaling factor of correlation coefficients is suggested by Fogel (see [Fog92a], p. 292).

[27]Notice, however, that these values are recommended by Fogel for low-dimensional problems. The range values, the upper bound c, and the population size μ depend on the problem and the available hardware.

Parameter	Occurs in		Default
	EP	meta-EP	
Range bounds u_i, v_i	$\times$	$\times$	$u_i = -50$
			$v_i = 50$
Upper bound c of σ_i		$\times$	$c = 25$
Proportionality constants β_i	$\times$		$\beta_i = 1$
Offset constants γ_i	$\times$		$\gamma_i = 0$
Meta-parameter ζ for self-adaptation		$\times$	$\zeta = 6$
Tournament size q	$\times$	$\times$	$q = 10$
Population size μ	$\times$	$\times$	$\mu = 200$

Table 2.2. Default settings of exogenous parameters of standard- and meta-Evolutionary Programming.

of $\mu = 1$ and elitist selection (which is guaranteed; see section 2.2.4), the resulting algorithm is identical to a (1+1)–ES having $\sigma = \sqrt{f(\vec{x})}$, where instead of the 1/5-success rule the step size is controlled by the objective function value directly. This implies direct applicability of the results known for a (1+1)–ES to this special Evolutionary Programming variant. While a transfer of the corridor model (2.27) may cause some problems due to negative objective function values, the simplified sphere model

$$\tilde{f}_2(\vec{x}) \quad = \quad \sum_{i=1}^{n} x_i^2 = r^2 \qquad\qquad (2.53)$$

can be used in combination with the optimal standard deviation $\sigma_2^* = 1.224 \cdot r/n$ (2.32) to obtain the result

$$\sqrt{\tilde{f}_2(\vec{x})} \quad = \quad r = \frac{\sigma_2^* n}{1.224} \quad . \qquad\qquad (2.54)$$

In other words, the standard deviation used by this variant of Evolutionary Programming is — in case of the sphere model — always a factor $n/1.224$ larger than the optimal standard deviation. Therefore, when the dimension of the objective function is increased, this algorithm is expected to perform worse than an algorithm that is able to retain the optimal standard deviation σ^*.

Using the convergence rate equation (2.30) for the sphere model in terms of variables φ_2, σ_2, r, and n, i.e.

$$\varphi_2 \quad = \quad \frac{\sigma_2}{\sqrt{2\pi}} \exp\left(-\frac{1}{8}\left(\frac{\sigma_2 n}{r}\right)^2\right) - \frac{\sigma_2^2 n}{4r}\left(1 - \operatorname{erf}\left(\frac{\sigma_2 n}{r\sqrt{8}}\right)\right) , \quad (2.55)$$

the convergence rate of a $(1+1)$-EP algorithm can be obtained easily by calculating $\tilde{\varphi}_2 = \varphi_2(\sigma_2 = r)$:

$$\tilde{\varphi}_2 = \left(\frac{1}{\sqrt{2\pi}} \exp\left(-\frac{n^2}{8} \right) - \frac{n}{4} \left(1 - \mathrm{erf}\left(\frac{n}{\sqrt{8}} \right) \right) \right) \cdot r \quad . \tag{2.56}$$

While the dependency of $\tilde{\varphi}_2$ on r is linear as in the case of φ_2^*, its dependency on n is more complicated than the simple inverse proportionality of φ_2^*. Indeed, $\tilde{\varphi}_2$ approaches zero much faster than φ_2^* does, as can be seen from the ratio

$$
\begin{aligned}
\phi_2(n) &:= \frac{\tilde{\varphi}_2}{\varphi_2^*} \\
&= \frac{n}{0.2025} \left(\frac{1}{\sqrt{2\pi}} \exp\left(-\frac{n^2}{8} \right) - \frac{n}{4} \left(1 - \mathrm{erf}\left(\frac{n}{\sqrt{8}} \right) \right) \right) ,
\end{aligned}
\tag{2.57}
$$

where the term $\exp(-n^2/8)$ quickly becomes dominating as n is increased. The ratio $\phi_2(n)$ is plotted over n in figure 2.7 and has a maximum for a value of n slightly above one. A more exact calculation[28] of n^* according to

$$\left. \frac{d\phi_2(n)}{dn} \right|_{n^*} = 0 \tag{2.58}$$

yields $n^* \approx 1.48$, which must be rounded to one due to the discrete nature of n. Only for values of $n \in \{1, \ldots, 6\}$, the theory predicts a convergence rate that is practically useful for the sphere model.

These calculations provide an impressive demonstration of the overall sensitivity of the search to the step size control in the case of high dimensionality. Fogel also recognizes the problem and indicates the use of

$$\beta_i = n^{-2} \tag{2.59}$$

as a scaling factor when n is increased beyond two [Fog92c]. Then, the standard deviation of standard Evolutionary Programming becomes

$$\sqrt{\frac{\tilde{f}_2(\vec{x})}{n^2}} = \frac{r}{n} = \frac{\sigma_2^*}{1.224} \tag{2.60}$$

in case of the sphere model, thus being scaled correctly as the number of variables is increased. Under these circumstances, only a minor difference between the performance of Evolution Strategies and standard Evolutionary Programming is expected on the sphere model.

---

[28] Without presenting the complete calculation, we mention that $\frac{d}{dz} \mathrm{erf}(z) = \frac{2}{\sqrt{\pi}} \exp(-z^2)$. Furthermore, the expression for $\frac{d\phi_2(n)}{dn}$ was simplified by using the approximation $\mathrm{erf}(z) \approx 1 - \frac{1}{\sqrt{\pi}z} \exp(-z^2)$ (see [Rec73], p. 111).

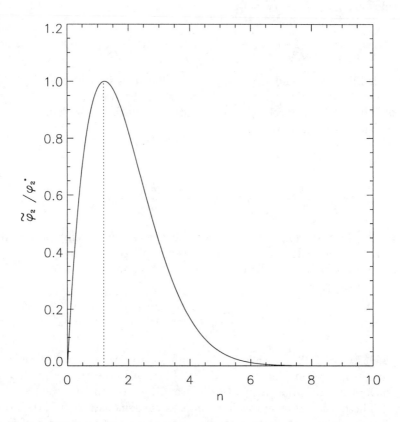

Fig. 2.7: Ratio of convergence rate for standard Evolutionary Programming ($\tilde{\varphi}_2$) and optimal convergence rate (φ_2^*) over the dimension (n) of the objective function sphere model.

In addition to the convergence rate theory from investigations on the sphere model, the global convergence theorem 7 from Evolution Strategies is also valid for standard Evolutionary Programming, if positive objective function values are guaranteed in order to prevent stagnation due to vanishing step sizes. However, for reasons of completeness, we will also summarize the convergence proof presented by Fogel, which is based on interpreting any possible population that may occur during evolution as a state of a finite Markov chain. To provide the background as far as necessary, the basic terminology on Markov chains is inserted here, following [Dör78] (pp. 400–430). A Markov chain is a special *stochastic process*, i.e. a time-dependent random variable.

Definition 2.7 (Stochastic process, Markov process)
A stochastic process is a family $(X(t))$, $t \in J \subseteq \mathbb{R}$, *of random vari-*

ables $X(t)$. In case $J = I\!N$, the stochastic process is called a process
with discrete time, *denoted* (X_k). *A stochastic process $X(t)$, $t \in J$, is*
called a Markov process*:* $\Longleftrightarrow$
$\forall k \geq 3$, $x_i \in I\!R$, $i \in \{1, \ldots, k\}$, $t_i \in J$ *with $t_i < t_{i+1}$ for $i \in$*
$\{1, \ldots, k-1\}$:

$$
\begin{aligned}
\mathcal{P}\{X(t_k) \leq x_k \mid X(t_{k-1}) = x_{k-1}, \ldots, X(t_1) = x_1\} = \\
\mathcal{P}\{X(t_k) \leq x_k \mid X(t_{k-1}) = x_{k-1}\} \quad .
\end{aligned}
\tag{2.61}
$$

If the number of states x_i *is finite or countable infinite, $X(t)$ is called a*
Markov chain.

In other words, the probability of the process being in a certain state
at time k only depends on the state at time $k-1$, not on any states the
process has passed earlier. The probabilities to go into state number j
at time $k + 1$ assuming the process is in state number i at time k,

$$
p_{ij}(k) \quad = \quad \mathcal{P}\{X_{k+1} = j \mid X_k = i\} \quad ,
\tag{2.62}
$$

are called *transition probabilities.* The Markov chain is called *ho-*
mogenous, if $p_{ij}(k)$ is independent of k. Then, transition probabilities
are denoted p_{ij}, and they are usually collected in the *transition matrix*
$\mathbf{P} = (p_{ij})$. Calculation of arbitrary l-step transition probabilities

$$
p_{ij}^{(l)} \quad = \quad \mathcal{P}\{X_{m+l} = j \mid X_m = i\}
\tag{2.63}
$$

is then possible by means of the *Chapman-Kolmogorov-equation:*

$$
p_{ij}^{(m+l)} \quad = \quad \sum_k p_{ik}^{(m)} p_{kj}^{(l)} \quad ,
\tag{2.64}
$$

which can also be expressed by matrix multiplication, since $\mathbf{P}^{(m+l)} = (p_{ij}^{(m+l)}) = \mathbf{P}^m \mathbf{P}^l$. Then, the probabilities $p_j(k)$ to be in state j at time
k can be calculated from a *start distribution* $p_j(0)$ by $\vec{P}(k) = \vec{P}(0)\mathbf{P}^k$.
Finally, we mention that a state i with $p_{ii} = 1$ is called *absorbing* (once
the process has entered an absorbing state, it can never leave that state).

After defining the state space, Fogel's argument is based on identifying the only absorbing state of a Markov chain as the union of all states
that contain the global optimum point. His state space is defined by
relying on the discretization of $I\!R$ that is used by any computer representation of real values, i.e. he argues implementation-based, really
investigating a grid-search algorithm. If $C \subset I\!R$ denotes the finite set
of numbers represented on a computer, $C^{n\mu}$ is the state space of the
Markov chain. This simplification leads to

Theorem 10 *Let the absorbing state be identified by index value* 1. *The probability* $p_1(k)$ *to enter the absorbing state at time step* k *is given by*

$$p_1(k) \;=\; \left(\vec{P}(0)\mathbf{P}^k\right)_1 = \vec{P}(0) \begin{pmatrix} 1 \\ \mathbf{N}_k\mathbf{R} \end{pmatrix} \quad , \tag{2.65}$$

where $\vec{P}(0)$ *is the arbitrary start distribution,* $\mathbf{P} = \begin{pmatrix} 1 & \vec{0} \\ \mathbf{R} & \mathbf{Q} \end{pmatrix}$ *denotes the transition matrix of the Markov chain,* $\mathbf{N}_k = \mathbf{I} + \mathbf{Q} + \ldots + \mathbf{Q}^{k-1}$, *and* $(\cdot)_1$ *denotes projection on the first component. Then,*

$$\lim_{k \to \infty} p_1(k) \;=\; \vec{P}(0) \begin{pmatrix} 1 \\ \cdot \\ \cdot \\ \cdot \\ 1 \end{pmatrix} = 1 \quad . \tag{2.66}$$

Proof: See [Fog92b], pp. 142–144.   Q.E.D.

The result is of extreme generality, based on the elitist property of selection that guarantees a monotone behavior of evolution, i.e. existence of an absorbing state, on discretization of the search state, and on the ability to get anywhere in the search space either in one step or many. Referring to the discussion presented in connection with theorem 1 (section 1.3), one has to recall that the true global optimum may differ arbitrarily from that identified by the algorithm. Furthermore, since theorem 10 relies on the discretization, it does not say anything about the convergence properties of Evolutionary Programming on objective functions $f : I\!\!R^n \to I\!\!R$.

For any discrete Markov chain, *waiting times* in states, i.e. the probabilities

$$\begin{aligned} \mathcal{P}\{X_{m+k+1} \neq j \mid X_m = X_{m+1} = \ldots = X_{m+k} = j\} = \\ p_{jj}^k(1 - p_{jj}) \end{aligned} \tag{2.67}$$

to stay in state j for k time steps, are distributed geometrically. This does, however, not allow for deriving convergence rate statements, since the steps of improvement of the best individuals' objective function value may be very small[29] (the Markov chain used in theorem 10 has approximately $|C|^{n\mu}$ states, where $|C|$ on modern digital computers is very large).

2.3   Genetic Algorithms

Genetic Algorithms are very likely to be the most widely known type of Evolutionary Algorithms, today receiving remarkable attention all over

---

[29]See also [BRS93] for a discussion of geometrical convergence of Evolutionary Programming.

the world. Probably the earliest predecessor of these algorithms emerged in the work of Fraser, a biologist who wanted to simulate evolution with special emphasis on the interaction of epistasis (see section 1.1.1) with selection [Fra57a, Fra57b, Fra60, Fra62]. This work as well as some other early approaches from biologists towards simulating evolution in order to improve understanding from the biological point of view are summarized by Goldberg ([Gol89a], pp. 89–103). As the work of Sumida, Houston, McNamara, and Hamilton on solving epistatic problems by using migration between semi-isolated subpopulations clearly demonstrates, biologists are still interested in Genetic Algorithms [SHMH90]. Sumida et al. apply the Genetic Algorithm to the problem of how a male bird allocates its time between singing and foraging and point towards further application possibilities of Genetic Algorithms in biology, e.g. investigations of game theoretic interactions between animals or learning rules of animals. In a different paper, Genetic Algorithms are discussed from a biologist's point of view, with a special emphasis on the relation between the biological source and the algorithmic imitation [Sum92].

However, Genetic Algorithms in their usual form are a development of Holland, computer scientist and psychologist at the University of Michigan. He summarized his work on *adaptive* and *reproductive plans* in 1975 in a book that serves as the starting point of nearly all known applications and implementations of Genetic Algorithms [Hol75]. While biologists intended to simulate biological systems using Genetic Algorithms, Holland pointed out how the natural search algorithm could be used in combination with problems that occur in practical application fields. But the goal of his work was broader, aiming at the development of a general theory of adaptive systems that communicate with their environment via a set of binary detectors (see [Hol75], pp. 6–30). In his earlier work he indicates that the population of a most general adaptive system would consist of individuals that represent computer programs, therefore allowing to represent rather complicated behaviour strategies [Hol62][30]. These ideas are picked up again in chapter 8 of [Hol75], where the "broadcast language" is defined, the predecessor of *Classifier Systems*, i.e. rule-based machine learning systems capable of generalization and inductive learning by means of GA-based evolution of rules[31].

---

[30]This reminds one of the earlier work of Friedberg on automatic programming, briefly discussed in section 1.4. Despite his early efforts, researchers working on automatic programming by Evolutionary Algorithms often refer to the Genetic Algorithm foundations. Using the term *"Genetic Programming Paradigm,"* Koza uses a Genetic Algorithm for the evolution of LISP programs (e.g. [Koz89, Koz90, Koz91, Koz92]), though even this idea was applied for the first time by others [FD87]. A syntactically simpler, special programming language was developed by Cramer two years earlier [Cra85]. Since the approaches have several problems, e.g. finding an appropriate fitness function, the halting problem, and brittleness of most programming languages to the effects of random changes (see [DeJ87] for a more detailed discussion), some researchers recently turned back to binary representations of simple assembler-like programming languages [Ray91].

[31]For more informations on Classifier Systems, the reader is referred to the in-

This interpretation of Genetic Algorithms as generalized adaptive systems is sometimes adopted by researchers when discussing the application possibilities to parameter optimization problems, e.g. ([DeJ85])[32]:

> *However, because of this historical focus and emphasis on function optimization applications, it is easy to fall into the trap of perceiving GAs themselves as optimization algorithms and then being surprised and/or disappointed when they fail to find an "obvious" optimum in a particular search space.*

Again, the central question concerns the interpretation of adaptation as a special optimization process or vice versa. Neither De Jong [DeJ92] nor Holland [Hol75] identified the differences between adaptation and optimization. As discussed in section 1.1 and 1.2, in our opinion there is no difference except that both terms have emerged from different disciplines, and we support the meliorisation interpretation in the following.

Holland himself pointed out how to interpret his reproductive plans in terms of genetics, economics, game-playing, pattern recognition, statistical inference, control, and parameter optimization (see [Hol75], chapter 3). De Jong laid the foundations to the latter application technique with his fundamental thesis [DeJ75], and many of the methods introduced by him are still the basic principles of most applications of Genetic Algorithms to real problems. A look at the conference proceedings of the "International Conference on Genetic Algorithms and Their Applications (ICGA)," held since 1985 in the U.S. every second year, provides an impression of the large number of successful parameter optimization applications of Genetic Algorithms [Gre85, Gre87a, Sch89, BB91, For93], thus the conception of Genetic Algorithms as optimization algorithms prevails.

The following presentation of Genetic Algorithms is restricted to continuous and binary parameter optimization problems, i.e. it is based on a classical understanding of Genetic Algorithms. Whenever the search space becomes more complex, e.g. in case of permutation spaces, matrix spaces, tree and graph spaces, or program spaces, the classical Genetic Algorithm can only be applied by constructing rather complicated encoding mappings for the representations. Alternatively, many researchers started to adapt the algorithm to the natural representation of the search space, thus developing new genetic operators that are suited to the special data structures. However, such modifications lead to algorithms showing enormous differences to the basic Genetic Algorithm, such that the boundaries to other Evolutionary Algorithms

---

troductory article of Booker, Goldberg, and Holland [BGH89]. More detailed introductions can be found in [SZ90] (chapter 6, pp. 139–173) and [Gol89a] (chapter 6, pp. 218–257).

[32]Note. From "Genetic Algorithms: A Ten Year Perspective" by K. DeJong, 1985. In Proceedings of the First International Conference on Genetic Algorithms, by J. J. Grefenstette, 1985, New Jersey: Lawrence Erlbaum Associates, INC. Copyright 1985 by Lawrence Erlbaum Associates, INC. Reprinted by permission.

become blurred. For an excellent discussion of Evolutionary Algorithms working on complex data structures by using specialized operators on a natural data representation (rather than natural operators — in the sense of Holland's original definitions — on a specialized representation), the reader is referred to [Mic92].

2.3.1 Representation and Fitness Evaluation

In contrast to both Evolution Strategies and Evolutionary Programming, Genetic Algorithms work on bitstrings of fixed length l, i.e.[33] $I = I\!B^l$. For pseudoboolean objective functions, this representation is directly applicable. More frequently, however, Genetic Algorithms are applied to continuous parameter optimization problems of the form

$$f : \prod_{i=1}^{n} [u_i, v_i] \to I\!R \qquad (2.68)$$

$(u_i < v_i)$ by interpreting the bitstring $\vec{a} = (a_1, \ldots, a_l) \in I\!B^l$ as the encoding of a vector $\vec{x} \in \prod_{i=1}^{n} [u_i, v_i]$. This process works by logically dividing the bitstring into n segments of (in most cases) equal length l_x, such that $l = n \cdot l_x$ and each segment $a_{i1}, \ldots, a_{il_x} \in I\!B^{l_x}$ of $\vec{a}$ encodes the corresponding object variable x_i.

Decoding of a segment works by decoding the bits into the corresponding integer value between 0 and $2^{l_x} - 1$ and then linearly mapping that integer to the real interval $[u_i, v_i]$, i.e. injective decoding functions $\Upsilon^i : I\!B^{l_x} \to [u_i, v_i]$ are assumed. Simple decoding of base two numbers to base ten numbers as used e.g. in [DeJ75] (p. 196) or [Mic92] (p. 34ff.) takes the form

$$\Upsilon^i(a_{i1}, \ldots, a_{il_x}) \quad = \quad u_i + \frac{v_i - u_i}{2^{l_x} - 1} \cdot \left(\sum_{j=0}^{l_x - 1} a_{i(l_x - j)} \cdot 2^j \right) \quad . \qquad (2.69)$$

This mechanism implies that in the continuous space of the original problem f only a search on grid points is performed, such that in general instead of the true global minimum point it can at the best be expected to find that grid point whose objective function value is the smallest within all grid points but may nevertheless differ by an arbitrary amount from the true global minimum (cf. theorem 1 of section 1.3). The number l_x of bits for encoding one object variable x_i together with the object variable range $[u_i, v_i]$ determines the distance Δx_i of two grid points being neighbors with respect to dimension i according to

$$\Delta x_i \quad = \quad \frac{v_i - u_i}{2^{l_x} - 1} \quad , \qquad (2.70)$$

i.e. accuracy of the results can be improved by increasing l_x.

---

[33]To distinguish between the dimension n of the objective function, and l of the binary vector, two different letters are used here.

Combining the segment-wise decoding functions Υ^i to an individual-decoding function $\Upsilon : I\!B^l \to \prod_{i=1}^{n} [u_i, v_i]$, $\Upsilon = \Upsilon^1 \times \ldots \times \Upsilon^n$, the vector $\vec{x} = \Upsilon(\vec{a})$ is obtained from a bitstring $\vec{a}$.

However, instead of the simple base two representation given in equation (2.69), it is now common practice to use a *Gray code* interpretation of the bitstring segments. Bethke was one of the first who indicated the advantages such a code might have on the search ([Bet81], pp. 100–103) due to representing adjacent integer values by bitstrings having Hamming distance one, i.e. when $i_1, i_2 \in \{0, \ldots, 2^{l_x} - 1\}$ denote the integer values represented by Gray-coded bitstring segments $\vec{a}_1, \vec{a}_2 \in I\!B^{l_x}$, we have

$$|i_1 - i_2| = 1 \quad \Rightarrow \quad \rho_H(\vec{a}_1, \vec{a}_2) = 1 \quad . \tag{2.71}$$

Note that this is an implication, *not* an equivalence: Even for a Gray code a change of a single bit may cause arbitrarily large changes to the corresponding integer values. To illustrate this observation, table 2.3 compares a three-bit standard binary code to a Gray code.

Integer	Standard	Gray
0	000	000
1	001	001
2	010	011
3	011	010
4	100	110
5	101	111
6	110	101
7	111	100

Table 2.3. Comparison of standard binary-coded and Gray-coded integers.

Conversions between standard and Gray code and vice versa for a standard-coded bitstring $\vec{a} = (a_1, \ldots, a_{l_x})$ and its Gray-coded counterpart $\vec{b} = (b_1, \ldots, b_{l_x})$ can be defined on the basis of an operator $\oplus$ that denotes addition modulo 2 on $I\!B$ (i.e. $0 \oplus 0 = 0$, $0 \oplus 1 = 1 \oplus 0 = 1$, $1 \oplus 1 = 0$) as follows [Wri91] ($\forall i \in \{1, \ldots, l_x\}$):

$$\gamma : \quad b_i = \begin{cases} a_i & , \text{ if } i = 1 \\ a_{i-1} \oplus a_i & , \text{ if } i > 1 \end{cases} \quad \text{Standard to Gray}$$

$$\tag{2.72}$$

$$\gamma^{-1} : \quad a_i = \bigoplus_{j=1}^{i} b_j \qquad \text{Gray to standard .}$$

For a Genetic Algorithm using Gray code, the decoding function of equation (2.69) must be extended to

$$\Upsilon_G^i(b_{i1}, \ldots, b_{il_x}) \;=\; u_i + \frac{v_i - u_i}{2^{l_x} - 1} \cdot \left(\sum_{j=0}^{l_x-1} \left(\bigoplus_{k=1}^{l_x-j} b_{ik} \right) \cdot 2^j \right) . \quad (2.73)$$

Due to the fact that Gray-coding has become a standard of modern implementations (see [CS88] for an experimental comparison of Gray code and standard code, indicating a better performance for the former), a Gray code is assumed in the follwing in most cases. Standard code and Gray code are distiguished here by indexing the standard code Υ_S when it is used.

Genetic Algorithms need a scaling function $\delta : I\!\!R \times \Theta_\delta \to I\!\!R^+$ to map objective function values $f(\Upsilon(\vec{x}))$ to positive real values, since the standard selection mechanism of Genetic Algorithms requires positive fitness values and highest fitness values for the best individuals. A variety of different scaling methods have been proposed by researchers, ranging from simple linear transformations to methods that calculate some population measures (e.g. the standard deviation of the objective function values within the current population) in order to perform an appropriate transformation. The following list of scaling methods (formulated for maximization tasks) intends to give an overview in view of a later discussion of the impact of scaling on the selection mechanism:

- *Linear static scaling* ([GB89], [Gol89a], p. 124):

$$\delta(f(\Upsilon(\vec{a})), \{c_0, c_1\}) \;=\; c_0 \cdot f(\Upsilon(\vec{a})) + c_1 , \quad (2.74)$$

where $c_0 \in I\!\!R - \{0\}$, $c_1 \in I\!\!R$ are exogenous constants.

- *Linear dynamic scaling* ([GB89]):

$$\delta(f(\Upsilon(\vec{a})), \{c_0, P(t)\}) \;=\; \begin{aligned} &c_0 \cdot f(\Upsilon(\vec{a})) \\ &- \min\{f(\Upsilon(\vec{a}_j)) \mid \vec{a}_j \in P(t) \} , \end{aligned} \quad (2.75)$$

where $P(t)$ denotes the current population and $c_0 \in I\!\!R - \{0\}$.

- *Logarithmic scaling* ([GB89]):

$$\delta(f(\Upsilon(\vec{a})), \{c_0\}) \;=\; c_0 - \log(f(\Upsilon(\vec{a}))) , \quad (2.76)$$

assuming a guaranteed positive objective function as well as $c_0 > \log(f(\vec{x})) \; \forall \vec{x} \in \prod_{i=1}^{n} [u_i, v_i]$.

- *Exponential scaling* ([GB89], [Gol89a], p. 124):

$$\delta(f(\Upsilon(\vec{a})), \{c_0, c_1, c_2\}) \;=\; (c_0 \cdot f(\Upsilon(\vec{a})) + c_1)^{c_2} , \quad (2.77)$$

where c_0 and c_1 are chosen as in case of the linear scaling methods. Michalewicz extended this method to *non-uniform scaling*, which

changes the exponent c_2 during the search according to a schedule
determined by a statistical population measure (the *span*) and the
generation counter t ([Mic92], pp. 63–66).

- *Sigma truncation*:
This method was originally introduced by Forrest in an implementation for solving the prisoner's dilemma problem in the form
(see [For85], p. 10 and pp. 54–55):

$$\delta(f(\Upsilon(\vec{a})), \{P(t)\}) \;=\; \frac{f(\Upsilon(\vec{a})) - (\bar{f} - \sigma(P(t)))}{\sigma(P(t))} \,, \qquad (2.78)$$

where $\bar{f} = \frac{1}{\mu} \sum_{i=1}^{\mu} f(\Upsilon(\vec{a}_i(t)))$ and $\sigma(P(t))$ denotes the standard
deviation of objective function values in $P(t)$. The original is re-
formulated in [Gol89a] (p. 124) as

$$\delta(f(\Upsilon(\vec{a})), \{c_0, P(t)\}) \;=\; f(\Upsilon(\vec{a})) - (\bar{f} - c_0 \cdot \sigma(P(t))) \,, \; (2.79)$$

and Michalewicz substitutes the first minus sign in that definition
by a plus (see [Mic92], p. 62).

Brill, Brown, and Martin applied sigma-truncation in the formulation

$$\delta(f(\Upsilon(\vec{a})), \{c_0, P(t)\}) \;=\; \frac{f(\Upsilon(\vec{a})) - (\bar{f} - c_0 \cdot \sigma(P(t)))}{2c_0 \cdot \sigma(P(t))} \quad (2.80)$$

to a feature selection problem in the context of neural network
classifiers [BBM92]. The parameter c_0 is used to control the bias
towards highly fit individuals. Except mentioning that this scaling method works relative to the current population, the authors
neither motivate their choice nor discuss the relevance of this scaling method for the success of their algorithm.

Altogether, the usefulness of sigma-truncation seems unclear both
from a theoretical and practical point of view.

Theoretical investigations on the interactions between scaling and
selection do not exist, which is plausible due to the complexity of such
efforts. However, even empirical comparisons of the performance of Genetic Algorithms relying on different scaling methods have not been
performed, such that the choice of a scaling method and its parameterization can be thought of as a "black art." Avoiding nonlinearities,
the confusions caused by sigma-truncation, and the oversimplification of
linear static scaling, we follow the linear dynamic scaling method from
Grefenstette's widely spread implementation according to [Gre87b]. As
a scaling baseline, it takes the worst individual of the population $\omega \in I\!N$

time steps before into account (using $\omega = 0$ during the first ω generations). In a formulation suitable for minimization tasks, it takes the form

$$
\begin{aligned}
\delta(f(\Upsilon(\vec{a})), \{P(t-\omega)\}) = \\
-f(\Upsilon(\vec{a})) + \max\{f(\Upsilon(\vec{a}_j)) \mid \vec{a}_j \in P(t-\omega)\} \quad ,
\end{aligned}
\tag{2.81}
$$

and Grefenstette suggests from experience to set $\omega = 5$ as a reasonable default value [Gre87b]. The parameter ω is called *scaling window*.

2.3.2   Mutation

The mutation operator of Genetic Algorithms was introduced by Holland as a "background operator" that occasionally changes single bits of individuals by inverting them[34] (see [Hol75], pp. 109–111). In analogy to the natural model (cf. the data given for spontaneous base pair mutation in section 1.1.3), the mutation probability $p_m \in [0,1]$ per bit is usually very small in Genetic Algorithms. Some common settings are $p_m = 0.001$ ([DeJ75], pp. 67–71), $p_m = 0.01$ [Gre86], and $p_m \in [0.005, 0.01]$ [SCED89]. In the latter study the authors additionally formulate heuristic rules indicating that performance is decreasing both for large population size ($\mu > 200$) combined with large mutation probability ($p_m > 0.05$) as well as for small population size ($\mu < 20$) combined with small mutation probability ($p_m < 0.002$).

The local form of the mutation operator, $m'_{\{p_m\}} : I \rightarrow I$, using bit-inversion for each position that undergoes mutation, produces a bitstring $\vec{a}' = (a'_1, \ldots, a'_l) = m'_{\{p_m\}}(a_1, \ldots, a_l) = m'_{\{p_m\}}(\vec{a})$ according to ($\forall i \in \{1, \ldots, l\}$):

$$
a'_i = \begin{cases} a_i & , \quad \text{if } \chi_i > p_m \\ 1 - a_i & , \quad \text{if } \chi_i \leq p_m \end{cases}
\tag{2.82}
$$

where $\chi_i \in [0,1]$ as usual denotes a uniform random variable sampled anew for each bit.

Small mutation rates, as Holland indicates, guarantee that an individual produced by mutation does not differ genetically very much from its ancestor. This statement is valid in genotype space, but as our observations from section 2.3.1 indicate it neither holds for a standard code nor for a Gray code when a nonlinear decoding function is in the game.

---

[34] Originally, Holland defined mutation of a certain bit as a substitution of that bit by a random element from the finite underlying alphabet, e.g. $\mathbb{B}$. However, most researchers interpret mutation as a real change instead of a random toss with probability one-half, and this more natural point of view is adopted here since it is in good agreement with the biological model where the simplest mutation event is a base pair change (see section 1.1).

2.3.3 Recombination

While mutation in Genetic Algorithms serves as an operator to reintroduce "lost alleles" into the population, i.e. bit positions that are converged to a certain value throughout the complete population and therefore could never be regained again by means of recombination, the *crossover* operator is emphasized as the most important search operator of Genetic Algorithms. The idea forming the background of crossover is that useful segments of different parents should be combined in order to yield a new individual that benefits from advantageous bit combinations of both parents. This way, longer and longer segments of high fitness are expected to emerge, finally leading to a good overall solution ([Hol75], pp. 97–106).

Crossover in Genetic Algorithms is always a sexual operator $r'_{\{p_c\}}$: $I^2 \to I$ that with probability p_c selects two parent individuals $\vec{s}$ and $\vec{v}$ from the population, recombines them to form two new individuals, and discards one of the results at random. Common proposed settings for the crossover probability are $p_c = 0.6$ [DeJ75], $p_c = 0.95$ [Gre86], and $p_c \in [0.75, 0.95]$ [SCED89]. The traditional *one-point crossover* introduced by Holland chooses one crossover position $\chi \in \{1, \ldots, l-1\}$ within the bitstrings at random and exchanges the bits to the right of that position between both individuals, resulting in ([Hol75], p. 98):

$$
\begin{aligned}
\vec{s}' &= (s_1, \ldots, s_{\chi-1}, s_\chi, v_{\chi+1}, \ldots, v_l) \\
\vec{v}' &= (v_1, \ldots, v_{\chi-1}, v_\chi, s_{\chi+1}, \ldots, s_l) \quad .
\end{aligned}
\tag{2.83}
$$

In connection with parameter optimization problems, however, the traditional one-point operator seems to be clearly inferior to other crossover operators with respect to the performance results. Extensive empirical studies concerning the performance of various crossover operators have been performed by Schaffer et al., published in several papers which shed some light on the relation between performance, parameterization and configuration of Genetic Algorithms [CES89, ECS89, SCED89].

The one-point crossover operator suffers from its *positional bias*, i.e. a strong dependence of the exchange probability on the bit positions, since as bit indices increase towards l their exchange probability approaches one. A generalization to *multi-point crossover* $r'_{\{p_c, z\}}$ allows of $z \geq 1$ crossover positions and exchanges each second segment between subsequent crossover positions. z crossover points $\chi'_1, \ldots, \chi'_z \in \{1, \ldots, l-1\}$ are chosen at random, such that $\chi'_k < \chi'_{k+1}$ $\forall k \in \{1, \ldots, z-1\}$, and if z is odd an additional point $\chi'_{z+1} = l$ is added by definition. For $z = 5$, a possible effect of 5-point crossover on two individuals is schematically shown in figure 2.8.

Whenever the number of crossover points is odd, the exchange probabilities turn out to be asymmetrically depending on the bit position, such that for symmetry reasons in most cases small, even numbers of crossover points are proposed, e.g. $z = 2$ [Gre87b], $z \in \{1, 2, 3, 4, 8\}$

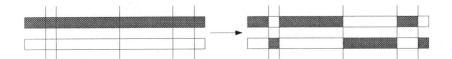

Fig. 2.8: Working mechanism of 5-point crossover (schematically).

([DeJ75], pp. 148–160), or $z \in \{1, 2, 4, 8, 12\}$ [ECS89], empirically indicating a value of $z = 8$ to be optimal[35]. However, the actual standard used in implementations is a two-point crossover, probably due to the wide dissemination of Grefenstette's implementation [Gre87b].

Further increasing the number of crossover points, one arrives at the *uniform crossover* operator as proposed by Syswerda [Sys89]. In case of uniform crossover exchange segments reduce to single bits, since for each bit the decision whether to exchange it or not is done by means of independent coin tosses. Comparing this operator to one-point crossover, Syswerda also reports better results for uniform crossover on a set of test functions including pseudoboolean problems as well as continuous ones. A number of additional crossover operators have been discussed in the literature, and during each of the main conferences on Genetic Algorithms a few new operators can be expected, especially when a non-traditional problem representation is used. Before we try to give a short overview of some further approaches, we mention that the multi-point crossover (with $z \geq 1$) and uniform crossover will be understood in the following as basic recombination operators used currently in Genetic Algorithms relying on binary representations. This collection may appear arbitrary, but it reflects (the author's overview of) the frequency of use of the operators as reported in the literature. Following the presentation of recombination as in section 2.1.3, these operators are summarized here as follows ($\chi'_1, \ldots, \chi'_z \in \{1, \ldots, l-1\}$ denote randomly sampled crossover positions, where $\chi'_k < \chi'_{k+1}$ and $\chi'_{z+1} = l$ if z is odd, $k \in \{1, \ldots, l\}$):

- z-point crossover $r_{\{p_c, z\}}$:

$$a'_i = \begin{cases} a_{S,i} &, \quad \forall i \, (\chi'_k < i \leq \chi'_{k+1}) \,, \; k \leq z, k \text{ odd} \\ a_{T,i} &, \quad \text{otherwise} \end{cases} \qquad (2.84)$$

- Uniform crossover $r_{\{p_c\}}$:

---

[35] It is an open question whether this number is valid in general. However, it seems very unlikely that the optimal number of crossover points should neither depend on the length of individuals nor on the dimension of the objective function and its topological properties. And it is surely pure chance that the number is identical to the maximum number of crossover points observed in nature (cf. section 1.1.2).

$$a_i' = \begin{cases} a_{S,i} \, , \chi > 1/2 \\ a_{T,i} \, , \chi \le 1/2 \end{cases} \qquad (2.85)$$

Indices S and T are again used to denote two parent individuals selected at random from the population. Multi-point crossover exchanges any segment between an odd-numbered and the next even-numbered crossover point, while other segments remain unchanged. The definition also includes the case $z = 1$, i.e. one-point crossover. A global decision whether to perform any crossover or not is made for each operator according to the outcome of one trial of the uniform random variable $\chi \in [0,1]$ in comparison to the crossover rate p_c, and whenever no crossover has to be performed the individual $\vec{a}$ is copied to the offspring population[36]. For each application of the crossover operator (each trial of χ), the z crossover points and both parents must be determined anew.

Without claiming completeness, a short informal description of the working mechanism of some more crossover operators is given in the following list:

- *Segmented crossover* [ECS89]:
  Segmented crossover works in a way similar to multi-point crossover, except that the number of crossover points is not fixed but may vary around an expectation value. This is achieved by a segment switch rate specifying the probability that a segment will end at any point in the string. If p denotes the switch rate, on average $l \cdot p$ crossover points can be expected.

- *Shuffle crossover* [ECS89]:
  This technique can be used in combination with any multi-point crossover. In order to reduce the positional bias of standard operators, shuffle crossover proceeds by randomly shuffling the bit positions of both parents in the same way, performing the multi-point operator and then unshuffling the result.

- *Punctuated crossover* [SM87]:
  The punctuated crossover operator is of special interest here, since it is the only known attempt to incorporate self-adaptation of some strategy parameters into Genetic Algorithms in the same way as it is done in Evolution Strategies and in Evolutionary Programming, i.e. by incorporating the strategy parameters into the genotype and evolving them just as object variables are evolved. Punctuated crossover is an effort to self-adapt both number and positions of crossover points for a multi-point crossover by adding l bits to the genotype that represent the crossover operator of the individual

---

[36]Within implementations, recombination is often applied deterministically to $100 \cdot p_c\%$ of the population, thus neglecting the probabilistic character of the crossover rate as proposed by Holland ([Hol75], p. 122).

(a one-bit indicates a crossover point). According to this description, object variable bits and corresponding bits of the crossover punctuations are exchanged between parents or remain unchanged, and the operator code itself is subject to crossover and mutation. In their experiments on a two-dimensional sphere model using 15 bits for each object variable, Schaffer and Morishima observed an emerging, time-dependent pattern of accumulated crossover points for certain bit positions[37].

The large number of different approaches to identify the best recombination operator by experimental comparison or to define a new, more powerful operator, can be interpreted as a clear indication that in at least some cases the operator proposed by Holland does not yield a satisfactory degree of performance. Moreover, some results suggest that the dominating role of crossover in Genetic Algorithms will diminish in the future in favor of mutation.

Concluding this section, some analogies of recombination in Evolution Strategies and Genetic Algorithms as well as important differences are discussed. Looking at the genotype, there is a clear correspondence between uniform crossover and discrete recombination. However, looking at the real-valued (in Genetic Algorithms the decoded) object variables it becomes apparent that no crossover operator obeys to the logical boundaries of object variables on the bitstring, i.e. crossover points may fall anywhere into the bitstring instead of being restricted to the positions $l_x, 2 \cdot l_x, \ldots, (n-1) \cdot l_x$. It would surely be a very interesting experiment to compare a boundary-restricted crossover in Genetic Algorithms to the corresponding unrestricted multi-point operator (compare also section 7.3) or to perform intensive experiments with punctuated crossover testing whether crossover points show a tendency to concentrate at boundaries of decoded object variables.

2.3.4 Selection

Just as in Evolutionary Programming, research in Genetic Algorithms emphasizes a selection mechanism using a probabilistic survival rule. By deriving an analogy to the game-theoretic *multi-armed bandit problem* (see section 2.3.7), Holland developed the *proportional selection* method in order to deal with the trade-off between further exploiting promising regions of the search space and exploring other regions at the same time (see [Hol75], chapter 5). The *survival probabilities* (also called *selection probabilities*)

$$p_s(\vec{a}) \;\; = \;\; \mathcal{P}\{\vec{a} \in s(P(t)) \mid \vec{a} \in P(t)\} \tag{2.86}$$

---

[37]The most obvious accumulations can be identified in their graphics around bit positions 17 and 28.

for proportional selection $s : I^\mu \rightarrow I^\mu$ are calculated according to the relative fitness of the individuals $\vec{a}_i(t) \in P(t) = \{\vec{a}_1(t), \ldots, \vec{a}_\mu(t)\}$, i.e. $(\forall i \in \{1, \ldots, \mu\})$:

$$p_s(\vec{a}_i(t)) = \frac{\Phi(\vec{a}_i(t))}{\sum\limits_{j=1}^{\mu} \Phi(\vec{a}_j(t))} . \qquad (2.87)$$

Obviously, this mechanism fails in the case of negative fitness or minimization tasks, if Φ would simply yield the objective function value without performing an appropriate scaling. On the other hand, any scaling technique manipulates selection probabilities and therefore the selection mechanism itself, such that the fundamental theoretical foundation of proportional selection becomes questionable in these cases.

According to the probability distribution defined on the offspring population by equation (2.87), μ samples are performed and the corresponding individuals are copied to the new parent population. It is useful to define the expected number of occurrences of individuals $\vec{a}_i(t) \in P(t)$ in the parent population after selection, which is denoted $\eta(\vec{a}_i(t))$ in the following. They are given by the relation

$$\eta(\vec{a}_i(t)) = \mu \cdot p_s(\vec{a}_i(t)) \qquad (2.88)$$

and are usually simply called *expected values*. Though this is trivial from a mathematical point of view, it is worth thinking about whenever proportional selection is used practically in an implementation, since we must agree to create a discrete number of copies for each individual, i.e. some method must be developed to convert expected values to integers. To further illustrate the problem, figure 2.9 shows all expected values that occurred during a typical run of a standard Genetic Algorithm[38] with population size $\mu = 100$ over 200 generations for a highly multimodal objective function[39].

Evidently, deviations from the average expected value one do not exceed an absolute value of one, except for the first generation, where a "superindividual" having an expected value close to three can be identified. During the run, expected values larger than 1.5 or smaller than 0.5 are rare. Therefore, in order to avoid sampling errors, i.e. large discrepancies between expected value and realized number of copies, a clever sampling algorithm for converting expected values to integer numbers of offspring is necessary. The most commonly used method is called "spinning wheel" or "roulette wheel" due to an analogy to a biased roulette wheel assigning to each individual a slot sized in proportion to its fitness ([Gol89a], pp. 11–12, [Bak87]):

---

[38]The algorithm used two-point crossover, proportional selection, and parameters $n = 30$, $l_x = 30$, $u_i = -50$, $v_i = 50$, $p_m = 0.001$, $p_c = 0.6$ (see also section 2.3.6).

[39]A generalized version of a function designed by Ackley. It is presented in detail in section 3.3.

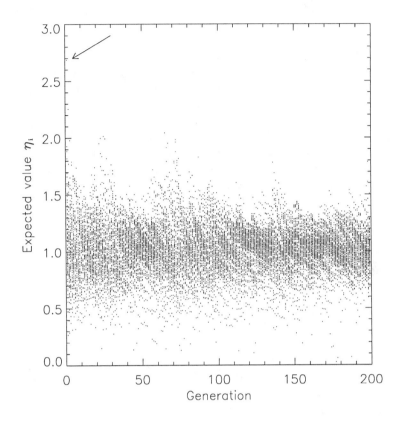

Fig. 2.9: Expected values η_i occurring during 200 generations of a typical run of a Genetic Algorithm. The objective function is highly multimodal, population size $\mu = 100$. The arrow indicates an individual in the initial population whose expected value is close to three. Notice that this exceptionally large expected value occurs only once within 200 generations and expected values below 0.5 respectively above 1.5 are only rarely observed. "Superindividuals" which are likely to dominate selection completely are never observed in this example.

(1) 1–1 map the individuals to contiguous segments of the real number line $[0, \mu)$, such that each individual's segment size is equal to its expected value.

(2) Generate a random number within $[0, \mu)$.

(3) Select the individual whose segment spans the random number.

(4) Repeat the process until the desired number of samples is obtained.

Baker analyzed several different algorithms for realizing such spinning wheel approaches with respect to their accuracy (measured in terms of *bias*, i.e. deviation between expected values and algorithmic sampling frequencies), precision (measured in terms of *spread*, i.e. the range of possible values for the number of copies an individual $\vec{a}_i$ receives by the selection mechanism[40]), and the computational complexity of the sampling algorithm [Bak87]. He developed an optimal sampling algorithm called *stochastic universal sampling* that combines zero bias, minimum spread, and an $\mathcal{O}(\mu)$ time complexity[41]. Being analogous to a spinning wheel with μ equally spaced pointers, the (tricky) algorithm can be used in combination with any expected value based selection mechanism and is chosen in most modern implementations. However, we should have in mind that it can only reduce sampling errors without avoiding them completely. To facilitate the reader to use stochastic universal sampling in his or her own implementation, we present the algorithmic formulation as given by Baker [Bak87].

Algorithm 7 (Stochastic universal sampling)

$$Sum := 0;$$
$$Ptr := \chi \in [0, 1);$$
for $i := 1$ **to** μ **do**
$$\qquad Sum := Sum + \eta(\vec{a}_i);$$
$$\qquad \textbf{while } (Sum > Ptr) \textbf{ do}$$
$$\qquad\qquad SelectInd(\vec{a}_i);$$
$$\qquad\qquad Ptr := Ptr + 1;$$
$$\qquad \textbf{od}$$
od

χ denotes a uniform random variable, and *SelectInd* simply copies the argument individual to the next parent population. Since implementation issues are critical for proportional selection, explanation of these topics seemed helpful. Whenever discussing probabilistic, expected-value based selection mechanisms in subsequent chapters, we will instead choose a pure mathematical description in terms of selection probabilities and assume an algorithmic realization based on stochastic universal sampling.

2.3.5 Other Components

The initialization of a population in Genetic Algorithms is performed by sampling a binary uniform random variable $l \cdot \mu$ times (independent coin

---

[40]In any case, we require a spread such that each individual receives either $\lfloor \eta(\vec{a}_i) \rfloor$ or $\lceil \eta(\vec{a}_i) \rceil$ copies.

[41]A function $g(n)$, $n \in \mathbb{N}$, is said to be $\mathcal{O}(h(n))$ ("order $h(n)$") if there exists a constant c such that $g(n) \le c \cdot h(n)$ for all but some finite (possibly empty) set of nonnegative values for n.

tosses), this way determining each bit of the start population $P(0) = \{\vec{a}_1(0), \ldots, \vec{a}_\mu(0)\}$ at random.

Due to the representation mechanism, a Genetic Algorithm enforces the existence of $2n$ inequality constraints

$$g_j(\vec{x}) = \begin{cases} x_j - u_j \geq 0 & , \forall j \in \{1, \ldots, n\} \\ v_{j-n} - x_{j-n} \geq 0 , \forall j \in \{n+1, \ldots, 2n\} , \end{cases} \tag{2.89}$$

which may be advantageous or disadvantageous depending on the actual problem. In any case, the necessity of these constraints requires the user of Genetic Algorithms to have some conjectures about the location of the interesting region of the search space. For some real-world optimization problems, this might be hard to come up with.

The termination criterion for Genetic Algorithms is often identical to the simple maximum number of generations $t_{\max}$ criterion as it was formulated in the context of Evolutionary Programming in equation (2.51) (see section 2.2.5). However, sometimes termination is also controlled by a genotype diversity measure that allows to assess the average convergence of all bit positions throughout the population, i.e. the *bias* measure defined by Grefenstette [Gre87b]. Denoting a single individual by $\vec{a}_i = (a_{i,1}, \ldots, a_{i,l})$ $(\forall i \in \{1, \ldots, \mu\})$ in order to distinguish its bits separately, the bias $b(P(t))$ of a population is calculated according to

$$b(P(t)) = \frac{1}{l \cdot \mu} \sum_{j=1}^{l} \max \left\{ \sum_{i=1}^{\mu} (1 - a_{i,j}), \sum_{i=1}^{\mu} a_{i,j} \right\} \in [0.5, 1.0] . \tag{2.90}$$

The value $b \in [0.5, 1.0]$ indicates the average percentage of the most prominent value in each position of the individuals. Smaller (larger) values of b indicate higher (lower) genotypic diversity. An alternative termination criterion for Genetic Algorithms can then be formulated by using b as follows:

$$\iota(P(t)) = \begin{cases} \text{true} , \text{if } b(P(t)) > b_{\max} \\ \text{false} , \text{otherwise,} \end{cases} \tag{2.91}$$

where $b_{\max} \approx 0.95 - 0.99$ is an exogenous parameter defining a lower bound of diversity that is required to be maintained in the population.

2.3.6   Conceptual Standard Algorithm

Following the presentation style of the preceding sections, the high-level algorithmic formulation of a standard Genetic Algorithm is presented in algorithm 8:

Algorithm 8 (Outline of a Genetic Algorithm)

$t := 0$;

$initialize\ P(0) := \{\vec{a}_1(0), \dots, \vec{a}_\mu(0)\} \in I^\mu$
  where $I = \{0, 1\}^l$;

$evaluate\ P(0):\ \{\Phi(\vec{a}_1(0)), \dots, \Phi(\vec{a}_\mu(0))\}$
  where $\Phi(\vec{a}_k(0)) = \delta(f(\Upsilon(\vec{a}_k(0))), P(0))$;

while $(\iota(P(t)) \neq \textbf{true})$ **do**

$recombine:\ \vec{a}'_k(t) := r'_{\{p_c, z\}}(P(t))\ \forall k \in \{1, \dots, \mu\}$;

$mutate:\ \vec{a}''_k(t) := m'_{\{p_m\}}(\vec{a}'_k(t))\ \forall k \in \{1, \dots, \mu\}$;

$evaluate:\ P''(t) := \{\vec{a}''_1(t), \dots, \vec{a}''_\mu(t)\}:$
  $\{\Phi(\vec{a}''_1(t)), \dots, \Phi(\vec{a}''_\mu(t))\}$ **where**
  $\Phi(\vec{a}''_k(t)) = \delta(f(\Upsilon(\vec{a}''_k(t))), P(t - \omega))$;

$select\ P(t + 1) := s(P''(t))$
  where $p_s(\vec{a}''_k(t)) = \Phi(\vec{a}''_k(t)) / \sum_{j=1}^{\mu} \Phi(\vec{a}''_j(t))$;

$t := t + 1$;

od

Within the framework provided by definition 2.1, the specialization of an Evolutionary Algorithm to a Genetic Algorithm is formalized in definition 2.8.

Definition 2.8 (Genetic Algorithm) *An Evolutionary Algorithm*

$$EA = (I, \Phi, \Omega, \Psi, s, \iota, \mu, \lambda)$$

is called Genetic Algorithm: $\Longleftrightarrow$

(1) $I = I\!B^l$,

(2) $\forall \vec{a} \in I$: $\Phi(\vec{a}) = \delta(f(\Upsilon(\vec{a})), \Theta_\delta)$, *where* $\delta : I\!R \times \Theta_\delta \to I\!R^+$ *denotes a scaling function as in equations (2.74)–(2.81) and* Υ *is a decoding function according to equation (2.69) or equation (2.73)*,

(3) $\Omega = \{m_{\{p_m\}} : I^\mu \to I^\mu, r_{\{p_c, z\}} : I^\mu \to I^\mu, r_{\{p_c\}} : I^\mu \to I^\mu\}$ *where the genetic operators are defined as in equation (2.82), equation (2.84), and, equation (2.85)*,

(4) $\Psi(P) = s(m_{\{p_m\}}(r_{\{p_c, z\}}(P)))$,

(5) $s : I^\mu \to I^\mu$, *the proportional selection operator, samples individuals according to the probability density function given by equation (2.87)*,

(6) *the termination criterion* ι *is given by (2.51) or (2.91), and*

(7) $\lambda = \mu$.

The extraction of a standard parameter setting for Genetic Algorithms from literature data is not a trivial task. In addition to the different suggestions for mutation rate and crossover rate as presented in sections 2.3.2 and 2.3.3, common settings for the population size are $\mu \in \{50, \ldots, 100\}$ [DeJ75], $\mu = 30$ [Gre86], and $\mu \in \{20, \ldots, 30\}$ [SCED89]. The length l of individuals depends on the precision Δx_i according to equation (2.70) that is required for each object variable. For reasons of comparability with Evolution Strategies and Evolutionary Programming, where a high precision of object variables is provided, we will assume a default value of $l_x = 30$ in the following, i.e. 30 bits are used to encode a single object variable. Depending on the particular application, however, a smaller number of bits per object variable may be absolutely sufficient[42]. The precision of the search grid provides an additional degree of freedom which the practitioner does not have at his disposal in case of Evolution Strategies and Evolutionary Programming. So far, the impact of the encoding length on the search process in Genetic Algorithms was not investigated in a systematic way. In section 6.2, we will present a (surprising) qualitative argument which indicates that the mutation operator may become more effective when l_x is large.

Finally, as mentioned in section 2.3.1, linear dynamic scaling with a scaling window $\omega = 5$ is considered a standard value. The critical exogenous parameters are summarized in table 2.4.

Parameter	Default
Mutation rate	$p_m = 0.001$
Recombination operator	$r_{\{0.6,2\}}$
Length per object variable	$l_x = 30$
Scaling window	$\omega = 5$
Population size	$\mu = 50$

Table 2.4. Default settings of exogenous parameters of a standard Genetic Algorithm.

The general notation $GA(l_x, p_m, r, \omega, \mu)$ is used in the following to indicate an instance of a Genetic Algorithm. The standard Genetic Algorithm is denoted by the tuple $GA(30, 0.001, r_{\{0.6,2\}}, 5, 50)$[43].

2.3.7 Theory

Most efforts on analyzing the behavior of Genetic Algorithms concentrate on the idea that the algorithm processes *schemata*, a term that

---

[42]Sometimes, this may also be necessary as demonstrated by the application of Genetic Algorithms for the optimization of Monte Carlo generator parameters in high energy physics (see [HBH92, Hah93]) where, due to statistical fluctuations of well-estimated magnitude, the precision is naturally restricted (the authors use 7–10 bits to encode parameters in a range $[0.1 - 0.9]$).

[43]Remember that the notation $r_{\{0.6,2\}}$ indicates a two-point crossover with application probability $p_c = 0.6$.

refers to similarity templates or hyperplanes in l-dimensional bit space $I\!B^l$. A schema describes a subset of strings that have similarities at certain string positions. To capture such similarities, schemata are defined to be strings of length l over the alphabet $\{0, 1, *\}$, and for a given schema $H \in \{0, 1, *\}^l$ a string $\vec{a} \in I\!B^l$ is called an *instance* of H iff whenever a position in H is specified (i.e. is either a 0 or a 1), this bit is identical to the corresponding bit in $\vec{a}$. The $*$ serves as a wildcard and matches both 0 and 1, thus allowing for arbitrarily general schemata. More formally, the set $\mathcal{I}(H)$ of all instances of a particular schema $H = (h_1, \ldots, h_l)$ is given by $\mathcal{I} : \{0, 1, *\}^l \to 2^I$ according to

$$
\begin{aligned}
\mathcal{I}(H) \quad = \quad & \{(a_1, \ldots, a_l) \mid \forall i \in \{1, \ldots, l\} : \\
& h_i \in \{0, 1\} \Rightarrow a_i = h_i\} \;.
\end{aligned}
\tag{2.92}
$$

As an example of a schema, consider $H = (01 * 1*)$ having the set of instances $\mathcal{I}(H) = \{(01010), (01011), (01110), (01111)\}$.

To measure specifity of schemata and to allow for an investigation of the effects of genetic operators on schemata, two measures on schemata were defined by Holland ([Hol75], p. 102, p. 110). The *order* $o(H)$ of a schema, $o : \{0, 1, *\}^l \to \{0, \ldots, l\}$ is given by the number of fixed positions of H, i.e.

$$
o(H) \quad = \quad |\{i \mid h_i \in \{0, 1\}\}| \;.
\tag{2.93}
$$

For example, $o(0 * *1*) = 2$, illustrating that two positions of the schema are specified. Besides the number of specified positions, their maximum distance is also of interest and captured by the *defining length* $\Delta(H)$ of a schema H according to $\Delta : \{0, 1, *\}^l \to \{0, \ldots, l-1\}$:

$$
\Delta(H) \quad = \quad \max\{i \mid h_i \in \{0, 1\}\} - \min\{i \mid h_i \in \{0, 1\}\} \;.
\tag{2.94}
$$

To refer to the previous example, the defining length is $\Delta(0 * *1*) = 4 - 1 = 3$.

Order and defining length of a schema $H(t)$ occurring in individuals of a population $P(t) = \{\vec{a}_1(t), \ldots, \vec{a}_\mu(t)\}$ are useful to calculate the *survival probabilities* of that schema under mutation and one-point crossover. The survival probability

$$
\mathcal{P}\{m'_{\{p_m\}}(\vec{a}_i(t)) \in \mathcal{I}(H(t)) \mid \vec{a}_i(t) \in \mathcal{I}(H(t))\}
\tag{2.95}
$$

for mutation is simply given by the expression

$$
(1 - p_m)^{o(H(t))} \;,
\tag{2.96}
$$

since the survival probability per defined position is $1 - p_m$. Often, p_m is chosen to be very small, such that the expression is simplified to the approximation $1 - o(H(t)) \cdot p_m$ (see [Gol89a], p. 32).

Calculation of the survival probability under one-point crossover,

$$
\begin{aligned}
&\mathcal{P}\{r'_{\{p_c,1\}}(\vec{a}_i(t), \vec{a}_j(t)) \in \mathcal{I}(H(t)) \mid \vec{a}_i(t) \in \mathcal{I}(H(t))\} \\
= \ &\mathcal{P}\{r'_{\{p_c,1\}}(\vec{a}_i(t), \vec{a}_j(t)) \in \mathcal{I}(H(t)) \mid \vec{a}_j(t) \in \mathcal{I}(H(t))\} \quad,
\end{aligned}
\tag{2.97}
$$

is slightly more complicated. We will present the precise form as derived by Holland ([Hol75], pp. 102–103), before the simplification is introduced. A schema is destroyed by one-point crossover whenever the crossover point falls within the schema's defining length, i.e. with probability $p_c \cdot \Delta(H(t))/(l-1)$. Furthermore, any recombination with an individual that is also an instance of schema $H(t)$ will automatically guarantee to preserve that schema. When $N(H(t)) = |\mathcal{I}(H(t)) \cap P(t)|$ denotes the number of instances of schema $H(t)$ that occur in population $P(t)$, only a proportion $1 - N(H(t))/\mu$ of the population can be expected to cause a desctruction of schema $H(t)$ under one-point crossover. Altogether, its survival probability amounts to

$$
1 - p_c \cdot \frac{\Delta(H(t))}{l-1} \cdot \left(1 - \frac{N(H(t))}{\mu}\right) \quad.
\tag{2.98}
$$

Often, however, small cross-product terms are neglected and the survival probability is simplified to $1 - p_c \cdot \Delta(H(t))/(l-1)$ (see [Gol89a], p. 32).

In this schema analysis of a Genetic Algorithm that uses one-point crossover, the selection operator is still missing. To investigate it in terms of schemata, the *average schema fitness*

$$
\Phi(H(t)) \quad = \quad \frac{1}{N(H(t))} \cdot \sum_{\vec{a}(t) \in \mathcal{I}(H(t)) \cap P(t)} \Phi(\vec{a}(t))
\tag{2.99}
$$

of all individuals in $P(t)$ that are instances of $H(t)$ as well as the average fitness

$$
\bar{\Phi}(t) \quad = \quad \frac{1}{\mu} \sum_{i=1}^{\mu} \Phi(\vec{a}_i(t))
\tag{2.100}
$$

of the population are used to formulate the general schema growth equation for proportional selection:

$$
N(H(t+1)) \quad = \quad N(H(t)) \cdot \frac{\Phi(H(t))}{\bar{\Phi}(t)} \quad.
\tag{2.101}
$$

Under the assumption that $H(t)$ is a schema of above average fitness, i.e.

$$
\Phi(H(t)) \quad = \quad \bar{\Phi}(t) + c \cdot \bar{\Phi}(t)
\tag{2.102}
$$

with a constant value of $c > 0$, after t time steps starting with $t_0 = 0$ one obtains the idealized equation

$$N(H(t+1)) \;=\; N(H(0)) \cdot (1+c)^t \;\;, \tag{2.103}$$

i.e. proportional selection allocates exponentially increasing (decreasing) numbers of trials to above (below) average schemata. Combining equation (2.101) and the survival probabilities (2.98) and (2.96), one obtains an estimate for the number of instances of a schema that occur at generation $t+1$ for a Genetic Algorithm using mutation, one-point crossover, and proportional selection, summarized in the *schema theorem* of Genetic Algorithms.

Theorem 11 (Schema Theorem)

$$N(H(t+1)) \;\geq\; N(H(t)) \cdot \frac{\Phi(H(t))}{\bar{\bar{\Phi}}(t)} \cdot$$
$$\left[1 - p_c \cdot \frac{\Delta(H(t))}{l-1} \cdot \left(1 - \frac{N(H(t))}{\mu} \right) \right] \cdot \tag{2.104}$$
$$(1 - p_m)^{o(H(t))}$$

Proof: All proof steps have been explained in detail in the text. Q.E.D.

Using the simplifications mentioned in the text, the schema theorem is often abbreviated to (see [Gol89a], p. 33)

$$N(H(t+1)) \;\geq\; N(H(t)) \cdot \frac{\Phi(H(t))}{\bar{\bar{\Phi}}(t)} \cdot$$
$$\left[1 - p_c \frac{\Delta(H(t))}{l-1} - o(H(t)) \cdot p_m \right] \cdot \tag{2.105}$$

The basic statement of the schema theorem is that short, low-order, above-average schemata (so-called *building blocks*) receive exponentially increasing trials in the following generations.

The usefulness of the exponential growth of above-average schemata was also confirmed theoretically by Holland, using a game-theoretic analogy to the problem how to allocate trials to the arms of a two-armed bandit in order to minimize the expected loss. It is assumed that mean and variance of both arms, (e_1, σ_1^2) and (e_2, σ_2^2), are known, but it is unknown which arm is associated with which mean-variance pair. While playing the arms of the bandit, we collect information about which arm is actually the *observed* best arm. However, the observed best is not necessarily the real best but may also be the second best, hence it is surely not the best strategy to give an equal number of trials to each arm and then to concentrate *all* remaining trials on the observed best arm (this would correspond to a classical decision theoretical approach).

Searching for the optimal allocation strategy, i.e. a strategy that minimizes the total expected loss, two potential sources of loss must be considered. First, the observed best may really be the second best, such that for each trial given to the observed best a loss of $|e_1 - e_2|$ is expected. Second, the observed best may really be the best, such that each trial dedicated to the observed second best amounts to a loss $|e_1 - e_2|$. Investigating this problem, Holland arrived at the following theorem for an optimal strategy (see [Hol75], pp. 77–78):

Theorem 12 *Given a total of N trials allocated to two random variables with means $e_1 > e_2$ and variances σ_1^2, σ_2^2 respectively, the minimum expected loss results when n, the number of trials allocated $\xi_{(2)}(N)$ (the random variable associated with the arm of lowest observed payoff after N trials), is[44]*

$$n \leq n^* \sim b^2 \ln \left(\frac{N^2}{8\pi b^4 \ln N^2} \right) , \quad b = \frac{\sigma_1}{e_1 - e_2} . \qquad (2.106)$$

Proof: The lengthy proof is omitted here; see [Hol75], pp. 78–83. Q.E.D.

Turning the equation around, Holland arrives at a result

$$N - n^* \sim N \sim \sqrt{8\pi b^4 \ln N^2} \exp \left(\frac{n^*}{2b^2} \right) , \qquad (2.107)$$

indicating an exponentially growing number of trials $N - n^*$ to be allocated to the observed best (see [Hol75], p. 83). The strategy, however, cannot be carried out as it would require knowledge of outcomes in advance. Therefore, it is interpreted as a guideline for the allocation of trials, and an extension to bandits having more than two arms allows for establishing the correspondence to schemata. A schema of order i is interpreted as an arm out of 2^j arms of one of $\binom{l}{j}$ different bandits existing for bitstrings of length l. Occurrence of such a schema in the population corresponds to a trial of the arm, and the average fitness of the schema corresponds to the average payoff of the arm.

Looking closer to the analogy, some problems can be identified:

- Most approximations used in Holland's proof of the theorem are only valid for very large trial numbers, corresponding to very large populations of Genetic Algorithms.

- Within any finite population, an exponentially increasing (decreasing) number of instances of a schema corresponds to either completely filling the population with instances of this schema or to a complete elimination of the schema from the population after a short time.

- Not all schemata are represented in a typical population.

---

[44]The notation $Y(t) \sim Z(t)$ indicates $\lim_{t \to \infty} Y(t)/Z(t) = 1$ for arbitrary functions $Y(t)$, $Z(t)$ of the same variable t [Hol75].

- Schemata of large defining length are likely to be destroyed by recombination, such that not all bandit problems are equally represented.

The schema processing argument also provides the reason for choosing a binary alphabet (*principle of minimal alphabets*), since it offers the maximum number of schemata of any discrete code, i.e. 3^l (see [Gol89a], pp. 80–82). For a k-ary alphabet in order to encode the same number of search points as a binary does, i.e. 2^l, a string of length

$$l' \ = \ l \cdot \frac{\ln 2}{\ln k} \tag{2.108}$$

is needed. Such a string is an instance of $(k+1)^{l'}$ schemata, a number that is always smaller than 3^l for $k > 2$.

The interpretation of Genetic Algorithms as schema processing machines is completed by the *implicit parallelism* result which states that the number of schemata processed at each generation is of order $\mathcal{O}(\mu^3)$, though only μ individuals are available in the population ([Gol89a], pp. 40–41).

These results on the schema processing qualities of Genetic Algorithms seem to give strong evidence for the importance of proportional selection and a binary alphabet. Investigations on the effect of new genetic operators were typically performed with respect to the schema disruption probabilities for building blocks (e.g. [SD91a, SD91b]). For a very long time, no alternatives to the "proved" optimal proportional selection method have been tested in Genetic Algorithms, and some efforts to incorporate new selection mechanisms are still not accepted in general (e.g. [Bak85, Whi89, BH91]). These alternative methods will be discussed in detail in chapter 5.

On the other hand, practitioners working on real-world problems with Genetic Algorithms tended towards nonbinary, problem-adequate representations, selection methods quite different from proportional selection, and problem-specific genetic operators (e.g. [Dav91c, Mic92]).

The gap between theory and practice of Genetic Algorithms, indicated by this short overview, seems to become larger. Nearly all theoretical work on Genetic Algorithms concentrates on the assumption of a binary alphabet, trying to characterize and identify pseudoboolean functions that are hard to optimize for a Genetic Algorithm (*deceptive* functions, e.g. [Gol87, LV90, BG91, DG91, PR92]). As it is now clear from theorem 4, however, it may well be the case that just these are the problems for which Genetic Algorithms *must* fail according to the construction of the problem and the provable limits of Genetic Algorithms.

The theoretical topic that is still missing before this section can be concluded concerns the global convergence with probability one. In view of the grid search character the global optimum point that one can only hope to identify is $\vec{a}^* \in I\!B^l$, which is really optimal for pseudoboolean functions but may be different from $\vec{x}^* \in \prod_{i=1}^{n}[u_i, v_i]$ for a continuous problem represented by a binary code.

The Markov chain argumentation (the absorbing state contains the global optimum) allows to derive the following convergence theorem [Har90]:

Theorem 13 *Let a Genetic Algorithm fulfil the following conditions:*

(1) The population sequence $P(0), P(1), \ldots$ is monotone, i.e. $\forall t$:

$$\min\{\Phi(\vec{a}(t+1)) \mid \vec{a}(t+1) \in P(t+1)\}$$
$$\leq \quad \min\{\Phi(\vec{a}(t)) \mid \vec{a}(t) \in P(t)\} ,$$

and

(2) $\forall \vec{a}, \vec{a}' \in I$ $\vec{a}'$ is reachable[45] from $\vec{a}$ by means of mutation and recombination.

Then

$$\mathcal{P}\{\lim_{t \to \infty} \vec{a}^* \in P(t)\} \quad = \quad 1 \quad . \tag{2.109}$$

Proof: The proof is given in [Har90] and, in a slightly different way for similar assumptions, in [EAH91]. It is also obtained in section 6.1 as a by-product of well-known Markov chain theory. Q.E.D.

Concerning the premises of the theorem, we mention that monotony can easily be achieved by using an *elitist* selection variant guaranteeing survival of the best individual[46]. Reachability is already assured by a mutation rate $p_m \in (0,1)$, since for two arbitrary individuals $\vec{a}, \vec{b} \in I$ and mutation $m'_{\{p_m\}} : I \to I$:

$$\mathcal{P}\{m'_{\{p_m\}}(\vec{a}) = \vec{b}\} \quad = \quad (1-p_m)^{l-\rho_H(\vec{a},\vec{b})} \cdot p_m^{\rho_H(\vec{a},\vec{b})} \quad . \tag{2.110}$$

Notice that this probability is maximized for $p^* = \rho_H(\vec{a}, \vec{b})/l$.
Proof: Both individuals differ in $\rho_H(\vec{a}, \vec{b})$ positions and are identical in $l - \rho_H(\vec{a}, \vec{b})$ positions. With probability p a single position is changed by mutation, while it remains identical with probability $1 - p$. The result follows immediately from the fact that single bit mutations are independent events, and it is clear that the reachability property holds for $1 > p_m > 0$:

$$1 > p_m > 0 \quad \Rightarrow \quad \forall \vec{a}, \vec{b} \in I : \; \mathcal{P}\{m'_{\{p_m\}}(\vec{a}) = \vec{b}\} > 0 \quad , \tag{2.111}$$

which completes the proof. Q.E.D.

Omitting the requirement for monotony in theorem 13, one can still prove (following an idea that was outlined by Rudolph) that the algorithm locates the global optimum by means of the reachability property. The resulting theorem 14 can be considered as the discrete analogue

---

[45]I.e. arbitrary points of $I\!\!B^l$ can be created by means of mutation and recombination from a point $\vec{a}$.

[46]See also definition 5.7 (section 5.1.6).

of theorem 3 for a one-individual population that evolves by means of mutation (a (1,1)-GA). The theorem uses the notation $\mathcal{B}(t) = \{\vec{a}(t) = \vec{a}^*\}$ to denote the event that a global optimum point is located at step t, and $\bar{\mathcal{B}}(t) = \{\vec{a}(t) \neq \vec{a}^*\}$:

Theorem 14 *If* $P\{\mathcal{B}(t) \mid \bar{\mathcal{B}}(t-1)\} \geq q_t \in [0,1]$, *and* $\sum_{t=1}^{\infty} q_t = \infty$, *then*[47]

$$\lim_{t \to \infty} P\{\mathcal{B}(t) \mid \bigwedge_{i=0}^{t-1} \bar{\mathcal{B}}(i)\} = 1 \quad . \tag{2.112}$$

Proof: From $P\{\mathcal{B}(t) \mid \bar{\mathcal{B}}(t-1)\} \geq q_t$, one can conclude that

$$P\{\bar{\mathcal{B}}(t) \mid \bar{\mathcal{B}}(t-1)\} \leq 1 - q_t \quad . \tag{2.113}$$

For independent events $\mathcal{B}(t)$, we have

$$
\begin{aligned}
0 &\leq P\{\bar{\mathcal{B}}(t) \mid \bigwedge_{i=0}^{t-1} \bar{\mathcal{B}}(i)\} \\
&\leq \prod_{i=1}^{t}(1 - q_i) \\
&\leq \prod_{i=1}^{t} \exp(-q_i) \\
&= \exp\left(-\sum_{i=1}^{t} q_i\right) \quad ,
\end{aligned}
\tag{2.114}
$$

and since $\lim_{t \to \infty} \exp\left(-\sum_{i=1}^{t} q_i\right) = 0$ one can conclude that the probability $P\{\bar{\mathcal{B}}(t) \mid \bigwedge_{i=0}^{t-1} \bar{\mathcal{B}}(i)\}$ tends towards zero for $t \to \infty$, such that the complementary probability approaches one. Notice that $p^l > 0$ is a lower bound for q_t which guarantees divergence of the sum of the q_t. Q.E.D.

Theorem 14 remains valid for larger populations and recombination, as long as reachability is assured with a certain, not too quickly decreasing minimum probability q_t. Essentially, however, the statement of the theorem is very trivial: Whenever we generate new points for a sufficiently long time, the global optimum will occur in the sequence generated this way. This argumentation, though completely valid, is useless when looking at a real-world application where a good solution is desired within reasonable waiting time. Under such conditions, convergence velocity is the main evaluation criterion for any optimization algorithm.

---

[47]The notation $\bigwedge_{i=0}^{t-1} \bar{\mathcal{B}}(i)$ indicates that $\bar{\mathcal{B}}(i)$ is valid for all values of $i \in \{0, \ldots, t-1\}$.

2.4 Summary

In the previous three sections much detailed information on Evolution Strategies, Evolutionary Programming, and Genetic Algorithms was presented in order to clarify their working principles as well as similarities and differences, both from a theoretical and a practical point of view. Some new theoretical results[48] were also presented, which may improve the understanding of the basic mechanisms of these algorithms. The most important characteristics of the algorithms discussed here are summarized in table 2.5 in order to give a quick overview.

Although all algorithms share an identical meta-model, each one emphasizes different features as being most important to a successfully modeled evolutionary process. Apart from representational issues, the most conspicuous difference is given by the interpretation of the role of genetic operators. In Evolutionary Programming, no recombination is used at all, while Genetic Algorithms claim for a dominating role of recombination, neglecting the influence of mutation nearly completely. Evolution Strategies use both operators, indicating a necessity to use recombination on strategy parameters in order to achieve successful self-adaptation, a process that, however, is indicated to work in Evolutionary Programming even without recombination. In order to explain this contradiction, it is necessary to investigate the combined influence of the particular selection, mutation (and recombination) operators used in Evolution Strategies and Evolutionary Programming on the efficiency of the self-adaptation process.

An analogy with repair-enzymes and mutator-genes can be used to summarize the evidence for biological self-control of mutation rates of nucleotide bases (see section 1.1.3). Both Evolution Strategies and Evolutionary Programming rely on these self-adaptation processes for step-size control and correlation of mutations. This concept was tested in the context of Genetic Algorithms only in form of the punctuated crossover operator discussed in section 2.3.3, but it never gained acceptance due to a combination of a lack of success and acknowledgement.

Both Evolutionary Programming and Genetic Algorithms insist on probabilistic selection, although differently implemented, referring to the character of selection in nature in the first case and to the multi-armed bandit analogy in the second case. In contrast to this, Evolution Strategies use a strictly deterministic selection mechanism, being *extinctive* in the sense of definitely excluding the worst individuals from being selected[49].

---

[48]These are the generalized recombination result for Evolution Strategies (section 2.1.3), the characterization of selection in Evolutionary Programming (section 2.2.4), the application of the convergence rate theory to Evolutionary Programming (section 2.2.7), and theorem 14 for a (1,1)-GA (section 2.3.7).

[49]See section 5.1.6 for a more formal definition of these terms.

	ES	EP	GA
Repre-sentation	Real-valued	Real-valued	Binary-valued
Fitness is	Objective function value	Scaled objective function value	Scaled objective function value
Self-adaptation	Standard deviations and rotation angles	None (standard-EP), variances (meta-EP), correlation coefficients	None
Mutation	Gaussian, main operator	Gaussian, only operator	Bit-inversion, background operator
Recom-bination	Discrete and intermediate, sexual and panmictic, important for self-adaptation	None	z-point crossover, uniform crossover, only sexual, main operator
Selection	Deterministic, extinctive or based on preservation	Probabilistic, extinctive	Probabilistic, based on preservation
Constraints	Arbitrary inequality constraints	None	Simple bounds by encoding mechanism
Theory	Convergence rate for special cases, $(1+1)$–ES, $(1 \overset{+}{,} \lambda)$-ES, global convergence for $(\mu+\lambda)$-ES	Convergence rate for speacial cases, $(1+1)$-EP, global convergence for $(1+1)$-EP	Schema processing theory, global convergence for elitist version

Table 2.5. Main characteristics of Evolutionary Algorithms. Explanations of terms are given in the text.

While in Evolutionary Programming some individuals are also excluded from selection, Genetic Algorithms make use of *preservation* in a sense that each individual receives a nonzero selection probability. Furthermore, the elitist property is implicit to selection in Evolutionary Programming, while it occurs in Evolution Strategies $((\mu+\lambda)$–ES) and Genetic Algorithms only if requested explicitly.

The constraint mechanism of Evolution Strategies is rather simple and can (in principle) be incorporated to the other algorithms (see section 2.1.5). A major difference occurs in Genetic Algorithms, where two-sided bounds on the object variables are mandatory for the encoding mechanism to work properly.

Finally, to mention the theoretical results, we have seen that a proof of global convergence with probability one exists for simplified versions of all algorithms, while results on the convergence rate are known only for Evolution Strategies and Evolutionary Programming for simple test functions. Theoretical investigations of Genetic Algorithms concentrate on the theory of schemata, which seems rather inappropriate to assess convergence rates of the algorithm. We will present a convergence rate analysis for a simplified Genetic Algorithm on a special objective function in chapter 6.

The indicated displacement of emphasis on components even between algorithms as similar as Evolution Strategies and Evolutionary Programming demonstrates a strong need for further research in order to identify the fundamental principles that lead to the design of successful Evolutionary Algorithms. Before we try to shed some light on the role of components especially in case of Genetic Algorithms, it is now time to conclude this chapter by relating the representational mechanisms used in Evolutionary Algorithms to biological counterparts, similar to the effort presented by Goldberg (see [Gol89a], pp. 21–22). To do so, we use the information in table 1.2 for describing the hierarchy of genetic information, and we present a similar table that shows a possibility to relate components of the algorithmic representation to the original, i.e. table 2.6.

The representation used in Genetic Algorithms emphasizes on the genotype due to its binary character, i.e. a correspondence of the binary alphabet to the quarternary alphabet of nucleotide bases can be identified. Then, one can either view a bitstring segment as a codon, thus implying an analogy of a single (decoded) object variable to a single amino acid, or we can view a bitstring segment as a complete gene by leaving out the codon level, which implies an analogy of a single object variable to a protein. Both points of view are equally inexact, the former because it leaves out the gene level, the latter because it does not supply us with the obvious interpretation of segment decoding. However, the latter seems preferable because the highly nonlinear code in Genetic Algorithms seems to correspond better to the gene-protein relation than to the codon-amino acid relation and is also a bit more consistent with viewing the decoded vector $\vec{x}$ as phenotype. Consequently, the genotype

Biology	ES	EP	GA
Nucleotide base	—	—	Binary digit $a_i \in I\!B$
Codon	—	—	—
Gene	Single x_i, σ_i, α_j	Single x_i, ν_i	Bitstring segment $(a_{i1}, \ldots, a_{il_x}) \in I\!B^{l_x}$
Chromosome	Complete vectors $\vec{x}, \vec{\sigma}, \vec{\alpha}$	Complete vectors $\vec{x}, \vec{\nu}$	Complete bitstring $\vec{a}$
Genotype	Collection of chromosomes $(\vec{x}, \vec{\sigma}, \vec{\alpha})$	Collection of chromosomes $(\vec{x}, \vec{\nu})$	Complete bitstring $\vec{a}$
Phenotype	Component $\vec{x}$	Component $\vec{x}$	Decoded structure $\vec{x} = \Upsilon(\vec{a})$

Table 2.6. Relation of artificial and natural information representation.

is made up of the complete binary vector that in turn corresponds to a single chromosome.

Since the phenotype is surely represented by that unit which undergoes an evaluation of its fitness in the environment, the object variable vector $\vec{x}$ can for all these Evolutionary Algorithms be interpreted as the phenotype. It is derived from the genotype in case of Evolution Strategies and Evolutionary Programming by a rather trivial mapping, i.e., a projection, since no explicit code is used. The complete genotype consists of the object variable vector and one or two strategy parameter vectors, and each vector represents a chromosome. It is straightforward to interpret single components of these vectors as genes.

However, the similarities between the algorithms and their natural origin are still crude, and even the seemingly closer correspondence of Genetic Algorithms gives by far no evidence for a more successful modeling. The many mappings that are used by nature to create the phenotype from the genotype are almost completely missing in Evolutionary Algorithms. Furthermore, even very simple individuals in nature are multicellular organisms, and recombination turned out to occur only in diploid, multicellular organisms. Finally, ontogenetical learning of individuals during their development and aging are processes that may turn out to improve Evolutionary Algorithms even further.

In any case, biological terminology is established for use in the field of Evolutionary Algorithms, such that an identification of and agreement on the meaning of biological terms in this context is urgently necessary. Of course, other assignments are possible, but they should in any case use biological terms in a correct context.

3

Artificial Landscapes

In order to facilitate an empirical comparison of the performance of Evolution Strategies, Evolutionary Programming, and Genetic Algorithms, a test environment for these algorithms must be provided in the form of several objective functions $f : I\!R^n \to I\!R$. Finding an appropriate and representative set of test problems is not an easy task, since any particular combination of properties represented by a test function does not allow for generalized performance statements. However, there is evidence from a vast number of applications that Evolutionary Algorithms are robust in the sense that they give reasonable performance over a wide range of different topologies.

Here, a set of test functions that are completely artificial and simple is used, i.e., they are stated in a closed, analytical form and have no direct background from any practical application. Instead, they allow for a detailed analysis of certain special characteristics of the topology, e.g. unimodality or multimodality, continuous or discontinuous cases, and others. If any prediction is drawn up for the behavior of Evolutionary Algorithms depending on such strong topological characteristics, the appropriate idealized test function provides a good instrument to test such hypotheses. Furthermore, since many known test sets have some functions in common, at least a minimal level of comparability of results is often guaranteed. Finally, before we can expect an algorithm to be successful in the case of hard problems, it has to demonstrate that it does not fail to work on simple problems.

On the other hand, the (public relations) effect of using artificial topologies is vanishingly small, since the test functions used are of no industrial relevance. This way, researchers working with such test functions can never rest on their industrial laurels.

A more legitimate objection against artificial topologies may be that they are possibly not representative of the "average complexity" of real-

137

world problems, and that some regularity features of their topology may inadmissibly speed up the search. However, most test function sets incorporate even multimodal functions of remarkable complexity, such that only the regularity argument counts against using an artifical function set.

Since we are mainly interested in an objective comparison and verification of some central research hypotheses, a set of artifical test functions seems most appropriate. This is in accordance with many researchers who had the idea to collect sets of test functions with specific properties and to use them as performance benchmarks. In the field of Evolutionary Algorithms, the most famous test sets are due to De Jong (see [DeJ75], pp. 196–210) and Schwefel (see [Sch77], pp. 319–354) for Genetic Algorithms and Evolution Strategies, respectively. Schwefel's test set, consisting of 62 functions that cover an enormous diversity of different topologies (and even highly constrained cases) is surely one of the most extensive function sets. Many other test functions are used in global optimization, and a brief overview of some popular functions is also given in [TŽ89] (pp. 183–186).

De Jong's test function set, consisting of five functions of unimodal and multimodal, continuous and discontinuous, and even noisy character, have been a standard for Genetic Algorithm benchmarks since 1975. Four of these functions are low-dimensional ones, such that especially in case of the only multimodal function (Shekel's foxholes, [She71]) a generalization of results is not possible. An arbitrary scaling of the dimension n is a necessary property of test functions in order to approach reasonable problem sizes (with $n > 20$). Furthermore, as Davis argued, it is quite likely that the location of the optimal solution at the exact middle point of the feasible range in each dimension as chosen by De Jong is advantageous for a Genetic Algorithm due to the high regularity of the bit pattern of the optimum point [Dav91b].

Finally, we mention that artificial test functions in Evolutionary Programming, including e.g. the sphere model, Rosenbrock's function[1] [Ros60], and the multimodal Bohachevsky function [BJS86], were also in most cases only tested with very low dimension [Fog92b].

For our purposes, it is most important to develop a small set of test functions that cover several important features, i.e. the set should

- consist exclusively of functions that are scalable with respect to their dimension n,

- include a unimodal, continuous function for comparison of convergence velocity,

---

[1]Both the sphere model and Rosenbrock's function are also members of Schwefel's and De Jong's test set. Though being unimodal, the latter function causes difficulties to some optimization methods due to the location of the optimum in a steep parabolic valley with a flat bottom. It caused Rosenbrock to invent his widely used method of rotating coordinates.

- include a step function with several flat plateaus of different height in order to test the behavior of Evolutionary Algorithms in case of absence of any local gradient information,

- cover multimodal functions of different complexity.

The function set does not incorporate pseudoboolean objective functions because Evolution Strategies and Evolutionary Programming are not applicable without major changes of the basic algorithms as introduced in chapter 2. Currently, Genetic Algorithms are useful for a wider range of problems than the two other algorithms described here. This extended generality is achieved by the introduction of an elaborate genotype-phenotype mapping (see section 2.3.1). Recently, Michalewicz presented an empirical investigation of the performance of a *hierarchy* of evolution programs (i.e., a partial ordering of different evolution programs such that the problem ranges to which they can be applied are increasingly general) and indicated that generality grows at the expense of performance [Mic93]. Though it is not intended here to check the validity of this conclusion, our findings in chapter 4 turn out to fit with this "rule".

In the following sections, we will introduce five test functions of our choice in detail, including a three-dimensional[2] graphic of their topology and an explanation of their basic properties. The meaning of "different complexity" as indicated in the last topic of the list presented above will also become clear when multimodal functions are discussed.

3.1 Sphere Model

The sphere model as an example of a continuous, strongly convex, unimodal function was already introduced in connection with the theory of Evolution Strategies in section 2.1.7. It serves as a test case for convergence velocity and is well known and widely used in all fields of Evolutionary Algorithms, occurring in the test sets of Schwefel, De Jong, and Fogel. For algorithms that use the self-adaptation mechanism for mutation step sizes, it provides an appropriate test environment due to the knowledge of optimal step sizes. The three-dimensional (i.e., $n = 2$) topology of the sphere model is shown in figure 3.1.

For reasons of completeness, we present the mathematical description including the default dimension, global minimum point (if known) and its objective function value, and the constraints that define the feasible range (for Genetic Algorithms) for each objective function. Furthermore, notation is redefined now, using f_1 to denote the sphere model:

$$f_1(\vec{x}) = \sum_{i=1}^{n} x_i^2 \tag{3.1}$$

---

[2]I.e., two object variables ($n = 2$) plus one dimension for the objective function value.

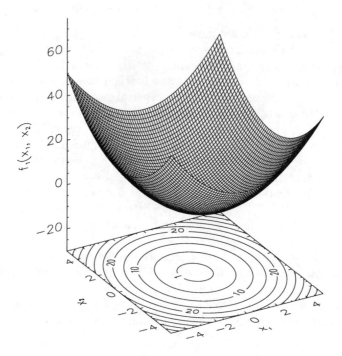

Fig. 3.1: Three-dimensional plot of the sphere model.

$$\vec{x}^* = (0,\ldots,0)^T \;;\; f_1^* = 0 \;;\; n = 30 \;;\; -40 \le x_i \le 60 \,.$$

3.2 Step Function

The background idea of the step function is to make the search more difficult by introducing small plateaus to the topology of an underlying continuous function. While De Jong did this for a simple linear function ([DeJ75], p. 200), we use a discretization of the sphere model obtained by summing over terms[3] $\lfloor x_i + 0.5 \rfloor^2$. As a result, the topology shown in figure 3.2 is discontinuous whenever for any $i \in \{1, \ldots, n\}$ $x_i = k + 0.5$ ($k \in I\!N$).

According to definition 1.5 each plateau corresponds to a local min-

---

[3] $\lfloor x \rfloor = \max\{i \in Z\!\!\!Z \mid i \le x\}$ denotes the largest integer value less than or equal to x.

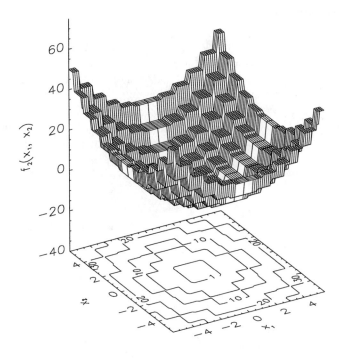

Fig. 3.2: Three-dimensional plot of the step function.

imum of the step function, which therefore is a multimodal function. The plateaus may cause considerable problems to the search process due to the absence of any improvement or worsening of objective function values of offspring located in the close neighborhood of parents, i.e. on a plateau there is no gradient information available for directing the search. Therefore, the search can only be expected to be successful by means of the collective learning process facilitated by a diverse population of solutions.

The global optimum of the step function is located at the plateau having $x_i \in [-0.5, 0.5)$ for all i, and other settings are identical to those for the sphere model, such that altogether the step function is formalized as follows:

$$f_2(\vec{x}) = \sum_{i=1}^{n} \lfloor x_i + 0.5 \rfloor^2 \qquad (3.2)$$

$$\vec{x}^{\,*} \in ([-0.5, 0.5))^n \ ; \ f_2^* = 0 \ ; \ n = 30 \ ; \ -40 \le x_i \le 60 \ .$$

3.3 Ackley's Function

Ackley's function is a continuous, multimodal test function obtained by modulating an exponential function with a cosine wave of moderate amplitude (see [Ack87], pp. 13–14). Originally, it was formulated by Ackley only for the two-dimensional case and is presented here in a generalized, scalable version. Its topology, as shown in figure 3.3, is characterized by an almost flat (due to the dominating exponential) outer region and a central hole or peak where modulations by the cosine wave become more and more influential.

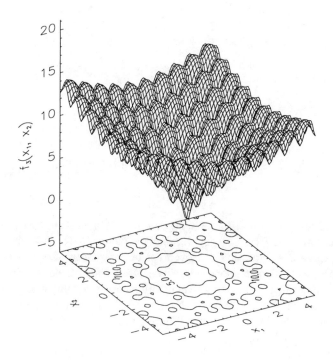

Fig. 3.3: Three-dimensional plot of the generalized function by Ackley.

As Ackley points out, this function causes moderate complications to the search, since though a strictly local optimization algorithm that performs hillclimbing would surely get trapped in a local optimum, a search strategy that scans a slightly bigger neighborhood would be able to cross intervening valleys towards increasingly better optima ([Ack87], p. 14). Therefore, Ackley's function provides a reasonable test case for the necessary combination of path-oriented and volume-oriented characteristics of a search strategy.

To facilitate its use for minimization and to achieve a standardization of the global minimum to an objective function value of zero, the function is formulated as follows:

$$f_3(\vec{x}) = -c_1 \cdot \exp\left(-c_2\sqrt{\frac{1}{n}\sum_{i=1}^{n}x_i^2}\right) - \exp\left(\frac{1}{n}\cdot\sum_{i=1}^{n}\cos(c_3\cdot x_i)\right) + c_1 + e$$

(3.3)

$$c_1 = 20 \; ; \; c_2 = 0.2 \; ; \; c_3 = 2\pi$$
$$\vec{x}^* = (0,\ldots,0)^T \; ; \; f_3^* = 0 \; ; \; n = 30 \; ; \; -20 \le x_i \le 30 \;.$$

In contrast to f_1 and f_2, the feasible range for object variables is smaller due to the fact that fitness differences in the outer regions of the topology become vanishingly small even for moderate dimensions and values for object variables.

3.4 Function after Fletcher and Powell

The highly multimodal function presented here is a typical representative of nonlinear parameter estimation (regression) problems as discussed in section 1.3. It was introduced for the first time by Fletcher and Powell in 1963 (see [FP63]) and also used by Schwefel in connection with Evolution Strategies (see [Sch77], pp. 327–328). A three-dimensional plot of this function is shown in figure 3.4.

In contrast to the other functions discussed in the previous sections, the function f_4 is not symmetric, but instead the extrema are randomly distributed over the search space. This way, the objective function has no implicit symmetry advantage that might simplify optimization for certain algorithms. The random location of extrema is achieved by using random matrices $\mathbf{A} = (a_{ij})$ and $\mathbf{B} = (b_{ij})$ in the following description of the problem:

$$f_4(\vec{x}) = \sum_{i=1}^{n}(A_i - B_i)^2$$

$$A_i = \sum_{j=1}^{n}(a_{ij}\sin\alpha_j + b_{ij}\cos\alpha_j)$$

(3.4)

$$B_i = \sum_{j=1}^{n}(a_{ij}\sin x_j + b_{ij}\cos x_j)$$

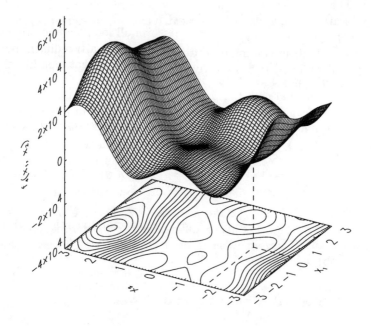

Fig. 3.4: Three-dimensional plot of the function after Fletcher and Powell.

$$\vec{x}^* = \vec{\alpha} \; ; \; f_4^* = 0 \; ; \; n = 30 \; ; \; -\pi \le x_i \le \pi$$

$$a_{ij}, b_{ij} \in [-100, 100] \; ; \; \alpha_j \in [-\pi, \pi] \; .$$

As Fletcher and Powell pointed out, there are up to 2^n extrema located in the search interval $|x_i| \le \pi$. In addition to the matrices $\mathbf{A}$ and $\mathbf{B}$, the vector $\vec{\alpha}$ is also chosen at random. Altogether, these are 1830 random numbers ($n = 30$) which are collected in appendix A.

3.5 Fractal Function

Natural forms that occur e.g. in mountains, canyons, coastlines, and plants are *fractal*, i.e. they show a substantial degree of *self-similarity*. While a mathematical definition requires self-similarity at all resolutions (i.e. the fractal object has no natural, implicit scale) and an infinite, recursive generation process, methods of fractal analysis can also be applied to objects where self-similarity stops at smaller resolution levels. Mountains exhibit their fractal properties by peaks and smaller peaks, rocks, and gravel, coastlines by bays, inlets, estuaries, rivulets, and ditches.

Mandelbrot recognized this fractal structure of nature and developed an underlying mathematical theory [Man83].

For a line segment having dimension one, self-similarity is assured by dividing it into $N \in I\!N$ equal segments which all look like the original segment scaled down by a factor of $N = N^{1/1}$. For a two-dimensional square, the same is true if it is divided into N parts that look like the original scaled down by a factor of $\sqrt{N} = N^{1/2}$.

Closely associated with the notion of self-similarity is the *fractal dimension* or self-similarity dimension, a generalization of the usual notion of dimensionality. In case of a fractal curve such as the *Koch curve*, however, one can prove that though its total length tends towards infinity if self-similarity on increasingly higher resolution is assured, the resulting curve does not cover all points of a plane. Hence, its dimension is larger than one, but smaller than two. Since the Koch curve is constructed such that dividing it into four pieces each piece is the original curve scaled down by a factor of three, it has fractal dimension d where $4^{1/d} = 3$, i.e. $d = \log(4)/\log(3) \approx 1.26$ (see [Man83], p. 36).

The details of fractal geometry cannot be discussed here, but in order to provide a motivation for introducing a fractal function as well as the basic idea of a fractal and the notion of fractal dimension, some excursion is necessary. Following an idea of Schwefel, the motivation to design a fractal objective function was twofold. First, a fractal function offers the possibility to control its degree of complexity by varying the fractal dimension. As the dimension is increased towards a value of two, the fractal complexity of the topology dominates the surface, while for dimensions close to one the topology is just continuous and smooth. Second, the fractal surface is likely to capture characteristics of noisy real-world objective functions.

The objective function introduced here is obtained by an appropriate modification of the famous *Weierstrass-Mandelbrot function* (e.g. see [Man83], pp. 388–390; [Fed88], pp. 26–30):

$$W(x) \;=\; \sum_{j=-\infty}^{\infty} \frac{\left(1 - \exp(ib^j x)\right) \cdot \exp(i\varphi_j)}{b^{(2-D)j}} \quad, \tag{3.5}$$

where i denotes the imaginary unit, $b > 1$ determines how much of the curve is visible for a given range of x, φ_j is an arbitrary phase angle, and D $(1 < D < 2)$ is believed to be the fractal dimension of W (as pointed out in [BL80], this is not yet proved).

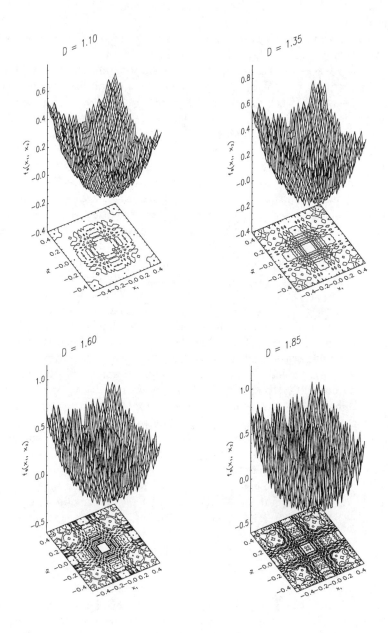

Fig. 3.5: Fractal function for different values of $D \in \{1.1, 1.35, 1.6, 1.85\}$.

From a mathematical point of view, W is a very interesting function because it is continuous but has no derivative at any point. This is also true for the simplified ($\varphi_j = 0$) real part:

$$C(x) = \sum_{j=-\infty}^{\infty} \frac{1 - \cos(b^j x)}{b^{(2-D)j}} , \tag{3.6}$$

the Weierstrass-Mandelbrot cosine fractal function[4]. For this function, D is known to be a *box dimension*[5] ([Fed88], p. 27).

As Berry and Lewis indicate, the function $C(x)$ consists of a general underlying trend and a fractal component, but the trend can only be estimated to [BL80]:

$$c(x) \approx \frac{x^{2-D}\Gamma(D-1)\cos(\frac{\pi}{2}(2-D))}{(2-D)\ln b} . \tag{3.7}$$

Since the trend depends on D and therefore hinders comparability of results for different values of D, we removed the trend as exactly as possible, finally superimposing a new trend that is independent of D in order to reintroduce a general shape of the topology. To achieve this, the *self-affinity*[6] of C, $C(bx) = b^{2-D}C(x)$, offers a good opportunity to relate all function values to $C(1)$ and to remove the trend by defining

$$C'(x) = \begin{cases} \frac{C(x)}{C(1)|x|^{2-D}} , & \text{if } x \neq 0 \\ 1 , & \text{if } x = 0 . \end{cases} \tag{3.8}$$

Summing up over n such one-dimensional functions, each of which is superimposed by a sphere model trend, we finally obtain

$$f_5(\vec{x}) = \sum_{i=1}^{n} \left(C'(x_i) + x_i^2 - 1 \right) \tag{3.9}$$

$$D = 1.85 ; \; b = 1.5 ; \; n = 20 ; \; -5 \leq x_i \leq 5 ,$$

where the constant 1 is subtracted in order to move function values of points close to the origin to an expected value of zero rather than one.

[4] Practically, the infinite sum is approximated as follows to calculate $C(x)$: Starting with $j = 0$ and alternating the sign of j, the summation process continues as long as the relative difference between the last and the actual partial sum exceeds a threshold value $\varepsilon_C = 10^{-8}$ or a maximum number of iterations is reached.

[5] Several different notions of dimension have been introduced to fulfil practical requirements. In case of the box dimension, the minimal number N_s of squares of side length s needed to cover the fractal object completely is counted for smaller and smaller values of s, and finally one obtains

$$D = -\lim_{s\to 0} \frac{\log(N_s)}{\log(s)} .$$

The box dimension D is also known under the term *Minkowski-dimension* (see [Jet89], p. 150).

[6] C is *not* self-similar.

Due to the numerical difficulties of f_5 it is impossible to indicate the exact position of the global minimum.

The three-dimensional topology of the objective function is shown in figure 3.5 for four different values of $D \in \{1.1, 1.35, 1.6, 1.85\}$. The general shape of the function is dominated by the sphere model, and the ruggedness of the surface increases remarkably as the value of the box dimension D is increased. This way, D is a parameter that allows for arbitrarily increasing or decreasing the complexity of this objective function.

3.6 Summary

Five artificial objective functions were introduced in this chapter to serve as a basis for empirical comparisons of Evolutionary Algorithms, i.e. the sphere model (section 3.1) and its step-function version (section 3.2), the generalized function by Ackley (section 3.3), the function after Fletcher and Powell (section 3.4), and a fractal function based on the Weierstrass-Mandelbrot cosine function (section 3.5). The latter three represent highly multimodal topologies that are expected to cause difficulties to the search process with respect to convergence reliability towards the global optimum.

In principle, all functions are arbitrarily scalable concerning the dimension, but in the case of the Fletcher-Powell function we restrict dimension to values up to $n = 30$ (otherwise, larger matrices would have to be presented in appendix A).

Except for the fractal function, all artificial objective functions introduced here are well known and used by several authors in connection with empirical investigations on Evolutionary Algorithms. At least in case of the Fletcher-Powell function and the fractal function we have good reason to claim that they have strong similarities to real-world problems. The next chapter will give a practical impression of both the complexity of the test functions and the problem solving capacity of Evolutionary Algorithms.

There is nothing more practical than a good theory.
Leonid Ilich Breznev (in V. Rich, Nature 1977, 270, pp. 470–1)

Theory is a good thing but a good experiment lasts forever.
Peter Leonidovich Kapitsa (Nature 1980, 288, p. 627)

4

An Empirical Comparison

Given the discussions about Evolutionary Algorithms from the previous chapters, we shall now apply them to the artificial topologies just presented. This will be done by simply running the algorithms in their standard forms (according to the definitions of standard forms as given in sections 2.1.6, 2.2.6, and 2.3.6) for a reasonable number of function evaluations on these problems. The experiment compares an algorithm that self-adapts n standard deviations and uses recombination (the Evolution Strategy), an algorithm that self-adapts n standard deviations[1] and renounces recombination (meta-Evolutionary Programming), and an algorithm that renounces self-adaptation but stresses the role of recombination (the Genetic Algorithm). Furthermore, all algorithms rely on different selection mechanisms.

With respect to the level of self-adaptation, the choice of the Evolution Strategy and Evolutionary Programming variants is fair, while the Genetic Algorithm leaves us no choice (i.e., no self-adaptation mechanism is used within the standard Genetic Algorithm). Concerning the population size the number of offspring individuals (λ) is adjusted to a common value of $\lambda = 100$ in order to achieve comparability of population sizes while at the same time limiting the computational requirements to a justifiable amount. This results in the following three algorithmic instances that are compared here (using the standard notation introduced in chapter 2)[2]:

- $ES(n, 0, r_{dI}, s_{(15,100)})$: An Evolution Strategy that self-adapts n

---

[1] To be precise, variances are self-adapted, but here emphasis is laid on identification of common qualitative properties.

[2] It is important to remember that these variants represent a kind of standard algorithms, which are compared here. Of course, it is possible to define variations which probably would result in a fairer comparison (e.g., by exchanging selection mechanisms in Genetic Algorithms), but this would contradict the intention to use the original algorithms.

standard deviations but does not use correlated mutations. Recombination is discrete on object variables and global intermediate on standard deviations, and the algorithm uses a (15,100)-selection mechanism.

- mEP(6, 10, 100): A meta-Evolutionary Programming algorithm that — by default — self-adapts n variances and controls mutation of variances by a meta-parameter $\zeta = 6$. The tournament size for selection and the population size amount to $q = 10$ and $\mu = 100$, respectively.

- GA(30, 0.001, $r_{\{0.6,2\}}$, 5, 100): A Genetic Algorithm that evolves a population of $\mu = 100$ bitstrings of length $l = 30 \cdot n$, each. The scaling window size for linear dynamic scaling is set to $\omega = 5$. Proportional selection, a two-point crossover operator with application rate 0.6 and a mutation operator with bit-reversal probability $1.0 \cdot 10^{-3}$ complete the algorithm.

The choice of appropriate measurements to assess the strengths and weaknesses of the Evolutionary Algorithms depends strongly on the goals envisaged. For our experimental purposes the objective functions are partitioned into two groups consisting of f_1 and f_2 in one group and f_3, f_4, f_5 in the second group. The members of the first group provide a good mechanism to test the *convergence velocity* of the algorithms, while the second group allows for assessing their *convergence reliability*, i.e. the capability to yield reasonably good solutions in case of highly multimodal topologies.

Since our intentions are different in both cases, these groups require different methods for evaluating the quality of the algorithms from a reasonably large set of repeated runs. These evaluation methods are discussed in the respective sections concerned with both groups of objective functions.

In general, since our point of view reflects the optimization aspect of Evolutionary Algorithms, we are interested in the development of the best individual existing in the population during the course of evolution, i.e. most graphical visualizations show the currently best objective function value as a function of the total number of evaluations. Since some selection mechanisms do not guarantee a monotonously improving course of evolution for the best individual (e.g. (μ, λ)-selection and proportional selection), practical applications often go one step further and record the development of the best function value discovered so far rather than the actually best. Though from a technical point of view this seems most appropriate, the first method is adopted here since it gives a better impression of the dynamic behavior of the algorithms[3].

---

[3]The difference is important in case of f_5.

4.1   Convergence Velocity: f_1, f_2

In order to assess the convergence velocity of Evolutionary Algorithms a measure is needed that is independent of the respective starting values and measures the relative rather than the absolute improvement. We adopt the method used by Schwefel (e.g. [Sch88]) and define the progress measure of a single run to be

$$ P \;\; = \;\; \ln \sqrt{\frac{f_{\min}(0)}{f_{\min}(T)}} \quad , \tag{4.1} $$

where $f_{\min}(i)$ refers to the best objective function value occurring in the parent population at generation i. A total of $T = 1000$ generations corresponding to $1 \cdot 10^5$ function evaluations are executed for all algorithms in each run.

To obtain statistically significant data, a sufficiently large number N of independent runs must be performed. Based on the hypothesis that the different progress values P_i ($i \in \{1, \ldots, N\}$) are normally distributed with expectation estimated by the average

$$ \bar{P} \;\; = \;\; \frac{1}{N} \sum_{i=1}^{N} P_i \tag{4.2} $$

and standard deviation estimated by the empirical standard deviation $\sqrt{V^2(P_i)}$, where

$$ V^2(P_i) \;\; = \;\; \frac{1}{N-1} \sum_{i=1}^{N} (P_i - \bar{P})^2 \quad , \tag{4.3} $$

we proceed as follows:

(1) The hypothesis of normally distributed P_i is checked by applying a *Kolmogorov-Smirnov* test to the data collected over $N = 100$ runs.

(2) If the test yields a positive answer, the number N' of independent runs can be calculated that must be performed in order to assure approximate repeatability of results with sufficiently high probability. To put this into concrete terms, we are interested in calculating a sample size N' such that with probability $1 - \alpha$ ("confidence") the result P of a new experiment obeys to a percentual exactness of $\varepsilon \cdot 100\%$ with respect to $\bar{P}$ obtained from these N' runs. The concrete values of α and ε remain to be chosen; typical values are 0.1, 0.05, or 0.01.

The application of a Kolmogorov-Smirnov test follows the description given e.g. in [HEK82] (pp. 183–189), [Kre65] (pp. 234–237). In contrast to the χ^2-test, the Kolmogorov-Smirnov test is well suited to a small sample size. The test requires the choice of a significance number α' such that the hypothesis (normally distributed progress data) holds with probability $1 - \alpha'$. For f_1, all progress value sets obtained from running each algorithm for $N = 100$ runs passed the test for a significance level $\alpha' = 0.01$, i.e. with probability 0.99 the hypothesis holds.

Based on this result, step two intends to keep results with high probability within a *confidence interval* $[\bar{P} \cdot (1 - \varepsilon), \bar{P} \cdot (1 + \varepsilon)]$ around the average progress. Again, $\alpha = 0.01$ and $\varepsilon = 0.01$ are set to the minimal usual values, i.e. we require a new experiment to yield with probability 0.99 a result that deviates from the average by no more than 1%. The number N' of runs necessary to assure this can be calculated under these circumstances according to the inequality

$$ N' \;\geq\; \left(\frac{t_{N'-1;1-\alpha/2}}{\varepsilon \cdot \bar{P}} \right)^2 \cdot V^2(P_i) \quad , \tag{4.4} $$

where the quantiles $t_{n;\gamma}$ of the t-distribution are tabulated or can be obtained from numerical approximations (see [HEK82], p. 736). The smallest integer N' satisfying inequality (4.4) gives the appropriate sample size.

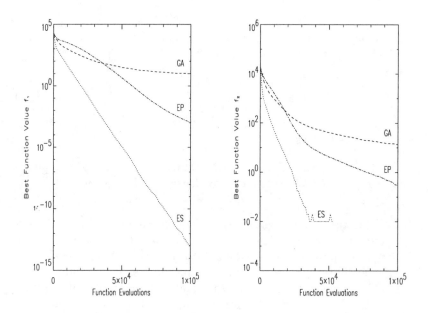

Fig. 4.1: Experimental results on f_1 (left) and f_2 (right).

Table 4.1 presents the corresponding data obtained by our initial sample of size $N = 100$ on function f_1 for the three algorithms. The first two columns contain the average initially best objective function values, i.e. $\bar{f}^1_{min}(0) = \frac{1}{N} \sum_{i=1}^{N} f^1_{min}(0)$, and the average final best objective function values, i.e. after $T = 1000$ generations. Furthermore, the average progress $\bar{P}$ and the resulting appropriate sample size N' are collected in the table.

	$\bar{f}^1_{min}(0)$	$\bar{f}^1_{min}(1000)$	$\bar{P}$	N'
ES	$2.119 \cdot 10^4$	$8.507 \cdot 10^{-14}$	21.37	127
EP	$1.435 \cdot 10^4$	$1.010 \cdot 10^{-3}$	8.31	68
GA	$1.822 \cdot 10^4$	9.581	3.80	89

Table 4.1. Objective function values and statistical test results for f_1.

From these results we accept a sample size of 100 runs for the objective functions f_1 and f_2 as a reasonable choice, though the statistical test can not be applied to f_2 due to the fact that both the Evolution Strategy and meta-Evolutionary Programming precisely attain the optimum function value zero in many of the 100 runs that were performed. Therefore, table 4.2 contains only the first two columns in analogy to table 4.1.

	$\bar{f}^2_{min}(0)$	$\bar{f}^2_{min}(t)$	
ES	$2.097 \cdot 10^4$	0	$(t = 540)$
EP	$1.426 \cdot 10^4$	$3.000 \cdot 10^{-1}$	$(t = 1000)$
GA	$1.827 \cdot 10^4$	$1.340 \cdot 10^1$	$(t = 1000)$

Table 4.2. Objective function values for f_2.

After 540 generations all runs of the Evolution Strategy located the optimal solution. Figure 4.1 gives a graphical impression of the behavior of the algorithms for both objective functions. In both cases the general pattern is very similar, indicating weak convergence velocity for the Genetic Algorithm, an intermediate result for meta-Evolutionary Programming, and best results for the Evolution Strategy which yields the expected linear convergence (see also [Sch88], pp. 187–188). Due to the logarithmic plot the corresponding curve for f_2 disappears when the average best objective function value is exactly zero. Both for the Genetic Algorithm and meta-Evolutionary Programming the local convergence rate (the slope of the curves) decreases over time, thus indicating that the necessary adjusment of the step size and mutation rate does not take place optimally.

4.2 Convergence Reliability: f_3, f_4, and f_5

In the case of multimodal functions like f_3, f_4, and f_5 the hypothesis to observe normally distributed data is completely unrealistic, since different runs must in general be expected to lead to different (at best) locally optimal solutions. A better method consists of performing a number of runs and creating a histogram that counts the relative frequency of runs that identified the same local optimum (or, at least, similar local optima) with respect to the objective function value. For Ackley's function f_3 and the Fletcher-Powell function f_4 we will give a demonstration of this method.

Again, the test plan consists of $N = 100$ independent runs for each algorithm on each test function except f_5, where due to the computational complexity of evaluating $C(x_i)$ (see section 3.5) a restriction to 50 runs and dimension $n = 20$ was necessary. Furthermore, the total number of generations is reduced to $T = 1000$ in case of f_5 in contrast to f_3 and f_4 where $T = 2000$ generations are permitted. This test plan is summarized in table 4.3.

Function	N	T	n
f_3	100	2000	30
f_4	100	2000	30
f_5	50	1000	20

Table 4.3. Test plan for multimodal functions.

The runs are prolonged to $2 \cdot 10^5$ function evaluations in order to get a better impression of the long-term behavior of the algorithms, and it will turn out that in some cases even longer runs would have been appropriate.

We continue with discussing the course of the average best objective function value for f_3, which is shown in figure 4.2. On Ackley's function both the Evolution Strategy and meta-Evolutionary Programming are characterizable by two phases. The first phase of slow improvement lasts for $\approx 2 \cdot 10^4$ (ES) respectively $\approx 6 \cdot 10^4$ (meta-EP) function evaluations and is followed by a second phase of faster improvement. These two phases reflect the topological properties of Ackley's function well, since the first phase corresponds to search in the multimodal regions far away from the origin while the second phase reflects the fine-tuning process in

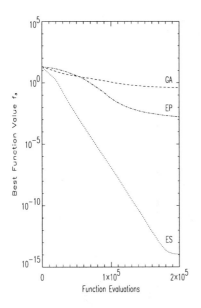
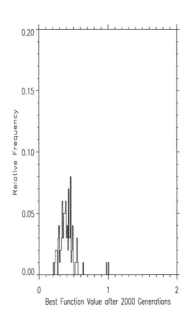

Fig. 4.2: Left: Experimental results on f_3. Right: Histogram of final best objective function values obtained from a Genetic Algorithm of f_3. The abscissa shows the range of best objective function values that occurred within 100 runs and is split up into segments of length 0.02. The ordinate shows the relative frequency of final best values falling into these segments.

the region of attraction of the global optimum finally located. The high convergence reliability of an Evolution Strategy and meta-Evolutionary Programming is clearly documented by the left part of figure 4.2 and the additional fact that a Kolmogorov-Smirnov test applied to their results indicates normally distributed progress data. In these cases a calculation of the appropriate sample size yields values as small as $N' = 4$ (Evolution Strategy) and $N' = 28$ (meta-Evolutionary Programming), respectively.

After 2000 generations, a Genetic Algorithm is not able to compete with the other Evolutionary Algorithms on f_3. The majority of runs located the globally optimum region characterized by objective function values below one, but a few runs seem to stagnate above this critical value. The right part of figure 4.2 shows a histogram of the final best objective function values obtained by the 100 runs of a Genetic Algorithm on f_3. The abscissa, split up into segments of length 0.02, each, shows the range of results that occurred within these runs. The ordinate shows the relative frequency of final best objective function values falling into these segments. The histogram reflects a distribution with a maximum located near 0.4 and nearly symmetrical distribution around this maximum.

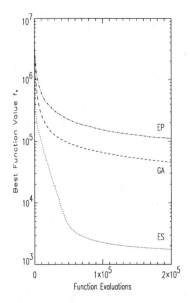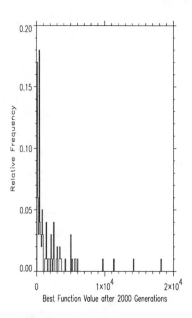

Fig. 4.3: Left: Experimental results on f_4. Right: Histogram of final best objective function values obtained from an Evolution Strategy on f_4. The abscissa shows the range of best objective function values that occurred within 100 runs and is split up into segments of length 100.0. The ordinate shows the relative frequency of final best values falling into these segments.

As indicated clearly by the left graphic shown in figure 4.3, the function f_4 after Fletcher and Powell causes extreme difficulties to all Evolutionary Algorithms, as can be concluded from the fact that $f_4^* = 0$ is reached by none of the curves at least approximately. For this function, Evolution Strategy runs are characterized by the histogram shown in the right part of figure 4.3. The abscissa axis is split up into segments of length 100.0, each, thereby impressively demonstrating the enormous amount of variation occurring in these 100 independent runs. In contrast to the histogram of the Genetic Algorithm for f_3 (right graphic in figure 4.2), this histogram identifies a large number of rather successful runs that yielded results better than 400.0 in objective function value (44 runs). The average quality of the runs decreases very much due to occasional runs stagnating in worse local optima with objective function values up to ≈ 18200.

The corresponding histograms for the Genetic Algorithm and meta-Evolutionary Programming are not shown here. Compared to that of the Evolution Strategy, they are shifted to much higher objective function values.

For technical application purposes, an engineer would be most interested in the best result obtained from a number of runs in case of a multimodal problem as hard as f_4. These values $f^i_{\min}(2000)$ $(i \in \{3,4\})$ are summarized for f_3 and f_4 in table 4.4 in addition to the average initial and final best objective function values $\bar{f}^i_{\min}(0)$ and $\bar{f}^i_{\min}(2000)$.

		f_3		
		$\bar{f}^3_{\min}(0)$	$\bar{f}^3_{\min}(2000)$	$f^3_{\min}(2000)$
ES		$2.114 \cdot 10^1$	$1.100 \cdot 10^{-14}$	$7.550 \cdot 10^{-15}$
EP		$2.069 \cdot 10^1$	$1.650 \cdot 10^{-3}$	$1.068 \cdot 10^{-3}$
GA		$2.080 \cdot 10^1$	$4.081 \cdot 10^{-1}$	$2.150 \cdot 10^{-1}$
		f_4		
		$\bar{f}^4_{\min}(0)$	$\bar{f}^4_{\min}(2000)$	$f^4_{\min}(2000)$
ES		$4.280 \cdot 10^6$	$1.749 \cdot 10^3$	$3.190 \cdot 10^{-1}$
EP		$3.302 \cdot 10^6$	$1.107 \cdot 10^5$	$2.997 \cdot 10^4$
GA		$3.088 \cdot 10^6$	$4.581 \cdot 10^4$	$1.032 \cdot 10^4$

Table 4.4. Average and overall final best objective function values for f_3 and f_4.

The most remarkable result presented in table 4.4 is the high quality of the best value obtained from an Evolution Strategy on f_4, especially when compared to the small diversity of results yielded by the other algorithms.

Finally, the results obtained for f_5 are collected in figure 4.4. The fractal function can be interpreted as a noisy variant of the sphere model such that the effect of the noise on the search increases as the origin is approached. Due to the zigzagging peaks close to the origin, several local optima with function values smaller than zero exist. Basically, the runs of the Evolutionary Algorithms on f_5 resemble the runs on the pure sphere model f_1 as long as the order of magnitude of the fractal portion is small compared to the sum of squares. This holds for the complete course of the experiments with a Genetic Algorithm and for the first $\approx 1.5 \cdot 10^4$ function evaluations of the Evolution Strategy and $\approx 4 \cdot 10^4$ function evaluations of meta-Evolutionary Programming, respectively. Then, the latter two algorithms exhibit different behavior which is completely due to their selection mechanisms, reflecting the difference between a comma-strategy and a plus-strategy (in other terms: a non-elitist and an elitist strategy). Evolutionary Programming guarantees a monotone course of evolution due to its elitist selection mechanism (see section 2.2.4 respectively section 5.1.6), such that due to the logarithmic plot the curve stops as soon as a local minimum of negative

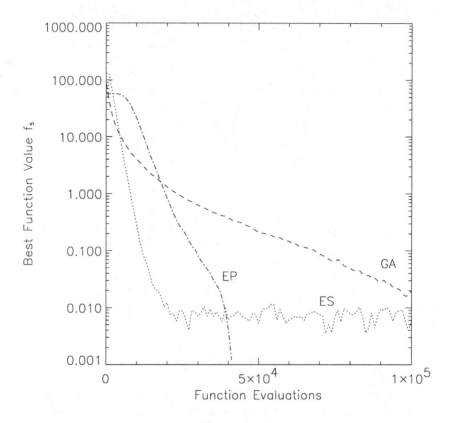

Fig. 4.4: Experimental results on f_5.

objective function value is located[4].

This is different in a (μ,λ)-Evolution Strategy. Due to the sharp and narrow peaks of the fractal function even small modifications of object variables may cause large deteriorations with respect to the objective function value. For this reason a non-elitist Evolution Strategy is just able to preserve objective function values within a level of fluctuation that corresponds to the order of magnitude of the fractal "noise." In technical applications it is often impossible to preserve a sharply restricted, narrow optimum, since the parameters of technical processes can only be fixed within tolerance intervals rather than on exact values. Therefore, stability of a solution in the sense of a sufficiently large, flat region of attraction is an important criterion for practical applic-

---

[4]Nevertheless, we stick to logarithmic plots with respect to the ordinate since they allow of observing the characteristics of the runs at all orders of magnitude.

ations. Furthermore, a non-elitist selection is required if the noise is dynamic over time rather than statically fixed as in the artificial examples discussed here (of course, the survivors could be re-evaluated, but this causes a computational overhead in comparison to the non-elitist strategy). Dynamic noise implies that individuals must not survive for more than one generation without being evaluated anew, because their objective function value is likely to become obsolete over time.

4.3 Summary

From the five objective functions tested empirically and the results reported here we can give only a statement of limited generality about the efficiency and effectiveness of these algorithms. However, since there is not yet enough theory available and the functions used here represent a good range of different topological features in higher dimensions, we are confident about the meaningfulness of the results. In addition, the results are confirmed by statistical tests in the unimodal case.

Our results provide strong evidence that a ranking of Evolutionary Algorithms in the order Evolution Strategy, meta-Evolutionary Programming, Genetic Algorithm (decreasing efficiency) appropriately reflects their performance on the test set (and parameterizations) chosen here. Test functions that yield another ordering of the methods are likely to exist. Furthermore, the encoding mechanism of Genetic Algorithms seems to extend their range of possible applications beyond the capabilities of Evolution Strategies and Evolutionary Programming.

The most critical problem of global optimization generally consists in finding an appropriate balance between the two conflicting goals of achieving high convergence velocity *and* high convergence reliability at the same time. In industrial applications this is a critical point due to the requirement to find a good solution quickly. Based on the results described in section 4.2 our recommendation for such cases must be to use the best result gained from a number of repeated runs or to use several strategies in parallel or for different phases of the search[5].

---

[5] An interesting step into this direction was presented by Peters, who developed a rule-based system which is able to switch between different optimization strategies according to the topological characteristics of the actual objective function and to modify the rule base according to the experience gained by different optimization strategies on different topologies [Pet91].

Part II

Extending Genetic Algorithms

This preservation of favourable variations and the rejection
of injurious variations, I call Natural Selection.
Variations neither useful nor injurious would not be affected
by Natural Selection, and would be left a fluctuating element,
as perhaps we see in the species called polymorphic.
Charles Darwin (The Origin of Species, 1859).
Penguin Books, Harmondsworth, England 1985 (p. 131).

Natural selection is a mechanism for generating
an exceedingly high degree of improbability.
Sir Ronald Aylmer Fisher (1890–1962).

5

Selection

The genetic operators summarized in the set Ω, i.e. mutation and recombination (and probably others, e.g. inversion) create new individuals in a completely undirected way. In Evolutionary Algorithms, the selection operator plays a major role by imposing a direction on the search process, i.e. a clear preference of those individuals which perform better according to the fitness measure Φ. Selection is the only component of Evolutionary Algorithms where the fitness of individuals has an impact on the evolution process.

The practical implementations of selection as discussed in sections 2.1.4, 2.2.4, and 2.3.4 seemingly contradict the biological viewpoint presented in section 1.1, where natural selection was emphasized not to be an active force but instead to be characterized by different survival and reproduction rates. However, artificial implementation models and biological reality are not necessarily contradicting each other. While in biological systems fitness can only be measured indirectly by differences in growth rates, fitness in Evolutionary Algorithms is a direct, well-defined and evaluable property of individuals. The biological struggle for existence (e.g. by predator-prey interactions, capabilities of somatic adaptation, and the particular physical properties of individuals) has no counterpart in computer implementations of standard Evolutionary Algorithms[1]. Therefore, an artificial abstraction of these mechanisms can use fitness measures to determine survival and reproduction a posteriori, since the struggle for existence is completely hidden

---

[1] The simulation of a more realistic struggle for existence is surely an interesting research field both for people interested in Artifical Life and for biologists.

163

in the evaluation process of individuals. The fact that different survival
and reproduction constitute selection is valid in both cases, but in Evolutionary Algorithms fitness is measurable and implies the survival and
reproduction behavior, which is just opposite to biological reality. This
is simply an implication of the fitness-centered intention which necessarily prevails design and application of these algorithms. Therefore, it
is just a logic consequence to model selection as an active, fitness-based
component of Evolutionary Algorithms.

However, *how* to model selection is by no means a simple problem.
In evolutionary biology, it is usually distinguished between *stabilizing*,
directed, and *disruptive* selection (see [Fut90], pp. 174–175). In the
case of stabilizing selection, intermediate phenotypes have best fitness
values, while disruptive selection is characterized by two or more distinct
phenotypes that are highly fit and by intermediate phenotypes of low
fitness (this assumes an – albeit unknown – ordering of phenotypes).
Finally, directed selection is characterized by a fairly monotone relation
between phenotype and fitness, where an extreme phenotype has best
fitness. The most famous example of directed selection at a single locus
is given by the frequency increase of 1% up to 90% of the black form of
a certain birch butterfly in England after the beginning of the industrial
revolution (see [Fut90], pp. 178–179).

Basically, this property of being more or less directed towards certain (i.e. the best) individuals in the actual population is the only
property common to all implementations of selection in Evolutionary
Algorithms[2]. Apart from this directedness, some rather different mechanisms have been developed and are currently in use. These selection
mechanisms are presented, analyzed, and compared to each other in the
following. Furthermore, a taxonomy of selection mechanisms providing
a simple but complete and useful characterization of existing approaches
is presented.

Selection deserves a great deal of attention since it is the component
mainly determining the character of the evolutionary search process to
be *volume-oriented* or *path-oriented*, corresponding to low respectively
high directedness in biological terminology. This is analogous to the
trade-off between good *convergence reliability* and high *convergence velocity* or, in other terms, reflects the idea of *exploration* of the search
space versus *exploitation* of information gained so far, a terminology
used by researchers in the field of Genetic Algorithms. Closely related is
the genotypic *diversity* of populations in genetic search, i.e. the range of
variation of genotypes that occurs within the population. The smaller
genotypic diversity, the more a population is crowded in the search space,
i.e. the search is path-oriented, exploitative. On the other hand, the
larger genotypic diversity, the more a population is distributed within
the search space, i.e. the search is volume-oriented, explorative. Con-

---

[2]It is probably worthwhile to explore the possibilities of simulating disruptive
selection in Evolutionary Algorithms.

sequently, measuring genotypic diversity of an evolution should allow for a characterization of the search in terms of these criteria. The idea to informally distinguish *"soft"* and *"hard"* selection mechanisms according to their emphasis on volume-oriented respectively path-oriented search is still another variation of the theme. Indeed, there is much empirical evidence available to agree with Whitley, who argues that population diversity and selective pressure are the only two primary factors in genetic search and that the main problem consists in the inverse relation of both [Whi89].

Table 5.1 summarizes the different dualistic terminology pairs that have been coined to denote the central trade-off in evolutionary search.

volume-orientation	path-orientation
convergence reliability	convergence velocity
exploration	exploitation
large genotypic diversity	small genotypic diversity
"soft" selection	"hard" selection

Table 5.1. Characterizations of the basic trade-off in evolutionary search.

Selective pressure is the instrument which enables the user of an Evolutionary Algorithm to influence these characteristics of the search. In the following section we will formalize the notion of selective pressure and analyze the most important selection mechanisms accordingly.

5.1 Selection Mechanisms

The analysis of the selection mechanisms presented in this section is based on a common formal notation of selection in terms of *selection probabilities* and a characterization in terms of the so-called *takeover time*.

The notion of selection probabilities was already introduced in section 2.3.4 to characterize the probability distribution of proportional selection. In the following, some basic assumptions will be made to simplify terminology and calculations:

(1) All individuals occurring in a population $P(t) = \{\vec{a}_1(t), \ldots, \vec{a}_\mu(t)\}$ are ordered with respect to fitness values $\Phi(\vec{a}_i(t))$, such that $\vec{a}_1(t)$ is the best individual, $\vec{a}_2(t)$ the second best, and so on.

(2) The individuals can be identified uniquely by means of their index $i \in \{1, \ldots, \mu\}$, such that selection probabilities

$$p_s(\vec{a}_i(t)) \;=\; \mathcal{P}\{\vec{a}_i(t) \in s(P(t)) \mid \vec{a}_i(t) \in P(t)\} \qquad (5.1)$$

can be abbreviated by p_i ($s : I^\mu \to I^\mu$ denotes a selection operator).

As a fundamental requirement to any selection operator, we emphasize that

$$\sum_{i=1}^{\mu} p_i \;=\; 1 \qquad (5.2)$$

must be fulfilled. Whenever equation (5.2) does not obviously hold, we will check its validity for the particular expressions derived for the selection probabilities.

The concept of *takeover time* was introduced by Goldberg and Deb in order to characterize the selective pressure imposed on the evolutionary search by particular selection mechanisms [GD91]. Their important work marks the first milestone towards a clear and conclusive analysis of the impact of different selection mechanisms. The takeover time approach reflects the effect of selection in absence of any genetic operator (such as recombination or mutation) by concentrating on the number of generations after which repeated application of selection yields a population consisting exclusively of copies of the best individual contained in the initial population. Initially, two classes of individuals are assumed to exist in the population: the single best individual and a class consisting of $\mu - 1$ worse individuals. By means of selection, the proportion of the best individual grows at the expense of the proportion of the worse class, until the population is completely filled by the best individual. More formally, this is captured by the following definition.

Definition 5.1 (Takeover time) *Let* EA $= (I, \Phi, \Omega, \Psi, s, \iota, \mu, \lambda)$ *denote an Evolutionary Algorithm with* $\Omega = \emptyset$ *(no genetic operators) and* $\Psi = s$ *(a consequence of an empty* Ω*). Furthermore,* $P(0)$ *denotes the initial population and* $\vec{a}'(0) \in P(0)$ *the single best individual occurring in* $P(0)$*. Assuming a termination criterion*

$$\iota(P(t)) \;=\; \{\vec{a}_1(t) = \vec{a}_2(t) = \ldots = \vec{a}_\mu(t) = \vec{a}'(0)\} \quad , \qquad (5.3)$$

the resulting running time

$$\tau_{EA'} \;=\; \min\{\, t \in I\!N \mid \iota(s^t(P(0))) = true \,\} =: \tau^* \qquad (5.4)$$

is called takeover time *of the selection operator s.*

The definition differs slightly from the formulation as used in [GD91], where τ^* is defined as the number of generations until the population contains $\mu - 1$ copies of the best individual rather than μ as required in definition 5.1. Apparently, this decision was made by Goldberg and Deb because some of their model equations cause technical complications when trying to solve them for a final best proportion of 1 rather than $1 - 1/\mu$. Nevertheless, the general validity of their arithmetical results does not suffer from this difference.

The basic assumption which indicates takeover time measures to be worthwhile relies on the idea that small takeover times characterize strong selective pressure, therefore corresponding to a path-oriented, exploitative search while large takeover times impose weak selective pressure on the search, i.e. characterize selection methods that cause a volume-oriented, explorative search. This intuition was confirmed empirically by Bäck and Hoffmeister, who measured population diversity in a Genetic Algorithm in terms of bias values calculated according to equation (2.90) [BH91]. These results in combination with the following takeover time characterization of selection methods clearly demonstrate the expected connection of small (large) takeover time and quickly (slowly) decreasing genotypic diversity even for a Genetic Algorithm with crossover and mutation enabled.

In the remainder of this section, we concentrate on four important selection mechanisms used in Evolutionary Algorithms, namely *proportional selection* (section 5.1.1), *ranking* (section 5.1.2), *tournament selection* (section 5.1.3), and (μ,λ)-*selection* (section 5.1.4) respectively $(\mu+\lambda)$-*selection* (section 5.1.4).

5.1.1   Proportional Selection

Goldberg and Deb analyzed the original proportional selection mechanism without scaling, i.e. $\Phi = f \circ \Upsilon$ [GD91]. The selection probabilities are then defined as usual according to

$$p_i = \frac{\Phi(\vec{a}_i)}{\displaystyle\sum_{j=1}^{\mu} \Phi(\vec{a}_j)} \quad . \tag{5.5}$$

Since the particular objective function f determines the selection probabilities p_i, Goldberg and Deb had to search for objective functions f that facilitated finding a solution of the proportionate reproduction equation. They succeeded for the two one-dimensional functions

$$f'(x) = x^c \tag{5.6}$$

and

$$f''(x) = \exp(c \cdot x) \tag{5.7}$$

where $c \neq 0$ is a constant. The takeover time results are presented in the next theorem.

Theorem 15 (Takeover time of proportional selection)
*The takeover time of proportional selection on the objective functions f'
and f'' is approximated by*

$$
\begin{aligned}
\tau_{f'}^* &\approx \frac{1}{c} \cdot (\mu \ln \mu - 1) \quad , \\
\tau_{f''}^* &\approx \frac{1}{c} \cdot \mu \ln \mu \quad .
\end{aligned}
\tag{5.8}
$$

Proof: See [GD91], pp. 72–75.   Q.E.D.

This leads to the important observation that the general takeover
time behavior of proportional selection is of the order $\mathcal{O}(\mu \ln \mu)$ regardless of the objective function being polynomial or exponential in x.

The result implies that even imposing a seemingly strong scaling
method such as exponential scaling (see section 2.3.1, equation (2.77))
does not change the general order of takeover time but works just by
changing the constant of proportionality. Goldberg and Deb draw a
conclusion about the reason for the development of scaling techniques
from their observation that the early growth ratio (when the proportion of best individuals is insubstantial) of proportional selection is high
while the late growth ratio (when the best occupy fifty percent of the
population) is likely to be low. This point of view is confirmed by their
simulation results which show an almost asymptotic growth towards the
best class proportion of one when no scaling is used [GD91].

To give an impression of the takeover time values under proportional
selection, table 5.2 presents some values calculated for f'' (with $c = 1$)
and $\mu \in \{10, 20, 30, 40, 50, 100, 200\}$.

		μ					
	10	20	30	40	50	100	200
τ	23	60	102	148	196	461	1060

Table 5.2. Takeover time values for proportional selection.

Comparing the result for $\mu = 100$ with the experimental results from
chapter 4, especially figures 4.1, 4.3, and 4.4, the transition from a period
of fast progress to a long period of slower progress can be identified for
the Genetic Algorithm somewhere around 100 generations. It can be sus-
pected that this reflects the transition from a high genotypic diversity
and crossover-based search to lower genotypic diversity and mutation-
based search. These two phases of the search process are also identified by Spears [Spe93]. The transition of emphasis from crossover to
mutation occurs earlier than predicted according to takeover times because the scaling technique used by the algorithm increases the selective

pressure of proportional selection remarkably. This increase of selective pressure caused by linear dynamic scaling can easily be demonstrated according to the following consideration: Assuming a maximization task and[3]

$$\Phi_i = f_i - c \qquad (5.9)$$

($c > 0$) according to the scaling equation (2.75) with $c_0 = 1$, the selection probabilities for proportional selection with scaling are given by

$$p_i' = \frac{f_i - c}{S_f - \mu \cdot c} \quad , \qquad (5.10)$$

where $S_f = \sum_{j=1}^{\mu} f_j$. Comparing p_i' to the unscaled selection probabilities $p_i = f_i/S_f$, we obtain the following result[4]:

$$\begin{aligned} p_i' > p_i &\iff f_i > \bar{f} \\ p_i' < p_i &\iff f_i < \bar{f} \end{aligned} \quad . \qquad (5.11)$$

The result clarifies that linear dynamic scaling increases the selection probabilities of above-average individuals and decreases selection probabilities of below-average individuals, i.e. selective pressure towards better individuals is increased.

5.1.2 Ranking

The term *ranking* or, more specifically, *linear ranking*, has been coined by Baker to denote a selection method for Genetic Algorithms which assigns selection probabilities solely on the basis of the rank i of individuals, completely ignoring absolute fitness values [Bak85, GB89]. Several advantages of such rank-based selection methods over proportional selection can be identified (see e.g. [BH91, Whi89]):

- Scaling is no longer necessary, thereby avoiding the drawbacks to find an appropriate scaling method and its parameter settings.

- Selective pressure can be controlled more directly by the ranking method than by scaling parameters.

- Ranking can speed up the search remarkably.

However, for several years rank-based methods did not receive much attention in Genetic Algorithm research — even though they are a standard in Evolution Strategies and Evolutionary Programming. The reason is very likely to be identified in its seemingly existing inconsistency with

---

[3] We use the abbreviations $\Phi_i = \Phi(\vec{a}_i(t))$ and $f_i = f(\Upsilon(\vec{a}_i(t)))$.

[4] It should be noticed here that $\bar{f} = S_f/\mu$.

the schema theorem (theorem 11). Whitley [Whi89, WS90] and Gold-berg (see [Gol89a], pp. 124–125), however, point out that the intent of the schema theorem is not violated by substituting the fitness ratio $\Phi(H(t))/\bar\Phi(t)$ by a rank-based expression. The fundamental properties of exponential growth and decline remain valid after such a change.

Baker's original method is called *linear ranking* due to its property of using a linear function to map indices i to selection probabilities respectively expected values. Assuming the maximal expected value η^+ is assigned to individual $\vec{a}_1$, i.e. $\eta^+ = \mu \cdot p_1$, the minimal expected value η^- is assigned to $\vec{a}_\mu$, i.e. $\eta^- = \mu \cdot p_\mu$, and a linear mapping of the form[5] (see [GB89]):

$$ p_i = \frac{1}{\mu} \cdot \left(\eta^+ - (\eta^+ - \eta^-) \cdot \frac{i-1}{\mu-1} \right) \quad , \qquad (5.13) $$

the constraints $\sum_{i=1}^{\mu} p_i = 1$ and $p_i \geq 0\ \forall i \in \{1, \ldots, \mu\}$ require that $1 \leq \eta^+ \leq 2$ and $\eta^- = 2 - \eta^+$.

The selective pressure of linear ranking can be varied by tuning the maximum expected value η^+, which controls the slope of the linear function. Usually, $\eta^+ = 1.1$ is recommended (see e.g. [Bak85]), i.e. on average the best individual is expected to be sampled 1.1 times within μ sampling steps. This is a rather moderate selective pressure, close to the extreme case of random walk ($\eta^+ = 1 \Rightarrow p_i = 1/\mu$).

---

[5]In his earlier paper, Baker explains the idea and presents the method indirectly by making the following three assumptions [Bak85]:

(1) Lower and upper *bounds* $\eta_{\min}, \eta_{\max}$ for expected values are related according to $\eta_{\min} = 2 - \eta_{\max}$.

(2) The difference of expected values between adjacent individuals is given by $\Delta\eta = |\eta_i - \eta_{i+1}| = 2(\eta_{\max} - 1)/\mu$.

(3) The expected value of the worst individual is $\eta^- = (\eta_{\max} - 1)/\mu$.

In contrast to equation (5.13), this distinction between bounds on expected values and maximal / minimal expected values themselves is artifical, confusing, and superfluous. However, in section 5.1.3 we will need to refer to the method specified indirectly by assumptions (1)–(3), such that it has to be transformed here into an explicit expression for p_i.

From the observation that, by assumption (3), $p_\mu = (\eta_{\max} - 1)/\mu^2$, and by assumption (2), $p_i - p_{i+1} = 2(\eta_{\max} - 1)/\mu^2$, a linear relation between p_i and i of the form

$$ p_i = \frac{1}{\mu} \cdot (\eta_{\max} - 1) \cdot \left(2 + \frac{1}{\mu} - \frac{2i}{\mu} \right) \qquad (5.12) $$

can be derived. Checking the sum condition (5.2) yields the result $\sum_{i=1}^{\mu} p_i = \eta_{\max} - 1$, i.e. this expression is only feasible in case $\eta_{\max} = 2$. Then, $\eta^+ = \mu \cdot p_1 = 2 - 1/\mu$ and $\eta^- = \mu \cdot p_\mu = 1/\mu$ are obtained, and for these (and only these) values of η^+, η^-, and $\eta_{\max}$, equations (5.13) and (5.12) are identical.

As Baker suggests a value $\eta_{\max} = 1.1$, we may suspect that he had already implemented the more general version (5.13) and was simply not aware of his misleading description of the method.

For deriving approximations of the takeover time in case of linear ranking, Goldberg and Deb [GD91] distinguished the case $\eta^+ = 2$ and $1 < \eta^+ < 2$, finally obtaining the results summarized in theorem 16.

Theorem 16 (Takeover time of linear ranking)
For linear ranking with $\eta^+ = 2$, the takeover time τ^* is approximated by[6]

$$\tau_2^* \approx \text{ld}\mu + \text{ld}(\ln \mu) \quad . \tag{5.14}$$

If $1 < \eta^+ < 2$, τ^* is approximated by

$$\tau_{\eta^+}^* \approx \frac{2}{\eta^+ - 1} \cdot \ln(\mu - 1) \quad . \tag{5.15}$$

Proof: See [GD91], pp. 77–78. Q.E.D.

Whitley has presented a linear ranking method equivalent to Baker's, which allows direct computation of the index $i - 1 \in \{0, \ldots, \mu - 1\}$ designating the selected individual [Whi89, MSB91]:

$$i = \left\lfloor \frac{\mu}{2(c - 1)} \cdot \left(c - \sqrt{c^2 - 4(c - 1)\chi} \right) \right\rfloor \quad . \tag{5.16}$$

Here, $\chi \in [0, 1]$ denotes a uniform random variable. Selection is then very conveniently performed by sampling χ for μ times and copying the individuals designated by the resulting index values to the next generation. The parameter c in equation (5.16) controls the selective pressure of the method, and for $1 < c \leq 2$ it is practically identical to linear ranking[7].

As for proportional selection, table 5.3 presents some numerical values of takeover times[8] for $\mu \in \{10, 20, 30, 40, 50, 100, 200\}$ and $\eta^+ \in \{1.1, 1.5, 1.9\}$.

---

[6]ld denotes the logarithm with base 2.

[7]This can be derived according to the consideration of χ as cumulative distribution function of index values, i.e. $\chi = \mathcal{P}\{i(\chi) \leq x\} =: F(x)$ and using (5.16) in its continuous generalization:

$$x = \frac{\mu}{2(c - 1)} \cdot \left(c - \sqrt{c^2 - 4(c - 1)F(x)} \right) \quad .$$

Solving for

$$F(x) = \frac{x}{\mu}(c - \frac{x}{\mu}(c - 1))$$

and calculating the continuous density function yields

$$\frac{\mathrm{d}F(x)}{\mathrm{d}x} = \frac{1}{\mu}(c - 2(c - 1)\frac{x}{\mu}) \quad ,$$

$\tau_{\eta^+}^*$		μ						
		10	20	30	40	50	100	200
η^+	1.1	43.94	58.89	67.35	73.27	77.83	91.90	105.87
	1.5	8.79	11.78	13.47	14.65	15.57	18.38	21.17
	1.9	4.88	6.54	7.48	8.14	8.65	10.21	11.76

Table 5.3. Takeover time values for linear ranking.

The strong general reduction of takeover times in contrast to proportional selection (see table 5.2) is striking in this table, clearly reflecting the $\mathcal{O}(\ln \mu)$ behavior of linear ranking. Furthermore, the influence of the control parameter η^+ on selective pressure reflects an enormous range of variability which can be controlled this way.

Of course, the ranking mechanism must not necessarily use a linear mapping of indices to selection probabilities. For instance, Michalewicz has used an exponential ranking method where selection probabilities are calculated according to (see [Mic92], p. 57):

$$p_i = c \cdot (1 - c)^{i-1} \quad , \tag{5.17}$$

where c $(0 < c \ll 1$, e.g. $c = 0.04)$ is a constant determining the best individuals' selection probability p_1. Such a method increases selective pressure by emphasizing even more on the best individuals. However, it is not widely used and does not fulfil the requirement (5.2), since

$$\sum_{i=1}^{\mu} p_i = 1 - (1 - c)^{\mu} < 1 \quad . \tag{5.18}$$

As we will demonstrate in the next section, this method is practically identical to tournament selection, i.e. it does not represent a qualitatively new selection mechanism.

5.1.3 Tournament Selection

The *q-tournament selection* method selects a single individual by choosing some number q of individuals randomly from the population and

---

i.e. the continuous analogue to the linear ranking equation (5.13) (for $c = \eta^+$, using $\eta^- = 2 - \eta^+$ in (5.13)).

[8]Of course, takeover times are positive integers, but within this and the following tables we present fractional values obtained from the takeover time equations. The reason is that we would like to give an impression of the general trends, which would vanish in some cases when the takeover times are rounded to integers.

selecting the best individual from this group to survive to the next generation. The process is repeated as often as necessary, i.e. μ times, to fill the new population [GD91]. A common *tournament size* is $q = 2$, i.e. binary tournaments.

A formalization of tournament selection in terms of selection probabilities is given in theorem 17.

Theorem 17 *The selection probabilities p_i ($i \in \{1, \ldots, \mu\}$) for q-tournament selection are given by*

$$p_i = \frac{1}{\mu^q} \cdot ((\mu - i + 1)^q - (\mu - i)^q) \quad . \tag{5.19}$$

Proof: An individual labeled by index i survives the tournament, if the index i is sampled at least once and, in addition, only index values from the set $\{i, i+1, \ldots, \mu\}$ are sampled at all within the q trials. Therefore, the number of combinatorial possibilities is given by the number of q-permutations with repetitions of indices from $\{i, i + 1, \ldots, \mu\}$, such that index i occurs with a multiplicity from $\{1, 2, \ldots, q\}$ *and* any index different from i occurs with a multiplicity from $\{0, 1, 2, \ldots, q - 1\}$.

According to the theory of generating functions, this number is given by the coefficient of the term $x^q/q!$ in the corresponding exponential generating function (see [Dör77], pp. 362–363):

$$
\begin{aligned}
(\exp(x) - 1) \cdot \exp(x)^{\mu - i} \\
= \exp(x)^{\mu - i + 1} - \exp(x)^{\mu - i} \\
= 1 + \sum_{q=1}^{\infty} ((\mu - i + 1)^q - (\mu - i)^q) \frac{x^q}{q!}
\end{aligned}
\tag{5.20}
$$

where the term $\exp(x) - 1$ characterizes index i to occur at least once, while $\exp(x)^{\mu - i}$ characterizes the $\mu - i$ remaining indices to occur in arbitrary multiplicities.

The coefficient $(\mu - i + 1)^q - (\mu - i)^q$ turns into the desired probability by observing that each of the q tournament members has a uniform sampling probability $1/\mu$.

Since $\sum_{i=1}^{\mu} (\mu - i + 1)^q = \mu^q + \sum_{i=1}^{\mu} (\mu - i)^q$, it is easy to confirm that the sum condition (5.2) is fulfilled.   Q.E.D.

Based on this result, it is easy to show that tournament selection and the nonlinear ranking method of Michalewicz (equation (5.17)) behave equivalently if $c = 1 - (1 - 1/\mu)^q$ is chosen in (5.17). This can be derived by inserting this value of c into (5.17), which yields

$$
\begin{aligned}
p_i &= \left(\left(1 - \frac{1}{\mu}\right)^{i-1} \right)^q - \left(\left(1 - \frac{1}{\mu}\right)^i \right)^q \\
&\approx \left(1 - \frac{i-1}{\mu}\right)^q - \left(1 - \frac{i}{\mu}\right)^q
\end{aligned}
\tag{5.21}
$$

by using the approximation $(1 - x)^i \approx 1 - ix$ for small x. The latter expression in (5.21) is equivalent to (5.19), and the error introduced by the approximation is practically negligible. This way, for $\mu = 100$ a value of $c = 0.04$ as proposed by Michalewicz corresponds directly with 4-tournament selection. From an algorithmic point of view, tournament selection is preferable because it does not require to keep the population sorted according to fitness values.

A derivation of the takeover time of tournament selection was also performed by Goldberg and Deb:

Theorem 18 (Takeover time of q-tournament selection)
For q-tournament selection, the takeover time τ^* is approximated by

$$\tau_q^* \approx \frac{1}{\ln q} \cdot (\ln \mu + \ln(\ln \mu)) \quad . \tag{5.22}$$

Proof: See [GD91], p. 80.   Q.E.D.

Comparing this to the result stated in theorem 16, the interesting conclusion is that takeover times of binary (i.e. $q = 2$) tournament selection and linear ranking with $\eta^+ = 2$ are identical in expectation [GD91]. With regard to selection probabilities for binary tournaments, however, the result $p_i = (2 - 2i/\mu + 1/\mu)/\mu$ obtained from theorem 17 agrees with linear ranking according to [Bak85] for $\eta_{\max} = 2$ (see footnote on page 170), i.e. with linear ranking as defined by equation (5.13) for $\eta^+ = 2 - 1/\mu$. Though this deviation does not spoil the takeover time results, it indicates that Goldberg and Deb refer to Baker's earlier specification.

Again, for some population sizes $\mu \in \{10, 20, 30, 40, 50, 100, 200\}$ and values of the control parameter[9] $q \in \{2, 3, 4, 5, 6, 7, 8, 9, 10\}$, table 5.4 presents the resulting numerical values of takeover time.

The table clearly confirms the expectation that the selective pressure is steadily increasing for growing values[10] of q. Furthermore, compared to linear ranking, tournament selection is always imposing stronger selective pressure on the search process, down to takeover times of just a few generations.

5.1.4 $(\mu+\lambda)$- and (μ,λ)-Selection

So far, selection methods that stem from the field of Genetic Algorithms were discussed. What is missing in this analysis is the discussion of

[9]Note that for $q = 1$ equation (5.19) turns into random walk ($p_i = 1/\mu$), corresponding to

$$\lim_{q \to 1} \tau_q^* = \infty \quad .$$

[10]It should also be noted that q might be chosen arbitrarily large, i.e., $q > \mu$ is allowed. However, as a takeover time smaller than one is practically not realizable, $\mu \cdot \ln \mu$ is an upper bound on reasonable values of q. For practical purposes, q will normally be chosen close to two.

τ_q^*		μ						
		10	20	30	40	50	100	200
	2	4.52	5.90	6.67	7.21	7.61	8.85	10.05
	3	2.86	3.73	4.21	4.55	4.80	5.58	6.34
	4	2.26	2.95	3.34	3.60	3.81	4.42	5.02
	5	1.95	2.54	2.87	3.10	3.28	3.81	4.33
q	6	1.75	2.28	2.58	2.79	2.94	3.42	3.89
	7	1.61	2.10	2.38	2.57	2.71	3.15	3.56
	8	1.51	1.97	2.22	2.40	2.54	2.95	3.35
	9	1.42	1.86	2.11	2.27	2.40	2.79	3.17
	10	1.36	1.78	2.01	2.17	2.29	2.66	3.03

Table 5.4. Takeover time values for q-tournament selection.

$(\mu+\lambda)$-selection and (μ,λ)-selection, methods which differ from the mechanisms discussed so far by three important properties:

- They are defined under the assumption of offspring and parent population having different sizes λ and μ, respectively.

- Both methods are completely deterministic, i.e. an argumentation on the basis of selection probabilities is not necessary.

- Both methods definitely exclude the worst individuals of the offspring population from the selection process rather than sampling them with small probabilities as the other selection mechanisms do.

A calculation of the takeover time for (μ,λ)-selection is quite straightforward, and the result is given in the next theorem.

Theorem 19 (Takover time of (μ,λ)-selection) *The takeover time of (μ,λ)-selection is given by*

$$\tau_{(\mu,\lambda)}^* = \frac{\ln \lambda}{\ln \frac{\lambda}{\mu}} . \tag{5.23}$$

Proof: The proof is based on counting N_t, the expected number of copies of the best individual contained in $P(t)$, starting with $N_0 = 1$. It is easy to see that for (μ,λ)-selection

$$N_0 = 1$$
$$N_1 = N_0 \cdot \frac{\lambda}{\mu}$$

$$N_2 = N_1 \cdot \frac{\lambda}{\mu}$$

$$\vdots \qquad \vdots \qquad\qquad\qquad (5.24)$$

$$N_t = \left(\frac{\lambda}{\mu}\right)^t .$$

Setting $N_{\tau^*} = \lambda$ and solving for τ^* yields the result.   Q.E.D.

This result considers the growth of a single individual seed within a population of size λ under the assumption that only a subset of cardinality μ of these may be selected (this implies $\lambda \geq \mu$). In terms of Evolution Strategies, this point of view characterizes the takeover time with respect to the offspring rather than the parent population, but this difference does not substantially affect the takeover time result.

This shift of emphasis, however, allows us to transfer (μ,λ)-selection to an Evolutionary Algorithm working with a population of constant size[11] λ by defining selection probabilities according to [BH91]:

$$p_i = \begin{cases} 1/\mu & , \quad 1 \leq i \leq \mu \\ 0 & , \quad \mu < i \leq \lambda \end{cases} \qquad (5.25)$$

The use of probabilities reflects well the uniform sampling process which forms the basis for recombination *and* (implicitly) reproduction in Evolution Strategies and is a fair method to fill the offspring population even if the quotient λ/μ is no integer value. In this formulation, (μ,λ)-selection is used in Genetic Algorithms in section 5.2. Understanding it as an expectation value, $\tau'^*_{(\mu,\lambda)}$ is still valid in the case of this modified probabilistic version of selection.

The selective pressure of (μ,λ)-selection is mainly determined by the ratio[12] λ/μ, which plays a role analogous to q and η^+ for tournament and linear ranking selection, respectively. Therefore, in table 5.5 the ratio λ/μ is varied in the leftmost column.

The row containing values for $\lambda/\mu = 7$ is of special importance, since this corresponds to the default selective pressure recommended for Evolution Strategies. For a (15,100)-strategy, an extremely small takeover time of slightly more than two generations results, and for $\lambda/\mu \geq 2$ selective pressure is always stronger than for comparable values for q-tournament selection. This gives a clear indication that Evolution Strategies and Evolutionary Programming must create a sufficient degree of diversity at each generation by means of mutation rather than

---

[11]This is not in correspondence with our usual terminology where μ denotes population size, but this is just a matter of terminology and can be solved by calling this a, say, (ϱ, μ)-strategy.

[12]C.f. our remark on theorem 8 at the end of section 2.1.7 on numerical evidence for this statement.

$\tau^*_{(\mu,\lambda)}$		λ						
		10	20	30	40	50	100	200
	1.1	24.16	31.43	35.69	38.70	41.05	48.32	55.59
	1.5	5.68	7.39	8.39	9.10	9.65	11.36	13.07
	2	3.22	4.32	4.91	5.32	5.64	6.64	7.64
	3	2.10	2.73	3.10	3.36	3.56	4.19	4.82
	4	1.66	2.16	2.45	2.66	2.82	3.32	3.82
$\frac{\lambda}{\mu}$	5	1.43	1.86	2.11	2.29	2.43	2.86	3.29
	6	1.29	1.67	1.90	2.06	2.18	2.57	2.96
	7	1.18	1.54	1.75	1.90	2.01	2.37	2.72
	8	1.10	1.44	1.64	1.77	1.88	2.21	2.55
	9	1.05	1.36	1.55	1.68	1.78	2.10	2.41
	10	1.00	1.30	1.48	1.60	1.70	2.00	2.30

Table 5.5. Takeover time values for (μ,λ)-selection.

relying on an initial diversity and recombination as Genetic Algorithms do[13].

The situation becomes more complicated in case of $(\mu+\lambda)$-selection. In order to guarantee survival of the μ best previous parent individuals, selection must be modeled as an (at least partially) deterministic process. For a calculation of the takeover time the number of copies of the best individual contained in the actual *and* in the preceding generation has to be considered. As in the proof of theorem 19, the first two elements of the growth sequence are $N_0 = 1$ and $N_1 = \lambda/\mu$, but now the recurrence relation turns into

$$N_{t+1} = \frac{\lambda}{\mu} \cdot (N_t + N_{t-1}) \quad , \qquad (5.26)$$

($t \geq 1$), since the best individual number grows in proportion to its portion within the actual and previous generation. Shifting the indices in equation (5.26) to $N_t = \frac{\lambda}{\mu} \cdot (N_{t-1} + N_{t-2})$ ($t \geq 2$), one observes a close similarity to the well-known Fibonacci-sequence, which would be obtained for the special case $\lambda/\mu = 1$.

Following standard methods for solving such recurrence relations (see [Liu68], pp. 60–61), the closed arithmetic expression

---

[13]Recall from section 2.1.5 that in Schwefel's implementation the search process starts from one individual (for reasons of fair comparison to "classical" methods).

$$N_t = \frac{\alpha_1^{t+1} - \alpha_2^{t+1}}{\sqrt{\frac{\lambda}{\mu} \cdot \left(\frac{\lambda}{\mu} + 4\right)}} \tag{5.27}$$

is obtained, where

$$\alpha_{1,2} = \frac{\lambda}{2\mu} \pm \frac{1}{2} \cdot \sqrt{\frac{\lambda}{\mu} \cdot \left(\frac{\lambda}{\mu} + 4\right)} \tag{5.28}$$

are the solutions of the characteristic equation $\alpha^2 - \alpha\lambda/\mu - \lambda/\mu = 0$ of equation (5.26).

$\tau^*_{(\mu+\lambda)}$		λ						
		10	20	30	40	50	100	200
	1.1	4.75	6.01	6.74	7.27	7.67	8.93	10.20
	1.5	3.30	4.18	4.70	5.07	5.35	6.24	7.12
	2	2.53	3.22	3.62	3.91	4.13	4.82	5.51
	3	1.86	2.39	2.70	2.91	3.08	3.60	4.12
	4	1.56	2.00	2.26	2.44	2.59	3.03	3.47
$\frac{\lambda}{\mu}$	5	1.38	1.77	2.00	2.16	2.29	2.68	3.08
	6	1.26	1.62	1.83	1.97	2.09	2.45	2.81
	7	1.17	1.50	1.70	1.84	1.95	2.28	2.62
	8	1.10	1.41	1.60	1.73	1.83	2.15	2.47
	9	1.05	1.35	1.52	1.65	1.74	2.05	2.35
	10	1.00	1.29	1.46	1.58	1.67	1.96	2.25

Table 5.6. Takeover time values for $(\mu+\lambda)$-selection.

Unfortunately, even the closed form (5.27) does not admit an analytical solution for τ^* when setting $N_{\tau^*} = \lambda$. At least, the equation for N_t can be checked with respect to the case of a large value of $\lambda/\mu \gg 4$, i.e. high selective pressure, which should cause takeover times to get close to those of (μ,λ)-selection. Neglecting the constant 4 in the terms for α_1, α_2, and N_t, we obtain $\alpha_1 \approx \lambda/\mu$, $\alpha_2 \approx 0$, and $N_t \approx (\lambda/\mu)^t$, the result for (μ,λ)-selection. Setting $\mu = 1$ and $N_{\tau^*} = \lambda$ in the exact equation (5.27), $\tau^* = 1$ meets our expectations to solve the equation. Table 5.6 presents the results obtained by numerically solving the equation $N_{\tau^*} = \lambda$ for the same values of λ respectively λ/μ as used in table 5.5.

As expected, the selective pressure of $(\mu+\lambda)$-selection is still larger than that of (μ,λ)-selection, since the parent individuals contribute to a

reduction of the takeover time. Furthermore, the takeover time values
for growing ratio λ/μ approach those of (μ,λ)-selection as predicted.

As any kind of selection that guarantees a monotonous evolution
process by means of an elitist strategy, $(\mu+\lambda)$-selection as defined here
is partially deterministic and refers to two different time steps of the
algorithms. This makes an analysis quite complicated, but does not
contribute important additional insights to our understanding and ordering of selection methods according to selective pressure. Therefore,
the following sections restrict attention to the probabilistic, not necessarily monotonous variants of selection.

5.1.5 Comparison of Takeover Times

In order to compare the selection mechanisms with respect to their selective pressure, we normalize population size within this section on a
value of λ (rather than μ). Based on this normalization, table 5.7 summarizes the results from the previous section.

Name	Selection Probability p_i	Takeover Time τ^*
Proportionate	$\Phi(\vec{a}_i)/\sum_{j=1}^{\lambda}\Phi(\vec{a}_j)$	$(\lambda\ln\lambda-1)/c$ for $\Phi(\vec{a})=x^c$ $(\lambda\ln\lambda)/c$ for $\Phi(\vec{a})=\exp(xc)$
Linear Ranking	$(\eta^+ - 2\cdot(\eta^+-1)\frac{i-1}{\lambda-1})/\lambda$	$\mathrm{ld}\lambda+\mathrm{ld}(\ln\lambda)$ for $\eta^+=2$ $\ln(\lambda-1)/(\eta^+-1)$ for $1<\eta^+<2$
(μ,λ)-selection	$\begin{cases} 1/\mu & , \quad 1\le i\le\mu \\ 0 & , \quad \mu<i\le\lambda \end{cases}$	$\ln\lambda/\ln(\lambda/\mu)$
q-tournament	$((\lambda-i+1)^q-(\lambda-i)^q)/\lambda^q$	$(\ln\lambda+\ln(\ln\lambda))/\ln q$

Table 5.7. Overview of takeover times for different selection mechanisms.

One fundamental observation from this table is the strong difference
between proportional selection having a takeover time of order $\mathcal{O}(\lambda\cdot\ln\lambda)$
and rank-based methods with a general takeover time of order $\mathcal{O}(\ln\lambda)$,
i.e. *a factor of λ faster*. Additionally, rank-based methods allow for an
explicit control of selective pressure while proportional selection does
not. These two arguments, higher selective pressure and better control
of selective pressure, are emphasized by many researchers who argue for
rank-based selection methods in Evolutionary Algorithms.

Rank-based methods support control of selective pressure within the complete range between random walk ($\tau^* = \infty$) and complete dominance of the best ($\tau^* = 1$), but the different methods available occupy different regions within this wide range. For $\eta^+ \to 1$ (linear ranking), $\mu \to \lambda$ ((μ,λ)-selection), and $q \to 1$ (q-tournament), all rank-based methods discussed here turn into random walk. Linear ranking yields a high resolution of selective pressure in the range where q-tournament allows only a choice between $q = 1$ (corresponding to $\eta^+ = 1$) and $q = 2$ (corresponding to $\eta^+ = 2$). For larger values of q, tournament selection quickly pushes forward into regions well covered by the extreme selective pressure of (μ,λ)-selection. Complete dominance of the best is achieved either by using q-tournament with $q = \lambda \cdot \ln \lambda$ or, much simpler, by (1,λ)-selection. Consequently, a general ordering of selection mechanisms according to increasing selective pressure, especially when default values[14] of the control parameters are assumed, looks as follows:

(1) Proportional selection.

(2) Linear ranking.

(3) Tournament selection.

(4) (μ,λ)-selection.

With respect to the consequences of high selective pressure (i.e., the $\mathcal{O}(\ln \lambda)$ variants) in Genetic Algorithms, Goldberg and Deb draw the conclusion that mutation must become an operator responsible for restoration of missing building blocks. They expect, however, this search by mutation to work only in case of relatively simple objective functions rather than being useful in general [GD91]. This question is picked up again in the experimental section 5.2.

5.1.6 A Taxonomy of Selection Mechanisms

Efforts to characterize and analyze selection mechanisms are rare, but according to the importance of selection they are necessary and useful. This section presents a classification of selection mechanisms, thereby introducing a terminology which seems useful for a complete and consistent characterization and for encountering possibilities that have not been tested so far. The classification criteria are given here in the format of a number of definitions, following [BH91], and each definition is motivated by a short introduction.

First, the distinction between *static* and *dynamic* selection mechanisms relies on rank-dependent versus absolute fitness-dependent selection probabilities. In the case of static selection probabilities, these can be calculated in advance and remain constant forever, while in the case of dynamic selection they have to be reevaluated at each generation. The

[14]I.e., $\eta^+ = 1.1$, $q = 2$, and $\lambda/\mu \approx 7$.

static variant is therefore characterized by constant, time-independent selection probabilities while in the dynamic case at least one selection probability varies over time.

Definition 5.2 (Static Selection) *A selection mechanism* $s : I^\gamma \to I^\mu$ *is called* static: $\Leftrightarrow$

$$\forall i \in \{1, \dots, \gamma\} \ \forall t \geq 0 : \ p_s(\vec{a}_i(t)) = c_i$$

where the c_i are constants.

Definition 5.3 (Dynamic Selection)
A selection mechanism $s : I^\gamma \to I^\mu$ *is called* dynamic: $\Leftrightarrow$

$$\exists i \in \{1, \dots, \gamma\} \ \neg\forall t \geq 0 : \ p_s(\vec{a}_i(t)) = c_i$$

where the c_i are constants.

Note that for a selection mechanism to be dynamic, just a single time varying selection probability is sufficient, i.e. not all selection probabilities are required to vary. Completely rank-based methods such as linear ranking and tournament selection are representatives of static selection while proportional selection is a classical dynamic method.

Furthermore, the property of excluding some individuals from selection by assigning them selection probabilities of zero is an important characteristic of some selection mechanisms. Such methods are called *extinctive* in the following, in contrast to selection methods based on *preservation*, which guarantee nonzero selection probabilities for all individuals.

Definition 5.4 (Selection based on preservation)
A selection mechanism $s : I^\gamma \to I^\mu$ *is based on* preservation: $\Leftrightarrow$

$$\forall i \in \{1, \dots, \gamma\} \ \forall t \geq 0 : \ p_s(\vec{a}_i(t)) > 0 \quad .$$

Definition 5.5 (Extinctive Selection)
A selection mechanism $s : I^\gamma \to I^\mu$ *is called* extinctive: $\Leftrightarrow$

$$\exists i \in \{1, \dots, \gamma\} \ \forall t \geq 0 : \ p_s(\vec{a}_i(t)) = 0 \quad .$$

Practically, extinctiveness exclusively concerns the worst individuals of a population, as in (μ, λ)-selection. From a more principal point of view, however, one might permit arbitrary ranks to be excluded from selection, e.g. the best or intermediate individuals. This motivates the distinction of *left extinctiveness* (some of the best individuals are excluded from selection) and *right extinctiveness* (some of the worst individuals are not taken into account by selection) made in [BH91]:

Definition 5.6 (Left and right extinctive selection)
A selection mechanism $s : I^\gamma \to I^\mu$ is called

$$
\begin{aligned}
\text{left extinctive:} \quad &\Leftrightarrow \quad \exists j \in \{1, \ldots, \gamma - 1\} \\
&\qquad \forall t \geq 0 : i \leq j \Rightarrow p_s(\vec{a}_i(t)) = 0 \quad, \\
\text{right extinctive:} \quad &\Leftrightarrow \quad \exists j \in \{2, \ldots, \gamma\} \\
&\qquad \forall t \geq 0 : i \geq j \Rightarrow p_s(\vec{a}_i(t)) = 0 \quad.
\end{aligned}
\tag{5.29}
$$

(μ,λ)-selection is an obvious representative of right extinctive selection, assuming $\mu < \lambda$. Left extinctiveness has never been tested in Evolutionary Algorithms, although it may prove useful in some situations to prevent superindividuals from dominating the population.

Finally, an important characterization of selection mechanisms consists in the *elitist* feature, a method which guarantees a monotonously improving course of evolution. In Genetic Algorithms, the elitist selection was introduced by De Jong, who investigated an algorithm which included the best individual of population $P(t)$ into population $P(t+1)$ if it was not transcribed to $P(t+1)$ by selection (see [DeJ75], p. 102). In other words, the best performing individual contained in a population is not allowed to become worse. The following definition extends this notion of elitism to include more than just one individual.

Definition 5.7 (Elitist Selection) *A selection mechanism $s : I^\gamma \to I^\mu$ is called k-elitist:* $\Leftrightarrow$

$$
\exists k \in \{1, \ldots, \gamma\} \; \forall t \geq 0 \; \forall i \in \{1, \ldots, k\} : f(\vec{x}_i(t)) \leq f(\vec{x}_i(t-1)) \quad.
$$

If $k = 1$, s is called elitist.

Definition 5.8 (Pure Selection) *A selection mechanism $s : I^\gamma \to I^\mu$ is called* pure *iff there is no $k \in \{1, \ldots, \gamma\}$ which satisfies the k-elitist condition.*

Of course, $(\mu+\lambda)$-selection is the natural example of a μ-elitist selection method. Practically, the selection method of Evolutionary Programming (section 2.2.4) is also elitist. All other selection mechanisms discussed so far are pure methods.

According to the main characterization criteria static-dynamic and extinctive-preservative, the classification shown in table 5.8 is obtained.

Generalizations to complete the table are indicated, i.e. the formulation of (μ,λ)-proportional selection as an example of dynamic, extinctive methods and (μ,λ)-linear ranking as well as (μ,λ)-tournament selection as extinctive variants of linear ranking and q-tournament, respectively[15].

---

[15]Random walk is added to the table since (μ,λ)-selection can in a similar sense be interpreted as extinctive version of random walk.

	Static	Dynamic
Based on preservation	(random walk) linear ranking q-tournament	proportional
(Right) Extinctive	(μ,λ)-selection (μ,λ)-*linear ranking* (μ,λ)-*tournament*	(μ,λ)-*proportional*

Table 5.8. Classification of selection mechanisms.

Consequently, all extinctive selection mechanisms turn into their pre-servative analogues by setting $\mu = \lambda$, such that the extinctive variants are just generalizations of their preservative original. The formulation of extinctive methods in terms of selection probabilities is obvious:

- (μ,λ)-proportional selection:

$$p_i = \begin{cases} \Phi(\vec{a}_i)/\sum_{j=1}^{\mu} \Phi(\vec{a}_j) & , \quad 1 \leq i \leq \mu \\ 0 & , \quad \mu < i \leq \lambda \end{cases} \quad . \tag{5.30}$$

- (μ,λ)-linear ranking:

$$p_i = \begin{cases} (\eta^+ - 2 \cdot (\eta^+ - 1) \cdot \frac{i-1}{\mu-1})/\mu & , \quad 1 \leq i \leq \mu \\ 0 & , \quad \mu < i \leq \lambda \end{cases} \quad . \tag{5.31}$$

- (μ,λ)-tournament:

$$p_i = \begin{cases} ((\mu - i + 1)^q - (\mu - i)^q)/\mu^q & , \quad 1 \leq i \leq \mu \\ 0 & , \quad \mu < i \leq \lambda \end{cases} \quad . \tag{5.32}$$

The first two of these mechanisms were already introduced in [BH91], and empirical investigations yielded strong evidence that the key factor of extinctive selection methods is determined by the degree of extinct-iveness (i.e. the ratio λ/μ) rather than by the original methods' char-acteristics. Therefore, the empirical investigations of selection methods presented in the following section concentrate on (μ,λ)-selection as the basic representative of the class of extinctive selection mechanisms and on the standard preservative versions of linear ranking and tournament selection.

5.2 Experimental Investigation of Selection

Within this section, the effect of varying selective pressure in a Genetic Algorithm is studied experimentally on the set of test functions from chapter 3. In particular, linear ranking, tournament selection, and (μ,λ)-selection are compared for varying selective pressure, and the results are discussed with respect to the theoretical investigations of section 5.1. Except the selection mechanism, the Genetic Algorithm is identical to the variant used in chapter 4, i.e. $l_x = 30$, $p_m = 0.001$, $r_{\{0.6,2\}}$, $\lambda = 100$. The test plan provides to use $(\mu,100)$-selection with[16] $\mu \in \{1, 2, 5, 10, 20, 30, 40, 50, 60, 70, 80, 90, 95\}$, linear ranking with $\eta^+ \in \{1.1, 1.2, 1.3, 1.4, 1.5, 1.6, 1.7, 1.8, 1.9, 2.0\}$ and tournament selection with $q \in \{2, 3, 4, 5, 6, 7, 8, 9, 10\}$. Furthermore, results are averaged over 20 runs instead of one hundred in order to perform the experiments within a reasonable amount of computing time (altogether, 105300 single runs of the Genetic Algorithm were required to obtain the data, and each run consisted of at least $1.0 \cdot 10^5$ evaluations of the objective function).

Similar to table 4.3, the test plan in terms of the number of runs N, the total number of generations T, and the dimension n of the objective function is summarized in table 5.9.

The tables which summarize the numerical data obtained in these experiments are collected in appendix B. Within these tables B.1–B.3, the average final best objective function values $\bar{f}^i_{\min}(T)$ and their empirical standard deviations $V^i_{\min}(T)$ are collected ($i \in \{1, \ldots, 5\}$ denotes the objective function number). The general results, however, can be grasped more easily from figures 5.1–5.5, which show $\bar{f}^i_{\min}(T)$ as a function of μ, q, and η^+, respectively.

Function	N	T	n
f_1	20	1000	30
f_2	20	1000	30
f_3	20	1000	30
f_4	20	2000	30
f_5	20	1000	20

Table 5.9. Test plan for selection experiments.

Wherever possible (due to the range of values on the ordinate axis), the Genetic Algorithm's result as obtained in chapter 4[17] is indicated

---

[16] The reader should notice here that recombination has no effect for $\mu = 1$, since after selection the population consists of λ identical individuals.

[17] I.e., with proportional selection and scaling window size $\omega = 5$.

by a dotted horizontal line in these figures.

The experimental results divide the set of objective functions into two classes, consisting of f_1 and f_3 in the first class and f_2, f_4, and f_5 in the second class. In the first class, increasing selective pressure unambigously improves the result of the Genetic Algorithm, while in the second case the effect of stronger selective pressure is much less clear. Both classes are discussed separately in the following sections.

5.2.1   Clear Improvement of Average Solutions: f_1, f_3

Both for the sphere model f_1 and for Ackley's function f_3 the results improve constantly as the selective pressure is increased. From figure 5.1 and figure 5.2, in combination with table B.1–B.3, the following observations concerning both functions can be formulated:

(1) Linear ranking yields better results than proportional selection. The result for linear ranking with $\eta^+ = 2$ is within the same order of magnitude as the result for tournament selection with $q = 2$, this way confirming their identical selective pressure theoretically shown in section 5.1.3. Increasing η^+ from 1.1 to 2.0 nearly monotonically improves the performance.

(2) Tournament selection with growing values of q further improves the performance. For $q = 10$, the objective function value corresponds well with objective function values obtained by $(\mu,100)$-selection for $\mu \approx [16-20]$, thus reflecting the almost identical selective pressure of 10-tournament selection and $(\mu,100)$-selection with μ in the range indicated above (see tables 5.4 and 5.5 for a confirmation).

(3) Decreasing μ in case of $(\mu,100)$-selection steadily improves performance, except $\mu = 1$ for f_3. A variation of μ allows for covering the widest range of possible final performance, i.e. 17 orders of magnitude for f_1 and 10 orders of magnitude for f_3.

The empirical standard deviations presented in tables B.1–B.3 indicate the statistical significance of these results. A further, surprising result is given by the small importance of recombination as indicated by the small decrease of performance when switching from $(2,100)$-selection to $(1,100)$-selection. Apparently, the recombination operator is relatively unimportant in case of these two objective functions, although for the sphere model the building block hypothesis certainly holds (the optimal solution is a combination of good partial solutions, i.e., substrings which represent object variables close to zero).

While the behavior obtained by varying selective pressure on f_1 is predictable, the result for the multimodal function f_3 are rather surprising. A plausible explanation relies on the fact that this function offers a path which steadily leads down towards the global optimum but does not correspond to the direction of steepest descent.

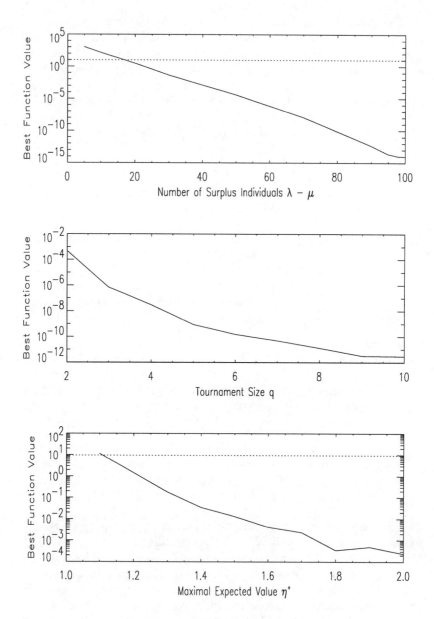

Fig. 5.1: The effect of varying selective pressure on objective function f_1. Upper graphic: $(\mu,100)$-selection with varying values of μ (expressed in terms of $\lambda - \mu$). Middle graphic: Tournament selection with varying values of q. Lower graphic: Linear Ranking with varying values of η^+. Function values are averaged over 20 runs and reflect the state of the search after $1 \cdot 10^5$ function evaluations. Reprinted by permission of IEEE Press from Th. Bäck: *Selective Pressure in Evolutionary Algorithms: A Characterization of Selection Mechanisms*, in *Proceedings of the First IEEE Conference on Evolutionary Computation*, volume I, p.61, fig. 2, copyright © 1994 IEEE Press.

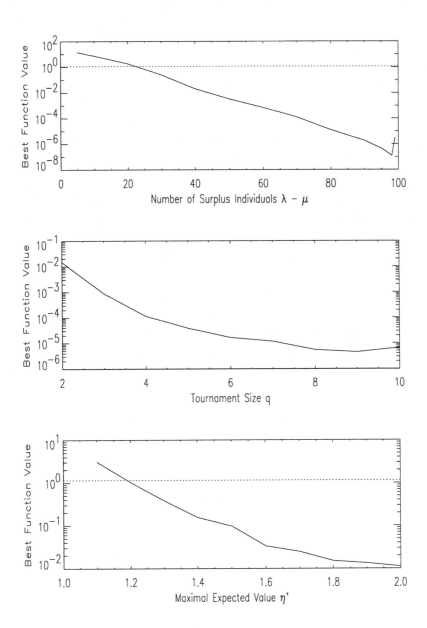

Fig. 5.2: The effect of varying selective pressure on objective function f_3. Upper graphic: $(\mu,100)$-selection with varying values of μ (expressed in terms of $\lambda - \mu$). Middle graphic: Tournament selection with varying values of q. Lower graphic: Linear Ranking with varying values of η^+. Function values are averaged over 20 runs and reflect the state of the search after $1 \cdot 10^5$ function evaluations.

If the algorithm would follow the latter path, it would converge suboptimally. Instead, it is able to probabilistically deviate from the gradient, thus missing the local optima located on the way downwards. Practically, these results confirm Ackley's function to be simpler than expected.

5.2.2   Ambiguous Results: f_2, f_4, f_5

For the test functions f_2 (step function), f_4 (Fletcher-Powell function), and f_5 (fractal function) the effect of varying selective pressure is less clear than for f_1 and f_3. Especially for f_2 and f_4 this observation is reflected by the large empirical standard deviations collected in appendix B. Consequently, as already pointed out in section 4.2, averaging the data is a more or less inappropriate method for performance evaluation, but the histogram technique used in that section would require an exceedingly large number of graphics to be applied here. Therefore, we restrict ourselves here on drawing the following conclusions from figures 5.3, 5.4, and 5.5:

(1) The performance differences between the selection methods are small (1–2 orders of magnitude), if compared with the performance differences which were obtained for f_1 and f_3.

(2) In comparison to proportional selection, the results show a statistically significant improvement by 1–2 orders of magnitude.

(3) On f_5, increasing selective pressure has a seemingly detrimental effect on the average best objective function value. Just for linear ranking with small values of η^+ the proportional selection result reported in section 4.2 is still improved, but according to the standard deviations reported in table B.3 the statistical significance is small. A conclusive explanation of the significantly bad results for high selective pressure (tournament and (μ,λ)-selection) is based on the assumption that the search quickly concentrates on suboptimal holes that cannot be left due to the low probability to hit a better hole by means of the mutation process. On the other hand, the suboptimal solution survives due to the combination of small mutation rate, high selective pressure, and recombination probability smaller than one, i.e., under these circumstances selection is "almost" elitist.

Table B.4 in appendix B provides some more information that may help to interpret the data, i.e. it summarizes the overall best objective function values obtained within the 20 experiments performed for each setting of selective pressure on f_2, f_4, and f_5. Comparing these values to the corresponding overall best results obtained by proportional selection as discussed in chapter 4, i.e. $f_{\min}^2(1000) = 6.0$, $f_{\min}^4(2000) = 1.032 \cdot 10^4$,

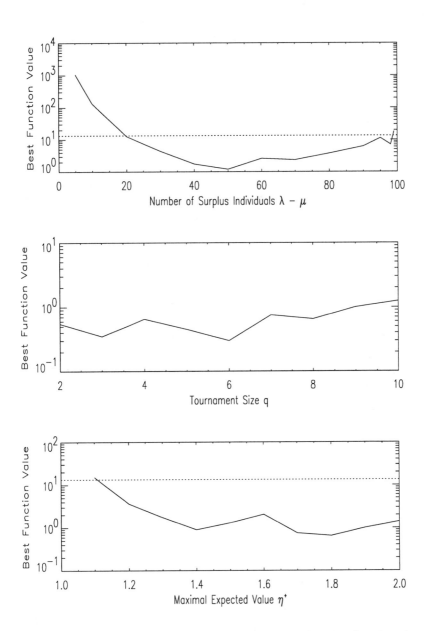

Fig. 5.3: The effect of varying selective pressure on objective function f_2. Upper graphic: $(\mu,100)$-selection with varying values of μ (expressed in terms of $\lambda - \mu$). Middle graphic: Tournament selection with varying values of q. Lower graphic: Linear Ranking with varying values of η^+. Function values are averaged over 20 runs and reflect the state of the search after $1 \cdot 10^5$ function evaluations.

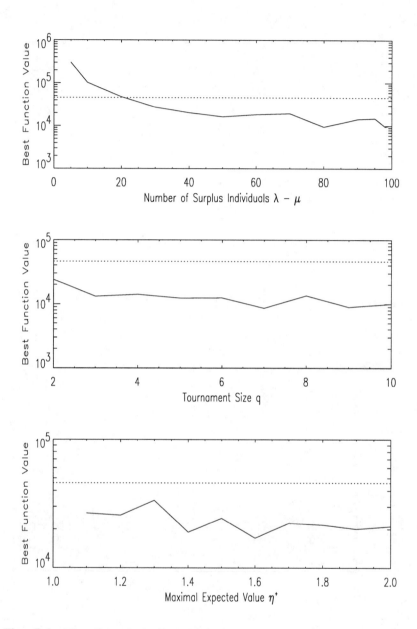

Fig. 5.4: The effect of varying selective pressure on objective function f_4. Upper graphic: $(\mu,100)$-selection with varying values of μ (expressed in terms of $\lambda - \mu$). Middle graphic: Tournament selection with varying values of q. Lower graphic: Linear Ranking with varying values of η^+. Function values are averaged over 20 runs and reflect the state of the search after $2 \cdot 10^5$ function evaluations.

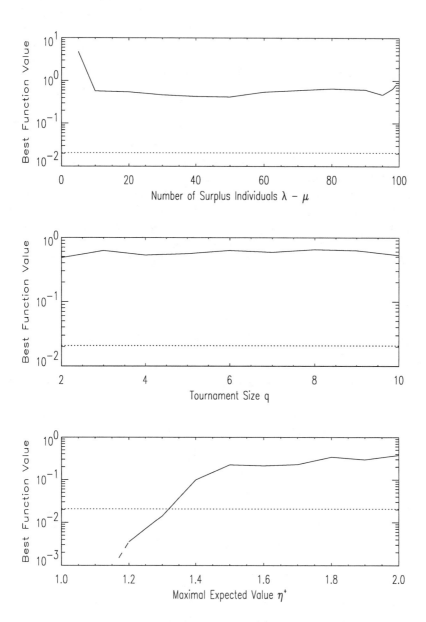

Fig. 5.5: The effect of varying selective pressure on objective function f_5. Upper graphic: $(\mu,100)$-selection with varying values of μ (expressed in terms of $\lambda - \mu$). Middle graphic: Tournament selection with varying values of q. Lower graphic: Linear Ranking with varying values of η^+. Function values are averaged over 20 runs and reflect the state of the search after $1 \cdot 10^5$ function evaluations.

and $f^5_{\min}(1000) = -6.808 \cdot 10^{-2}$, the effect of increasing selective pressure becomes clearer: Although the mean variation of results is still quite high, increasing selective pressure in case of the functions f_2 and f_4

- improves the average quality of results and

- improves the best solution found within a number of runs.

The latter property can well be identified in table B.4. For f_2, the optimal solution is identified at least once in nearly all experiments. On the Fletcher-Powell function f_4, solutions down to $1.248 \cdot 10^2$ ((20,100)-selection) are evolved[18]. For f_5, however, nearly all types of selective pressure led to the identification of a hole of negative objective function value in at least one of the 20 runs, thus indicating that the results on f_5 have low significance. In fact, one might argue well that as soon as the objective function values achieved by a non-elitist strategy reach the size of the fractal "noise," no meaningful conclusion can be drawn from the results.

5.2.3   A Note on Scaling

As already indicated in section 2.3.1 and 5.1.1, the effect of using a scaling method on selective pressure cannot be neglected. On the other hand, the proportional selection method in its unscaled version (i.e., setting $\Phi = f \circ \Upsilon$) is not applicable whenever negative objective function values are possible. Scaling methods help to overcome this problem, but, as clarified by Grefenstette and Baker, the schema theorem (theorem 11) no longer appropriately describes the allocation of trials to schemata when scaling is used [GB89]. The reason is identified in the fact that the schema theorem allocates trials on the basis of fitness rather than objective function values. By shifting emphasis on the ordering of schemata according to objective function values[19], Grefenstette and Baker clarified that the exponential growth property still holds for linearly scaled objective function values, but is usually violated by nonlinear scaling methods such as logarithmic or exponential scaling [GB89].

In terms of selective pressure, however, even linear scaling methods modify the behavior of a Genetic Algorithm. If we assume a minimization task, then even the smallest change of selection probabilities requires at least a scaling with respect to the actual generation, i.e., a scaling window $\omega = 0$ (c.f. section 5.1.1)[20]:

---

[18]This is, however, still a poor solution when compared to the desired function value of zero, but the intention is *not* to run the algorithm as long as necessary to achieve this quality. Instead, interest concentrates on comparing results after a certain, predefined number of evaluations.

[19]This way, a rank-based argument is introduced, essentially demonstrating that exponential growth of above-average schemata holds for any rank-based method.

[20]Remember our convention that $S_f = \sum_{j=1}^{\mu} f_j$.

$$p_i = \frac{c(t) - f_i}{\mu \cdot c(t) - S_f} \quad . \tag{5.33}$$

According to equation 2.81, $c(t) = \max\{f(\Upsilon(\vec{a}_j)) \mid \vec{a}_j \in P(t)\}$ denotes the worst objective function value in generation t. For a scaling reference point $c(t - w)$ from an older generation, selection probabilities

$$p_i' = \frac{c(t - w) - f_i}{\mu \cdot c(t - w) - S_f} \tag{5.34}$$

are obtained. The inequality

$$c(t - w) > c(t) \quad , \tag{5.35}$$

meaning that the worst individual at generation t performs better (in terms of objective function value) than the worst individual w generations before, is likely to hold for $w > 0$. Consequently, in analogy to the result (5.11), we obtain

$$\begin{aligned} p_i > p_i' &\iff f_i < \bar{f} \\ p_i < p_i' &\iff f_i > \bar{f} \quad , \end{aligned} \tag{5.36}$$

i.e., better than average individuals are likely to receive larger selection probabilities for $w > 0$ than for $w = 0$, at the cost of worse than average individuals. The magnitude of the effect should depend on the absolute difference $c(t-w)-c(t)$, which scales according to the objective function values and the setting of w.

For a practical confirmation of this result an additional experiment with proportional selection and $w \in \{0,5\}$ was performed to compare the default window size setting to a window size of zero. As before, following the test plan in table 5.9, the results presented in table 5.10 in terms of average final best objective function values and their standard deviations were obtained.

These results demonstrate the correctness of our prediction and support the suspicion formulated in section 5.1.1 that takeover times as calculated for proportional selection are larger than takeover times in realistic implementations where proportional selection is combined with scaling. It seems impossible, however, to derive a theoretical prediction of takeover time for such a combination, since already the derivation of theorem 15 required considerable assumptions [GD91]. Therefore, one has to be content with the qualitative argumentation presented above.

5.3 Summary

The predominating basic idea throughout this chapter postulates the possibility of characterizing the selective pressure of selection methods

ω	f_1		f_2	
	$\bar{f}^1_{\min}(1000)$	$V^1_{\min}(1000)$	$\bar{f}^2_{\min}(1000)$	$V^2_{\min}(1000)$
0	$8.541 \cdot 10^1$	$2.650 \cdot 10^1$	$8.405 \cdot 10^1$	$1.687 \cdot 10^1$
5	$1.067 \cdot 10^1$	4.476	$1.325 \cdot 10^1$	3.985
ω	f_3		f_4	
	$\bar{f}^3_{\min}(1000)$	$V^3_{\min}(1000)$	$\bar{f}^4_{\min}(1000)$	$V^4_{\min}(1000)$
0	1.608	$4.694 \cdot 10^{-1}$	$7.889 \cdot 10^4$	$2.318 \cdot 10^4$
5	1.055	$3.987 \cdot 10^{-1}$	$4.318 \cdot 10^4$	$2.393 \cdot 10^4$
ω	f_5			
	$\bar{f}^5_{\min}(1000)$	$V^5_{\min}(1000)$		
0	$3.108 \cdot 10^{-1}$	$1.345 \cdot 10^{-1}$		
5	$-6.209 \cdot 10^{-4}$	$4.598 \cdot 10^{-2}$		

Table 5.10. Average final best objective function values and their standard deviations for proportional selection with $\omega \in \{0, 5\}$ for objective functions f_1–f_5.

such as proportional selection, tournament selection, linear ranking, and (μ,λ)-selection by their takeover time (see definition 5.1) and selection probabilities. The analysis was initiated by Goldberg and Deb [GD91] and completed here to obtain results for all selection mechanisms mentioned above. This is summarized in the overview table 5.7.

It turned out that proportional selection is characterized by large takeover times of order $\mathcal{O}(\lambda \cdot \ln \lambda)$ in contrast to the other methods with takeover behavior of order $\mathcal{O}(\ln \lambda)$. The experiments presented in section 5.2 clearly confirm proportional selection to have the smallest selective pressure of all methods compared. Indeed, the selective pressure of unmodified proportional selection turned out never to be used in implementations due to the necessity of introducing scaling methods for negative objective function values and minimization tasks. In section 5.2.3 the effect of linear scaling to increase selective pressure of proportional selection was demonstrated and qualitatively confirmed by an analysis.

A further comparison of the $\mathcal{O}(\ln \lambda)$ methods, namely linear ranking, tournament selection, and (μ,λ)-selection, led to the conclusion that — from a theoretical point of view, assuming standard parameter settings — selective pressure of these mechanisms increases in the order linear ranking / tournament selection / (μ,λ)-selection. This theoretical expectation was confirmed by the experiments on objective functions f_1 and f_3 presented in section 5.2.1.

In case of the more complicated surfaces f_2, f_4, and f_5 the results presented in section 5.2.2 are characterized by a wide range of quality variation, but both the average quality and the best result obtained within all runs turned out to improve in comparison to proportional selection when stronger selection is used. No unambigiously "best" selective pressure, however, could be identified in these cases.

Rank-based methods in contrast to proportional selection clearly demonstrated that they allow for an effective control of selective pressure by just *one* control parameter (η^+, q, and μ, respectively) with predictable, direct effects on selective pressure. In case of proportional selection no such control parameter is provided except those which are introduced by a scaling method (see equations (2.74)–(2.77) in section 2.3.1). But the effect of varying the scaling method's parameter(s) on selective pressure is in general unpredictable. Introducing more than one control parameter for selective pressure seems also unreasonable since parameterization possibilities of the algorithm should be reduced as far as possible in order to maintain its robustness and applicability even for inexperienced users[21].

In general, we conclude that selective pressure is confirmed to provide a major control mechanism for the search process, with strong evidence to recommend rank-based selection methods rather than the uncontrollable proportional selection. The helpful effect of high selective pressure becomes even more interesting when taking into account that new genotypic diversity is generated by mutation at a very low rate ($p_m = 0.001$) and that as a consequence of selective pressure the effect of crossover is rather small. This leads to the consideration whether a combined increase of selective pressure *and* mutation rate may further enhance the search process and how the role of crossover may be clarified. The next chapter aims at a deeper understanding of the mutation operator in Genetic Algorithms, both for pseudoboolean functions and for encoded parameter optimization applications.

---

[21] *Boltzmann tournament selection*, introduced to Genetic Algorithms by Goldberg [Gol90], provides an example of a selection method controlled by several parameters. A deeper analysis or practical application is not performed here due to several reasons, including a missing guideline for parameter settings and missing dissemination and acceptance of the method. The basic idea is to transform the probabilistic acceptance rule of *Simulated Annealing* (see e.g. [vLA87]), an optimization method based on thermodynamical models of cooling and crystallization in a state of lowest energy. The original method operates by creating one "offspring" solution in the vicinity of the actual "parent," accepting improvements in any case and worsenings according to an exponentially decreasing function of "temperature." Transferring the method to populations in Genetic Algorithms, Goldberg does not clarify how to decrease the temperature parameter (the cooling schedule). Furthermore, he gives no hint after how many iterations of the algorithm a temperature decrease should take place. Due to the method's complexity, a takeover time analysis seems hopeless, but Mahfoud succeeded in calculating the selection probabilities [Mah91].

*Not surprisingly, there is much confusion about
the role of mutation in genetics (both natural and artificial).
Perhaps it is the result of too many B movies detailing the exploits
of mutant eggplants that consume mass quantities of Tokyo or Chicago,
but whatever the cause of the confusion, we find that mutation plays
a decidedly secondary role in the operation of genetic algorithms.*
David E. Goldberg (Genetic Algorithms in Search,
Optimization, and Machine Learning; Addison-Wesley 1989, p. 14).

In the beginning was the word and by mutations came the gene.
[WORD–WORE–GORE–GONE–GENE].
Michael A. Arbib (in C. H. Waddington, editor:
Towards a Theoretical Biology, Vol. 2; Edinburgh University Press 1969, p. 323).

6

Mutation

In section 1.1.3 it was clarified that a variety of different, more or less
drastic changes of the genome are summarized under the term *mutation*
by geneticists and evolutionary biologists. Several mutation events are
within the bounds of possibility, ranging from single base pair changes
to genomic mutations. The phenotypic effect of genotypic mutations,
however, can hardly be predicted from knowledge about the genotypic
change.

In general, advantageous mutations have a relatively small effect
on the phenotype[1], i.e., their expression does not deviate very much
(in phenotype space) from the expression of the unmutated genotype
([Fut90], p. 85). More drastic phenotypic changes are usually lethal or
become extinct due to a reduced capability of reproduction. The discussion, to which extent evolution based on phenotypic macro-mutations
in the sense of *"hopeful monsters"* is important to facilitate the process of speciation, is still ongoing[2] (such macromutations have been

---

[1] At least in the observable, well-adapted situation. In a period of adaptation into
a novel adaptive zone, this might be quite different.

[2] Evolution by macro-mutations and the concept of *punctuated equilibria* [EG72]
must not be confused. The latter theory tries to explain gaps in the fossile record by
the assumption that rapid phenotypic changes during a speciation period alternate
with relatively long periods of stasis, but it is not based on the occurrence of macro-
mutations (see [Fut90], pp. 454–460). In contrast to punctuated equilibria, classical
gradualism (the Darwinian point of view) assumes evolution to proceed by slow
(gradual) but steady changes which are not accelerated during speciation. Both
points of view are discussed e.g. in [Gou82] (slightly biased). Most realistic, however,

observed and classified for the fruitfly *Drosophila melangonaster*, see [Got89], p. 286). Actually, only a few data sets are available to assess the phylogenetic significance of macro-mutations completely, but small phenotypical effects of mutation are clearly observed to be predominant. This is the main argument justifying the use of normally distributed mutations with expectation zero in Evolutionary Programming and Evolution Strategies. It reflects the emphasis of both algorithms on modeling phenotypic rather than genotypic change.

The model of mutation is quite different in Genetic Algorithms, where bit reversal events (see section 2.3.2) corresponding with single base pair mutations in biological reality implement a model of evolution on the basis of genotypic changes. As observed in nature, the mutation rate used in Genetic Algorithms is very small (cf. section 2.3.2). In contrast to the biological model, it is neither variable by external influences nor controlled (at least partially) by the genotype itself (cf. section 1.1.3).

Holland defined the role of mutation in Genetic Algorithms to be a secondary one, of little importance in comparison to crossover (see [Hol75], p. 111):

> *Summing up: Mutation is a "background" operator, assuring that the crossover operator has a full range of alleles so that the adaptive plan is not trapped on local optima.*

Referring to Holland's work, most Genetic Algorithms implemented and applied since that time apply the mutation operator with a constant, small mutation rate in the range $[0.001, 0.01]$ (see section 2.3.2). Researchers often overlooked a suggestion also presented by Holland to use a time-dependent, deterministic mutation rate schedule which reduces the mutation rate towards zero ([Hol75], pp. 121–123). According to Holland, this might be useful in case of application tasks, but only very few attempts to vary the mutation rate over time are reported in literature: Both Davis and Fogarty observed a remarkable improvement of performance by varying the mutation rate over time. Davis developed a general deterministic heuristic to adapt operator application probabilities based on the observed performance of offspring[3] [Dav89]. Fogarty used several deterministic, decreasing schedules for the mutation rate [Fog89]. Schaffer et al. performed a computationally costly empirical study about the interrelation between population size, individual length, and mutation rate, and arrived at an empirical expression of the form

---

seems a neo-Darwinian combination of these theories: Fundamental changes are fast, but morphological changes are not restricted to speciation processes (see [Fut90], p. 456).

The observation of phenomena in the behavior of Evolutionary Algorithms which admit an interpretation as punctuated equilibria was reported by several researchers, e.g. see [Sch88, CMR91a]. An attempt towards a theoretical explanation in case of Genetic Algorithms is reported in [VL91].

[3]This causes a credit assignment problem, because in principle one must also reward an operator that set the stage for this production, and so on.

$p_m \approx 1.75/(\mu\sqrt{l})$ by curve fitting of their experimental data [SCED89]. This expression, though not being time-dependent, seems to confirm the result obtained theoretically by Hesser and Männer, who arrived at a general expression of the form

$$p_m(t) \;=\; \sqrt{\frac{c_1}{c_2}} \cdot \frac{\exp(-c_3 t/2)}{\mu\sqrt{l}} \;, \qquad (6.1)$$

where the constants c_1, c_2, and c_3 are estimated from heuristic arguments [HM91, HM92].

Within this chapter, the usefulness of a time-varying mutation rate for Genetic Algorithms is proven for some simple objective functions. The underlying algorithm is as simple as possible in order to facilitate mathematical analysis and is presented in section 6.1. The investigation of three simple objective functions yields some insight into the principal differences between unimodal and multimodal pseudoboolean optimization problems as well as standard binary code versus Gray code for parameter optimization tasks. The results are useful for formulating some general rules for the application of Genetic Algorithms and help to explain some of the observed behaviors they exhibit in parameter optimization applications.

6.1 Simplified Genetic Algorithms

The simplest algorithm to start with is called a (1+1)-GA in the following. As the terminology suggests, the algorithm constitutes a kind of discrete analogy to the (1+1)–ES (see section 2.1.7). The algorithmic formulation of the (1+1)-GA is given below:

Algorithm 9 ((1+1)-Genetic Algorithm)

> $t := 0$;
> *initialize* $P(0) := \{\vec{a}(0)\} \in I$ **where** $I = \{0, 1\}^l$;
> *evaluate* $P(0):$ $\{\Phi(\vec{a}(0))\}$ **where** $\Phi = f$;
> **while** $(\iota(P(t)) \neq$ **true**) **do**
> > *mutate:* $\vec{a}'(t) := m_{\{p_m\}}(\vec{a}(t))$;
> > *evaluate:* $P'(t) := \{\vec{a}'(t)\} :$
> > > $\{\Phi(\vec{a}'(t))\}$ **where** $\Phi = f$;
> > *select:* $P(t+1) := s_{(1+1)}(P(t) \cup P'(t))$;
> > $t := t + 1$;
>
> **od**

Using the standard notation for Evolutionary Algorithms, the (1+1)-GA is defined by the components $I = I\!B^l$, $\Phi = f$, $\Omega = \{m_{\{p_m\}} : I \to I\}$, $\Psi = s_{(1+1)} \circ m_{\{p_m\}}$, $\iota : I \to \{\text{true}, \text{false}\}$ as usual, and $\mu = \lambda = 1$. This algorithm is the canonical simplification of a Genetic Algorithm to match the general idea of an (1+1)-EA (one parent creates one offspring by mutation; the better one survives).

In contrast to the (1+1)-ES, however, algorithm 9 lacks any rule comparable to the 1/5-success rule for updating the mutation probability during the search, but it searches with a constant mutation probability. It is by no means clear whether a general modification rule is recommendable in the discrete case or whether modifying p_m is useful at all (except the indications gained from experimental investigations).

To shed some light on this question, algorithm 9 is formalized here as a finite Markov chain (see definition 2.7) and analyzed in detail for a simple unimodal pseudoboolean function. This method collects all information about the optimization problem and the structure of the (1+1)-GA in the transition matrix according to the following construction:

(1) In the most general case, each state z_i of the chain corresponds to exactly one bit string $\vec{a} \in \mathbb{B}^l$ and the chain has $k = 2^l$ states. We assume a maximization task in the following and identify states uniquely by their index $i \in \{0, \ldots, k-1\}$, i being the integer value represented by the bit string which belongs to state z_i. Without loss of generality state 0 is assumed to represent the global optimum. p_{ij} denotes the mutation-based transition probability from state number i to state number j. Furthermore, states are assumed to be ordered by fitness values f_i of the corresponding bit strings, such that $f_0 > f_1 > \ldots > f_{k-1}$.

(2) Because the elitist selection mechanism does not allow for a worsening of quality, transitions into states of higher index than the actual one are not allowed:

$$ i < j \;\Rightarrow\; p_{ij} = 0 \quad . \tag{6.2} $$

(3) Whenever $i > j$, an improvement is still possible for $p_m \in (0, 1)$:

$$ i > j \;\Rightarrow\; p_{ij} > 0 \quad . \tag{6.3} $$

(4) The remaining probability describes stagnation of the process in a state i:

$$ p_{ii} \;=\; 1 - \sum_{j<i} p_{ij} \quad . \tag{6.4} $$

Following this construction, the globally optimal bit string(s) is(are) described by the *absorbing* state 0 ($p_{00} = 1$) and the other states $T = \{1, 2, \ldots, k-1\}$ form a *transient* class of states (i.e. a class of states that may be left by a sequence of transitions; see e.g. [Goo88], p. 154). Moreover, the Markov chain itself is absorbing, since every state is either absorbing or transient. Therefore, starting in a transient state, the process is guaranteed to reach an absorbing state after a finite number of steps ([Goo88], p. 158). In other words: Assuring a monotonic course of evolution (existence of an absorbing state) and reachability (the remaining states form a transient class) yields the result of global convergence with probability one "for free" by well-known Markov chain results[4] (cf. theorem 13 and 14).

Furthermore, according to this construction method the transition matrix $\mathbf{P}$ is already in the block form

$$\mathbf{P} = \begin{pmatrix} \mathbf{I} & \mathbf{0} \\ \mathbf{R} & \mathbf{Q} \end{pmatrix} , \qquad (6.5)$$

where $\mathbf{I}$ is a quadratic unit matrix describing the absorbing state(s) (here, $\mathbf{I} = 1$), $\mathbf{R}$ describes movement from transient to absorbing states, and $\mathbf{Q}$ describes the movement among transient states. Then, assuming the process starts in state i, the expected number of steps $E_i(t)$ until an absorbing state (representing the global optimum) is reached can in principle be calculated according to theorem 20 (see e.g. [Goo88], pp. 161–162).

Theorem 20 *Let t be the number of steps taken until an absorbing state is reached. Then $t < \infty$ and*

$$E_i(t) = \sum_{j \in T} n_{ij} , \qquad (6.6)$$

where $\mathbf{N} = (n_{ij}) = (\mathbf{I} - \mathbf{Q})^{-1}$.

The theorem provides a real aid, but analytical solutions for $E_i(t)$ are in practical cases often excluded due to the matrix inversion involved. Numerical evaluations are possible, however, and will be used in the following to investigate a bit counting problem.

6.1.1   The Counting Ones Problem

We focus on the "One Max" ([Ack87], pp. 83–87) or "counting ones" problem $f : \mathbb{B}^l \to \{0, \ldots, l\}$:

$$f(\vec{a}) = \sum_{i=1}^{l} a_i , \qquad (6.7)$$

which is unimodal and an easy problem for Genetic Algorithms to solve, because it supports the building block hypothesis well [Sys89]. Due to its

---

[4] Moreover, a canonical Genetic Algorithm which does not keep track of the best solution found over time was recently shown by Rudolph to be *not* globally optimal convergent since the Markov chain is *ergodic* under such circumstances (there exists a unique limit distribution for the state of the chain with nonzero probability to be in any state at any time) [Rud94]. Probably, just this difference between absorbing and ergodic Markov chains provides the mathematical key for distinguishing between optimization (absorbing) and adaptation (ergodic). This point of view coincides well with the answer given by De Jong [DeJ93] to the question for this difference he raised before [DeJ92].

simplicity the problem promises to be a good candidate for an analysis, based on the calculation of several probability quantities according to definition 6.1.

Definition 6.1 *Assuming a mutation operator $m_{\{p_m\}}$ and an actual bit string $\vec{a}$, the following probabilities are defined with respect to the objective function (6.7):*

$$
\begin{aligned}
p_{\vec{a}}^+ &= \mathcal{P}\{f(m_{\{p_m\}}(\vec{a})) > f(\vec{a})\} && \text{Improvement probability} \\
p_{\vec{a}}^+(k) &= \mathcal{P}\{f(m_{\{p_m\}}(\vec{a})) = f(\vec{a}) + k\} && \text{k-step improvement prob.} \\
& && (0 \le k \le l - f(\vec{a})) \\
p_{\vec{a}}^0 &= \mathcal{P}\{f(m_{\{p_m\}}(\vec{a})) = f(\vec{a})\} && \text{Stagnation prob.} \qquad (6.8) \\
p_{\vec{a}}^-(k) &= \mathcal{P}\{f(m_{\{p_m\}}(\vec{a})) = f(\vec{a}) - k\} && \text{k-step failure prob.} \\
& && (0 \le k \le f(\vec{a})) \\
p_{\vec{a}}^- &= \mathcal{P}\{f(m_{\{p_m\}}(\vec{a})) < f(\vec{a})\} && \text{Failure prob.}
\end{aligned}
$$

In accordance with section 2.1.7, the term success probability *is used to denote* $p_{\vec{a}}^+ + p_{\vec{a}}^0 = \mathcal{P}\{f(m_{\{p_m\}}(\vec{a})) \ge f(\vec{a})\}$.

The relations $p_{\vec{a}}^+(0) = p_{\vec{a}}^-(0) = p_{\vec{a}}^0$, $p_{\vec{a}}^+ = \sum_{k=1}^{l-f(\vec{a})} p_{\vec{a}}^+(k)$, $p_{\vec{a}}^- = \sum_{k=1}^{f(\vec{a})} p_{\vec{a}}^-(k)$, and $p_{\vec{a}}^+ + p_{\vec{a}}^- + p_{\vec{a}}^0 = 1$ are required to hold for these probabilities. If $p_{\vec{a}}^- := 0$ as for an elitist selection mechanism, $p_{\vec{a}}^0 = 1 - p_{\vec{a}}^+$ is an immediate consequence.

Since $f(\vec{a})$ provides sufficient information for a calculation of transition probabilities, the counting ones problem allows for a remarkable reduction of the number of states from 2^l to $l + 1$ by means of the construction

$$
S_i = \{\vec{a} \in I\!B^l \mid f(\vec{a}) = l - i\} \quad , \tag{6.9}
$$

where S_i is the set of strings represented by state z_i (these sets form the equivalence classes of the equivalence relation induced on $I\!B^l$ by setting $\vec{a}_i R \vec{a}_j \Leftrightarrow f(\vec{a}_i) = f(\vec{a}_j)$). It is just this reduction of the number of states which makes the problem manageable.

The k-step improvement probabilities correspond with the transition probabilities they are sought for: $p_{ij} = p_{\vec{a}}^+(i - j)$ where $f(\vec{a}) = l - i$, $i > j$.

The next step involves calculation of the k-step improvement probabilities. Surprisingly, they turn out to be obtainable from the improvement probabilities in a simpler way than calculating them directly. The result is summarized in theorem 21 [Bäc92b]:

Theorem 21 *Let $\vec{a} \in I\!B^l$ and $f_a := f(\vec{a})$. Let p denote the mutation probability and $q = 1 - p$. Then:*

$$
p_{\bar{a}}^{+} = \sum_{i=0}^{f_a} \binom{f_a}{i} p^i q^{f_a-i} \cdot \sum_{j=i+1}^{l-f_a} \binom{l-f_a}{j} p^j q^{l-f_a-j} \quad ,
$$

$$
p_{\bar{a}}^{-} = \sum_{i=0}^{l-f_a} \binom{l-f_a}{i} p^i q^{l-f_a-i} \cdot \sum_{j=i+1}^{f_a} \binom{f_a}{j} p^j q^{f_a-j} \quad , \tag{6.10}
$$

$$
p_{\bar{a}}^{0} = \sum_{i=0}^{f_a} \binom{f_a}{i} \binom{l-f_a}{i} p^{2i} q^{l-2i} \quad .
$$

Proof: A proof for $p_{\bar{a}}^{+}$ is given by distinguishing the following two cases:

(1) None of the f_a one-bits in $\bar{a}$ mutates (probability q^{f_a}). Then, at least one zero-bit up to all $l - f_a$ zero-bits must undergo mutation in order to increase the number of ones, i.e. there are between $j = 1$ and $j = l - f_a$ mutations of zero-bits. The choice, which of the bits is mutated, is arbitrary, such that $\binom{l-f_a}{j}$ choices exist to mutate j bits (probability p^j) and to leave the remaining $l - f_a - j$ bits unmutated (probability q^{l-f_a-j}). Combining this, the first case result in an improvement probability

$$
p_1^{+} = q^{f_a} \cdot \sum_{j=1}^{l-f_a} \binom{l-f_a}{j} p^j q^{l-f_a-j} \quad .
$$

(2) Between $i = 1$ and $i = f_a$ one-bits are mutated to zero-bits. Then, in order to increase the number of ones in spite of this initial loss, at least $j = i+1$ up to $j = l - f_a$ zero-bits must be mutated. Part (1) of the proof gives us the probability

$$
\sum_{j=i+1}^{l-f_a} \binom{l-f_a}{j} p^j q^{l-f_a-j}
$$

for the mutation of j zero-bits. This has to be multiplied by the probability of mutating i one-bits, summing over all values of i:

$$
p_2^{+} = \sum_{i=1}^{f_a} \left[\binom{f_a}{i} p^i q^{f_a-i} \cdot \left(\sum_{j=i+1}^{l-f_a} \binom{l-f_a}{j} p^j q^{l-f_a-j} \right) \right] \quad .
$$

For $i = 0$, the expression in the rectangular brackets reduces to p_1^{+}. Therefore, $p_{\bar{a}}^{+} = p_1^{+} + p_2^{+}$ is obtained by simply extending the index range to $i = 0, \ldots, f_a$, which completes the proof. The expression for $p_{\bar{a}}^{-}$ is derived by an analogous calculation (just exchanging zeroes and ones, i.e. $l - f_a$ and f_a).

Furthermore, stagnation can be incorporated into both expressions for $p_{\bar{a}}^+$ and $p_{\bar{a}}^-$ by starting the inner sum at $j = i$ instead of $j = i + 1$, indicating that at least the same number of zeroes and ones must be mutated. Taking *only* the summand for $j = i$ in the inner sum yields the expression for $p_{\bar{a}}^0$.

As a final check of these results, we demonstrate that the probabilities $p_{\bar{a}}^+$, $p_{\bar{a}}^-$, and $p_{\bar{a}}^0$ sum to unity. To simplify notation, the abbreviations $c_i = \binom{l-f_a}{i} p^i q^{l-f_a-i}$ and $d_j = \binom{f_a}{j} p^j q^{f_a-j}$ are used, i.e. $p_{\bar{a}}^+ = \sum_{i=0}^{f_a} d_i \sum_{j=i+1}^{l-f_a} c_j$, $p_{\bar{a}}^- + p_{\bar{a}}^0 = \sum_{i=0}^{l-f_a} c_i \sum_{j=i}^{f_a} d_j$. An explicit notation of the sum and reordering of terms yields:

$$
\begin{aligned}
(p_{\bar{a}}^- + p_{\bar{a}}^0) + p_{\bar{a}}^+ \;=\; & c_0 \cdot (d_0 + d_1 + d_2 + \ldots + d_{f_a}) \\
+\; & c_1 \cdot (d_1 + d_2 + \ldots + d_{f_a}) \\
+\; & c_2 \cdot (d_2 + \ldots + d_{f_a}) \\
& \;\;\vdots \\
+\; & c_{f_a} \cdot d_{f_a} \\
+\; & d_0 \cdot (c_1 + c_2 + \ldots + c_{f_a} + \ldots + c_{l-f_a}) \qquad (6.11) \\
+\; & d_1 \cdot (c_2 + \ldots + c_{f_a} + \ldots + c_{l-f_a}) \\
& \;\;\vdots \\
+\; & d_f \cdot (c_{f_a+1} + \ldots + c_{l-f_a}) \\
=\; & \sum_{i=0}^{l-f_a} c_i \sum_{j=0}^{f_a} d_j \;\;.
\end{aligned}
$$

As $\sum_{j=0}^{f_a} \binom{f_a}{j} p^j q^{f_a-j} = 1$ and $\sum_{i=0}^{l-f_a} \binom{l-f_a}{i} p^i q^{l-f_a-i} = 1$, the proof is completed.   Q.E.D.

By an immediate consequence of the proof of theorem 21, the k-step probabilities result from taking into account *only* the summand for $j = i + k$ in the inner sum of the expressions for the improvement and failure probabilities:

$$
\begin{aligned}
0 \le k \le l - f_a \;:\quad p_{\bar{a}}^+(k) &= \sum_{i=0}^{f_a} \binom{f_a}{i}\binom{l-f_a}{i+k} p^{2i+k} q^{l-2i-k} \;\;, \\
& \hspace{4cm} (6.12) \\
0 \le k \le f_a \;\;\;\;\;:\quad p_{\bar{a}}^-(k) &= \sum_{i=0}^{l-f_a} \binom{l-f_a}{i}\binom{f_a}{i+k} p^{2i+k} q^{l-2i-k} \;\;.
\end{aligned}
$$

Though all formalism is provided now to evaluate expression (6.6), this is postponed here for a while for two reasons: First, it is instructive to compare the behavior of success probabilities with the corresponding $(1+1)$–ES results. Second, we actually do not know which mutation rate p is the most appropriate choice for the algorithm (besides the empirical indications described in section 2.3.2).

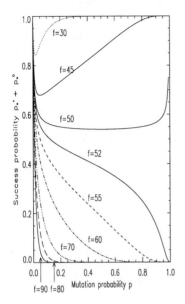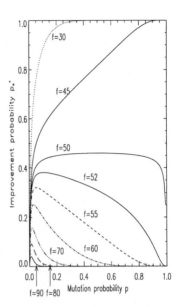

Fig. 6.1: Left: Success probabilities $p_{\tilde{a}}^{+} + p_{\tilde{a}}^{0}$ for varying mutation rate p, different values of $f_a \in \{30, 45, 50, 52, 55, 60, 70, 80, 90\}$, and $l = 100$. Right: The corresponding curves for improvement probabilities $p_{\tilde{a}}^{+}$.

In figure 6.1 it is shown how the success probability $p_{\tilde{a}}^{+} + p_{\tilde{a}}^{0}$ (left part) and the improvement probability $p_{\tilde{a}}^{+}$ (right part) depend on the mutation rate p for different values of f_a (i.e., distance to the optimum) and $l = 100$. Since a (1+1)-algorithm interprets offspring with a fitness value equal to the parents' fitness as a success, the left graphic provides an appropriate description of the dependency. For $f_a > 50$, all curves in the left figure behave similarly, attaining their maximum for $p \to 0$ and quickly decreasing as p increases. This behavior is well in correspondence with the lower part of figure 2.4 for the (1+1)–ES. In both cases — the discrete and the continuous one — success probabilities are maximized as the "step size" — and, consequently, the convergence velocity — are vanishing.

The improvement probability curves are characterized for $f_a > 50$ by clear maxima occurring for small values of p. The difference between success (including stagnation) and improvement (excluding stagnation) plays a major role in the analysis of the discrete algorithm while it is unimportant in the continuous case[5].

---

[5]The reason is very fundamental: For a continuous random variable X, $\mathcal{P}\{X = x\} = 0 \; \forall x \in \mathbb{R}$ since $\mathcal{P}$ denotes a probability density function.

These curves indicate that for a maximization of improvement probabilities during a run the optimal mutation rate p^* strongly depends
on the distance to the optimum, quickly decreasing as the optimum is
approached. However, the argument that in order to obtain an optimal
mutation rate schedule improvement probabilities

$$p_{\bar{a}}^+ \;=\; \sum_{k=1}^{l-f_a} p_{\bar{a}}^+(k) \tag{6.13}$$

have to be maximized is only partially correct. Indeed, for the unimodal
counting ones problem it is more appropriate to maximize the expected
local convergence velocity

$$\varphi_{(1+1)} \;=\; \sum_{k=0}^{l-f_a} k \cdot p_{\bar{a}}^+(k) \quad , \tag{6.14}$$

which weights improvements according to their magnitude. Equation
(6.13) incorporates all possible improvements equally, and maximizing
its value means to maximize the chance of an improvement regardless
of the resulting gain in fitness. In case of equation (6.14), just the expected fitness gain is maximized, which is certainly the best choice for a
unimodal objective function. For multimodal objective functions it may
be interesting to utilize mutation rate schedules based on maximizing
the improvement probability rather than convergence velocity.

The left part of figure 6.2 shows the course of $\varphi_{(1+1)}$ for $l = 100$ and
different values $f_a \in \{50, 52, 55, 60, 70, 80, 90\}$ over the mutation rate p.
Similar to the improvement probability curves (figure 6.1, right), optimal
mutation probability and convergence velocity are quickly decreasing as
the optimum is approached.

The optimal mutation probability schedule is shown in the right part
of figure 6.2 (dashed curve), obtained by numerical methods for values
$f_a \in \{50, \ldots, 99\}$. Though the analytical determination of the derivative
$d\varphi_{(1+1)}(l, f_a, p)/dp$ is simple, the resulting equation

$$\left. \frac{d\varphi_{(1+1)}(l, f_a, p)}{dp} \right|_{p=p^*} \;=\; 0 \tag{6.15}$$

cannot be solved for p^*. Finding an analytically useful approximation
of $p_{\bar{a}}^+(k)$ is also a hard problem which could not be solved successfully.
According to the hyperbolic shape of the curve and the special values
$p^*(l/2) = 1/2$ and $p^*(l-1) = 1/l$, however, the approximation

$$p^*(f_a) \;\approx\; \frac{1}{2(f_a + 1) - l} \tag{6.16}$$

turned out to be a reasonable choice (see also [Bäc92b]). The corresponding curve is also shown in the right part of figure 6.2 (dotted curve). Furthermore, the graphic shows the result (solid curve) which is obtained by

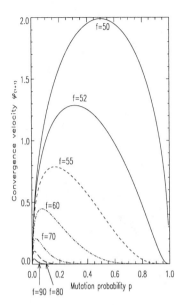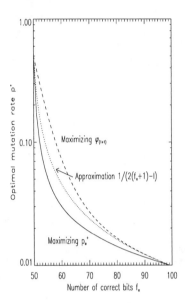

Fig. 6.2: Left: Convergence velocity $\varphi_{(1+1)}$ for varying mutation rate p, different values of $f_a \in \{50, 52, 55, 60, 70, 80, 90\}$, and $l = 100$. Right: The dependence of the optimal mutation rate p^* on the number f_a of already correct bits, where p^* is obtained by maximizing convergence velocity $\varphi_{(1+1)}$ (dashed curve) respectively by maximizing improvement probability $p_{\vec{a}}^+$ (normal curve). The dotted curve represents the approximation used in the text.

maximizing the improvement probability (equation (6.13)) rather than the convergence velocity. The corresponding mutation probabilities are clearly smaller than those for equation (6.14) and reflect the missing emphasis on the magnitude of improvements.

Independently from these investigations, Mühlenbein addressed the same question for the optimal mutation rate in case of the counting ones problem [Müh92]. His approach, however, is based on an *approximation* of the improvement probability under the assumption that the f_a ones are not changing back to zeroes:

$$p_{\vec{a}}^+ \approx (1-p)^{f_a} \cdot \left(1 - (1-p)^{l-f_a}\right) \quad , \tag{6.17}$$

where the first term denotes the probability to leave f_a ones unchanged and the second term denotes the probability to mutate at least one zero bit[6]. Expression (6.17) is easy to maximize, which yields

---

[6]This approximation was already derived as the first part of the proof of theorem 21, i.e., p_1^+ in that proof, as can be seen by remembering the identity $\sum_{j=0}^{l-f_a} \binom{l-f_a}{j} p^j q^{l-f_a-j} = 1$.

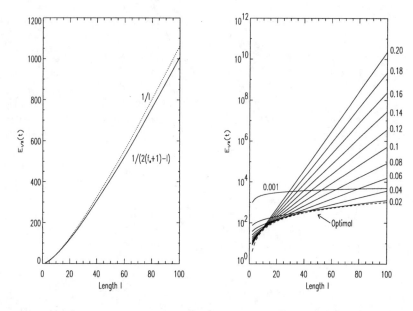

Fig. 6.3: Left: The expected time to absorption $E_{l/2}(t)$ for bit string lengths $l \in \{2, \ldots, 100\}$, calculated on the basis of the different approximations $p^* = 1/(2(f_a + 1) - l)$ and $p^* = 1/l$. Right: The corresponding curves for different, length-independent settings of the mutation rate $p \in \{0.001, 0.02, 0.04, 0.06, 0.08, 0.10, 0.12, 0.14, 0.16, 0.18, 0.20\}$.

$$p^*(f_a) \approx 1 - \left(\frac{f_a}{l}\right)^{\frac{1}{1-f_a}} \approx \frac{1}{l} \ , \qquad (6.18)$$

i.e. a mutation rate control which is independent of the distance to the optimum, constant, and identical for all individuals in the population. Using this result, Mühlenbein derived the expression

$$E_{l/2}(t) = e \cdot l \cdot \ln(l/2) \qquad (6.19)$$

for the expected number of steps, assuming $p^* = 1/l$ and the process starts at $f_a = l/2$ (which is surely a reasonable assumption for random initialization) [Müh92]. At the cost of using an approximation for p^*, this method allows for the derivation of the explicit analytical expression (6.19) for the expected absorption time, and Mühlenbein indicates the $\mathcal{O}(l \cdot \ln l)$ estimate to be valid for any unimodal pseudoboolean function.

The difference between the mutation rate schedules (6.18) and (6.16) is undoubtedly striking, and the amount of the error implied by approximation (6.18) remains to be analyzed. To do so, expression (6.6) was numerically evaluated for $i = l/2$ and values of $l \in \{2, \ldots, 100\}$ (larger values were prevented due to the computational effort required for performing these calculations with the necessary precision), using equation (6.16) for calculating the transition probabilities. The resulting curve for $E_{l/2}(t)$ is compared to the absorption time as obtained by approximation (6.18) in the left part of figure 6.3.

The graph in figure 6.3 (left) clarifies the validity of the $\mathcal{O}(l \cdot \ln l)$ estimate. The small difference concerning the expected time to absorption implies the consequence that the most time-consuming part of optimization consists in fine-tuning of the last few bits, i.e. the remarkably different schedules for p^* spend most of their time in almost optimal states of the Markov chain. In such states, the mutation probability has a value of (almost) $1/l$ for both schedules, and the number of steps needed for each further improvement is close to l per still incorrect bit position. This way, the large waiting times in the final phase of the search are responsible for the fact that the initially strong advantage of the schedule given by equation (6.16) results only in a small advantage with respect to the total time to absorption[7].

To confirm these results, experimental runs with a $(1+1)$-GA were performed for the spot checks $l = 50$ and $l = 100$, using both approximations (6.16) and (6.18). Starting from a bit string initialized with $l/2$ one bits and zero bits, $N = 1000$ independent runs were performed and the resulting times to absorption were averaged over these experiments. The resulting mean values $\bar{t}$ and the empirical standard deviations $V(t)$ are compared to the theoretical values $E_{l/2}(t)$ in table 6.1.

The mean values $\bar{t}$ are in overwhelming correspondence with the theoretically predicted values. The empirical standard deviations $V(t)$ are relatively large, however, indicating that the absorption time may vary considerably between single runs.

So far, all mutation rate settings depended at least on l, the length of the bit string. The right part of figure 6.3 demonstrates the effect of ignoring also the rule $p \approx 1/l$. Here, the curves represent constant, length-independent mutation rate settings ranging over the set $p \in \{0.001, 0.02, 0.04, 0.06, 0.08, 0.10, 0.12, 0.14, 0.16, 0.18, 0.20\}$, and they give a striking demonstration of the impact of inappropriately chosen mutation rates. For $p = 0.02$, the curve nestles against the optimal schedule in the vicinity of $l = 50$ and is just slightly worse for other values of l in the range discussed here. Further increasing the mutation rate, however, quickly changes the expected absorption time into an $\mathcal{O}(e^l)$ curve, i.e., being no better (except a constant) than complete enumeration!

A mutation rate such as $p = 0.001$ which is too small for the complete range of string lengths investigated here turns out to be a generally more

---

[7]An important question for further research is raised by asking for the time required to achieve a certain *approximation* of the optimum. The difference between both mutation rate schedules discussed here will certainly increase in favour of equation (6.16) as the approximation error is permitted to increase.

l	$p^* = 1/l$		
	$\bar{t}$	$V(t)$	$E_{l/2}(t)$
50	$4.379 \cdot 10^2$	$1.619 \cdot 10^2$	$4.375 \cdot 10^2$
100	$1.061 \cdot 10^3$	$3.296 \cdot 10^2$	$1.063 \cdot 10^3$
l	$p^* = 1/(2(f_a + 1) - l)$		
	$\bar{t}$	$V(t)$	$E_{l/2}(t)$
50	$4.051 \cdot 10^2$	$1.649 \cdot 10^2$	$4.135 \cdot 10^2$
100	$1.013 \cdot 10^3$	$3.396 \cdot 10^2$	$1.009 \cdot 10^3$

Table 6.1. Experimental spot checks for the expected time to absorption $E_{l/2}$, $l \in \{50, 100\}$, and both optimal schedules for p^*. In addition to the mean time $\bar{t}$, the empirical standard deviation $V(t)$ is shown. The data is averaged over $N = 1000$ experiments.

reasonable choice by far than a mutation rate which is by the same factor larger than the optimal rate (e.g., compare $p = 0.001$ and $p = 0.1$ for $l = 100$).

6.1.2 Reflections on Convergence Velocity

Within this section we extend the notion of a (1+1)-GA according to algorithm 9 to a $(\mu \overset{+}{,} \lambda)$-GA without recombination. Algorithmically, this step is performed by omitting recombination within the standard algorithm 8 and substituting proportional selection by $(\mu+\lambda)$- respectively (μ,λ)-selection as indicated in section 5.1.4.

In order to derive an equation for the expectation of the progress rate of the population average just as presented for the Evolution Strategy in theorem 8, an expression for $p_\nu(k)$ as introduced in equations (2.35) and (2.37) has to be derived. In contrast to section 2.1.7, the discrete character of the underlying distribution implies a more general combinatorial expression for the probability density function $p_\nu(k)$ of the ν-th order statistics. The reason is that the chance of ties is nonzero, since more than exactly one offspring individual as in the continuous case may have identical fitness values, i.e. occupy the $(\lambda - \nu + 1)$-th best position (remember that we consider a maximization task and assume an order statistics to be arranged in increasing order, i.e., $f_{\tilde{a}_1} \leq f_{\tilde{a}_2} \leq \cdots \leq f_{\tilde{a}_\lambda}$).

A realization of the event $\{f_{\tilde{a}_\nu} = k\}$ may occur in $\nu \cdot (\lambda - \nu + 1)$ different ways as follows: $\nu - i - 1$ outcomes are less than k (for $i = 0, 1, \ldots, \nu - 1$), $\lambda - \nu - j$ outcomes are larger than k (for $j = 0, 1, \ldots, \lambda - \nu$), and the remaining $\lambda - (\nu - 1 - i) - (\lambda - \nu - j) = i + j + 1$ observations equal k. As there are $\binom{\lambda}{\nu - 1 - i}$ ways to choose offspring individuals covering a distance less than k and $\binom{\lambda - (\nu - 1 - i)}{\lambda - \nu - j}$ possibilities for the better ones, we obtain:

$$
p_\nu(k) = \sum_{i=0}^{\nu-1} \binom{\lambda}{\nu-1-i} \sum_{j=0}^{\lambda-\nu} \binom{\lambda-(\nu-1-i)}{\lambda-\nu-j} \cdot \\
p_{k'=k}^{i+j+1} \cdot p_{k'<k}^{\nu-1-i} \cdot p_{k'>k}^{\lambda-\nu-j} \quad .
\tag{6.20}
$$

Notice that if exactly one single $(\lambda-\nu+1)$-th best offspring individual exists, $i + j + 1 = 1$ is required, i.e. $i = 0$ and $j = 0$. In this case, equation (6.20) reduces to the version (2.37) discussed in section 2.1.7.

For the counting ones problem introduced in section 6.1.1, one can easily derive the probabilities $p_{k'=k}$, $p_{k'>k}$, and $p_{k'<k}$ for an offspring individual to cover a distance k, a larger one, or a smaller one, respectively $(-f_a \le k \le l - f_a)$:

$$
p_{k'=k} = \begin{cases} p_a^+(k) & , \ k \ge 0 \\ p_a^-(-k) & , \ k < 0 \end{cases}
$$

$$
p_{k'>k} = \begin{cases} \displaystyle\sum_{i=k+1}^{l-f_a} p_a^+(i) & , \ k \ge 0 \\ \displaystyle\sum_{i=k+1}^{-1} p_a^-(-i) + \sum_{i=0}^{l-f_a} p_a^+(i) & , \ k < 0 \end{cases}
\tag{6.21}
$$

$$
p_{k'<k} = 1 - p_{k'=k} - p_{k'>k} \quad .
$$

From equations (6.20) and (6.21) it is possible to formulate an exact expression for the expected convergence velocity of a $(1 \overset{+}{,} \lambda)$-GA. The result is stated in theorem 22 [Bäc92b]:

Theorem 22 *The expectation of the convergence velocity* $\varphi_{(1 \overset{+}{,} \lambda)}$ *for the counting ones problem is given by*

$$
\varphi_{(1 \overset{+}{,} \lambda)}(l, f_a, p) = \sum_{k=k_{\min}}^{l-f_a} k \cdot p_\lambda(k)
$$

$$
= \sum_{k=k_{\min}}^{l-f_a} k \cdot \sum_{i=1}^{\lambda} \binom{\lambda}{i} \cdot p_{k'=k}^i \cdot p_{k'<k}^{\lambda-i}
$$

$$
= \sum_{k=k_{\min}}^{l-f_a} k \cdot \left(p_{k'\le k}^\lambda - p_{k'<k}^\lambda \right) \quad ,
$$

where $k_{\min} = -f_a$ *for a* $(1,\lambda)$-GA *and* $k_{\min} = 0$ *for a* $(1+\lambda)$-GA.

Proof: According to the order $f_{\bar{a}_1} \le f_{\bar{a}_2} \le \cdots \le f_{\bar{a}_\lambda}$, the best individual is considered by setting $\nu = \lambda$. From equation (6.20) we obtain

$$p_\lambda(k) = \sum_{i=0}^{\lambda-1} \binom{\lambda}{\lambda-i-1} \cdot p_{k'=k}^{i+1} \cdot p_{k'<k}^{\lambda-1-i}$$

$$= \sum_{i=1}^{\lambda} \binom{\lambda}{i} \cdot p_{k'=k}^{i} \cdot p_{k'<k}^{\lambda-i}$$

$$= \sum_{i=0}^{\lambda} \binom{\lambda}{i} \cdot p_{k'=k}^{i} \cdot p_{k'<k}^{\lambda-i} - p_{k'<k}^{\lambda}$$

$$= p_{k'\leq k}^{\lambda} - p_{k'<k}^{\lambda}$$

by shifting the index and using the basic identity $\binom{\lambda}{\lambda-i} = \binom{\lambda}{i}$ as well as the binomial theorem with[8] $p_{k'\leq k} = p_{k'<k} + p_{k'=k}$.   Q.E.D.

As for the (1+1)-GA, the optimal mutation rate schedule maximizing φ can be calculated by numerical methods for a (1+λ)-GA with varying values of λ. First, however, we concentrate on the behavior of $\varphi_{(1+\lambda)}$ and $\varphi_{(1,\lambda)}$ for varying values of p and $\lambda \in \{1,2,5,10,20\}$, $f_a \in \{60,80\}$ ($l = 100$ as usual). The resulting curves of the convergence velocity behavior are shown in figure 6.4.

At first glance, a striking similarity between these graphics and figure 2.5 is observed, reflecting a qualitatively identical behavior. With the exception of the (1,1)-strategy, all progress curves quickly attain a maximum as p increases, and decrease as p is further increased beyond its optimal setting. As p grows further, the convergence velocity quickly becomes negative for (1,λ)-strategies, and the curves for these strategies exhibit the general shape of a quadratic parabola (which is to be expected from theory on Evolution Strategies; see e.g. [BRS93]). In contrast to this, the convergence velocity of (1+λ)-strategies remains positive, however quickly approaching zero as p is growing. Comparing the plots for $f_a = 60$ (left) and $f_a = 80$ (right), the range of useful mutation rates shrinks down considerably as the optimum is approached, i.e., as f_a grows. Correspondingly, the convergence velocity also dwindles remarkably.

Figure 6.4 also indicates a growth of optimal mutation rates as λ increases, an effect which can be interpreted by taking into account the redundancy of creating λ descendants allows for risky experiments with a larger mutation rate. Again, the optimal mutation rate schedules can be calculated numerically for different values of λ, and the resulting curves for $\lambda \in \{1,2,5,10,20,30,40,50\}$ as shown in the left part of figure 6.5 clearly demonstrate this impact of λ on the optimal schedule of p as the number of correct bits increases. Towards the end, where the close vicinity of the optimum $l = 100$ is reached, all curves are merging back into the already known optimal (1+1)-GA schedule, thus demonstrating the dominant role of an $1/l$ control for optimizing the last few bits.

[8]$p_{k'\leq k}$ is of course just the distribution function of the random variable k; $p_{k'=k}$ is its density.

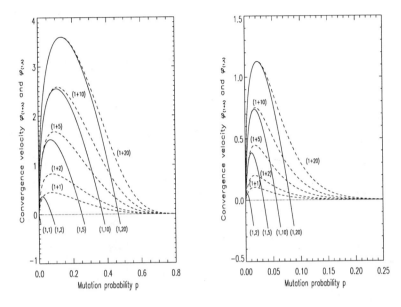

Fig. 6.4: Local Convergence velocity $\varphi_{(1+\lambda)}$ and $\varphi_{(1,\lambda)}$ over the mutation rate p for $\lambda \in \{1, 2, 5, 10, 20\}$, $l = 100$, and $f_a = 60$ (left) respectively $f_a = 80$ (right).

The treatment of a $(1+\lambda)$-GA automatically raises the question for the speedup in terms of generations achieved by creating $\lambda > 1$ individuals from one common ancestor. This question is of some importance due to the availability of massively parallel hardware and the excellent suitability of Evolutionary Algorithms for implementation on such machines (see e.g. [Hof91] for an overview). Then, leaving communication times unconsidered, speedup with respect to the number of generations coincides with computation time speedup.

Since we do not possess an analytical approximation for the optimal mutation rate schedule of an $(1+\lambda)$-GA, i.e. a schedule depending on f_a, λ, and l, the best choice is to use $p^* = 1/l$ in the following. As demonstrated in section 6.1.1, this approximation is unlikely to cause an extreme distortion of the results.

On these conditions, the expected time to absorption $E_{l/2,\lambda}(t)$ can be calculated numerically by theorem 20, now using the transition probabilities

$$p_{ij} \;=\; p_{f_a}(i-j) =: p_\lambda(i-j) \quad \text{where} \quad f_a = l - i, \; i > j \quad , \quad (6.22)$$

and, according to equation (6.20) and (6.21):

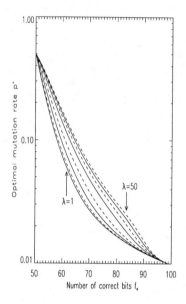
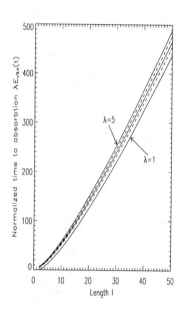

Fig. 6.5: Left: The dependence of the optimal mutation rate p^* on the number $f_{\vec{a}}$ of already correct bits for a $(1 + \lambda)$-GA with $\lambda \in \{1, 2, 5, 10, 20, 30, 40, 50\}$. Right: Normalized expected time to absorption $\lambda \cdot E_{l/2,\lambda}(t)$ for $\lambda \in \{1, 2, 3, 4, 5\}$ and $l \in \{2, \ldots, 50\}$ (larger values for λ and l are not numerically evaluable due to the required precision of calculations).

$$p_\lambda(k) = \sum_{i=1}^{\lambda} \binom{\lambda}{i} \left(p_{\vec{a}}^+(k)\right)^i \cdot \left(1 - p_{\vec{a}}^+(k) - \sum_{j=k+1}^{l-f_a} p_{\vec{a}}^+(j)\right)^{\lambda-i} \quad (6.23)$$

A numerical evaluation of equation (6.6) with the necessary arithmetical precision turns out to require a tremendous computational effort, placing strong restrictions on the range of λ and l for which results are presented here. These ranges include values for $\lambda \in \{1, 2, 3, 4, 5\}$ and $l \in \{2, \ldots, 50\}$, and the resulting curves for the normalized expected time to absorption $\lambda \cdot E_{l/2,\lambda}(t)$ are collected in the right graphic shown in figure 6.5.

These curves seem to give a clear indication that the speedup with respect to the number of generations is almost linear rather than being of logarithmic order as for an Evolution Strategy on the sphere model. This result can be analyzed further by a theoretical argumentation similar to the approximation used by Mühlenbein to derive the result $E_{l/2,1}(t) = e \cdot l \cdot \ln(l/2)$ [Müh92].

The search is assumed to proceed exclusively by one bit changes, a realistic basic assumption since $p^* = 1/l$. This implies the setting $k = 1$

and $i = 0$ in equation (6.12) and yields:

$$
\begin{aligned}
p_{\bar{a}}^+(1) &\approx (l - f_a)p(1 - p)^{l-1} \\
&= (l - f_a)\frac{1}{l}\left(1 - \frac{1}{l}\right)^{l-1} \quad \text{for } p = p^* \qquad (6.24) \\
&\approx \frac{l - f_a}{e \cdot l} \quad ,
\end{aligned}
$$

using the approximation $(1 - 1/l)^{l-1} \approx e^{-1}$. Furthermore, equation (6.23) is simplified by taking just one single best individual (i.e., the case $i = 1$) into account:

$$
\begin{aligned}
p_{l-f_a,l-f_a-1} &= p_\lambda(1) \\
&\approx \lambda \cdot p_{\bar{a}}^+(1) \cdot (1 - p_{\bar{a}}^+(1))^{\lambda-1} \qquad (6.25) \\
&\approx \lambda \cdot \frac{l - f_a}{e \cdot l} \cdot \left(1 - \frac{l - f_a}{e \cdot l}\right)^{\lambda-1} \quad .
\end{aligned}
$$

The probabilities $p_{i,i-1} = p_{l-f_a,l-f_a-1}$ (remember that $f_a = l - i$) are now the only non-vanishing off-diagonal elements of the transition matrix (the diagonal elements are $1 - p_{i,i-1}$), and the expected waiting time to leave state i of the Markov chain is $1/p_{i,i-1}$. Consequently, the total expected time to absorption is given by

$$
\begin{aligned}
E_{l/2,\lambda}(t) &\approx \sum_{f_a=l/2}^{l-1} \frac{1}{p_{l-f_a,l-f_a-1}} \\
&= \sum_{i=1}^{l/2} \frac{e \cdot l}{\lambda \cdot i \left(1 - \frac{i}{e \cdot l}\right)^{\lambda-1}} \qquad (6.26) \\
&= \frac{e \cdot l}{\lambda} \cdot \sum_{i=1}^{l/2} \frac{1}{i} \cdot \frac{1}{\left(1 - \frac{i}{e \cdot l}\right)^{\lambda-1}} \quad ,
\end{aligned}
$$

and a lower bound for the exponential function of λ in the denominator is given for $i = l/2$ by

$$
\left(1 - \frac{i}{e \cdot l}\right)^{\lambda-1} \geq \left(1 - \frac{1}{2e}\right)^{\lambda-1} = 0.816^{\lambda-1} \quad , \qquad (6.27)
$$

such that[9]

[9] Using the fact that

$$
\lim_{m \to \infty} \left(\sum_{k=1}^{m} \frac{1}{k} - \ln m\right) = \gamma = 0.5772\ldots
$$

(Euler's constant) (e.g., [AS65], p. 68).

$$\dot{E}_{l/2,\lambda}(t) \;\leq\; \frac{e\cdot l}{\lambda\left(1-\frac{1}{2e}\right)^{\lambda-1}}\cdot(\ln(l/2)+\gamma) \quad. \tag{6.28}$$

For two reasons, this is a crude upper bound on the expected time to absorption: First, the algorithm approaches the optimum quickly, i.e. most of the terms $(1-i/(e\cdot l))^{\lambda-1}$ in the denominator are close to one (however, as λ grows the term becomes quickly smaller). Second, the mutation rate $p = 1/l$ becomes increasingly less optimal as λ is growing. Taking into account that Mühlenbein's approximation (6.19) already omits the additional summand γel, it can be concluded that for small values of λ, $i \in I\!N$, $i \geq 2$:

$$E_{l/i,\lambda}(t) \;\approx\; \frac{E_{l/i,1}(t)}{\lambda} \quad, \tag{6.29}$$

where the initial bit string's fitness is generalized now to a fraction l/i (i.e., $E_{l/i,\lambda}(t) \approx e\cdot l\cdot \ln(l/i)/(\lambda\cdot c_i^{\lambda-1})$ where $c_i = 1 - 1/(e\cdot i)$).

These results for a $(1+\lambda)$-GA were also tested experimentally for $l \in \{50,100\}$ and $\lambda \in \{1,2,3,4,5,10,20,30,40,50,60,70,80,90,100\}$, and the results, averaged over $N = 100$ experiments for each setting of λ and l, are summarized in table 6.2 ($l = 50$) and 6.3 ($l = 100$).

For each setting of λ and l the measured mean time to absorption $\bar{t}$, the empirical standard deviation $V(t)$ of these times, and the calculated speedup in terms of generations, i.e. $\bar{t}_1/\bar{t}_\lambda$, are shown in the table. Additionally, for $\lambda \in \{1,2,3,4,5\}$ and $l = 50$, the numerically calculated time to absorption (from the calculations performed for the right graphic in figure 6.5) occur in this table and turn out to be in good agreement with the measured values. As λ increases further, the speedup decreases remarkably and is far from being linear but instead resembles a logarithmic curve, as can be concluded from figure 6.6, showing the measured speedup $\bar{t}_1/\bar{t}_\lambda$ over λ. In contrast to the impact of λ, increasing the bit string length l increases the speedup (for λ being held constant). This observation can be explained by equation (6.26) since for growing l the denominator $(1-i/(e\cdot l))^{\lambda-1}$ approaches one for the most time-consuming values of i (i.e., for small i).

One source of error for large values of λ is to be identified in the no longer reasonable simplification (6.25), which assumes exactly one single best offspring to exist. For large λ, however, this assumption is almost surely incorrect, and for $\lambda > l$ redundancy in the offsprings' objective function values is clearly expected to occur. In summary, one can say that the approximations (6.25) and (6.28) are only valid for $p = 1/l$ and small λ and that a better approximation, due to the difficulty introduced by the sum in equation (6.26), is currently not available.

Finally, to conclude these reflections on convergence velocity, the case $\mu > 1$ remains to be analyzed. To do so, one has to focus on the expected convergence velocity of the average of the μ best individuals as outlined in section 2.1.7, following equation (2.35). In other words,

λ	$l = 50$			
	$\bar{t}_\lambda$	$V(t)$	$\bar{t}_1/\bar{t}_\lambda$	$E_{l/2,\lambda}(t)$
1	$4.280 \cdot 10^2$	$1.881 \cdot 10^2$		$4.443 \cdot 10^2$
2	$2.186 \cdot 10^2$	$7.601 \cdot 10^1$	1.96	$2.275 \cdot 10^2$
3	$1.589 \cdot 10^2$	$5.653 \cdot 10^1$	2.69	$1.553 \cdot 10^2$
4	$1.264 \cdot 10^2$	$4.982 \cdot 10^1$	3.39	$1.192 \cdot 10^2$
5	$9.773 \cdot 10^1$	$3.653 \cdot 10^1$	4.38	$9.766 \cdot 10^1$
10	$5.734 \cdot 10^1$	$1.584 \cdot 10^1$	7.46	
20	$3.243 \cdot 10^1$	7.343	13.20	
30	$2.631 \cdot 10^1$	5.049	16.27	
40	$2.257 \cdot 10^1$	4.269	18.96	
50	$2.086 \cdot 10^1$	3.315	20.52	
60	$1.944 \cdot 10^1$	3.040	22.02	
70	$1.817 \cdot 10^1$	2.606	23.56	
80	$1.743 \cdot 10^1$	2.133	24.56	
90	$1.699 \cdot 10^1$	2.397	25.19	
100	$1.613 \cdot 10^1$	1.574	26.53	

Table 6.2. Experimental results for the expected time to absorption in case of a $(1+\lambda)$-GA with $p = 1/l$, $l = 50$, and $\lambda \in \{1, 2, 3, 4, 5, 10, 20, 30, 40, 50, 60, 70, 80, 90, 100\}$. In addition to the mean time $\bar{t}_\lambda$, the empirical standard deviation $V(t)$ and the measured speedup $\bar{t}_1/\bar{t}_\lambda$ are shown. The data is averaged over $N = 100$ experiments.

the parent population is assumed to be reduced to one single representative of average quality $\bar{f}_a$. In reality, however, this assumption is surely not true as it neglects population diversity and the resulting potential to create a number of well–performing descendants from already better-than-average parents at the cost of parents which are worse than average, thus having a smaller chance to contribute to the μ best offspring. Though population diversity plays a major role for the observed power of Evolutionary Algorithms (especially concerning convergence reliability and self-adaptation), its inclusion into the formal analysis of such algorithms remains an open field of further research.

Furthermore, even the restriction to the convergence velocity of the average of the μ best suffers from the discrete nature of the objective function which enforces rounding of the average. To overcome these difficulties, the simulation results discussed here were obtained under the condition of μ parent individuals with exactly identical objective function values f_a, and the local convergence velocity $\varphi_{(\mu+\lambda)}$ was measured

λ	$l = 100$		
	$\bar{t}_\lambda$	$V(t)$	$\bar{t}_1/\bar{t}_\lambda$
1	$1.065 \cdot 10^3$	$3.474 \cdot 10^2$	
2	$5.425 \cdot 10^2$	$1.542 \cdot 10^2$	1.96
3	$3.869 \cdot 10^2$	$1.245 \cdot 10^2$	2.75
4	$2.860 \cdot 10^2$	$8.526 \cdot 10^1$	3.72
5	$2.254 \cdot 10^2$	$6.271 \cdot 10^1$	4.72
10	$1.275 \cdot 10^2$	$3.438 \cdot 10^1$	8.34
20	$7.596 \cdot 10^1$	$1.725 \cdot 10^1$	13.99
30	$6.064 \cdot 10^1$	$1.314 \cdot 10^1$	17.53
40	$4.920 \cdot 10^1$	7.798	21.65
50	$4.605 \cdot 10^1$	8.073	23.13
60	$4.243 \cdot 10^1$	5.824	25.10
70	$3.895 \cdot 10^1$	4.356	27.34
80	$3.712 \cdot 10^1$	4.300	28.69
90	$3.625 \cdot 10^1$	4.244	29.38
100	$3.410 \cdot 10^1$	3.442	31.23

Table 6.3. Experimental results for the expected time to absorption in case of a $(1+\lambda)$-GA with $p = 1/l$, $l = 100$, and $\lambda \in \{1, 2, 3, 4, 5, 10, 20, 30, 40, 50, 60, 70, 80, 90, 100\}$. In addition to the mean time $\bar{t}_\lambda$, the empirical standard deviation $V(t)$ and the measured speedup $\bar{t}_1/\bar{t}_\lambda$ are shown. The data is averaged over $N = 100$ experiments.

as the difference between the average fitness of the μ best members of the offspring population and f_a. The resulting local convergence velocity $\varphi_{(\mu+\lambda)}(l, f_a, p)$ was measured for $l = 100$, $p = 0.01$, $f_a \in \{60, 80\}$ and for $\mu \in \{1, \ldots, 30\}$, $\lambda \in \{\mu, \ldots, 100\}$, and each value for φ results from averaging over $N = 100$ experiments. The measured relationship between $\varphi_{(\mu+\lambda)}$ and the settings of μ and λ are shown in the right graphic of figure 6.7 ($f_a = 60$) and 6.8 ($f_a = 80$), respectively.

Theoretically, the convergence velocity $\varphi_{(\mu\overset{+}{,}\lambda)}(l, \bar{f}_a, p)$ of the average of the μ best individuals is obtained from equation (6.20) as

$$\varphi_{(\mu\overset{+}{,}\lambda)}(l, \bar{f}_a, p) = \frac{1}{\mu} \sum_{k=k_{min}}^{l-\bar{f}_a} k \cdot \sum_{\nu=\lambda-\mu+1}^{\lambda} p_\nu(k) , \qquad (6.30)$$

where $k_{min} = -\bar{f}_a$ for a (μ,λ)-GA and $k_{min} = 0$ for a $(\mu+\lambda)$-GA. Notice that since we are interested in the maximal improvements the index ν takes the values $\lambda - \mu + 1, \ldots, \lambda$.

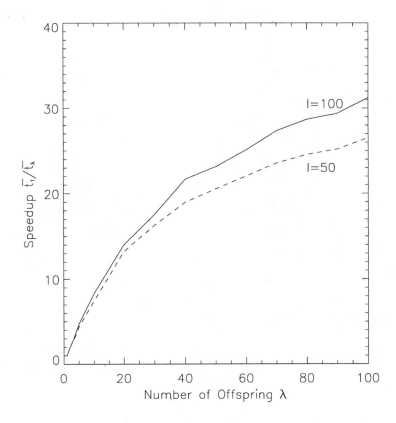

Fig. 6.6: Speedup $\bar{t}_1/\bar{t}_\lambda$ for a $(1+\lambda)$-GA with $\lambda \in \{1, 2, 3, 4, 5, 10, 20, 30,$ $40, 50, 60, 70, 80, 90, 100\}$ for $l = 50$ and $l = 100$, respectively, with $p = 1/l$. Each data point reflects the mean of $N = 100$ experiments.

In addition to performing the simulation experiments as outlined above, the theoretical prediction (6.30) is numerically evaluated for the settings of l, p, $\bar{f}_a$, μ, and λ given above. The resulting theoretical plots are shown in the left part of figure 6.7 ($\bar{f}_a = 60$) respectively figure 6.8 ($\bar{f}_a = 80$).

Both graphics clearly confirm the correctness of the theoretical results also for the case $\mu > 1$. As expected, the convergence velocity for any constant value of λ is maximized if $\mu = 1$. From the previous investigations on the total speedup achieved by a $(1+\lambda)$-strategy (figure 6.6), the steadily decreasing slope of the curve for $\mu = 1$ as λ increases is no surprise. As μ increases, the range of λ-values where φ depends linearly on λ also increases. For instance, if $\mu = 30$ the dependency is strictly linear over the range of values considered here, while as μ be-

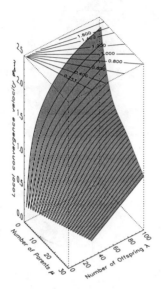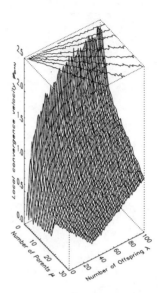

Fig. 6.7: Local convergence velocity $\varphi_{(\mu+\lambda)}$ for $p = 0.01$, $l = 100$, and $f_a = 60$. The number of parents μ varies in the range $\{1, \ldots, 30\}$, the offspring population size λ in the range $\{\mu, \ldots, 100\}$. The left plot shows the theoretically predicted shape of the convergence velocity landscape; the right plot reflects the experimental results.

comes smaller the slope of the curves starts to decline at smaller values of λ. Concerning the influence of the ratio λ/μ on convergence velocity, the lines of equal convergence velocity shown on top of the graphics clarify that $\varphi_{(\mu+\lambda)}$ is constant for any constant ratio λ/μ, i.e., $\varphi_{(\mu+\lambda)} \propto \lambda/\mu$. This result is in agreement with the corresponding results for Evolution Strategies mentioned at the end of section 2.1.7.

As a final observation from figures 6.7 and figures 6.8 we notice that $\varphi_{(\lambda\overset{+}{,}\lambda)}$ seems to be constant, regardless of the value of λ. This observation can also be derived theoretically from results about the distribution of the sample mean

$$L_\lambda(k) = \frac{1}{\lambda} \sum_{\nu=1}^{\lambda} p_\nu(k) \quad , \tag{6.31}$$

which is known to be asymptotically normal with expectation $E(L_\lambda) = E(K)$ (see [ABN92], p. 110, pp. 227–229), where the random variable K is sampled according to the density function $p_{k'=k}$ (i.e., the common distribution of the improvements of the offspring individuals). In more explicit form, we have

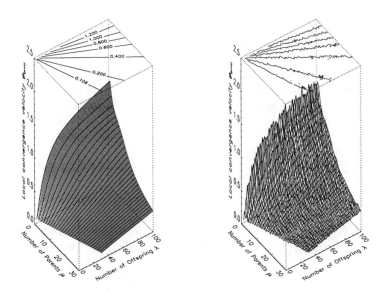

Fig. **6.8:** Local convergence velocity $\varphi_{(\mu+\lambda)}$ for $p = 0.01$, $l = 100$, and $f_a = 80$. The number of parents μ varies in the range $\{1, \ldots, 30\}$, the offspring population size λ in the range $\{\mu, \ldots, 100\}$. The left plot shows the theoretically predicted shape of the convergence velocity landscape; the right plot reflects the experimental results.

$$
\begin{aligned}
E(L_\lambda) &= \sum_{k=k_{\min}}^{l-\bar{f}_a} k \cdot L_\lambda(k) &= \varphi_{(\lambda\overset{+}{,}\lambda)} = E(K) \\
&= \sum_{k=k_{\min}}^{l-\bar{f}_a} k \cdot p_{k'=k} &= \varphi_{(1\overset{+}{,}1)}
\end{aligned}
\tag{6.32}
$$

This interesting result, which is experimentally as well as theoretically confirmed, would have consequences for Evolutionary Programming — which uses a stochastic $(\mu+\mu)$-selection and no recombination — if all offspring individuals were sampled from the same distribution. This is not the case, however, since by means of the self-adaptation mechanism the distributions are different for all individuals.

6.1.3   The Role of the Binary Code

The simplicity of the counting ones problem turned out to provide a good entry point for the analysis of simplified Genetic Algorithms. More interestingly, however, would be an investigation of the impact of the binary code used to apply Genetic Algorithms to other than pseudoboolean optimization tasks. In order to analyze the role of the binary code — both the standard code and, as an alternative, the Gray code — the algorithm is reduced here again to the (1+1)-GA. For the basic terminology concerning the binary representation mechanism, the reader is referred to section 2.3.1.

To simplify things as far as possible, we start by using the standard mechanism of decoding a bit string to a single integer value, i.e., we use equation (2.69) with $l_x = l$, $n = 1$, $u = 0$, $v = 2^l - 1$, resulting in an objective function $g : \mathbb{B}^l \to \{0, \ldots, 2^l - 1\}$:

$$g(a_1 \ldots a_l) = \sum_{i=0}^{l-1} a_{l-i} \cdot 2^i \quad . \tag{6.33}$$

As in case of the counting ones problem, a maximization task is assumed here, i.e. g attains its optimum for the bit string consisting of one bits only. However, this property cannot be assumed to hold in general, such that g is generalized here to a function g' as follows:

$$g'(\vec{a}) = \begin{cases} g(\vec{a}) \ , \ \text{if } g(\vec{a}) \le w \\ -1 \ \ , \ \text{if } g(\vec{a}) > w \end{cases} \tag{6.34}$$

for an arbitray $w \in \{1, \ldots, 2^l - 1\}$. g' is a kind of truncated version of g, attaining its optimal value just for the bit string $\vec{a}^*$ that represents w.

Neither for g nor for g' a closed analytical expression for the improvement probability according to the style of theorem 21 can be presented. At least, the probabilities can be described indirectly by means of the bit string level probabilities for arbitrary, mutation-based transitions according to equation (2.110):

$$\begin{aligned} p_{\vec{a}}^+ &= \sum_{i=g'(\vec{a})+1}^{w} \mathcal{P}\{g'(m_{\{p_m\}}(\vec{a})) = i\} \\ &= \sum_{i=g'(\vec{a})+1}^{w} \mathcal{P}\{m_{\{p_m\}}(\vec{a}) = g^{-1}(i)\} \quad , \end{aligned} \tag{6.35}$$

where g^{-1} denotes the inverse function of g (the restriction of g' to $\{0, \ldots, w\}$ is invertible). This way, transition probabilities

$$\mathcal{P}\{g'(m_{\{p_m\}}(\vec{a})) = i\} \tag{6.36}$$

of the objective function are reduced to transition probabilities on bit strings. Similarly, it is straightforward to describe the k-step improvement probability[10] $(0 \le k \le w - g'(\vec{a}))$

---

[10]In the following, we always assume $g'(\vec{a}) > -1$ as these are the interesting cases. Including $g'(\vec{a}) = -1$, the resulting probabilities require to make a distinction of cases which is lengthy but not of any help for the following considerations.

$$p_{\vec{a}}^{+}(k) \;=\; \mathcal{P}\{m_{\{p_m\}}(\vec{a}) = g^{-1}(g'(\vec{a}) + k)\} \quad , \qquad (6.37)$$

the stagnation probability $p_{\vec{a}}^{0} = \mathcal{P}\{m_{\{p_m\}}(\vec{a}) = g^{-1}(g'(\vec{a})) = \vec{a}\} = (1 - p)^{l}$, the k-step failure probability $p_{\vec{a}}^{-}(k) = \mathcal{P}\{m_{\{p_m\}}(\vec{a}) = g^{-1}(g'(\vec{a}) - k)\}$ $(0 \le k \le g(\vec{a}))$, and the failure probability

$$p_{\vec{a}}^{-} \;=\; \sum_{i=0}^{g'(\vec{a})-1} \mathcal{P}\{m_{\{p_m\}}(\vec{a}) = g^{-1}(i)\} + \\ \sum_{i=w+1}^{2^{l}-1} \mathcal{P}\{m_{\{p_m\}}(\vec{a}) = g^{-1}(i)\} \quad . \qquad (6.38)$$

For small l the success probabilities can be evaluated numerically, but due to the large number of states (2^{l}) a Markov chain analysis including the calculation of absorption times remains almost impossible.

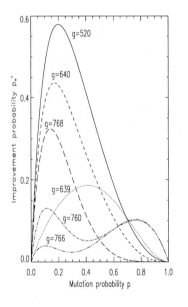 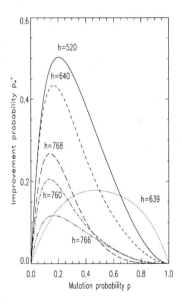

Fig. 6.9: Left: Improvement probabilities $p_{\vec{a}}^{+}$ for varying mutation rate p, different objective function values $g'_a \in \{520, 639, 640, 760, 766, 768\}$ and $l = 10$, $w = 822$. Right: The corresponding curves for the objective function h'.

In addition to g, we define also a function h which is intended to model the Gray code rather than the standard binary code. h simply interprets the bit string as a Gray coded integer by converting it to the corresponding standard code, using the conversion function γ^{-1} according to equation (2.72), and applies g:

$$h(\vec{a}) \;=\; g(\gamma^{-1}(\vec{a})) \;. \tag{6.39}$$

As before, a more realistic modification of h is defined by setting

$$h'(\vec{a}) \;=\; \begin{cases} h(\vec{a}) \;, & \text{if } h(\vec{a}) \le w \\ -1 \;, & \text{if } h(\vec{a}) > w \;, \end{cases} \tag{6.40}$$

and the formulation of improvement, stagnation, and failure probabilities is completely analogous to the corresponding probabilities for g'.

Similar to the investigation of the counting ones problem, it seems appropriate to pay attention to the improvement probabilities $p_{\vec{a}}^+$. While the string length $l = 10$ is chosen in order to keep the problems numerically manageable within reasonable time, the choice of $w = 822$ was performed arbitrarily (however, $w > 2^{l-1}$ was intended). To obtain an overview of the new situation concerning the dependency of $p_{\vec{a}}^+$ on the mutation probability p, all cases for $g'(\vec{a}), h'(\vec{a}) \in \{512, \ldots, 821\}$ were evaluated and figure 6.9 displays some interesting and representative spot checks at $g'(\vec{a}), h'(\vec{a}) \in \{520, 639, 640, 760, 766, 768\}$.

Both for g' (left part) and h' (right part) figure 6.9 reflect a surprising diversity of different behaviors. Some curves are in good correspondence with the expectations according to the experience gained from the counting ones problem. But for some distances to the optimum g' turns out to imply a multimodal improvement probability function, attaining its global optimum for a remarkably large mutation probability ($p^* \approx 0.8$ for $g'(\vec{a}) = 766$). This anomaly does not occur in case of h'. Furthermore, we notice that both for g' and h' the shape of curves for similar objective function values (e.g., 639 and 640) may differ considerably.

The reason for multimodality in the improvement probability function $p_{\vec{a}}^+$ is to be identified in the fact that the pseudoboolean function g' may itself become multimodal[11] for $w < 2^l - 1$, while h' remains unimodal. To see the multimodality of g', consider $g'^{-1}(767) = 1011111111$ which is a local maximum since no change of a single bit can yield an improvement[12] (remember that $g'(1111111111) = -1$). The function h' is unimodal for any w by construction of the Gray code which always assures for $\vec{a} \neq \vec{a}^*$ existence of $\vec{b} \in \mathcal{N}_1(\vec{a})$ such that $g(\gamma^{-1}(\vec{b})) = g(\gamma^{-1}(\vec{a})) + 1$.

An investigation of the convergence velocity

$$\varphi_{(1+1)}(l, \vec{a}, p) \;=\; \sum_{k=0}^{w-g'(\vec{a})} k \cdot p_{\vec{a}}^+(k) \tag{6.41}$$

still exhibits further strange properties of g' and h', as concerning $\varphi_{(1+1)}$ both g' and h' show an extreme diversity of optimal mutation rates.

---

[11]Local optima of pseudoboolean functions are defined by means of the $\mathcal{N}_1$-neighborhood; see equation (1.25).

[12]A more detailed example is given in [Bäc93].

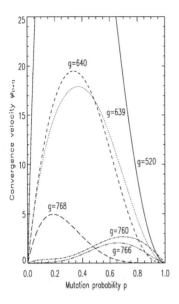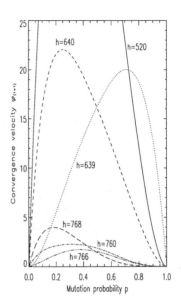

Fig. 6.10: Left: Convergence velocity $\varphi_{(1+1)}$ for varying mutation rate p, different values of $g'_a \in \{520, 639, 640, 760, 766, 768\}$ and $l = 10$, $w = 822$. Right: The corresponding curves for the objective function h'.

Figure 6.10 clarifies this statement by plots of the local convergence velocity $\varphi_{(1+1)}$ over p for g' (left) and h' (right). Now, both objective functions clearly possess discontinuous optimal mutation rate schedules which are by no means monotonically decreasing as the optimum is approached (e.g., notice the transitions $g' = 766 \rightarrow g' = 768$ and $h' = 639 \rightarrow h' = 640$ — although no Hamming cliffs exist in case of h', the optimal mutation rate for $h'^{-1}(639) = 1101000000$ is much larger than for $h'^{-1}(640) = 1111000000$).

To answer the question for the optimal mutation rate schedule, both criteria are taken into account here for a comparison: Maximization of the local convergence velocity $\varphi_{(1+1)}(l, \vec{a}, p)$ respectively maximization of the improvement probability $p_{\vec{a}}^{+}(l, \vec{a}, p)$. Both strategies yield irregular schedules of the optimal mutation rate, as can be seen from figure 6.11, which confronts the optimal schedules obtained for g' (left) and h' (right).

The schedule obtained from maximizing $p_{\vec{a}}^{+}$ shows sharp peaks and a highly discontinuous structure for both objective functions, but for g' an additional curiousness is identified in the range of objective function values around 767 (compare the left part of figure 6.9, demonstrating the optimum jump occurring in this range). The large optimal mutation

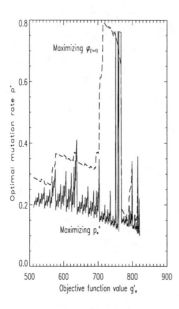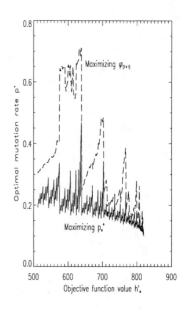

Fig. 6.11: Left: Dependency of the optimal mutation rate p^* on the actual objective function value $g'_a \in \{512, \ldots, 821\}$, where p^* is obtained by maximizing convergence velocity $\varphi_{(1+1)}$ (dashed curve) respectively by maximizing improvement probability $p_{\bar{a}}^+$ (normal curve). Right: The corresponding curves for the objective function h'.

rate in this range reflects the necessity to change several bit simultaneously for overcoming a local optimum in the boolean fitness landscape. A second difference of both schedules for g' and h' concerns the proximity of w, where the Gray code shows much smaller fluctuations of the optimal mutation rate than the standard code, thus reflecting the observation that fine-tuning of almost optimal solutions is simplified by a Gray code. The dashed curves, resembling the monument valley silhouette, correspond to the maximization of $\varphi_{(1+1)}$ and exhibit a higher degree of order than the other curves as they possess only a small number of wide peaks. These peaks indicate ranges of bit strings where a large progress can be achieved by changing multiple bits, thus clarifying that for the Gray code multiple bit changes may be helpful, while they are sometimes *necessary* for the standard code to achieve any progress at all.

Some experimental investigations concerning the time to absorption were performed for g' and h' in order to clarify the distinguishing properties of both encoding methods. Both optimal mutation rate schedules p_1^* (according to the improvement probability) and p_2^* (according to the convergence velocity) and the setting $p = 1/l$ are compared according to

l	w	g'			h'		
		$\bar{T}(p_1^*)$	$\bar{T}(p_2^*)$	$\bar{T}(1/l)$	$\bar{T}(p_1^*)$	$\bar{T}(p_2^*)$	$\bar{T}(1/l)$
8	206	79.1	83.8	812.3	56.5	52.9	76.4
9	411	87.6	87.2	1745.4	71.2	69.0	86.4
10	822	221.3	212.8	4227.1	89.8	95.1	132.4
11	1644	576.4	567.2	6403.5	132.6	121.9	156.0
12	3288	2160.5	2160.5	34225.1	157.5	140.2	187.1
13	6576	6185.5	5821.6	390072.1	157.0	160.8	205.7

Table 6.4. Experimental results concerning the mean time to absorption $\bar{T}$ for g' and h' with optimal mutation rate schedules p_1^* (according to the improvement probability) and p_2^* (according to the convergence velocity) and constant mutation rate $p = 1/l$ for different string lengths $l \in \{8, 9, 10, 11, 12, 13\}$. Each value reflects the mean over $N = 100$ experiments.

the mean time to absorption $\bar{T}(p)$, averaged over $N = 100$ experiments, for values of $l \in \{8, 9, 10, 11, 12, 13\}$ and initial objective function values 2^{l-1} in each case. According to our choice $w = 822$ for $l = 10$, the other values of w are — wherever possible — chosen by multiplying (dividing) by subsequent powers of 2 as l increases (decreases). The results are summarized in table[13] 6.4.

The table clarifies several important points: First, there does not exist a significant difference between both optimized mutation rate schedules. Second, the Gray code clearly enables the algorithm to find the optimal solution within time complexity $\mathcal{O}(l \cdot \ln l)$ and turns out to benefit just slightly from using an optimized mutation rate schedule rather than the $1/l$ heuristic. As known from section 6.1.1, the observed behavior is typical for unimodal pseudoboolean functions. Third, and most critical, the standard code engenders remarkable difficulties to the search by the existence of local optima the process may get trapped in. Overcoming local optima by means of an optimized mutation rate is possible, but the required search time increases dramatically when compared to the Gray code. If the mutation rate is simply fixed at a value of $1/l$, however, using the standard code becomes a hopeless method for optimizing g' within a reasonable amount of time (notice that l is ridiculously small).

---

[13]The table does not contain empirical standard deviations, but as an important remark we point out that standard deviations are in all cases in the same order of magnitude as the mean values.

6.2 Summary

Some progress concerning the role of mutation in Genetic Algorithms has been achieved by the results presented in section 6.1. Certainly, the role of mutation is not as unimportant as claimed by some researchers in the field. This observation from section 5.2, where mutation in combination with strong selective pressure turned out to yield surprisingly good results, was confirmed by theoretical investigations in sections 6.1.1 and 6.1.2.

The analysis of the unimodal pseudoboolean counting ones problem with respect to the optimal mutation rate control, convergence velocity and expected time to absorption yields several important results illustrating the principles of search algorithms traversing the boolean hypercube by bit mutation and selection. Based on the improvement probabilities derived in theorem 21, maximization of the convergence velocity led to an optimal mutation rate schedule which depends on the bit string length and the actual distance to the optimum, clarifying the inappropriateness of a constant mutation rate control which is independent of the dimension of the boolean space. Further investigations demonstrated that the most critical factor is given by the dimension l, which may turn the algorithm unusable if the mutation rate is chosen too large compared to $1/l$. Under such circumstances, time complexity quickly becomes exponential in l, in contrast to the time complexity $\mathcal{O}(l \cdot \ln l)$ achievable for $p = 1/l$. The latter heuristic turns out to be rather good as — according to numerical calculations for the true optimal mutation rate schedule — it can be improved by approximately just 5% when the optimal schedule is known (which is clearly not the case in general).

However, the results present an explanation of the observation of some researchers who reported improved velocity of a Genetic Algorithm using a mutation rate that decreases over time.

Increasing the offspring population size beyond $\lambda = 1$ still increases the deviation of the optimal mutation rate schedule from the $1/l$ heuristic. For small $\lambda > 1$ the speedup in terms of generations was shown to be linear, but it decreases as λ is further increased. On a larger scale, the dependency of the speedup on λ seems to be of logarithmic order as for Evolution Strategies. Additionally, the speedup depends on l in such a way that increasing l improves the speedup for a constant value of λ.

If $\mu > 1$ is also allowed, the ν-th order statistics according to equation (6.20) serves as a useful tool to describe the expected progress of the average objective function value of the μ best individuals. As demonstrated by figures 6.7 and 6.8, the resulting expression (6.30) for $\varphi_{(\mu \overset{+}{,} \lambda)}(l, \bar{f}_a, p)$ provides a correct and useful convergence velocity characterization for Evolutionary Algorithms based on mutation and selection and a discrete probability density function $p_{k'=k}$. In case of a continuous probability density function the theoretical approach presented here specializes to the results presented by Schwefel for Evolution Strategies (see equation (2.37)).

The simplest possible parameter optimization problems, following the general style of applying Genetic Algorithms to continuous optimization problems, were discussed in section 6.1.3. Though the objective functions discussed here — a single-parameter standard binary code and a single-parameter Gray code — seem to differ considerably from the counting ones problem, our investigations clarified that the Gray code problem and the counting ones problem belong to one class while the standard binary code plays the strange role. The fundamental advantage of the Gray code was identified by its unimodality in the decoding process, while in contrast to this the standard code may cause a multimodality in the mapping of bit strings to integer values. Assuming a mutation rate $p = 1/l$, the Gray code behaves logarithmically with respect to its time complexity as expected from knowledge about the counting ones problem. The same mutation rate control may be disastrous for the standard code as demonstrated by the exponentially growing time to absorption reported in table 6.4.

Searching for an optimal mutation rate schedule yields a highly discontinuous dependency of the mutation rate on the distance to the optimum, if improvement probabilities are maximized. For the standard code, occasionally occurring mutation rates above one half reflect the *necessity* to change several bits simultaneously for leaving local optima (crossing "Hamming cliffs"). Using an optimized mutation rate schedule considerably reduces the time to absorption for the standard code, but it remains much inferior to the Gray code results.

In real-world applications, however, multimodality of the objective function may cause a multimodal pseudoboolean fitness function although the decoding process remains unimodal by using the Gray code. Under such circumstances the resulting pseudoboolean problem may suffer from the same difficulties as the standard code does, but it is at least known that the Gray code does not create multimodality by its own as the standard code does. Consequently, using a Gray code in combination with a mutation rate $p = 1/l$ is the most reasonable recommendation for applying Genetic Algorithms to parameter optimization problems.

The highly discontinuous shape of the optimal mutation rate schedules presented in figure 6.11 can surely not be modeled by some kind of simple analytical expression for calculating the most appropriate mutation rate. Instead, it might give reason to develop a different idea which is based on providing a set of highly diverse, different mutation rates to the population members rather than restricting mutation probabilities to a single, constant one. For performing mutation, each individual may serve itself from the pool of available probabilities, and the probabilities may also undergo evolution by means of mutation and recombination, but trying to preserve their diversity at the same time. This idea, essentially similar to the self-adaptation processes of Evolution Strategies (see section 2.1) and Evolutionary Programming (see section 2.2), was already tested for mutation in Genetic Algorithms but has to be improved further to carry full conviction (see [Bäc92c] for the outline of a possible method to create sufficient diversity and for preliminary experimental results).

To conclude this chapter, we take the opportunity to present a speculative explanation of the remarkable convergence velocity reported in section 5.2.1 for a $(1,100)$-GA with $l = 900$ and $p = 0.001$ on the sphere model. Evidently, the algorithm gains its success solely from mutation and strong selective pressure. Assuming $p = 1/l$ (which is not completely correct for the result we refer to), we make the simplification that mutation changes *exactly* one single bit per application. This assumption requires *separability* of the objective function, i.e. a form $f(\vec{x}) = \sum_{i=1}^{n} f_i(x_i)$ where the f_i are one-dimensional subfunctions. Such a simplification excludes all really challenging examples of objective functions (by neglecting polygeny).

The central question to understand the algorithms' behavior on the 30-dimensional sphere model concerns the probability distribution imposed on the decoded parameter space by mutation in the bit string space. In general, this question is hard to answer because the probability distribution depends on the encoded parameter *itself*: If the individual representing a parameter value consists of k ones and $l - k$ zeros, the number of zeros (ones) will increase (decrease) by one with probability $1 - k/l$ (k/l). In other words, the closer the parameter value approaches its optimal value, the smaller becomes the probability to approach it even further; the optimum has a kind of repellor effect.

The *absolute value* $|\Delta x|$ of the change of the decoded parameter x, however, has a distribution which is invariant and independent of x (or, more exactly, its bit string representation). The density of this distribution is implicitly given by the probabilities $\mathcal{P}\{|\Delta x| = 2^i\} = 1/l$ $\forall i \in \{0, \ldots, l-1\}$, and the distribution function results from the observation that

$$\mathcal{P}\{2^0 \leq |\Delta x| \leq 2^k\} = \frac{k+1}{l} . \tag{6.42}$$

Generalizing this to a piecewise continuous distribution function for arbitrary[14] $|\Delta x| \in [2^{-1}, 2^{l-1}]$, we obtain

[14]There are basically two ways to obtain a continuous distribution and density function here: Extending the $|\Delta x|$ range as performed in the text, such that

$$\int_{2^{-1}}^{2^{l-1}} \frac{1}{lx \ln 2} \, dx = 1 ,$$

or using

$$\int_{1}^{2^{l-1}} \frac{1}{lx \ln 2} \, dx = 1 - 1/l ,$$

$$F_{|\Delta x|}(x) \;=\; \begin{cases} 0 & ,\; x \leq 2^{-1} \\ \left(\frac{\ln x}{\ln 2} + 1\right)/l & ,\; 2^{-1} \leq x \leq 2^{l-1} \\ 1 & ,\; x \geq 2^{l-1} \end{cases} \qquad (6.43)$$

and the density function is

$$f_{|\Delta x|}(x) \;=\; \frac{1}{lx \ln 2} \quad . \qquad (6.44)$$

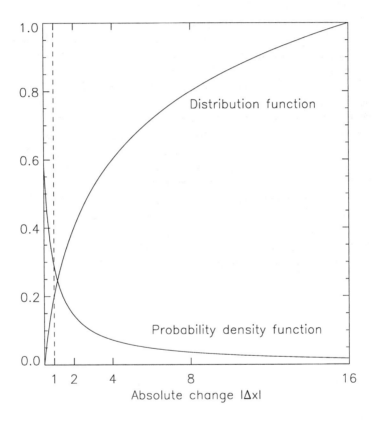

Fig. 6.12: Distribution function and probability density function of the continuous generalization describing the effect of the binary mutation operator for bit string length $l = 5$.

These considerations clarify that within the range of possible changes $[1, 2^{l-1}]$ smaller variations are more likely to occur than larger ones. Figure 6.12 visualizes this for $l = 5$.

and the argument that the continuous version implies $l \to \infty$, i.e., the representation of infinitely many points.

In contrast to the distribution of $|\Delta x|$, which is invariant and does not undergo adaptation during the optimization process, the distribution of Δx changes remarkably as its portion for $\Delta x > 0$ becomes "full of holes" as the optimum is approached, thus making further improvements less likely. For an elitist strategy the negative part of the distribution is essentially cut off, but to achieve an improvement just the few isolated positive changes have to be realized.

This model may explain some observations concerning the behavior of Genetic Algorithms for parameter optimization. First, a large number of bits l_x encoding a single parameter offers advantages since many bits are likely to offer a still non-vanishing portion of the useful branch of the density function even if the optimum is already approached in Euclidean space. Second, as long as there is a sufficient portion of the probability density function available for improvements, smaller improvements are more likely to occur than larger ones, i.e. the distribution has a general shape that qualitatively resembles those used by Evolution Strategies and Evolutionary Programming.

Based on these considerations, it is likely to be possible to demonstrate that for unimodal objective functions such as the sphere model, a Genetic Algorithm using mutation and strong selection may reach a convergence velocity of the same order as Evolution Strategies (see [MSV93] for a similar argument into this direction). However, as the mutation operator most likely changes just one variable at a time, this holds only for separable objective functions, such that the general claim made by Mühlenbein et al. not to change too many variables at the same time does not hold for really interesting problems. A number of questions are still open here for further research.

*The discovery of appropriate variables for biology
is itself an act of creation.*
Brian C. Goodwin (in C. H. Waddington, editor:
Towards a Theoretical Biology, Vol. 2; Edinburgh University Press 1969).

7

An Experiment in Meta-Evolution

So far, the basic knowledge about setting up the parameters of Evolutionary Algorithms stems from a lot of empirical work and few theoretical results. The standard guidelines for parameters such as crossover rate, mutation probability, and population size as well as the standard settings of the recombination operator and selection mechanism were presented in chapter 2 for the Evolutionary Algorithms.

In the case of Evolution Strategies and Evolutionary Programming, the self-adaptation mechanism for strategy parameters solves this *parameterization problem* in an elegant way, while for Genetic Algorithms no such technique is employed. Chapter 6 served to identify a reasonable choice of the mutation rate, but no theoretically confirmed knowledge about the choice of the crossover rate and the crossover operator is available. With respect to the optimal population size for Genetic Algorithms, Goldberg presented some theoretical arguments based on maximizing the number of schemata processed by the algorithm within fixed time, arriving at an optimal size $\lambda^* = 3$ for serial implementations and extremely small string length[1] [Gol89b]. However, as indicated in section 2.3.7 and chapter 6, it is by no means clear whether the schema processing point of view is appropriately preferred to the convergence velocity investigations presented in section 2.1.7 and chapter 6. As pointed out several times, we prefer the point of view which concentrates on a convergence velocity analysis.

Consequently, the search for useful parameter settings of a Genetic Algorithm constitutes an optimization problem by itself, leading to the idea of using an Evolutionary Algorithm on a higher level to evolve optimal parameter settings of Genetic Algorithms. Due to the existence

---

[1]In case of parallel implementations, his result indicates — not surprisingly — to make population size as large as possible. Furthermore, his results also showed an exponential dependence on string length l, which makes them unusable for any reasonable string length.

of two logically different levels in such an approach, it is reasonable to call it a *meta-evolutionary algorithm*[2]. By concentrating on meta-evolution in this chapter, we will radically deviate from the biological model, where no two-level evolution process is to be observed but the self-adaptation principle can well be identified (as argued in chapter 2). However, there are several reasons why meta-evolution promises to yield some helpful insight into the working principles of Evolutionary Algorithms:

First, meta-evolution provides the possibility to test whether the basic heuristic and the theoretical knowledge about parameterizations of Genetic Algorithms is also evolvable by the experimental approach, thus allowing us to confirm the heuristics or to point at alternatives. This is of special interest for discrete parameters determining the *configuration* of the algorithms, i.e., the choice of crossover operator and selection mechanism.

Second, the new Evolutionary Algorithm for the meta-level is designed to search a space consisting of continuous parameters (p_c, p_m, η^+) and discrete parameters (μ, λ, tournament size q, number of crossover points z, selection operator s, crossover operator r, elitist flag e) at the same time, such that a mixture of concepts from Evolution Strategies and Genetic Algorithms seems to be appropriate on the meta-level. By combining continuous and discrete parameters to form structures that undergo optimization, we naturally arrive at a prototype algorithm for handling *nonlinear mixed-integer problems*, which are also of much interest for industrial applications[3]. Due to the lack of applicable algorithms, such problems are usually handled by optimizing discrete and continuous parameters separately, thus assuming total separability of the discrete and continuous components of the problem. Often, however, the (discrete) design process is performed "by hand," and just the remaining continuous parameters are optimized. For instance, Lohmann uses the term *structure evolution* to denote the discrete design process and he decouples it to a large extent from the continuous parameter optimization process in his implementation for evolving structures in visual systems. In addition, he introduces isolation of subpopulations which contain individuals representing similar structures for competition [Loh91, Loh92a, Loh92b]. Herdy investigates multipopulation algorithms to self-adapt single global parameters of Evolution Strategies such as the isolation time [Her92] or the population size. In contrast to their work, the evolutionary optimization principle is simply transferred to individuals that combine discrete and continuous variables, implying the possibility of simultaneous modification of all variables by mutation.

Third, the meta-evolution process can be implemented efficiently on a parallel computer, thus allowing for still relatively small but reason-

---

[2] The reader should be careful not to confuse this with the term meta-EP used by Fogel to denote self-adaptation of variances in Evolutionary Programming (see section 2.2).

[3] As an example, consider any kind of problem where only a limited number of fixed components are permitted for some variables, e.g. in case of material constants.

able numbers of function evaluations performed by each of the Genetic Algorithms which are to be evolved. In this way, the number of individuals is just limited by the number of processors available. Some information about the parallel machine and software enviroment used for the experiments is given in appendix D.

Of course, the meta-evolution approach also has disadvantages, e.g. concerning the parameter settings of the meta-algorithm *itself*. Seemingly, the problem is shifted one level upwards this way, but the meta-level parameterization is likely to be more robust than the parameterizations of Genetic Algorithms themselves. A more serious problem consists in defining a useful fitness function to assess the quality of Genetic Algorithms. It is easily solved if maximization of convergence velocity is intended, but maximizing convergence reliability is a much harder and in general unsolvable problem. The experiments presented in section 7.3 will therefore concentrate on convergence velocity.

Grefenstette is the only researcher who has so far reported results of a meta-evolution approach [Gre86]. He allowed for a variation of population size, crossover probability, mutation rate, generation gap[4], scaling window, and selection strategy (proportional selection, pure or elitist). The parameter space was discretized even for the continuous parameters by using a coarse grid allowing for eight respectively sixteen different settings of each parameter in order to employ a Genetic Algorithm also on the meta-level. Furthermore, Grefenstette used the *online-* and *offline-performance* measure[5], which is not the best measure for solving static optimization problems as discussed in this work.

The approach presented here differs remarkably from those of Grefenstette due to the qualitatively new meta-algorithm, the fitness measure for individuals, and the characteristics of the search space (higher dimension, partially different parameters, continuous variation of the continuous parameters). In the remainder of this chapter a brief overview of parallel Evolutionary Algorithms is presented (section 7.1) before discussing the meta-Evolutionary Algorithm (section 7.2) and the experimental test results (section 7.3).

---

[4]The percentage of the population to be replaced during each generation; the remainder is chosen (at random) to survive intact. The generation gap allows for shifting from the generation-based basic working scheme towards the extreme of just creating one new individual per "generation" (c.f. the introductory remarks in section 2.2). See [DS93] for a more detailed discussion of the generation gap topic.

[5]These measures, introduced by De Jong (see [DeJ75], pp. 10–13), yield the average fitness of *all* tested structures over the course of the search (online) respectively the average of the *best* fitness found between generations zero and t for all $t \in \{0, \ldots, \tau_{GA}\}$ (offline; τ_{GA} denotes the running time of the algorithm). In other words, online performance and offline performance are moving averages over all respectively the best individuals found so far, thus incorporating the complete history of the process.

7.1 Parallel Evolutionary Algorithms

A basic advantage of all Evolutionary Algorithms lies in the inherent parallelism of the algorithms, reflecting the character of organic evolution to proceed simultaneously on organizational levels such as individuals, populations, and species. Moreover, parallel implementations of Evolutionary Algorithms are easily scalable to larger populations, thus providing a good potential to exploit even massively parallel hardware. A description of the generally existing possibilities to parallelize Evolutionary Algorithms was recently presented by Hoffmeister [Hof91].

Without going into too much detail here, the two main approaches and their biological inspiration, i.e., the *migration model* and the *diffusion model*, are mentioned here.

In case of the migration model, a population is divided into a number of independent — isolated — subpopulations, so-called *demes* (see [Fut90], p. 146). These subpopulations evolve in isolation most of the time, but occasionally individuals *migrate* between a subpopulation and its neighbors. Selection as well as recombination are restricted by this approach to work in each subpopulation as usual, such that each subpopulation may evolve towards different locally optimal regions of the search space. Migration events offer the chance to recombine favorable information of one deme with information evolved in another deme, such that still uncovered regions of the search space may be tested.

The migration model aims at preserving the diversity between different subpopulations, such that the frequency of migration events is a critical new parameter introduced by this concept. Migrating good information at each generation will almost unify all subpopulations to one large population, without strong differences to a standard Evolutionary Algorithm. According to the results presented by Tanese, performance degrades if migration happens too frequently or too infrequently, and values between 5 and 20 generations served as useful settings [Tan87, Tan89]. According to Hoffmeister, three further parameters are necessary to characterize the migration policy completely [Hof91]: The number of individuals to exchange, a strategy for choosing the emigrants, and a replacement strategy to incorporate the immigrants. Usually, the best individuals are migrated and replace the worst individuals of the target population, but less deterministic (and more realistic, i.e., more natural) schemes may be thought of. Apart from some experimental results concerning migration rate and the number of migrants, no systematic experimental or theoretical investigations of these parameters are reported in the literature. Pettey and Leuze presented an analysis of a migration model with the aim of demonstrating that their parallel Genetic Algorithm (presented in [PLG87]) conforms with the schema theorem (theorem 11) in order to justify "efficiency" of the algorithm [PL89], but this is by no means related to the basic assumption that convergence reliability is increased by migration model approaches nor does it say something about the speedup achieved by parallelism. Some further results obtained by migration models on the basis of Genetic Algorithms are reported by Cohoon et al. [CHMR87, CMR91b, CMR91a] and Starkweather et al. [SWM91, WS90], while Rudolph implemented the corresponding model using Evolution Strategies [Rud91].

In contrast to the migration model, where parallelization is exploited on the level of populations (e.g., by assigning each deme to its own processor, coarse-grained parallelism), the diffusion model concentrates on interactions of individuals within a single population. In this case, parallelization is performed on the level of individuals (fine-grained parallelism), resulting in a large number of interacting parallel processes of low complexity, such that a high communication bandwidth is necessary for the target machine. This approach requires a parallelization of the Evolutionary Algorithm itself rather than adding a migration concept to the algorithm.

Usually, a fine-grained parallel Evolutionary Algorithm restricts communication of individuals to a local neighborhood structure, such that recombination and selection are applied locally within these neighborhoods. This way, advantageous genetic information may arise at different points in the topological interaction structure and spread slowly over the population, an imagination which has served to coin the term diffusion model. According to its local characteristics, the diffusion model requires a modification of the selection mechanism in order to be locally applicable (e.g., standard proportional selection would require knowledge of the populations' total fitness, a global measure). In addition to this, the neighborhood size and the interaction structure play an important role for maintaining diversity (see e.g. [GS90], pp. 142–151, for a discussion of these topics). A discussion of critical components of massively parallel implementations of Genetic Algorithms was recently presented by Gorges-Schleuter (concerning local mating structures) [GS92] and Collins and Jefferson (with respect to a comparison of global — panmictic — selection and local selection strategies, indicating strong advantages of the latter) [CJ91]. As a third representative of massively parallel Genetic Algorithms, we mention the implementation of Spiessens and Manderick who also reported an improved convergence reliability offered by local selection and recombination techniques [SM90, SM91b].

Though this overview can hardly be complete (and is not intended to be), it should suffice to clarify that these approaches try to exploit the — if communication overhead is neglected — almost linear speedup of parallel implementations and to emphasize convergence reliability by incorporating local operations and restricted information exchange. This way, parallelism might serve as a basis to implement faster, scalable, and biologically more appropriate Evolutionary Algorithms.

To conclude this brief overview, it seems useful to mention the role of the available parallel hardware for choosing a coarse-grained or fine-grained parallel implementation. Massively parallel machines with a large number of relatively simple processors and high communication bandwidth (such as the Connection Machine) are appropriately used for

implementing the diffusion model. On the contrary, the migration model
requires few communication and relatively few parallel processes but
processors capable of running a complete Evolutionary Algorithm, each.
Consequently, an MIMD-machine[6] is recommendable in the second case
while an SIMD-machine[7] suffices in the first case. Of course, however,
the diffusion model can be implemented also on machines with few processors by topologically subdividing the total population into parts running on single processors. As recently clarified by Sprave, such an implementation can be extended to a mixture of migration and diffusion
model by adding migration between topological subcomponents of the
population structure to the implementation [Spr93].

For a more detailed consideration of hardware and communication
issues, the reader is referred to the work of Hoffmeister [HS90b, Hof91].

7.2   The Algorithm

A parallelization of the meta-evolution approach is desirable due to the
enormous computational effort required to evaluate each generation of
the meta-Evolutionary Algorithm. This way, parallelism serves just to
speed up the algorithm rather than introducing some qualitatively new
feature. Consequently, the algorithm is appropriately implemented by
a so-called *master-slave* approach, i.e., a global instance (the meta-EA)
controls a number of worker processes running in parallel, where each
worker process evaluates one of the Genetic Algorithms, corresponding
to an individual of the master's population. This implies that the population size of the meta-algorithm is identical to the number of slave
processes. The communication between master and slaves proceeds in a
completely synchronous way, following the generation sequence passed
by the meta-algorithm. For evaluating the meta-algorithm's population,
each individual is interpreted as description of a Genetic Algorithm and
passed to the slaves, which run the Genetic Algorithms and deliver an
evaluation result to the master. In order to facilitate a fair comparison
of the fitness of GA parameterizations, each slave algorithm is allowed
to run for a fixed number of function evaluations. This arrangement also
assures similar total running times of all slave algorithms (presupposing
that each slave process runs on its own processor) and guarantees idle
times caused by the generation-based synchronization to be as short as
possible. The master-slave concept is illustrated in figure 7.1.

Following the formalization of Evolutionary Algorithms as introduced in definition 2.1, a meta-Evolutionary Algorithm is formally characterized by the fact that its space of individuals I possesses a component
which also describes an Evolutionary Algorithm. Definition 7.1 captures

---

[6]Multiple Instruction stream, Multiple Data stream.
[7]Single Instruction stream, Multiple Data stream.

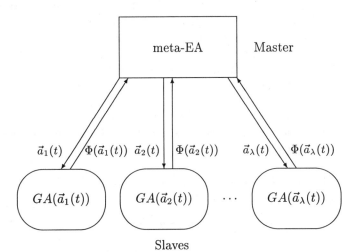

Fig. 7.1: Structure of the master-slave implementation of a meta-Evolutionary Algorithm, which is running as the master-process. At each generation of the master, each slave evaluates one of the meta-EA's individuals by running the Genetic Algorithm specified by that individual. Reprinted by permission of Springer-Verlag from Th. Bäck: *Parallel Optimization of Evolutionary Algorithms*, in Davidor, Schwefel, Männer: *Parallel Problem Solving from Nature — PPSN III*, Lecture Notes in Computer Science 866, p. 420, fig. 1, copyright © Springer-Verlag Berlin Heidelberg 1994.

this property.

Definition 7.1 (Meta-Evolutionary Algorithm)
An Evolutionary Algorithm $\text{EA} = (I, \Phi, \Omega, \Psi, s, \iota, \mu, \lambda)$, $I = A_x \times A_s$, *is called a* meta-Evolutionary Algorithm, *iff a family*

$$(\text{EA}')_{A_x} \;=\; (I', \Phi', \Omega', \Psi', s', \iota', \mu', \lambda')_{A_x} \tag{7.1}$$

of Evolutionary Algorithms exists such that $\forall t, \vec{a}_i(t) = (\vec{x}_i(t), \vec{y}_i(t)) \in A_x \times A_s$:

$$\Phi(\vec{a}_i(t)) \;=\; \mathcal{F}(P'(\tau_{\text{EA}'(\vec{x}_i(t))})) \;\;, \tag{7.2}$$

where $\mathcal{F} : (I')^{\mu'} \to I\!\!R$ *denotes a fitness function for populations* $P'(t)$ *of Evolutionary Algorithms (e.g.,* $\mathcal{F}(P'(t)) = \min\{\Phi'(\vec{a}'_i(t)) \mid \vec{a}'_i(t) \in P'(t)\}$).

The definition clarifies that each "object variable" component $\vec{x}_i(t) \in A_x$ of the meta-EA specifies a slave-algorithm $\text{EA}' = \text{EA}'(\vec{x}_i(t))$. The fitness function Φ of the meta-algorithm is evaluated according to the final population $P'(\tau_{\mathrm{EA}'(\vec{x}_i(t))})$, where $\tau_{\mathrm{EA}'(\vec{x}_i(t))}$ denotes the running time (definition 2.3) of the Evolutionary Algorithm specified by $\vec{x}_i(t)$. One of the simplest methods to evaluate the quality of $\mathrm{EA}'(\vec{x}_i(t))$ is just to use the best objective function value that occurs in the final population, and this method is chosen here to evolve algorithms with high convergence velocity.

Since it is intended here to apply meta-evolution to algorithms which are basically Genetic Algorithms, extended by some additional selection and recombination mechanisms, the object variable set A_x of the meta-Evolutionary Algorithm has the following structure:

$$
\begin{aligned}
A_x \;=\; & [0,1] \times [0,0.5] \times [1,2] \times \{1,\ldots,20\} \times \\
& \{1,\ldots,100\} \times \{1,\ldots,100\} \times \{1,\ldots,8\} \times \qquad (7.3) \\
& \{P,R,C,T\} \times \{S,U,D,\_\} \times \{0,1\} \;\;.
\end{aligned}
$$

An element $\vec{x} \in A_x$ consists of the components

- crossover probability $p_c' \in [0,1]$,

- mutation rate $p_m' \in [0,0.5]$,

- maximal expected value $\eta'^{+} \in [1,2]$ for linear ranking selection (cf. section 5.1.2),

- tournament size $q' \in \{1,\ldots,20\}$ for tournament selection (cf. section 5.1.3),

- parent population size[8] $\mu' \in \{1,\ldots,100\}$,

- offspring population size $\lambda' \in \{1,\ldots,100\}$,

- number of crossover points[9] $z' \in \{1,\ldots,8\}$,

- selection operator[10]

$$
s' \;=\; \begin{cases}
s_{\{(\mu',\lambda'),\omega'\}} & (P) \;\;,\;\; (\mu,\lambda)\text{-proportional} \\
s_{\{(\mu',\lambda'),\eta'+\}} & (R) \;\;,\;\; (\mu,\lambda)\text{-linear ranking} \\
s_{\{(\mu',\lambda'),q'\}} & (T) \;\;,\;\; (\mu,\lambda)\text{-tournament} \\
s_{(\mu',\lambda')} & (C) \;\;,\;\; (\mu,\lambda)\text{-selection} \;\;,
\end{cases}
\qquad (7.4)
$$

---

[8]The most general algorithms discussed here allow for $\mu' \neq \lambda'$, thus introducing the extinctive variants of proportional selection, linear ranking, and tournament selection (cf. section 5.1.6) to GAs.

[9]The maximum of eight points stems from the empirical observation reported in section 2.3.3.

[10]See section 5.1.6 for a presentation of these selection mechanisms.

- recombination operator[11]

$$
r' = \begin{cases}
r_{\{p'_c, z'\}} & (S) \quad, \quad \text{standard } z'\text{-point} \\
r_{\{p'_c\}} & (U) \quad, \quad \text{uniform} \\
r_{d\{p'_c\}} & (D) \quad, \quad \text{sexual, discrete} \\
id & (\_) \quad, \quad \text{no recombination} \quad,
\end{cases}
\tag{7.5}
$$

- elitist flag e' (if the value is one, the elitist[12] version of the selection mechanism is used).

The search space defined this way consists of three continuous and seven discrete variables, using symbols rather than numbers to denote the selection and recombination operator (just for reasons of readability). There exist some relations between certain variables, however, which cause a variation of the dimension of the search space during the search, i.e.:

(1) The crossover probability p'_c is superfluous if $\mu' = 1$ or $r' = id$ (no recombination) is fulfilled.

(2) The number of crossover points z' is unimportant if $\mu' = 1$ or $r' \neq r_{\{p'_c, z'\}}$ (standard z'-point crossover).

(3) The maximal expected value η'^{+} is used only if (μ, λ)-linear ranking is enabled ($s' = s_{\{(\mu', \lambda'), \eta'^{+}\}}$).

(4) The tournament size q' is used only if (μ, λ)-tournament selection is enabled ($s' = s_{\{(\mu', \lambda'), q'\}}$).

Furthermore, the constraint $\mu' \leq \lambda'$ is required to hold for parent and offspring population size. Boundary conditions $u_i \leq x_i \leq v_i$ concerning the range of values allowed for each variable x_i ($i \in \{1, \ldots, 6\}$) are assured by the meta-algorithm by setting $x_i = u_i$ (v_i) whenever the range of possible values would be left by a mutation at the lower bound u_i (upper bound v_i).

The master-algorithm which was developed to handle the mixed-integer problem raised by the meta-algorithm combines concepts from Evolution Strategies to mutate six parameters (p'_c, p'_m, η'^{+}, q', μ', λ') and self-adapt their standard deviations and concepts from Genetic Algorithms to define mutation on the remaining four parameters (z', s', r', e'). Consequently, the strategy parameter set $A_s = \mathbb{R}_+^6$ is used for the meta-EA, and based on the object variable terminology $x_1 = p'_c$,

---

[11]$id : I^\mu \to I^\mu$ denotes the identity mapping, i.e. $id(P) = P$.
[12]See definition 5.7.

$x_2 = p'_m$, $x_3 = \eta'^+$, $x_4 = q'$, $x_5 = \mu'$, $x_6 = \lambda'$, $x_7 = z'$, $x_8 = s'$, $x_9 = r'$, $x_{10} = e'$, the mutation operator of the meta-algorithm works as follows:

$$
\begin{aligned}
\sigma'_i &= \sigma_i \cdot \exp(\tau' \cdot N(0,1) + \tau \cdot N_i(0,1)) && \forall i \in \{1,\ldots,6\} \\
x'_i &= x_i + \sigma'_i \cdot N_i(0,1) && \forall i \in \{1,2,3\} \\
x'_i &= x_i + \lfloor \sigma'_i \cdot N_i(0,1) \rfloor && \forall i \in \{4,5,6\}
\end{aligned}
$$

$$
x'_7 = \begin{cases} x_7 & , \ \chi > p_m \\ u \in \{1,\ldots,8\} & , \ \chi \le p_m \end{cases}
$$

$$
x'_8 = \begin{cases} x_8 & , \ \chi > p_m \\ u \in \{P,R,C,T\} & , \ \chi \le p_m \end{cases} \tag{7.6}
$$

$$
x'_9 = \begin{cases} x_9 & , \ \chi > p_m \\ u \in \{S,U,D,\_\} & , \ \chi \le p_m \end{cases}
$$

$$
x'_{10} = \begin{cases} x_{10} & , \ \chi > p_m \\ u \in \{0,1\} & , \ \chi \le p_m \end{cases} .
$$

The variables $x_1,\ldots,x_6$ are mutated just as in Evolution Strategies, ($n = 6 \Rightarrow \tau' = 1/\sqrt{12}$, $\tau = 1/\sqrt{2\sqrt{6}}$), except that in order to yield integer values the fractional parts of the changes of x_4, x_5, and x_6 remain unconsidered. The initialization of all variables is performed randomly uniform within the search space, and standard deviations are initialized to one sixtieth of the total range of values allowed for the object variables (i.e., $\sigma_1(0) = 1/60$, $\sigma_2(0) = 1/120$, $\sigma_3(0) = 1/60$, $\sigma_4(0) = 20/60$, $\sigma_5(0) = 100/60$, $\sigma_6(0) = 100/60$).

In the case of $x_7,\ldots,x_{10}$ the underlying discrete alphabet is of low cardinality, such that uniform mutation is applied similar to the mutation in Genetic Algorithms[13]. $\chi \in [0,1]$ denotes a uniform random variable sampled to decide for each of these four variables whether the uniform mutation operator is applied, according to the meta-algorithm's mutation rate p_m.

In addition to mutation, a recombination operator $r_{di} : I^\mu \to I^\lambda$ in the style of Evolution Strategies is used by the meta-algorithm, applying discrete recombination to object variables and intermediate recombination to the strategy parameters $\vec{\sigma} = (\sigma_1,\ldots,\sigma_6)$. The mutation probability for uniform mutation is fixed to a value $p_m = 0.05$, and due to some technical restrictions regarding the number of available processors a (4,30)-selection strategy is chosen for the master algorithm.

Altogether, the resulting algorithm is a new heuristic for searching spaces of inhomogeneous structure, e.g. mixed-integer problem spaces. Though the combination of concepts from Evolution Strategies and Genetic Algorithms seems to be straightforward, no comparable approach

---

[13]It is a serious problem to decide at which cardinality of the alphabet one should switch from uniform mutation to a mutation operator that prefers smaller changes to large ones, and it is not solvable at all when there exists no notion of a distance measure on the discrete space (e.g., on $\{P,R,C,T\}$).

was discussed in the literature so far. The feasibility of this combination technique is evaluated in the following section with respect to the meta-evolution of convergence velocity.

7.3 Evolving Convergence Velocity

Within this section we concentrate on performing experiments with the sphere model, aiming at the evolution of a Genetic Algorithm with maximum convergence velocity. Furthermore, the experiment serves as a method to investigate the capabilities of the new meta-algorithm.

In order to perform the experiments, the meta-algorithm was allowed to run for 50 generations, corresponding to 1504 executions of Genetic Algorithms. Conducting such an experiment requires a considerable amount of computing time[14], such that each slave-algorithm has to be restricted with respect to its computational effort by the following measures: The running time is limited to 10^4 function evaluations, i.e., $\iota(P'(t)) = \text{true} \Leftrightarrow \mu' + \lambda' \cdot t > 10^4$, the problem dimension is chosen to be[15] $n = 20$ (rather than 30, as before), and each slave-algorithm is executed twice to yield the average final best objective function value of both runs as result. Therefore, we may think of a noisy objective function which is optimized by the meta-algorithm, and we conclude from section 4.2 that the algorithm used here is also suitable to cope with such circumstances. Notice, however, that the comparison of Genetic Algorithms is fair with respect to their initial populations, which are guaranteed to be identical for all individuals of the meta-algorithm and for each of the two independent runs. In order to check results for their general validity, the algorithms obtained by the meta-evolution process are also verified by executing them for a statistically significant number of serial runs and averaging the results.

The test plan consists of the following increasingly generalized experiments:

(1) The population sizes are fixed at values $\mu' = \lambda' = 50$ and the selection operator is fixed to proportional selection. Except the discrete recombination operator, these restrictions define an evolution experiment within the space of standard Genetic Algorithms. This experiment serves to verify whether the meta-algorithm is able to evolve an appropriate mutation rate that does not deviate too much from $1/l = 1/600 \approx 0.00167$. In addition to this, the crossover operator and its application rate are of high interest. The search space dimension in case of this experiment is just 4–5, depending on the recombination operator.

---

[14] Approximately sixteen hours per experiment in case of the problem size presented here.

[15] Using $l_x = 30$ as defined in section 2.3.6 to be the standard setting.

(2) The population sizes remain fixed, but the selection operator is allowed to vary. This experiment serves to evolve the appropriate selection mechanism (tournament selection with a maximum value of q') and a mutation rate that reflects the higher selective pressure. Furthermore, the influence (if any) of the crossover operator is investigated under expected conditions of strong selective pressure. Due to the fixation of μ' and λ', the search space dimension varies in the range 4–8.

(3) The complete search space according to equation (7.3) is permitted. This experiment is used to verify the expectation that an extinctive selection operator and relatively large mutation rates should evolve according to the results from chapter 6. The dimension of the search space varies in the range 6–10, depending on the recombination and selection operators.

The initial and final populations in case of experiment (1) are shown in tables[16] 7.1 and 7.2, respectively. As to be expected, the initial population (table 7.1) is very diverse. By chance, it includes some algorithms that perform relatively well. In this early stage of the search the mutation rate p'_m of the slave algorithms dominates the fitness function completely. Most mutation rates are much too large and cause an extremely bad fitness of the corresponding individuals. Due to this dominating role of mutation it is not surprising to identify the best individuals having relatively small mutation rates.

After running the meta-algorithm for 50 generations, the population shown in table 7.2 is obtained. This final result has to be interpreted in view of the fact that the fitness function is noisy. Thus, some remaining fitness differences obtained for very similar individuals are surely caused by this fact, and we concentrate on observations of a more global nature: The population has converged to a small range of genotypic diversity, and the small selective pressure of proportional selection meets our expectation to evolve mutation rates close to $1/l$ with a surprisingly high accuracy. Mutation rates which are larger or smaller than this value cause a degradation of fitness (if all other parameters are approximately constant). The inappropriate selection mechanism prevents the algorithms from exploiting the benefits of larger mutation rates.

Crossover — in this case a uniform crossover operator — turns out to have a clear impact on the search. A crossover probability close to one as observed for all individuals in the final population gives some evidence to apply recombination in general to all individuals of a population as performed in Evolution Strategies. The concentration on uniform crossover clarifies the potential usefulness of highly disruptive recombination operators and confirms some empirical observations recently reported by other researchers (e.g., [Sys89, SD91b, SE91]).

---

[16]Within this and all following tables, the values of parameters that have no impact on the behavior of the Genetic Algorithm according to the rules (1)–(4) are just omitted for reasons of clarity of the presentation.

p_c'	p_m'	z'	r'	e'	Φ
0.469	0.02122	—	D	1	$6.43204 \cdot 10^2$
0.239	0.02183	—	D	1	$6.85113 \cdot 10^2$
0.975	0.03561	—	_	1	$1.74747 \cdot 10^3$
0.247	0.04263	8	S	1	$2.42679 \cdot 10^3$
0.265	0.10329	—	_	1	$3.46830 \cdot 10^3$
0.424	0.05198	1	S	0	$4.77329 \cdot 10^3$
0.573	0.10501	—	D	1	$5.10812 \cdot 10^3$
0.194	0.15447	4	S	1	$5.99915 \cdot 10^3$
0.442	0.24631	—	_	1	$8.07875 \cdot 10^3$
0.323	0.35874	6	S	0	$8.39357 \cdot 10^3$
0.999	0.33714	3	S	0	$8.70468 \cdot 10^3$
0.283	0.09659	4	S	0	$8.79064 \cdot 10^3$
0.325	0.26309	—	_	1	$8.79426 \cdot 10^3$
0.280	0.19972	5	S	0	$8.84707 \cdot 10^3$
0.764	0.49582	—	U	0	$9.08696 \cdot 10^3$
0.198	0.49794	—	U	1	$9.16742 \cdot 10^3$
0.486	0.33294	—	_	1	$9.54032 \cdot 10^3$
0.233	0.22491	3	S	0	$9.65002 \cdot 10^3$
0.695	0.43110	—	U	1	$9.80524 \cdot 10^3$
0.175	0.26968	—	_	0	$9.82232 \cdot 10^3$
0.135	0.22431	—	D	0	$9.84021 \cdot 10^3$
0.154	0.28594	—	U	0	$1.01346 \cdot 10^4$
0.356	0.47504	2	S	1	$1.01738 \cdot 10^4$
0.143	0.47290	—	U	1	$1.03939 \cdot 10^4$
0.738	0.38947	—	_	0	$1.03988 \cdot 10^4$
0.916	0.36282	—	_	0	$1.04819 \cdot 10^4$
0.446	0.47438	8	S	1	$1.04929 \cdot 10^4$
0.152	0.45008	5	S	1	$1.08379 \cdot 10^4$
0.568	0.47423	—	U	1	$1.11591 \cdot 10^4$
0.044	0.45816	—	U	0	$1.18575 \cdot 10^4$

Table 7.1. Initial population (generation 50) of the meta-evolution experiment using proportional selection ($\omega' = 5$, $\mu' = \lambda' = 50$). Reprinted by permission of Springer-Verlag from Th. Bäck: *Parallel Optimization of Evolutionary Algorithms*, in Davidor, Schwefel, Männer: *Parallel Problem Solving from Nature — PPSN III*, Lecture Notes in Computer Science 866, p. 423, table 1 (left), copyright © Springer-Verlag Berlin Heidelberg 1994.

p'_c	p'_m	z'	r'	e'	Φ
0.969	0.00151	—	U	1	$3.924470 \cdot 10^0$
0.956	0.00118	—	U	1	$4.784130 \cdot 10^0$
0.957	0.00153	—	U	1	$5.086330 \cdot 10^0$
0.956	0.00160	—	U	1	$5.600480 \cdot 10^0$
0.957	0.00137	—	U	1	$5.616090 \cdot 10^0$
0.959	0.00151	—	U	1	$5.999380 \cdot 10^0$
0.957	0.00181	—	U	1	$6.543100 \cdot 10^0$
0.963	0.00130	—	U	1	$6.615280 \cdot 10^0$
0.960	0.00144	—	U	1	$7.188730 \cdot 10^0$
0.964	0.00153	—	U	1	$7.522640 \cdot 10^0$
0.961	0.00297	—	U	1	$8.227170 \cdot 10^0$
0.956	0.00142	—	U	1	$8.264990 \cdot 10^0$
0.958	0.00110	—	U	1	$8.523150 \cdot 10^0$
0.961	0.00140	—	U	1	$8.546150 \cdot 10^0$
0.965	0.00134	—	U	1	$9.338230 \cdot 10^0$
0.964	0.00127	—	U	1	$9.521460 \cdot 10^0$
0.957	0.00208	—	U	1	$9.761820 \cdot 10^0$
0.961	0.00184	—	U	1	$1.000500 \cdot 10^1$
0.960	0.00191	—	U	1	$1.219270 \cdot 10^1$
0.957	0.00160	—	U	1	$1.238260 \cdot 10^1$
0.967	0.00141	—	U	1	$1.310300 \cdot 10^1$
0.968	0.00144	—	U	1	$1.464350 \cdot 10^1$
0.956	0.00146	—	U	1	$1.589780 \cdot 10^1$
0.960	0.00130	—	U	1	$1.780140 \cdot 10^1$
0.956	0.00105	—	U	1	$1.874710 \cdot 10^1$
0.959	0.00121	—	U	1	$1.893150 \cdot 10^1$
0.964	0.00119	—	U	1	$1.994610 \cdot 10^1$
0.961	0.00066	—	U	1	$2.083210 \cdot 10^1$
0.954	0.00146	—	U	0	$2.172610 \cdot 10^1$
0.964	0.00164	—	U	1	$2.373870 \cdot 10^1$

Table 7.2. Final population (generation 50) of the meta-evolution experiment using proportional selection ($\omega' = 5$, $\mu' = \lambda' = 50$). Reprinted by permission of Springer-Verlag from Th. Bäck: *Parallel Optimization of Evolutionary Algorithms*, in Davidor, Schwefel, Männer: *Parallel Problem Solving from Nature — PPSN III*, Lecture Notes in Computer Science 866, p. 423, table 1 (right), copyright © Springer-Verlag Berlin Heidelberg 1994.

Such strong mixing of genetic information, however, requires the invention of an elitist selection mechanism in order to counterbalance the danger of generating no improvement at all by too disruptive joint processes of crossover and mutation.

p'_c	p'_m	η'^+	q'	z'	s'	r'	e'	Φ
0.469	0.02122	—	5	—	T	D	1	$4.433580 \cdot 10^1$
0.247	0.04263	—	12	8	T	S	1	$2.595720 \cdot 10^2$
0.239	0.02183	—	—	—	P	D	1	$6.851130 \cdot 10^2$
0.424	0.05198	—	18	1	T	S	0	$8.542280 \cdot 10^2$
0.975	0.03561	—	—	—	P	_	1	$1.747470 \cdot 10^3$
0.283	0.09659	—	12	4	T	S	0	$2.331720 \cdot 10^3$
0.573	0.10501	—	14	—	T	D	1	$3.297110 \cdot 10^3$
0.265	0.10329	—	—	—	P	_	1	$3.468300 \cdot 10^3$
0.194	0.15447	—	10	4	T	S	1	$4.727340 \cdot 10^3$
0.135	0.22431	—	20	—	T	D	0	$6.791590 \cdot 10^3$
0.442	0.24631	—	—	—	P	_	1	$8.078750 \cdot 10^3$
0.175	0.26968	1.662	—	—	R	_	0	$8.094380 \cdot 10^3$
0.323	0.35874	—	7	6	T	S	0	$8.484820 \cdot 10^3$
0.999	0.33714	—	—	3	P	S	0	$8.704680 \cdot 10^3$
0.916	0.36282	1.110	—	—	R	_	0	$8.860660 \cdot 10^3$
0.486	0.33294	—	6	—	T	_	1	$9.001140 \cdot 10^3$
0.764	0.49582	—	—	—	P	U	0	$9.086960 \cdot 10^3$
0.198	0.49794	1.189	—	—	R	U	1	$9.150990 \cdot 10^3$
0.152	0.45008	1.031	—	5	R	S	1	$9.156780 \cdot 10^3$
0.568	0.47423	—	5	—	T	U	1	$9.301270 \cdot 10^3$
0.154	0.28594	1.044	—	—	R	U	0	$9.361540 \cdot 10^3$
0.738	0.38947	1.034	—	—	R	_	0	$9.362140 \cdot 10^3$
0.280	0.19972	—	—	5	C	S	0	$9.752010 \cdot 10^3$
0.695	0.43110	—	3	—	T	U	1	$9.976610 \cdot 10^3$
0.233	0.22491	—	—	3	C	S	0	$9.989270 \cdot 10^3$
0.356	0.47504	—	—	2	P	S	1	$1.017380 \cdot 10^4$
0.446	0.47438	—	—	8	C	S	1	$1.032690 \cdot 10^4$
0.325	0.26309	—	—	—	C	_	1	$1.079370 \cdot 10^4$
0.143	0.47290	—	7	—	T	U	1	$1.123730 \cdot 10^4$
0.044	0.45816	—	—	—	P	U	0	$1.185750 \cdot 10^4$

Table 7.3. Initial population of the meta-evolution experiment using fixed values of $\mu' = 50$ and $\lambda' = 50$.

The initial population of experiment (2), shown in table 7.3, clarifies the importance of the mutation rate in the same way as table 7.1 does. Again, the diversity of fitness values is remarkable and the best individual combines tournament selection ($q' = 5$) and a small mutation rate (notice that in case of the second best individual the higher selective pressure caused by $q' = 12$ is not able to counterbalance the increase of the mutation rate in comparison to the best individual).

p'_c	p'_m	η'^+	q'	z'	s'	r'	e'	Φ
0.955	0.00665	—	20	—	T	D	0	$2.846310 \cdot 10^{-3}$
0.964	0.00663	—	20	—	T	D	1	$2.886790 \cdot 10^{-3}$
0.941	0.00642	—	20	—	T	D	1	$4.716110 \cdot 10^{-3}$
0.995	0.00660	—	20	—	T	D	0	$5.032290 \cdot 10^{-3}$
0.880	0.00664	—	20	—	T	D	0	$5.522910 \cdot 10^{-3}$
0.962	0.00663	—	20	—	T	D	1	$5.647140 \cdot 10^{-3}$
1.000	0.00666	—	20	—	T	D	0	$6.760060 \cdot 10^{-3}$
0.932	0.00665	—	20	7	T	S	0	$9.123820 \cdot 10^{-3}$
0.954	0.00665	—	20	—	T	D	1	$9.952810 \cdot 10^{-3}$
0.992	0.00663	—	20	—	T	D	0	$1.006900 \cdot 10^{-2}$
0.042	0.00667	—	20	—	T	U	1	$1.030840 \cdot 10^{-2}$
0.968	0.00670	—	20	—	T	D	0	$1.113980 \cdot 10^{-2}$
0.998	0.00674	—	20	—	T	D	0	$1.126770 \cdot 10^{-2}$
0.956	0.00664	—	20	—	T	D	0	$1.299640 \cdot 10^{-2}$
0.991	0.00662	—	20	—	T	D	0	$1.305160 \cdot 10^{-2}$
0.997	0.00665	—	20	—	T	D	1	$1.343140 \cdot 10^{-2}$
0.004	0.00664	—	20	—	T	D	1	$1.411990 \cdot 10^{-2}$
0.956	0.00664	—	20	—	T	D	0	$1.476430 \cdot 10^{-2}$
0.008	0.00660	—	20	—	T	D	0	$1.744520 \cdot 10^{-2}$
0.960	0.00674	—	20	—	T	D	1	$1.905440 \cdot 10^{-2}$
0.942	0.00676	—	20	—	T	D	0	$2.096840 \cdot 10^{-2}$
0.982	0.00663	—	20	—	T	D	0	$2.175460 \cdot 10^{-2}$
0.951	0.00665	—	20	—	T	D	1	$2.253590 \cdot 10^{-2}$
0.932	0.00660	—	20	—	T	D	1	$2.457020 \cdot 10^{-2}$
0.941	0.00673	—	20	—	T	D	0	$3.487040 \cdot 10^{-2}$
0.929	0.00662	—	20	—	T	D	1	$3.763210 \cdot 10^{-2}$
0.958	0.00658	—	20	—	T	D	0	$4.038440 \cdot 10^{-2}$
0.015	0.00656	—	20	—	T	D	1	$5.688240 \cdot 10^{-2}$
0.994	0.00661	—	20	—	T	D	0	$6.734520 \cdot 10^{-2}$
0.974	0.00664	—	—	—	P	D	0	$1.305450 \cdot 10^{2}$

Table 7.4. Final population (generation 50) of the meta-evolution experiment using fixed values of $\mu' = 50$ and $\lambda' = 50$.

After 50 generations, the population shown in table 7.4 was evolved by the meta-algorithm. As to be expected, tournament selection with $q' = 20$ characterizes all individuals[17]. This setting of q' implies a strong

---

[17]With one exception: The worst individual is characterized by proportional selec-

preference of the three best individuals during selection, such that re-combination may have some impact on the search performed by the slave algorithms. Neither the crossover probability nor the recombination op-erator, however, confirm this assumption. Though generally a crossover probability close to one is observed, very small crossover probabilities occur in the population without significantly degrading the fitness of individuals. Furthermore, the occurrence of 7-point crossover does not cause a strong difference with respect to the fitness, such that the dom-ination of discrete recombination seems to be an event caused by chance.

Concerning the mutation rate, a surprisingly clear convergence of p'_m towards a value of $p'_m \approx 0.0066$ is observed in table 7.4. This value is about four times the value of $1/l$ as evolved by proportional selection in table 7.1. The experiment provides an impressive confirmation of the increase of the optimal mutation rate and convergence velocity as select-ive pressure respectively the surplus of offspring generated by extinctive selection increases (notice that tournament selection with $q' = 20$ comes close to a $(1,50)$-selection method).

To conclude the discussion of experiment (2), we indicate that the 1-elitist property is not really of importance in case of the sphere model and relatively strong selective pressure, since improvements are easy to achieve in the early phase of the search to which the algorithms are restricted by limiting the number of function evaluations to 10^4.

Experiment (3) allows for the additional variation of the parent and offspring population sizes μ' and λ'. This way, any kind of extinctive selection method may be evolved by the meta-algorithm.

As expected, the initial population of this experiment, shown in table 7.5, consists of highly diverse Genetic Algorithm descriptions. As in experiments (1) and (2), the mutation rate is the key factor that de-termines the fitness of individuals, and the best individual benefits from the combination of a relatively small mutation rate and strong selective pressure.

Table 7.6 shows the meta-algorithm's population after running for 50 generations. The fitness of the best performing individuals has im-proved now by approximately seven orders of magnitude. Expecially the mutation rate column of this table reveals a complete convergence of this parameter to a value of $p'_m = 0.00383$. The average step size for p'_m amounts to about 10^{-9}, the smallest value of σ_i permitted at all. The fact that p'_m is smaller than for experiment (2), but larger than for experiment (1) can well be explained by considering again the selective pressure: $(7,17)$-tournament selection with $q' = 20$ as obtained in this

---

tion, introduced by a mutation event. Such disastrous discrete mutations may occur at any time since the meta-algorithms' mutation rate for discrete parameters remains constant. Due to its extremely bad fitness value, such a mutation is quickly removed from the population. As a solution of this problem, the component-wise application probabilities of uniform mutation events (for z', s', r', e') should probably also un-dergo self-adaptation, this way allowing these parameters to adjust on fixed values. Currently, however, we do not consider this a serious problem because it concerns only a few worst individuals (if any) in the population.

p'_c	p'_m	η'^+	q'	μ'	λ'	z'	s'	r'	e'	Φ
0.202	0.01062	—	—	12	28	—	C	U	1	$2.48201 \cdot 10^1$
0.283	0.09659	—	12	6	16	4	T	S	1	$1.83496 \cdot 10^3$
0.950	0.06581	1.236	—	46	73	—	R	U	0	$3.96824 \cdot 10^3$
0.162	0.06007	—	—	5	14	—	P	D	0	$4.51741 \cdot 10^3$
0.092	0.08388	—	—	3	11	—	C	D	0	$5.66094 \cdot 10^3$
0.606	0.29313	1.066	—	33	98	4	R	S	0	$5.85423 \cdot 10^3$
0.496	0.21327	—	—	9	61	—	C	U	1	$6.24783 \cdot 10^3$
0.880	0.29778	—	—	7	98	—	C	D	0	$6.52485 \cdot 10^3$
0.901	0.24549	—	—	26	84	8	C	S	1	$6.53671 \cdot 10^3$
0.473	0.17765	1.874	—	15	15	—	R	U	1	$7.84848 \cdot 10^3$
0.844	0.17145	—	—	58	74	2	C	S	1	$8.01979 \cdot 10^3$
0.999	0.33714	—	—	11	84	3	P	S	1	$8.03596 \cdot 10^3$
0.227	0.20959	1.469	—	2	12	5	R	S	1	$8.09145 \cdot 10^3$
0.854	0.26478	1.488	—	80	98	—	R	D	1	$8.42532 \cdot 10^3$
0.180	0.24580	—	—	73	81	6	C	S	0	$8.61893 \cdot 10^3$
0.922	0.38617	1.336	—	12	14	—	R	U	1	$8.68986 \cdot 10^3$
0.154	0.28594	1.044	—	38	77	—	R	U	0	$9.06912 \cdot 10^3$
0.152	0.45008	1.031	—	90	90	5	R	S	0	$9.29234 \cdot 10^3$
0.998	0.33453	1.036	—	65	66	—	R	_	0	$9.35776 \cdot 10^3$
0.982	0.22989	—	—	36	52	—	P	_	1	$9.40567 \cdot 10^3$
0.205	0.23960	—	3	7	20	—	T	_	0	$9.41534 \cdot 10^3$
0.595	0.46653	1.247	—	38	40	—	R	U	1	$9.60902 \cdot 10^3$
0.303	0.39338	—	18	38	71	5	T	S	1	$9.69947 \cdot 10^3$
0.764	0.49582	—	—	9	58	—	P	U	1	$1.01754 \cdot 10^4$
0.198	0.49794	1.189	—	22	32	—	R	U	1	$1.11008 \cdot 10^4$
0.814	0.46578	1.265	—	5	11	—	R	_	1	$1.11710 \cdot 10^4$
0.678	0.26395	—	—	5	5	—	C	U	1	$1.14654 \cdot 10^4$
0.230	0.30343	—	12	9	11	—	T	D	0	$1.17944 \cdot 10^4$
0.625	0.37873	—	—	11	30	—	C	_	1	$1.18864 \cdot 10^4$
0.685	0.31320	—	10	7	14	7	T	S	0	$1.36929 \cdot 10^4$

Table 7.5. Initial population of the meta-evolution experiment using the complete search space A_x.

experiment (see table 7.6) is essentially a (1,17)-selection as can easily be confirmed by calculating the selection probability[18] $p_1 = 0.9542$ of the best parent individual. The selective pressure is clearly much stronger than for proportional selection, hence the mutation rate is larger (about a factor of 2.5) than in experiment (1).

---

[18]This is done by using theorem 17 with $\mu = 7$, $q = 20$, $i = 1$.

p'_c	p'_m	η'^+	q'	μ'	λ'	z'	s'	r'	e'	Φ
0.421	0.00383	—	20	7	17	—	T	U	0	$2.164470 \cdot 10^{-6}$
0.421	0.00383	—	20	7	17	—	T	U	0	$2.164470 \cdot 10^{-6}$
0.573	0.00383	—	20	7	17	—	T	U	0	$2.712040 \cdot 10^{-6}$
0.404	0.00383	—	20	7	17	—	T	U	1	$3.473870 \cdot 10^{-6}$
0.570	0.00383	—	20	7	17	—	T	U	0	$3.621860 \cdot 10^{-6}$
0.424	0.00383	—	20	7	17	—	T	D	0	$4.720930 \cdot 10^{-6}$
0.413	0.00383	—	20	7	17	—	T	U	0	$9.608950 \cdot 10^{-6}$
0.414	0.00383	—	20	7	17	—	T	U	0	$1.012210 \cdot 10^{-5}$
0.592	0.00383	—	20	7	19	—	T	U	0	$1.420130 \cdot 10^{-5}$
0.582	0.00383	—	20	7	19	—	T	U	0	$1.420130 \cdot 10^{-5}$
0.418	0.00383	—	20	7	17	—	T	U	0	$1.573790 \cdot 10^{-5}$
0.423	0.00383	—	20	7	17	—	T	U	0	$1.819870 \cdot 10^{-5}$
0.419	0.00383	—	20	7	17	—	T	U	0	$2.168210 \cdot 10^{-5}$
0.417	0.00383	—	20	7	19	—	T	U	0	$2.720590 \cdot 10^{-5}$
0.383	0.00383	—	20	7	17	—	T	U	0	$3.121010 \cdot 10^{-5}$
0.383	0.00383	—	20	7	17	—	T	U	0	$3.249550 \cdot 10^{-5}$
0.571	0.00383	—	20	7	20	—	T	U	0	$4.695690 \cdot 10^{-5}$
0.568	0.00383	—	20	7	17	—	T	U	0	$4.912150 \cdot 10^{-5}$
0.412	0.00383	—	20	7	17	—	T	U	0	$5.726070 \cdot 10^{-5}$
0.416	0.00383	—	20	7	19	—	T	U	0	$7.530270 \cdot 10^{-5}$
0.400	0.00383	—	20	7	20	—	T	U	0	$8.602180 \cdot 10^{-5}$
0.439	0.00383	—	20	7	19	—	T	U	0	$9.137410 \cdot 10^{-5}$
0.415	0.00383	—	20	7	19	—	T	U	0	$9.137410 \cdot 10^{-5}$
0.426	0.00383	—	20	7	17	—	T	U	0	$1.507170 \cdot 10^{-4}$
0.394	0.00383	—	20	7	17	—	T	U	0	$1.610950 \cdot 10^{-4}$
0.593	0.00383	—	20	7	19	—	T	U	0	$7.921950 \cdot 10^{-4}$
0.558	0.00383	—	20	7	17	—	T	U	0	$1.032500 \cdot 10^{-3}$
0.586	0.00383	—	20	7	19	—	T	U	0	$1.736870 \cdot 10^{-3}$
0.424	0.00383	1.330	20	7	17	—	R	U	0	$4.471430 \cdot 10^{-2}$
0.552	0.00383	—	20	7	17	—	M	U	0	$1.720780 \cdot 10^{-1}$

Table 7.6. Final population (generation 50) of the meta-evolution experiment using the complete search space A_x. Reprinted by permission of Springer-Verlag from Th. Bäck: *Parallel Optimization of Evolutionary Algorithms*, in Davidor, Schwefel, Männer: *Parallel Problem Solving from Nature — PPSN III*, Lecture Notes in Computer Science 866, p. 424, table 2, copyright © Springer-Verlag Berlin Heidelberg 1994.

On the other hand, the tournament selection scheme with $\mu' = 50$ and $q' = 20$ as obtained from experiment (2) is essentially very similar to an extinctive selection method which emphasizes on the best 1–3 individuals. The optimal mutation rate for (1,17)-selection is smaller than for the selection scheme from experiment (2) because the offspring population size is smaller. This observation is in good agreement with the results from chapter 6 for increasing values of λ (see the left part of figure 6.5).

All individuals shown in table 7.6 are characterized by a parent population size of 7 and an offspring population size of 17–20. The fact that μ' does not reduce to a value of one is currently not explainable. The interpretation as a confirmation of the usefulness of recombination, which is here in almost all cases the uniform crossover operator, does not seem to be sufficient for three reasons: First, the occurrence of a discrete recombination operator (for the 6-th best individual) without any strong impact on the fitness value indicates the choice of the operator to be unimportant. Second, the still high degree of diversity for p'_c indicates the role of crossover to be even more questionable, since p'_c does not significantly affect the final fitness value. Third, the strong selective pressure reduces genotypic diversity within the parent individuals in such a way that all parents are almost identical, which implies crossover to be useless.

It is worthwhile to observe that the two worst individuals contained in the population suffer from their selection mechanisms, which deviate from tournament selection due to mutation events. These individuals, however, go extinct by means of the meta-algorithms' (4,30)-selection in the next step of the algorithm.

In order to verify the two-run fitness measures obtained for the best individuals as reported so far, the corresponding algorithms were also evaluated by running them for $N = 100$ independent experiments and averaging the data (as in chapter 4). The resulting algorithms

- $\text{GA}_{(1)} = \text{GA}(l'_x = 30, p'_m = 0.00151, r_{\{p'_c=0.969\}}, s_{\{(50,50),\omega'=5\}}, 1-\text{elitist})$
  (experiment (1)),

- $\text{GA}_{(2)} = \text{GA}(l'_x = 30, p'_m = 0.00665, r_{d\{p'_c=0.955\}}, s_{\{(50,50),q'=20\}})$
  (experiment (2)), and

- $\text{GA}_{(3)} = \text{GA}(l'_x = 30, p'_m = 0.00383, r_{\{p'_c=0.421\}}, s_{\{(7,17)\}}, 1-\text{elitist})$
  (experiment (3))

are compared to the standard Genetic Algorithm according to section 2.3.6 and the algorithm

$$\text{GA}^+ = \text{GA}(l'_x = 30, p'_m = 0.001667, s_{\{(1,5)\}}, 1-\text{elitist})\quad,$$

which is supposed to be a good choice for the sphere model according to existing knowledge about the optimal mutation rate and the relation of offspring and parent population size. Table 7.7 compares the averaged best results $\bar{f}_{\min}$ after $10^4/\lambda'$ generations (including their empirical standard deviations $V_{\min}$) to the results obtained by the meta-evolution experiment as an average of two runs.

Experiment	$\bar{f}_{\min}$	$V_{\min}$	Meta-EA, $f_{\min}$
$GA_{(1)}$	$2.331 \cdot 10^0$	$3.328 \cdot 10^0$	$3.924 \cdot 10^0$
$GA_{(2)}$	$2.270 \cdot 10^{-2}$	$3.885 \cdot 10^{-2}$	$2.846 \cdot 10^{-3}$
$GA_{(3)}$	$7.312 \cdot 10^{-5}$	$1.730 \cdot 10^{-4}$	$2.164 \cdot 10^{-6}$
GA^+	$2.197 \cdot 10^{-3}$	$6.098 \cdot 10^{-3}$	—
Standard-GA	$1.032 \cdot 10^2$	$8.289 \cdot 10^1$	—

Table 7.7. Average final best objective function values obtained by running different Genetic Algorithms for $N = 100$ independent experiments, compared to the corresponding results obtained from the experiment with a meta-Evolutionary Algorithm.

The general quality assessment achieved by the meta-evolution approach is well confirmed by the data obtained from the mass runs. Surprisingly, the $GA_{(3)}$-algorithm performs better than the GA^+-variant. Indeed, the latter is not optimal due to the extreme impact of the mutation rate, which has an optimal value larger than $1/l$ when $\lambda > \mu$ (again, the reader is referred to section 6.1.2). For instance, an experiment with GA^+ and $p'_m = 0.004$ resulted in an average best performance of $\bar{f}_{\min} = 6.413 \cdot 10^{-5}$ ($V_{\min} = 3.400 \cdot 10^{-4}$), which is close to the result obtained by $GA_{(3)}$ and confirms the role of crossover to be unimportant.

The result clarifies again how critical an appropriate choice of the mutation rate has to be considered. Low selective pressure as in case of proportional selection considerably restricts the range of useful mutation rates to a tiny interval centered close to $1/l$. Higher selective pressure shifts the upper bound of this interval (and the optimal rate itself) to larger values. A theoretical approach towards a description of the interdependency between selective pressure (respectively the degree of extinctiveness) and the optimal mutation rate therefore proves again to be of real interest.

7.4 Summary

The meta-Evolutionary Algorithm presented in this chapter is motivated by three different aspects concerning the meta-algorithm, the interpretation of the results obtained from the evolution process, and implementational issues.

First, the meta-algorithm itself presents an example of the potential usefulness of Evolutionary Algorithms in the field of mixed integer problems, i.e., optimization problems which combine discrete and continuous variables. This way, a mixture of search space characteristics typical for Evolution Strategies (Evolutionary Programming) and Genetic Algorithms results, such that the idea to combine concepts of both algorithms arises naturally. Consequently, the algorithm presented in section 7.2 uses a hybrid mutation operator and self-adapts strategy parameters for just six out of a total of ten parameters while the remaining are modified by uniform mutation. The resulting algorithm, though not at all perfectly tuned, clearly demonstrated its principal effectiveness in the experiments performed on the application task to evolve Genetic Algorithms of maximum convergence velocity. Interpreting this as a successful study of the feasibility of tackling mixed integer optimization problems by Evolutionary Algorithms, an encouraging new field of future applications is opened for further work, especially concerning the practical use of Evolutionary Algorithms.

Second, the algorithms which were evolved as best individuals within the final population of the meta-algorithm served to confirm some of our knowledge about parameter settings of Genetic Algorithms. This is especially true for the mutation rate, which is by far the most critical parameter influencing the performance of Genetic Algorithms. The mutation rates that were evolved are perfectly in agreement with the results from chapter 6 (though these were obtained for a different objective function), indicating an optimal rate in the vicinity of $1/l$ which shifts to larger values when the degree of extinctiveness (the selective pressure) is increased.

Concerning the recombination operator, results are much less meaningful. The role of crossover clearly diminishes as selective pressure is increased, but also for proportional selection (table 7.1) only a general conclusion about a small advantage gained by using a highly disruptive recombination operator (uniform crossover) may be drawn. Understanding crossover and its potential benefits for Genetic Algorithms not only from a schema theory point of view, but also concerning its impact on convergence velocity and reliability, presents one of the real challenges for further research on Genetic Algorithms. This aspect of Genetic Algorithms, which are in most cases understood and applied in the sense of optimization algorithms, becomes even more important due to the strong emphasis laid on the crossover operator.

Finally, a hint is given to the new generation of parallel machines using processors much more powerful than available for the experiment described here (see appendix D). Then, the feasibility of a meta-evolution approach to gain considerable knowledge about the parameterizations of Genetic Algorithms is remarkably improved, implying several possibilities such as

- increasing the number of function evaluations performed during each single experiment of a slave algorithm,

- reducing the noisy component of the fitness function by averaging over a larger number of independent runs performed by each slave algorithm, and

- trying to evolve algorithms of high convergence reliability by the development of an appropriate fitness function.

The last topic deserves some further explanation and requires one to remember the convergence reliability assessment presented in section 4.2, where the quality distribution obtained from a large number of independent long runs served as a criterion. To design an appropriate fitness function, the relative frequency of runs that fall into the best range of results might provide a starting point. Though it requires a huge amount of computing time, such an approach may be worthwhile due to the fact that even less empirical (and theoretical) knowledge than for the case of maximizing convergence velocity is currently available to guide the search for parameterizations of Genetic Algorithms that support convergence reliability.

Hofstadter's Law: It always takes longer than you expect,
even when you take into account Hofstadter's Law.
Douglas J. Hofstadter (in: Goedel, Escher, Bach
Cambridge, MA: Harvester, 1979, p. 152).

Summary and Outlook

Within the total of seven chapters presented here on the topic of Evolutionary Algorithms there are a number of crude but nevertheless powerful simplifications of the model of organic evolution. Chapter 1 clarified that Evolutionary Algorithms, if they are interpreted as global optimization algorithms, are not to be confused with the oversimplified concept of uniform random search. Instead, they rely on keeping the history insofar as the subsequent generation is created at each step of the evolution process from the current generation maintained by the algorithm. In other words: Evolutionary Algorithms are representatives of the mathematical concept of a Markov process (respectively chain, in discrete spaces).

Concerning the convergence reliability of Evolutionary Algorithms, the theoretical property of global convergence with a probability of one holds for all variants that use an elitist selection method and guarantee a reachability property of mutation which is basically assured by working with nonzero mutation rate in Genetic Algorithms (respectively with nonzero standard deviation in Evolution Strategies and Evolutionary Programming). These results are summarized in theorem 7, 10, and 13, which are based on the general convergence theorem 3 for global random search algorithms respectively on well-known results on absorbing Markov chains.

In contrast to convergence reliability investigations where the focus is on the explorative character of the search, convergence velocity analysis emphasizes the exploitation of information collected about a promising region or point in the search space. Both properties are contradictory and cause a trade-off that dominates behavior and control of Evolutionary Algorithms. Nevertheless, convergence velocity investigations so far were known only for Evolution Strategies (see section 2.1.7) but can easily be transferred to standard Evolutionary Programming as demonstrated in section 2.2.7. The result provides a clear indication that the step-size control of standard EP is useless for even moderately large dimensions of the search space and for objective functions that possess a non-vanishing global optimum. More advanced versions of Evolutionary Programming overcome this problem by a self-adaptive control of strategy parameters quite similar to the technique used in Evolution Strategies.

An attempt towards the mathematical analysis of convergence velocity properties of simplified Genetic Algorithms was presented for the first time in chapter 6 of this work, using the counting ones objective function. Based on a calculation of the improvement probability of bit strings subject to mutation, convergence velocities and optimal mutation rate schedules were calculated for a $(1,\lambda)$-GA with $\lambda \geq 1$, and it turned out that the optimal setting of the mutation rate p_m depends on the bit string length l *and* the actual objective function value $f(\vec{a})$ of the bit string $\vec{a}$. However, in case of this particular objective function, the approximation $p_m \approx 1/l$ serves as a good rule of thumb for parameterizing the Genetic Algorithm, and this result is likely to be generalizable for any unimodal pseudoboolean objective function.

Choosing a mutation rate that is just a bit too large (where the bottom line is understood to be the optimal setting), the impact on the search process is disastrous. The time complexity of the algorithm quickly drops from $\mathcal{O}(l \log l)$ to exponential behavior in l.

This observation explains why researchers in the field of Genetic Algorithms steadily warn against trying to strengthen the role of mutation by increasing p_m, and it is also in good agreement with the result from molecular Darwinism (section 1.1.4) indicating optimal search conditions to be provided by a mutation rate just below the error threshold. This borderline between ideal conditions for evolution and dissolving information corresponds directly with the transformation of computational complexity from subquadratic to exponential observed for the mutation-based Genetic Algorithm.

Concerning the number of offspring individuals λ, an increasing value of λ results in an increasing optimal mutation rate setting and an increasing convergence velocity. For small λ, the effect on convergence velocity turns out to be linear, but it changes into a logarithmic curve as λ grows further. By interpreting an increase of λ as a growth of selective pressure this observation may serve as an explanation of the speedup observed under conditions of increasingly stronger selective pressure.

The analysis presented in section 6.1.2 extends the convergence velocity investigations towards a (μ,λ)-GA without recombination. Based on the theory of order statistics, an expression for the progress rate of the average objective function value of the μ parents is derived and confirmed by experimental data. In addition to the expected behavior of decreasing convergence velocity as μ is increased for constant λ, the results confirm the assumption that $\varphi_{(\mu,\lambda)}$ is proportional to the ratio λ/μ.

A convergence velocity analysis of the simple Genetic Algorithm for binary encoded parameter optimization problems was attempted in section 6.1.3. This numerical investigation clearly demonstrates the strong nonlinearities introduced by both the standard code and the Gray code, and the optimal mutation rate schedule turns out to be absolutely unpredictable and highly discontinuous. The standard code, however, reveals an additional disadvantage for mutation due to the existence of local optima within the binary hypercube landscape, a property that definitely does not occur when a Gray code is used. Based on these investigations, a Gray code is identified as the preferred choice whenever a continuous parameter optimization problem is given for optimization by a Genetic Algorithm.

As clarified in chapter 6 (and also confirmed by the experiments in chapter 7), optimal mutation rate, selective pressure, and convergence velocity are tightly coupled insofar as increasing (decreasing) selective pressure implies an increase (decrease) of the optimal mutation rate and of the convergence velocity. While an analysis respectively quantification of convergence velocity and optimal mutation rate are presented in chapter 6, chapter 5 presents a quantification of the notion of selective pressure and an analyzation of the selective pressure of commonly used selection mechanisms. This analysis is based on measuring the takeover time as introduced by Goldberg and calculating the selection probabilities of individuals. The theoretical analysis indicates an order of selection methods according to selective pressure such that proportional selection $<$ ranking $<$ tournament selection $< (\mu\overset{+}{,}\lambda)$-selection, and this result is well confirmed by empirical investigations. Once more, the extremely small selective pressure of proportional selection clarifies the reason why early work on Genetic Algorithms always resulted in the claim to use very small mutation rates and to neglect the impact of mutation on the search process almost completely.

All theoretical results on the relation between optimal mutation rate, selective pressure, and convergence velocity are confirmed by the experiments reported in chapter 7. This is especially true for proportional selection, where mutation rates in the close vicinity of $1/l$ are evolved by the meta-algorithm, while for stronger selective pressure considerably larger mutation rates are observed.

The experiment on meta-evolution includes another important aspect which is related to the point of view that understands Evolution Strategies, Evolutionary Programming, and Genetic Algorithms as instances of the concept of a general Evolutionary Algorithm. Chapter 2 captures this idea and presents a formal framework for Evolutionary Algorithms, including concepts such as the generation transition function, population sequence, and running time. This general approach offers the advantage of clarifying the similarities and differences of the approaches and helps to identify important points of contact where knowledge about one algorithm may be helpful for understanding another algorithm. On a higher level of abstraction, the question for universal principles and concepts for the development and application of Evolutionary Algorithms is still far from being solved but will surely gain some additional in-

sights from the generalization provided here. In any case, according to
the meta-algorithm structure presented in section 7.2 the combination
of principles from Evolution Strategies and Genetic Algorithms yields
an algorithm that is useful for tackling mixed integer optimization problems.

However, the current situation for applying Evolutionary Algorithms
is still unfavourable from a practical point of view concerning the flexibility of available software implementations. Standard algorithms as
presented in chapter 2 are often not sufficient to cope with all demands
made by the actual practical optimization problem, such that extensions by special, problem-specific features such as special representations
of solutions, feasibility-preserving operators (or other methods for constraint handling), varying dimension of the search space, mixed search
spaces, and others are to be implemented. Consequently, the currently
most favorable practical work consists in the development of a flexible
Evolutionary Algorithm description language (or a library extension of
a programming language) that allows for the specification of arbitrarily
complex Evolutionary Algorithms and provides easy and comfortable
data handling and visualization facilities. In addition to a first proposal by Jankowski et al. towards the realization of a programming language PROBIOL (programming in biology) for Evolutionary Algorithms
[JMRS89], no other attempt into this direction was reported. The development of such a programming language (of course, providing also
standard implementations for the common Evolutionary Algorithms) is
an important and challenging project that could be able to yield a remarkable simplification of scientific as well as application-oriented work
in the field of Evolutionary Algorithms.

In addition to experimental investigations, the theoretical understanding of Evolutionary Algorithms is a research field of increasing
importance where many questions still remain to be answered. Some of
the most interesting ones are related to the role of recombination — a
chapter that has been completely omitted in this work. A new book by
Rechenberg [Rec94] includes a convergence velocity analysis of discrete,
panmictic recombination in Evolution Strategies, and a similar investigation for Genetic Algorithms is very desirable in order to understand
the impact of crossover analytically. Much theoretical work on crossover
in Genetic Algorithms focuses on schema disruption probabilities and
gives some insight into the properties of different recombination operators, but the debate on the pros and cons of crossover versus mutation
still expresses a certain lack of understanding, especially for crossover.

As a long term goal of theoretical research both an analysis of the
working principles of self-adaptation and a general characterization of
the approximation quality that can be achieved by Evolutionary Algorithms, depending on the degree of complexity of the objective function, seem to be of high interest. Self-adaptation of strategy parameters
is still a concept that is grounded on empirical findings and hard to
accept and understand for those who are not used to working with Evol-

ution Strategies or Evolutionary Programming. A theoretical foundation would present an undeniable confirmation, explaining the high success that has been observed when using this technique.

Concerning the problem complexity, it is quite clear that Evolutionary Algorithms should be useful in a range of problem complexities somewhere between unimodal, smooth functions (too easy) and needle-in-a-haystack problems (having equal objective function values at all points except the global optimum), but general complexity measures are still to be developed (if this is possible at all). This seems to be simpler for the binary search space, where the maximum Hamming distance for leaving a local optimum might serve as such a complexity measure. Based on such a measure, it is very desirable to characterize the expected time complexity of an algorithm to obtain a certain approximation of the global optimum with a certain probability — in the sense of PAC-learning (probably approximately correct) in computational learning theory (see e.g. [Val84, BEHW89]). Though such a project is currently unrealistic, it might be possible to obtain results at least for some appropriately defined classes of objective functions and to characterize their "learnability" by an — even simplified — Genetic Algorithm.

Many problems remain still unsolved, but Evolutionary Algorithms are of interest in fields as diverse as one can imagine: They may serve as optimization algorithms for almost any industrial application purposes, as simulation tools for biological evolution processes and more general simulations based on a kind of "evolutionary dynamics," and as learning algorithms in Artificial Intelligence, such that the general research field is still expected to grow over the coming years.

Appendices

A

Data for the Fletcher-Powell Function

The objective function after Fletcher and Powell as presented in section 3.4 is described by the $n \times n$ matrices $\mathbf{A}$ and $\mathbf{B}$ with random entries $a_{ij}, b_{ij} \in [-100, 100]$ and the random optimum location $\vec{\alpha} \in [-\pi, \pi]^n$. For $n = 30$, the vector $\vec{\alpha}$ and matrices $\mathbf{A}$ and $\mathbf{B}$ are presented here. Since the function is intended to be scalable for dimensions $1 \leq n \leq 30$ we use the convention that for $n < 30$ the upper left $n \times n$ submatrix and the subvector consisting of the first n entries of $\vec{\alpha}$ describe the objective function. The vector $\vec{\alpha}$ is given by:

$$
\vec{\alpha} = (\quad
\begin{array}{rrrrr}
0.435934 & 0.550595 & -1.283410 & -0.0734284 & -2.6051900 \\
2.104100 & 1.867540 & -3.012750 & 0.8628350 & 0.0666833 \\
2.336110 & -0.658149 & -3.112430 & -3.0755600 & 0.8418540 \\
-0.692549 & 3.062840 & -0.917399 & 0.2111350 & -1.4526100 \\
2.482440 & 2.008340 & 0.906190 & -0.1087510 & 0.6348730 \\
1.458810 & 1.240920 & 2.303110 & -2.3116000 & -2.1476100
\end{array}
$$
$$).$$

Due to space restrictions the matrices $\mathbf{A}$ and $\mathbf{B}$ are presented on the following pages by splitting rows into two subrows of 15 entries, each. For instance, the first row of matrix $\mathbf{A}$ is obtained by concatenation of the first and second row of the matrix as presented here.

$$(a_{ij}) =$$

-78	28	53	-9	75	-55	-62	20	-88	95	-71	-70	36	-4	-76
38	13	-30	77	61	-25	-65	37	22	-88	24	-45	-61	30	0
-13	-50	-98	20	-40	-62	-68	-6	16	58	-98	2	10	67	0
-75	0	-22	-60	-88	-90	-18	59	61	2	-95	69	-15	-28	20
27	73	63	81	15	92	0	59	63	62	97	-22	-49	66	-93
-43	71	-97	-81	74	37	80	-51	-93	-85	99	-30	-8	76	14
59	-23	39	98	11	26	-25	-49	-77	-36	66	-43	30	26	-52
80	-60	96	47	96	-87	-5	-28	43	24	-28	81	19	-68	69
-44	-58	-49	-9	-22	5	-27	35	95	-70	60	71	-83	23	77
78	13	68	-8	71	39	-76	-5	25	1	6	-76	-74	-5	92
0	81	30	1	-52	-32	-56	-70	31	-53	75	-12	41	14	-51
10	22	-84	10	17	46	90	99	-15	-37	89	-67	64	-55	-23
16	49	-39	-66	42	-63	47	80	-58	17	-56	26	-92	-54	-25
-8	-52	-66	52	-73	62	-69	-31	5	73	30	17	-43	-17	-94
90	-50	-17	-11	69	92	-49	2	-2	35	64	-38	-6	92	-98
20	31	-80	95	52	91	76	-67	53	32	76	-83	47	-74	66
-6	2	-32	1	51	-17	2	86	-12	-77	95	37	-68	23	-57
99	-97	-98	69	94	40	62	25	66	27	39	24	-37	-5	-97
65	-7	19	95	9	-44	10	96	-85	13	-13	-17	-25	95	37
68	-40	-76	31	-84	69	-45	-62	-38	60	24	-35	-2	83	0
-22	-97	-89	81	4	45	-6	-6	52	68	-34	21	47	55	52
92	92	65	-56	-90	-93	-25	-53	21	-10	38	-90	-69	-74	-78
54	59	61	-54	-74	51	67	77	-58	-61	29	36	-1	-52	52
-31	-34	-61	-60	-52	47	-77	-88	70	89	-26	66	28	7	57
50	-42	-71	-4	73	66	-93	-82	15	13	-95	-86	4	-48	-49
-10	41	-41	10	2	-4	-73	-18	-51	21	69	12	-91	-30	-5
-21	11	-45	-76	68	96	-63	15	70	-35	39	-1	-94	44	-91
27	32	20	-9	11	-77	-43	-63	77	98	67	-81	37	-81	-6
-67	6	74	-2	-42	36	-92	84	91	-43	-23	-3	78	-4	-32
-48	30	38	-29	-7	-20	64	51	6	56	-73	22	86	-67	-43
-30	-68	92	2	76	-22	-72	-97	86	50	-11	80	-82	54	26
68	-94	90	-8	-48	-87	20	80	84	70	-78	95	-23	-30	60
-67	-45	68	-20	80	-25	-26	-21	-35	60	86	99	-17	30	-55
-77	50	-91	31	-49	-52	-42	-70	-2	-65	-7	-43	45	-53	89
-50	8	-31	-62	-7	-5	-60	-26	-91	42	46	90	-37	-49	-2
-14	50	-56	93	-43	-98	-17	-69	-76	-61	47	36	-76	-20	87
-99	21	29	-59	-28	2	-80	38	-98	-41	4	-49	0	-52	74
-29	99	53	-4	56	-87	43	-44	-30	-7	-97	-39	-93	18	-5
97	96	12	-62	89	34	68	-76	-24	0	-95	-85	-2	54	-34
94	20	17	21	71	13	4	10	98	29	16	-88	-47	22	22
-76	29	-76	21	87	-41	64	-40	-76	-93	-58	5	87	-31	48
-57	78	-56	-17	93	-93	-69	1	-4	-15	-95	56	50	-30	-64
-26	34	72	75	-86	30	-17	4	-28	-69	54	-92	-89	2	65
-93	71	-36	-66	38	-65	57	-51	55	-96	-83	84	-37	-73	21
2	-69	99	-64	-10	-95	-29	18	89	-17	11	-14	-96	62	-9
-53	4	67	-45	59	-13	-8	-88	85	64	91	43	55	-99	-96
-44	15	12	-2	54	-61	52	-36	-27	-61	32	60	-88	54	-47
-10	-93	-42	-49	-23	90	-33	-40	-43	56	48	74	-50	26	52
-69	92	-77	27	-14	-91	-74	80	-66	-33	30	-44	69	-87	-53
3	31	-61	-66	84	90	99	6	-93	-74	-54	-78	4	-77	-53
93	44	-14	81	78	75	-60	-2	54	66	60	-54	86	77	-43
-22	-51	3	5	-6	1	62	-68	-78	42	47	34	-30	88	-31
5	70	11	-26	-30	28	76	91	-10	-89	90	27	42	49	-95
63	83	45	-90	-7	42	-72	13	92	89	-92	-31	64	64	82
29	18	88	-66	-20	-54	59	-23	7	-18	-30	-15	82	-60	-59
-6	-35	11	71	-19	93	59	-67	45	-33	76	-67	-23	-25	-26
76	-48	42	27	-15	24	-44	-3	12	80	26	14	-35	97	-71
26	-9	-54	-36	87	-87	14	-6	-87	89	-14	-12	62	39	93
53	-39	38	-54	84	56	-51	-37	98	-18	-3	69	50	-3	-38
-20	48	-33	-40	83	38	-30	-95	0	38	57	34	-63	-46	-57

$b_{ij}) =$

97	-25	-78	-27	85	0	-55	68	61	-57	88	2	-9	-44	-52
-11	-72	10	-33	-19	56	68	-55	-54	-10	1	-65	14	-19	64
30	25	-32	-1	15	-5	28	92	99	42	-83	21	10	82	-45
76	75	46	58	74	75	12	-86	-11	0	-29	-17	15	-58	59
87	-31	-92	-47	25	-68	76	-43	-87	92	-58	-25	-88	-45	89
82	-40	85	96	78	43	-61	-99	-22	-57	-37	65	-26	-65	-20
31	-37	6	27	-1	3	76	-70	73	-15	0	-97	71	-66	7
-43	63	-62	-44	-82	-62	38	-39	88	60	67	90	97	-96	51
13	-19	85	-59	-18	63	-62	39	77	5	6	-38	-88	3	-63
0	-6	66	-32	-91	-92	-56	-24	48	-34	-10	95	57	91	64
64	82	-5	5	-25	-69	70	21	16	27	40	-37	-31	45	-28
35	58	23	50	3	83	-41	90	-63	36	-51	6	-66	95	-15
41	-61	60	69	-16	24	22	43	2	54	5	54	74	-88	-99
-26	12	85	45	88	-64	79	8	-44	9	-96	-95	-82	2	56
38	81	5	30	-45	0	2	-72	-17	53	-95	-93	22	38	-4
50	-39	-30	43	-65	-33	-72	-99	-78	45	-82	-22	40	68	-41
-57	77	83	2	-61	27	-3	-3	-76	54	86	73	-25	-65	41
50	-33	-42	3	-40	96	-3	92	67	37	68	-45	0	99	13
13	31	78	-12	17	-69	67	-70	26	-23	29	90	40	-69	53
10	32	86	81	-17	-26	-61	-85	-75	70	-12	35	22	-64	-28
72	-18	-52	-66	-73	-85	-23	-50	64	70	17	38	5	87	-44
-43	-37	51	-40	-15	80	93	60	-52	13	0	-63	98	-42	39
86	-84	-3	49	54	-27	93	42	-38	37	84	-7	-33	20	-59
41	-98	-49	-23	-89	-2	-44	25	95	19	-49	-43	54	-3	-3
95	8	3	-21	20	-10	-46	-91	72	53	-56	1	15	-36	20
93	29	32	7	67	-89	-64	93	88	-8	-4	9	-78	-96	30
-25	1	41	-7	28	60	1	-82	33	-47	79	-42	10	63	99
81	6	89	11	-50	26	51	47	80	14	-96	-47	-98	78	-43
9	-39	-93	-90	4	23	31	-29	-9	93	0	-86	-61	-27	-86
-64	-96	-61	43	-76	10	65	-89	-85	95	-6	96	2	56	-38
94	-98	25	40	-88	-77	-84	-58	-75	-29	-88	-42	95	28	2
31	-50	66	79	47	-55	-60	-6	-30	36	97	-43	-59	-39	-46
1	18	-74	44	-50	-34	-56	-49	27	-73	-87	-51	-91	40	-9
31	-78	66	-63	25	69	-18	46	87	69	-70	20	40	73	72
95	-33	-42	-62	-20	-18	-33	-33	-73	17	65	27	-27	63	0
60	5	42	47	75	-12	90	-68	10	33	-34	7	-70	-43	74
86	33	3	-23	17	-75	14	-40	-48	34	31	-51	-77	-79	-98
94	-44	30	-47	-28	-28	-79	56	-47	-32	-33	-93	14	28	83
80	-4	-28	-77	35	-74	-62	-76	-78	-72	84	-96	-12	-63	40
62	-67	-35	22	-72	9	14	-57	-71	43	-55	55	9	-18	-93
61	89	-28	72	26	30	74	-34	-7	17	34	67	-23	98	-88
-14	-6	36	-55	-38	14	28	-42	-69	46	54	-72	9	10	-13
-48	18	-73	32	-9	-52	-62	82	-5	-34	-28	40	41	-66	-87
-73	15	-19	-3	85	-16	19	35	94	-20	-72	-54	26	27	-85
-82	37	-18	86	30	-65	-65	-18	89	-13	-59	0	23	-80	-55
-48	-73	70	-2	-51	-10	-96	-80	39	-2	41	68	-61	-68	20
-94	80	-52	50	38	1	4	50	-34	19	-41	-8	-9	-94	9
-82	23	-14	45	41	57	69	7	67	25	-40	-22	53	93	0
-83	-91	2	-43	90	-8	-44	-42	82	71	34	-54	48	-85	-42
-28	6	-19	18	-14	0	-58	-43	3	59	-56	78	52	-72	-63
5	23	84	46	-65	47	-37	-95	28	-59	10	13	85	-48	-95
-98	9	-67	-19	29	35	62	73	30	51	-21	22	-53	90	47
-52	-42	-81	7	-85	1	-30	75	95	24	-13	-27	15	99	79
47	-1	89	61	29	96	-38	-28	-26	-14	-8	-39	18	-79	91
11	-53	-82	77	96	-72	58	-82	-93	26	-63	-72	-29	56	84
60	97	-84	-89	-63	14	-59	-50	10	-8	18	97	52	90	81
-47	67	-53	-32	-5	45	-86	-43	51	-87	-82	46	64	-45	3
-35	59	55	36	-43	-83	49	-3	-83	57	71	62	68	3	-83
80	67	-14	42	-70	-10	-66	73	-7	92	93	93	78	-62	-74
-51	16	11	-12	15	-95	-46	13	-74	-82	-38	19	-75	-39	33

B

Data from Selection Experiments

The tables B.1–B.4 collected in this appendix summarize numerical data obtained by the selection experiments discussed in section 5.2. The data is organized as follows:

- Tables B.1–B.3 illustrate the impact of varying selective pressure in $(\mu,100)$-selection (table B.1), tournament selection (table B.2), and linear ranking (table B.3). For each objective function the average final best objective function values $\bar{f}^i_{\min}(T)$ and their empirical standard deviations $V^i_{\min}(T)$ are presented ($i \in \{1,\ldots,5\}$). The data is averaged over $N = 20$ runs.

- Table B.4 emphasizes the objective functions f_2, f_4, and f_5 by presenting the corresponding overall final best objective function values $f^i_{\min}(T)$ found within the 20 runs for the different selection methods and selective pressure settings.

For a more detailed discussion of these results and graphical illustrations, the reader is referred to section 5.2.

μ	f_1		f_2	
	$\bar{f}^1_{\min}(1000)$	$V^1_{\min}(1000)$	$\bar{f}^2_{\min}(1000)$	$V^2_{\min}(1000)$
1	$1.067 \cdot 10^{-14}$	$1.167 \cdot 10^{-15}$	$1.795 \cdot 10^1$	8.666
2	$1.041 \cdot 10^{-14}$	0	7.050	8.432
5	$2.351 \cdot 10^{-14}$	$2.941 \cdot 10^{-14}$	$1.120 \cdot 10^1$	7.804
10	$4.368 \cdot 10^{-13}$	$5.003 \cdot 10^{-13}$	6.200	5.357
20	$7.372 \cdot 10^{-11}$	$1.093 \cdot 10^{-10}$	3.750	4.339
30	$1.181 \cdot 10^{-8}$	$1.955 \cdot 10^{-8}$	2.350	3.731
40	$6.568 \cdot 10^{-7}$	$1.313 \cdot 10^{-6}$	2.600	4.210
50	$3.883 \cdot 10^{-5}$	$5.685 \cdot 10^{-5}$	1.200	2.567
60	$1.241 \cdot 10^{-3}$	$5.885 \cdot 10^{-4}$	1.750	3.596
70	$4.231 \cdot 10^{-2}$	$2.543 \cdot 10^{-2}$	4.400	5.471
80	2.902	1.848	$1.275 \cdot 10^1$	8.663
90	$1.391 \cdot 10^2$	$6.724 \cdot 10^1$	$1.323 \cdot 10^2$	$3.297 \cdot 10^1$
95	$1.103 \cdot 10^3$	$3.205 \cdot 10^2$	$1.056 \cdot 10^3$	$2.505 \cdot 10^2$

μ	f_4		f_5	
	$\bar{f}^3_{\min}(1000)$	$V^3_{\min}(1000)$	$\bar{f}^4_{\min}(2000)$	$V^4_{\min}(2000)$
1	$3.072 \cdot 10^{-6}$	$1.292 \cdot 10^{-5}$	$9.931 \cdot 10^3$	$8.340 \cdot 10^3$
2	$1.244 \cdot 10^{-9}$	$5.611 \cdot 10^{-9}$	$9.620 \cdot 10^3$	$7.990 \cdot 10^3$
5	$4.370 \cdot 10^{-7}$	$4.273 \cdot 10^{-7}$	$1.504 \cdot 10^4$	$1.315 \cdot 10^4$
10	$1.834 \cdot 10^{-6}$	$1.522 \cdot 10^{-6}$	$1.440 \cdot 10^4$	$1.533 \cdot 10^4$
20	$1.246 \cdot 10^{-5}$	$7.448 \cdot 10^{-6}$	$9.501 \cdot 10^3$	$6.502 \cdot 10^3$
30	$1.220 \cdot 10^{-4}$	$1.088 \cdot 10^{-4}$	$1.953 \cdot 10^4$	$1.533 \cdot 10^4$
40	$7.002 \cdot 10^{-4}$	$4.438 \cdot 10^{-4}$	$1.842 \cdot 10^4$	$1.212 \cdot 10^4$
50	$3.316 \cdot 10^{-3}$	$1.379 \cdot 10^{-3}$	$1.639 \cdot 10^4$	$1.415 \cdot 10^4$
60	$2.087 \cdot 10^{-2}$	$1.156 \cdot 10^{-2}$	$2.033 \cdot 10^4$	$1.392 \cdot 10^4$
70	$2.516 \cdot 10^{-1}$	$2.789 \cdot 10^{-1}$	$2.725 \cdot 10^4$	$2.172 \cdot 10^4$
80	1.826	$2.915 \cdot 10^{-1}$	$4.770 \cdot 10^4$	$2.794 \cdot 10^4$
90	7.261	$9.424 \cdot 10^{-1}$	$1.030 \cdot 10^5$	$4.593 \cdot 10^4$
95	$1.386 \cdot 10^1$	$8.608 \cdot 10^{-1}$	$3.017 \cdot 10^5$	$6.835 \cdot 10^4$

μ	f_5	
	$\bar{f}^5_{\min}(1000)$	$V^5_{\min}(1000)$
1	$8.084 \cdot 10^{-1}$	$4.415 \cdot 10^{-1}$
2	$6.505 \cdot 10^{-1}$	$3.794 \cdot 10^{-1}$
5	$4.690 \cdot 10^{-1}$	$3.742 \cdot 10^{-1}$
10	$6.151 \cdot 10^{-1}$	$4.342 \cdot 10^{-1}$
20	$6.523 \cdot 10^{-1}$	$4.133 \cdot 10^{-1}$
30	$5.954 \cdot 10^{-1}$	$3.651 \cdot 10^{-1}$
40	$5.442 \cdot 10^{-1}$	$3.914 \cdot 10^{-1}$
50	$4.170 \cdot 10^{-1}$	$3.208 \cdot 10^{-1}$
60	$4.294 \cdot 10^{-1}$	$4.253 \cdot 10^{-1}$
70	$4.667 \cdot 10^{-1}$	$4.083 \cdot 10^{-1}$
80	$5.460 \cdot 10^{-1}$	$4.215 \cdot 10^{-1}$
90	$5.738 \cdot 10^{-1}$	$4.838 \cdot 10^{-1}$
95	4.791	2.213

Table B.1. Average final best objective function values and their standard deviations for $(\mu,100)$-selection with varying values of μ on functions f_1–f_5.

q	f_1		f_2	
	$\bar{f}^1_{\min}(1000)$	$V^1_{\min}(1000)$	$\bar{f}^2_{\min}(1000)$	$V^2_{\min}(1000)$
2	$4.702 \cdot 10^{-4}$	$4.514 \cdot 10^{-4}$	$5.500 \cdot 10^{-1}$	$9.445 \cdot 10^{-1}$
3	$7.016 \cdot 10^{-7}$	$1.390 \cdot 10^{-6}$	$3.500 \cdot 10^{-1}$	$5.871 \cdot 10^{-1}$
4	$2.974 \cdot 10^{-8}$	$8.446 \cdot 10^{-8}$	$6.500 \cdot 10^{-1}$	2.007
5	$8.856 \cdot 10^{-10}$	$1.357 \cdot 10^{-9}$	$4.500 \cdot 10^{-1}$	2.012
6	$1.539 \cdot 10^{-10}$	$2.047 \cdot 10^{-10}$	$3.000 \cdot 10^{-1}$	$4.702 \cdot 10^{-1}$
7	$4.899 \cdot 10^{-11}$	$5.917 \cdot 10^{-11}$	$7.500 \cdot 10^{-1}$	2.023
8	$1.316 \cdot 10^{-11}$	$1.394 \cdot 10^{-11}$	$6.500 \cdot 10^{-1}$	2.033
9	$3.257 \cdot 10^{-12}$	$4.188 \cdot 10^{-12}$	1.000	2.753
10	$3.011 \cdot 10^{-12}$	$4.468 \cdot 10^{-12}$	1.250	2.712

q	f_3		f_4	
	$\bar{f}^3_{\min}(1000)$	$V^3_{\min}(1000)$	$\bar{f}^4_{\min}(2000)$	$V^4_{\min}(2000)$
2	$1.476 \cdot 10^{-2}$	$7.241 \cdot 10^{-3}$	$2.391 \cdot 10^4$	$1.483 \cdot 10^4$
3	$8.694 \cdot 10^{-4}$	$7.023 \cdot 10^{-4}$	$1.318 \cdot 10^4$	$9.094 \cdot 10^3$
4	$1.141 \cdot 10^{-4}$	$7.126 \cdot 10^{-5}$	$1.411 \cdot 10^4$	$8.636 \cdot 10^3$
5	$3.863 \cdot 10^{-5}$	$2.761 \cdot 10^{-5}$	$1.237 \cdot 10^4$	$9.180 \cdot 10^3$
6	$1.658 \cdot 10^{-5}$	$1.302 \cdot 10^{-5}$	$1.250 \cdot 10^4$	$1.172 \cdot 10^4$
7	$1.167 \cdot 10^{-5}$	$1.025 \cdot 10^{-5}$	$8.640 \cdot 10^3$	$1.073 \cdot 10^4$
8	$5.441 \cdot 10^{-6}$	$3.734 \cdot 10^{-6}$	$1.353 \cdot 10^4$	$1.074 \cdot 10^4$
9	$4.468 \cdot 10^{-6}$	$3.320 \cdot 10^{-6}$	$8.964 \cdot 10^3$	$8.489 \cdot 10^3$
10	$6.570 \cdot 10^{-6}$	$5.639 \cdot 10^{-6}$	$1.003 \cdot 10^4$	$7.927 \cdot 10^3$

q	f_5			
	$\bar{f}^5_{\min}(1000)$	$V^5_{\min}(1000)$		
2	$4.825 \cdot 10^{-1}$	$4.078 \cdot 10^{-1}$		
3	$6.208 \cdot 10^{-1}$	$4.303 \cdot 10^{-1}$		
4	$5.299 \cdot 10^{-1}$	$4.675 \cdot 10^{-1}$		
5	$5.579 \cdot 10^{-1}$	$4.115 \cdot 10^{-1}$		
6	$6.253 \cdot 10^{-1}$	$3.262 \cdot 10^{-1}$		
7	$5.873 \cdot 10^{-1}$	$4.644 \cdot 10^{-1}$		
8	$6.465 \cdot 10^{-1}$	$4.157 \cdot 10^{-1}$		
9	$6.246 \cdot 10^{-1}$	$3.481 \cdot 10^{-1}$		
10	$5.287 \cdot 10^{-1}$	$4.202 \cdot 10^{-1}$		

Table B.2. Average final best objective function values and their standard deviations for tournament selection with varying values of q on functions f_1–f_5.

η^+	f_1		f_2	
	$\bar{f}^1_{\min}(1000)$	$V^1_{\min}(1000)$	$\bar{f}^2_{\min}(1000)$	$V^2_{\min}(1000)$
1.1	$1.149 \cdot 10^1$	3.718	$1.515 \cdot 10^1$	4.826
1.2	1.438	1.546	3.650	3.422
1.3	$1.798 \cdot 10^{-1}$	$1.110 \cdot 10^{-1}$	1.750	2.712
1.4	$3.462 \cdot 10^{-2}$	$2.468 \cdot 10^{-2}$	$9.000 \cdot 10^{-1}$	2.221
1.5	$1.312 \cdot 10^{-2}$	$1.184 \cdot 10^{-2}$	1.300	2.867
1.6	$4.151 \cdot 10^{-3}$	$4.300 \cdot 10^{-3}$	2.050	3.720
1.7	$2.322 \cdot 10^{-3}$	$2.460 \cdot 10^{-3}$	$7.500 \cdot 10^{-1}$	2.221
1.8	$3.427 \cdot 10^{-4}$	$2.982 \cdot 10^{-4}$	$6.500 \cdot 10^{-1}$	2.033
1.9	$4.890 \cdot 10^{-4}$	$6.728 \cdot 10^{-4}$	1.000	2.000
2.0	$2.346 \cdot 10^{-4}$	$1.870 \cdot 10^{-4}$	1.400	2.062

η^+	f_3		f_4	
	$\bar{f}^3_{\min}(1000)$	$V^3_{\min}(1000)$	$\bar{f}^4_{\min}(2000)$	$V^4_{\min}(2000)$
1.1	3.069	$4.560 \cdot 10^{-1}$	$2.670 \cdot 10^4$	$1.481 \cdot 10^4$
1.2	1.030	$3.153 \cdot 10^{-1}$	$2.570 \cdot 10^4$	$1.322 \cdot 10^4$
1.3	$3.843 \cdot 10^{-1}$	$2.733 \cdot 10^{-1}$	$3.353 \cdot 10^4$	$2.302 \cdot 10^4$
1.4	$1.564 \cdot 10^{-1}$	$1.036 \cdot 10^{-1}$	$1.891 \cdot 10^4$	$1.241 \cdot 10^4$
1.5	$9.767 \cdot 10^{-2}$	$1.187 \cdot 10^{-1}$	$2.432 \cdot 10^4$	$1.362 \cdot 10^4$
1.6	$3.334 \cdot 10^{-2}$	$1.117 \cdot 10^{-2}$	$1.705 \cdot 10^4$	$1.232 \cdot 10^4$
1.7	$2.468 \cdot 10^{-2}$	$1.156 \cdot 10^{-2}$	$2.228 \cdot 10^4$	$1.202 \cdot 10^4$
1.8	$1.510 \cdot 10^{-2}$	$5.235 \cdot 10^{-3}$	$2.161 \cdot 10^4$	$1.581 \cdot 10^4$
1.9	$1.336 \cdot 10^{-2}$	$7.100 \cdot 10^{-3}$	$2.004 \cdot 10^4$	$1.304 \cdot 10^4$
2.0	$1.120 \cdot 10^{-2}$	$4.484 \cdot 10^{-3}$	$2.105 \cdot 10^4$	$1.390 \cdot 10^4$

η^+	f_5			
	$\bar{f}^5_{\min}(1000)$	$V^5_{\min}(1000)$		
1.1	$-6.311 \cdot 10^{-2}$	$1.405 \cdot 10^{-2}$		
1.2	$3.547 \cdot 10^{-3}$	$1.524 \cdot 10^{-1}$		
1.3	$1.421 \cdot 10^{-2}$	$1.997 \cdot 10^{-1}$		
1.4	$9.893 \cdot 10^{-2}$	$2.415 \cdot 10^{-1}$		
1.5	$2.228 \cdot 10^{-1}$	$2.773 \cdot 10^{-1}$		
1.6	$2.114 \cdot 10^{-1}$	$3.160 \cdot 10^{-1}$		
1.7	$2.270 \cdot 10^{-1}$	$3.265 \cdot 10^{-1}$		
1.8	$3.400 \cdot 10^{-1}$	$3.171 \cdot 10^{-1}$		
1.9	$2.954 \cdot 10^{-1}$	$2.763 \cdot 10^{-1}$		
2.0	$3.777 \cdot 10^{-1}$	$4.410 \cdot 10^{-1}$		

Table B.3. Average final best objective function values and their standard deviations for linear ranking with varying values of η^+ on functions f_1–f_5.

μ	$f^2_{\min}(1000)$	$f^4_{\min}(2000)$	$f^5_{\min}(1000)$
1	1	$6.144 \cdot 10^2$	$-8.252 \cdot 10^{-2}$
2	0	$1.854 \cdot 10^2$	$-3.460 \cdot 10^{-2}$
5	0	$1.437 \cdot 10^3$	$-3.313 \cdot 10^{-2}$
10	0	$4.048 \cdot 10^2$	$-2.828 \cdot 10^{-2}$
20	0	$1.248 \cdot 10^2$	$-2.349 \cdot 10^{-2}$
30	0	$2.464 \cdot 10^3$	$2.446 \cdot 10^{-2}$
40	0	$2.598 \cdot 10^3$	$7.163 \cdot 10^{-3}$
50	0	$1.988 \cdot 10^3$	$-5.077 \cdot 10^{-2}$
60	0	$3.323 \cdot 10^3$	$-1.102 \cdot 10^{-1}$
70	0	$6.339 \cdot 10^3$	$-9.583 \cdot 10^{-2}$
80	1	$1.456 \cdot 10^4$	$-8.904 \cdot 10^{-2}$
90	$6.500 \cdot 10^1$	$3.195 \cdot 10^4$	$3.722 \cdot 10^{-2}$
95	$5.590 \cdot 10^2$	$1.661 \cdot 10^5$	$2.179 \cdot 10^0$
q	$f^2_{\min}(1000)$	$f^4_{\min}(2000)$	$f^5_{\min}(1000)$
2	0	$6.054 \cdot 10^2$	$-1.218 \cdot 10^{-1}$
3	0	$1.421 \cdot 10^3$	$-9.895 \cdot 10^{-2}$
4	0	$1.126 \cdot 10^3$	$-5.507 \cdot 10^{-2}$
5	0	$5.445 \cdot 10^2$	$-7.057 \cdot 10^{-2}$
6	0	$8.139 \cdot 10^2$	$-8.071 \cdot 10^{-3}$
7	0	$1.528 \cdot 10^2$	$-5.795 \cdot 10^{-2}$
8	0	$7.512 \cdot 10^2$	$-9.180 \cdot 10^{-2}$
9	0	$8.614 \cdot 10^2$	$-1.271 \cdot 10^{-1}$
10	0	$1.055 \cdot 10^3$	$-2.779 \cdot 10^{-2}$
η^+	$f^2_{\min}(1000)$	$f^4_{\min}(2000)$	$f^5_{\min}(1000)$
1.1	$1.000 \cdot 10^1$	$8.743 \cdot 10^3$	$-8.652 \cdot 10^{-2}$
1.2	0	$3.506 \cdot 10^3$	$-1.316 \cdot 10^{-1}$
1.3	0	$6.719 \cdot 10^3$	$-1.243 \cdot 10^{-1}$
1.4	0	$2.852 \cdot 10^3$	$-1.216 \cdot 10^{-1}$
1.5	0	$2.757 \cdot 10^3$	$-1.358 \cdot 10^{-1}$
1.6	0	$4.414 \cdot 10^3$	$-1.295 \cdot 10^{-1}$
1.7	0	$7.720 \cdot 10^3$	$-1.026 \cdot 10^{-1}$
1.8	0	$1.292 \cdot 10^3$	$-1.180 \cdot 10^{-1}$
1.9	0	$1.214 \cdot 10^3$	$-1.305 \cdot 10^{-1}$
2.0	0	$1.989 \cdot 10^3$	$-1.063 \cdot 10^{-1}$

Table B.4. Overall final best objective function values found within 20 runs on f_2, f_4, and f_5 for different selection methods with varying selective pressure.

C

Software

In order to facilitate the experiments with Evolution Strategies, Evolutionary Programming, and Genetic Algorithms, a software environment was implemented which aims at providing a standardized user interface and output data format for these algorithms. The resulting software system is described here briefly by extensively referring the reader to chapters 2 and 5 wherever an explanation of specific parts of the algorithms seems necessary. Since the internals of Evolutionary Algorithms are assumed to be well known, our focus is on explaining the graphical user interface EVOS 1.0 (section C.2.1) and the data collection principles used to evaluate experiments (section C.3). Besides using the interface EVOS 1.0, the Evolutionary Algorithms may also be parameterized by command line options, i.e. for running them on machines without the graphics facilities required to run EVOS 1.0. This stand-alone usage is pointed out in section C.2.2. Section C.2.3 gives a short description of the online visualization features provided by the software. First, however, the overall structure of the software system is outlined.

C.1 Overview

Altogether, the software consists of the following four components:

- EVOS 1.0: The graphical user interface which allows for a convenient setup of experiments with Evolutionary Algorithms.

- *GENEsYs* 2.0: A Genetic Algorithm implemented after the widely used standard software package GENESIS 4.5 by Grefenstette (see [Gre87b]; [Dav91c], pp. 374–377).

- EPS 1.0: A combined implementation of Evolution Strategies and Evolutionary Programming. The Evolution Strategy part is based on Schwefel's implementations according to the descriptions given in [Sch80, Sch81b, HS90a]. The Evolutionary Programming component has no publicly available model and was implemented according to the description in Fogel's thesis [Fog92b].

275

- gnuplot 3.4: A public domain software tool for graphical visualization of data. See section C.2.3 for detailed information.

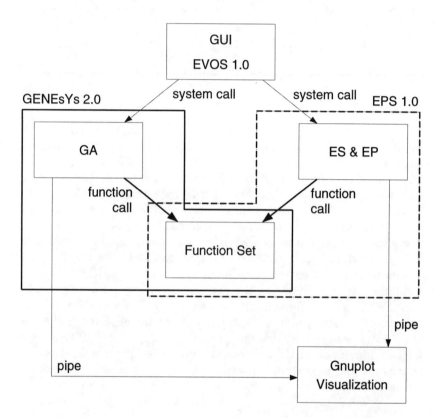

Fig. C.1: Architecture of the Evolutionary Algorithm software environment.

Both the EPS 1.0 and *GENEsYs* 2.0 software share a set of test functions such that for comparative experiments all algorithms can be applied to the same objective functions. The coupling between the graphical user interface EVOS 1.0 and EPS 1.0 respectively *GENEsYs* 2.0 is
achieved by a UNIX "system" call, such that EPS 1.0 and *GENEsYs* 2.0
can be used independently of EVOS 1.0 without recompiling, if desired.
This way, flexibility and applicability are guaranteed even if no graphical
environment is available (see the EVOS 1.0 user's manual for the system
requirements to run the user interface).

Similarly, the communication to gnuplot 3.4 works via the UNIX
"pipe" facility and is controlled by a special program option for EPS 1.0
respectively *GENEsYs* 2.0, such that the Evolutionary Algorithms are
also independent of the availability of gnuplot 3.4.

The resulting overall system architecture is shown in figure C.1, where the meaning of connecting arrows is indicated by the labels "system call," "pipe," and "function call."

C.2   Usage

C.2.1   The Graphical User Interface Evos 1.0

The Evos 1.0 user interface was designed under OpenWindows© with SUN Microsystem's OpenWindows Developer's Guide 3.0© under SunOS 4.1.3©. We are very grateful to Martin Schütz who perfectly realized our pretentious ideas about the functionality of Evos 1.0, which in the current version allows for a comfortable setup of experiments.

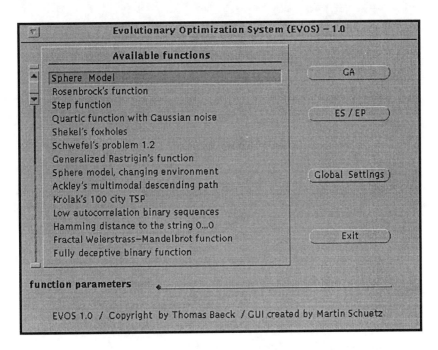

Fig. C.2: The base window of Evos 1.0.

The base window as obtained after starting Evos 1.0 (by the command evos &) is shown in figure C.2. Choosing an objective function is achieved by a mouseclick (select) on the function's name in the scroll window which makes up the left part of the base window. A double click on the objective function displays some help information about the function within a special help window. Certain parameter setting possibilities of the selected objective function are also displayed in this window. These option control possibilities of objective functions usually vary between different functions, such that options to objective functions must be given separately in the field "function parameters", e.g., entering –L –60.0 –H 40.0 sets the range of object variables to $[-60.0, 40.0]$.

Global Settings

Clicking the button "Global settings" in the Evos 1.0 base window yields a new window where parameter settings can be entered that are independent of the special Evolutionary Algorithm to be applied. The "Global settings" window is shown in figure C.3.

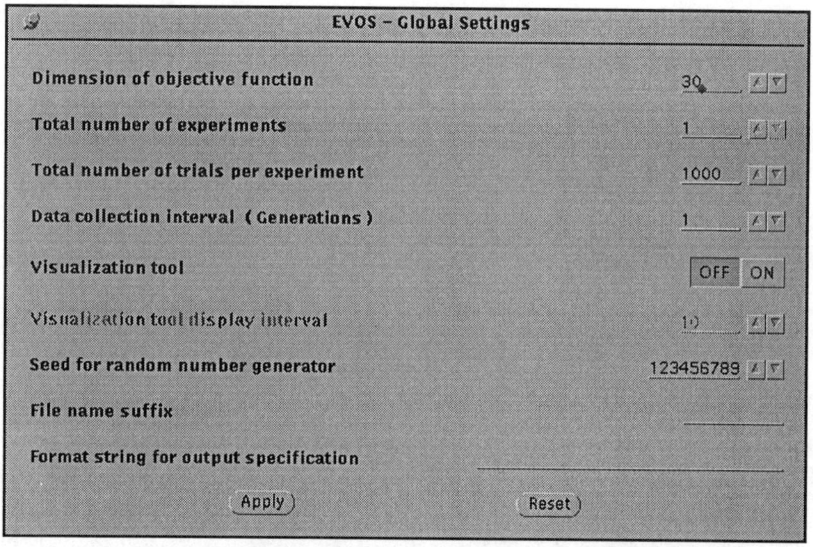

EVOS – Global Settings	
Dimension of objective function	30
Total number of experiments	1
Total number of trials per experiment	1000
Data collection interval (Generations)	1
Visualization tool	OFF ON
Visualization tool display interval	10
Seed for random number generator	123456789
File name suffix	
Format string for output specification	
Apply	Reset

Fig. C.3: The global settings window.

The window offers the following parameter setting possibilities:

- Dimension of the objective function, i.e., n.

- The total number of experiments, i.e., the number of independent optimizations of the same function. The resulting data is obtained by averaging over these experiments; the variances of the data are also calculated and stored.

- The total number of trials per experiment, where trials means function evaluations.

- The data collection interval, specified in generations, determines the frequency of data collection actions which add data about the state of optimization to the corresponding files.

- The visualization tool (see section C.2.3) may be switched on or off, and in the latter case a number of generations, the visualization tool display interval, defines the time between subsequent updates of the graphic.

- The random number generator seed, determining an entry point for the generation of a (deterministic) sequence of pseudo random numbers.

- The file name suffix, designating the directory name where the data of the actual run will be collected. A directory with this name is created by *GENEsYs* 2.0 respectively EPS 1.0 when optimization is started. Normally, a default mechanism creates relatively cryptic directory names which characterize the main parameters of the run (in stand-alone usage, the option -q for EPS 1.0 and *GENEsYs* 2.0 just causes the programs to print the name of the directory which would be created when running the algorithms, and exits the programs).

- A format string for output specifications. Beyond the data which is collected by default, the user may be interested in examining more and specialized information about the optimization process. This may include object variable values, standard deviations, and rotation angles for some few up to all individuals, and may cause the accumulation of a considerable amount of data. The format string allows for specifying exactly which data should be collected and is formulated in a simple, context-free language[1]. As an example, consider the format string
$$x:1,2,4\text{-}10s:2,4i:*$$
indicating the following data to be reported: Object variables $x_1, x_2, x_4, \ldots, x_{10}$ and standard deviations σ_2, σ_4 for all individuals[2].

In order to enable the new settings, the user must finally click the button "Apply" and the window will disappear. The button "Reset" discards all changes by turning back to the default values.

Genetic Algorithm

Selecting the button "GA" in the EVOS 1.0 base window opens a window for setting parameters which are specific to a Genetic Algorithm. This Genetic Algorithm control window as shown in figure C.4 is divided into control regions responsible for setting parameters related to the recombination, mutation, and selection mechanism, and for some other exogenous parameters such as population sizes (parent population size

---

[1] For the exact syntax, see the user's guide to EVOS 1.0 [SB93].

[2] Note that the identification of individuals works by integer values such that the best individual is designated by number 1.

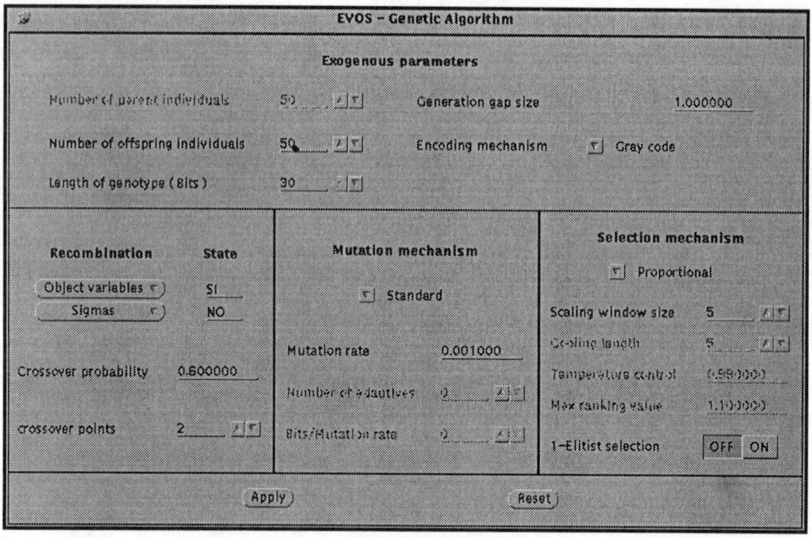

Fig. C.4: The parameter setting window for Genetic Algorithms.

μ and offspring population size λ), total genotype length l (for pseudo-boolean functions) respectively l_x (for continuous problems, the default assumption), generation gap, and encoding mechanism.

Most of the parameter setting possibilities should be clear from section 2.3. Extensions provided by *GENEsYs* 2.0 concern the Boltzmann selection method and the prototypical adaptive mutation rate feature; more detailed informations about these mechanisms are given in the "User's Guide to *GENEsYs* 1.0" [Bäc92a]. As common in the window of Evos 1.0, the button "Reset" reinstalls the default parameters. Alternatively, the button "Apply" starts the optimization run.

Evolution Strategies and Evolutionary Programming

Due to their similarities, the parameterization of Evolution Strategies and Evolutionary Programming is summarized under Evos 1.0 into a single window which is reached from the base window by clicking the button "ES & EP". As both algorithms are implemented within the Eps 1.0 software, this allows also for mixing concepts from Evolution Strategies and Evolutionary Programming for performing experiments (e.g., running Evolutionary Programming with recombination).

The window for setting parameters of the Evolution Strategy respectively of Evolutionary Programming is shown in figure C.5.

As for Genetic Algorithms, the control window is divided into regions for recombination, mutation, selection, and a region for some general exogenous parameters. The latter are enabled or disabled according to

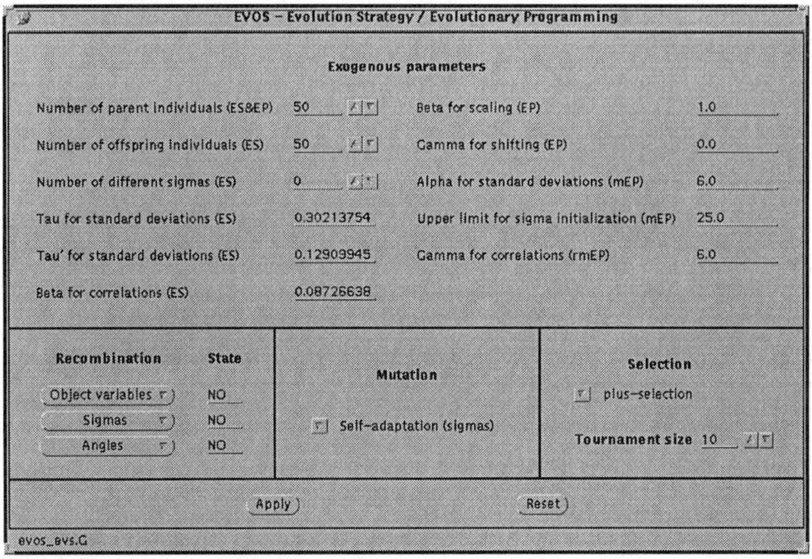

Fig. C.5: The parameter setting window for Evolution Strategies and Evolutionary Programming.

the choice of the mutation mechanism which is mainly responsible for controlling the algorithm's character. The right part of the exogenous parameter region is related to Evolutionary Programming and allows for controlling (from top to bottom) β_i and γ_i for standard EP, ζ for meta-EP, c for initialization of variances in meta-EP, and ϖ for Rmeta-EP (see sections 2.2.1 and 2.2.5).

As the possible parameter settings for recombination, mutation, and selection are self-explanatory from sections 2.1 and 2.2, we abstain from a detailed explanation and conclude by mentioning that (in the same way as for the Genetic Algorithm) optimization is started by the button "Apply" while "Reset" restores the default settings.

C.2.2   Stand–alone Usage

Both *GENEsYs* 2.0 and Eps 1.0 can also be used independently of the user interface Evos 1.0. For this purpose, the corresponding programs ga and eps are equipped with a simple UNIX command line option interface. This interface is not discussed here in full detail, but instead we refer to the calls ga -h respectively eps -h which provide the online help information of these programs. In combination with the previous description of Evos 1.0 and chapter 2, the meaning of the options should easily become clear. For detailed explanations, the interested reader is referred to the user's manual [Bäc92a].

In addition to the usual command line structure, the ga and eps programs provide the feature to submit special, function-dependent options to objective functions (the permissible options are also displayed as part of the help information). The general format of a call to ga or eps is then as follows:

```
ga/eps <some_options> -f <No.> { <options_to_function> }
                       <more_options>
```

Here, the options in curly brackets are function-specific options for the objective function numbered <No.>. It is important to note that the curly-bracketed function-specific options must directly follow the function number specification. The list of available objective functions is also displayed on the help option -h; a more detailed description may be found in the user's manual [Bäc92a].

C.2.3 Visualization of Runs

As indicated above, the current state of optimization may optionally be visualized by means of graphically displaying the course of the best, average, and worst objective function value contained in the actual population over the number of generations. As a visualization tool, the public domain software[3] gnuplot 3.4 is used and communication proceeds via the UNIX "pipe" command, such that the independence of the availability of gnuplot 3.4 is guaranteed and all software components remain usable in stand-alone modus.

Figure C.6 shows a possible layout of the screen when *GENEsYs* 2.0 runs under Evos 1.0 with the visualization tool being enabled.

C.3 Data Collection

When running a Genetic Algorithm, Evolution Strategy, or Evolutionary Programming, the respective program creates — depending on the amount of data specified to be collected — a number of files in the directory created for the experiment. The following list gives a brief description of the purpose of these files:

- log: General logging activities and information about the final best individual are collected in the log file. Its contents normally consist of timing information (start and end time of the experiment), the parameter settings of the run, and, for each of the independent optimization experiments, the full specification of the best individual found in the last generation of the experiment. This individual is saved in the general format

$$t \quad x_1 \ldots x_n \; f(x_1, \ldots, x_n) \; \sigma_1 \ldots \sigma_{n_\sigma} \; \alpha_1 \ldots \alpha_{n_\alpha} \; .$$

---

[3]For information about the gnuplot 3.4 software and how to obtain it, see [WK93].

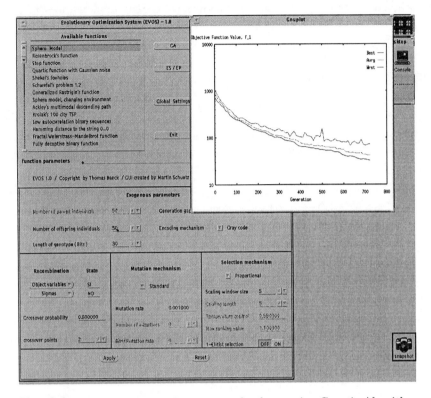

Fig. C.6: The screen layout for an example of a running Genetic Algorithm with visualization enabled.

- out: Contains accumulated population data for all independently performed experiments of the actual run, with the general fields generation number, number of function evaluations, number of lost alleles[4], number of converged alleles[5], bias value (see section 2.3.5), online- and offline-performance (for historical reasons; see e.g. [DeJ75], pp. 10–13), best, average, and worst objective function value found in the actual generation.

While these are the data fields for a Genetic Algorithm, for Evolution Strategies and Evolutionary Programming the generation number, number of function evaluations, the best objective function value found so far, the actual best, average, and worst objective function value, the actually minimal, average, and maximal

---

[4] After [Gre87b], the number of bit positions in which at least 95% of the population has the same value.

[5] After [Gre87b], the number of bit positions in which 100% of the population has the same value.

standard deviation, and eventually the actually minimal, average, and maximal rotation angle are collected.

To achieve compatibility for post-processing of the data, the out-file always contains the actually best objective function value in column number eight.

- rep, var: These files contain the averages (rep) respectively variances (var) of the results collected in the out-file for several experiments. Therefore, the rep and var file reflect the accumulated data from a number of independent experiments performed for identical parameter settings but different seeds of the random number generator.

- obj, sig, alp: If a format string is specified for additional data collection purposes (creation of the log, out, rep and var files happens by default), the data for object variables (obj), standard deviations (sig), and rotation angles (alp) is collected in these files in the order specified in the format string, each line starting with the generation number. For each generation these files contain as many lines as individuals are specified in the format string.

Note that the total size of the data files out, obj, sig, alp may quickly grow to megabytes of data if the data collection options of *GENEsYs* 2.0 respectively EPS 1.0 are not used carefully.

D

The Multiprocessor Environment

The experiments reported in chapter 7 were performed on a transputer-based multiprocessor system available at the Computer Science Department of the University of Dortmund, Germany. A transputer system is an example of an MIMD-machine based on asynchronous execution[1] and a synchronous communication[2] concept by *message passing*, i.e., each processor has exclusive access to its own main memory[3] and communicates with other processors by sending messages via *links* (physical connections between processors). Due to its relatively powerful processors and the asynchronous parallelism, such a system represents the most general instance of a parallel computer.

In order to provide the reader with an overview, sections D.1 and D.2 give a short introduction to the hardware and the operating system, respectively.

D.1 The Transputer System

The T800-transputer of INMOS consists of a 32-bit CPU with a fast on-chip RAM (up to 4kB), a communication subsystem — the so-called link interface — for the four external links, an external memory interface for accessing the processors memory, and an additional 64-bit floating point unit (FPU) (see e.g. [TW91], p. 155; [INM88], chapter 3). These components are connected by a 32-bit internal bus. The performance of a T800 is indicated to be 1.2 MFLOPS (1.9 peak) on 20 MHz devices [TW91].

The system available for our experiments consists of 48 transputers with 4MB of local memory per processor. The physical interconnection

---

[1]There is no global control unit that assures synchronization of operations of different processors.

[2]A message transfer between processors is finished when the message is accepted by the receiver. Asynchronous communication, however, can easily be simulated by adding a process responsible for buffering incoming messages.

[3]In contrast to *shared memory* concepts where communication is achieved by writing to respectively reading from the common memory.

topology of the transputer network is currently chosen to be a 6×8 grid for some technical reasons concerning an update of the operating system, but such a topology is not optimal with respect to the communication structure and the resulting communication times[4].

The access to the transputer network is facilitated by the connection to a host computer which provides services such as the file system and the I/O-periphery. In our case, the host computer is a SUN SPARC1+, which allows for the transputer system access via an S-bus connected to a BBK-S4 card which provides four link adapters to connect the host with entry points of the network (in our case, the four corners of the 6×8 transputer grid, connected at the borders to form a torus structure).

D.2 The Helios Operating System

The distributed operating system Helios was designed for a topology-independent use on a variety of transputer-based system configurations. It is based on the *client-server* model which distinguishes programs into clients, i.e. programs that ask for access to a system resource by sending a request, and servers, programs that control the system resource access.

Important examples of Helios servers are the network-server, which is responsible for loading the Helios nucleus to all transputers of the network, and the task force manager (TFM), a server responsible for distributing an application over the network. The TFM is started by the network server during the system boot process, which is initiated by the I/O server of the host machine (see [Per91]).

The programming philosophy under Helios concentrates on independent, active (running) programs — so-called *tasks* — that communicate by using pipes. Within programming languages such as C (FORTRAN and Pascal are also supported) these pipes are represented by descriptors and communication is implemented by **read** and **write** statements in application programs. A group of tasks which forms a parallel application program is called a *task force*, and the description of logical communication topologies of task forces is possible by using the *component distribution language* (CDL). The four parallel constructors of CDL are (see [Vee90], pp. 13–22):

- |: The *pipe-constructor*, which defines an unidirectional pipe between two programs A and B (A | B).

- <>: The *subordinate-constructor*, defining a bidirectional pipe (A <> B).

---

[4]It is advisable to consider a topological optimization with respect to the average distance between any two arbitrary nodes of the network. This was performed in the past for a smaller network by using an Evolutionary Algorithm and yielded a highly irregular optimal connection structure [Kni92] (see also [Rad90] for such a network optimization example).

- ||| : The *interleave-constructor* defines a farm topology that automatically includes a *load balancer*, i.e. a program which guarantees a balanced usage of worker programs. The interleave constructor is in most cases combined with a replicator [N] which specifies the number of workers (A [N] ||| W denotes a farm with load balancer and N worker processes).

- ^^ : The *parallel* constructor defines no communication between two programs.

The combination of CDL and communication on the basis of pipes allows for an abstraction from the physical topology of the network. Virtually any logical communication topology can be specified in CDL, thus providing full flexibility for user application software. The CDL script that specifies the communication structure of a task force is compiled into a description the task force manager uses to distribute tasks over the network and to provide the pipes as requested.

In case of the meta-evolution experiment, the desired logical topology according to figure 7.1 is identical to a farm without load balancer. The latter is not required due to the generational synchronization of the parallel algorithm. According to the example presented by Veer (see [Vee90], pp. 48–53), the CDL script

$$\text{Meta-EA (, } [\lambda] \text{ <> GA)}$$

specifies the topology of figure 7.1. The replicator [λ] defines λ instances of the Genetic Algorithm to communicate with the meta-Evolutionary Algorithm by bidirectional pipes. The Genetic Algorithm is just a serial implementation, extended by the read and write communication calls, and the meta-algorithm is implemented according to the specification presented in section 7.2, also extended by read and write communication instructions.

E

Mathematical Symbols

Within this appendix, we present a list of the major important mathematical symbols used in the text. A short indication of its meaning is given for each of these symbols. Furthermore, for most of the notations (except some rather general ones) the page number of its first occurrence is indicated. Page numbers are underlined if the corresponding quantity is (semi-) formally defined on that page.

Symbol	Short description	Page
∇f	Gradient of f.	<u>44</u>
$\nabla^2 f$	Hessian of f.	<u>44</u>
$\vec{\alpha}$	Vector of rotation angles.	68
α'	Significance level for Kolmogorov-Smirnov test.	152
β	Mutation parameter for rotation angles in Evolution Strategies.	72
β_i	Proportionality constants in Evolutionary Programming.	93
$\Gamma(\cdot)$	Gamma function.	49
$\gamma(\cdot)$	Standard to Gray code conversion.	<u>110</u>
$\gamma^{-1}(\cdot)$	Gray to standard code conversion.	<u>110</u>
γ_i	Offset values in Evolutionary Programming.	93
$\Delta(\cdot)$	Defining length of a schema.	<u>124</u>
$\delta(\cdot, \cdot)$	Scaling function.	111
ε_σ	Minimum standard deviation in Evolution Strategies.	72
$\varepsilon_{\Phi,1}, \varepsilon_{\Phi,2}$	Termination criterion constant in Evolution Strategies.	81
ζ	Mutation parameter in meta-Evolutionary Programming.	94
η	Expected value.	<u>118</u>
$\eta_{\max}, \eta_{\min}$	Expected value bounds.	170
η^+, η^-	Minimal and maximal expected value.	170

289

Bibliography

[AS65]   M. Abramowitz and I. A. Stegun, editors. *Handbook of Mathematical Functions with Formulas, Graphs, and Mathematical Tables*. Dover Publications, New York, 1965.

[Ack87]   D. H. Ackley. *A connectionist machine for genetic hillclimbing*. Kluwer, Boston, 1987.

[AHU74]   A. V. Aho, J. E. Hopcroft, and J. D. Ullman. *The Design and Analysis of Computer Algorithms*. Addison Wesley, Reading, MA, 1974.

[ASS90]   A. N. Antamoshkin, V. N. Saraev, and E. S. Semenkin. Optimization of unimodal monotone pseudoboolean functions. *Kybernetika*, 26(5):432–442, 1990.

[ABN92]   B. C. Arnold, N. Balakrishnan, and H. N. Nagaraja. *A First Course in Order Statistics*. Wiley Series in Probability and Mathematical Statistics. Wiley, New York, 1992.

[Atm92]   W. Atmar. The philosophical errors that plague both evolutionary theory and simulated evolutionary programming. In Fogel and Atmar [FA92], pages 27–34.

[Bäc92a]   Th. Bäck. A User's Guide to *GENEsYs 1.0*. Report of the Systems Analysis Research Group, Universität Dortmund, Fachbereich Informatik, 1992.

[Bäc92b]   Th. Bäck. The interaction of mutation rate, selection, and self-adaptation within a genetic algorithm. In Männer and Manderick [MM92], pages 85–94.

[Bäc92c]   Th. Bäck. Self–Adaptation in Genetic Algorithms. In F. J. Varela and P. Bourgine, editors, *Proceedings of the First European Conference on Artificial Life*, pages 263–271. The MIT Press, Cambridge, MA, 1992.

[Bäc93]   Th. Bäck. Optimal mutation rates in genetic search. In Forrest [For93], pages 2–9.

[BH91]   Th. Bäck and F. Hoffmeister. Extended selection mechanisms in genetic algorithms. In Belew and Booker [BB91], pages 92–99.

[BHS91]   Th. Bäck, F. Hoffmeister, and H.-P. Schwefel. A survey of evolution strategies. In Belew and Booker [BB91], pages 2–9.

[BHS92]   Th. Bäck, F. Hoffmeister, and H.-P. Schwefel. Applications of evolutionary algorithms. Report of the Systems Analysis Research Group SYS–2/92, Universität Dortmund, Fachbereich Informatik, February 1992.

[BRS93]   Th. Bäck, G. Rudolph, and H.-P. Schwefel. Evolutionary programming and evolution strategies: Similarities and differences. In D. B. Fogel and W. Atmar, editors, *Proceedings of the 2nd Annual Conference on Evolutionary Programming*, pages 11–22. Evolutionary Programming Society, San Diego, CA, 1993.

293

[Bak85]   J. E. Baker. Adaptive selection methods for genetic algorithms. In Grefenstette [Gre85], pages 101–111.

[Bak87]   J. E. Baker. Reducing bias and inefficiency in the selection algorithm. In
Grefenstette [Gre87a], pages 14–21.

[Bea93]   J. C. Bean. Genetics and random keys for sequences and optimization. Technical Report 92–43, Department of Industrial and Operations Engineering, The
University of Michigan, Ann Arbor, MI, 1993.

[BN93]   J. C. Bean and B. A. Norman. Random keys for job shop scheduling. Technical Report 93–7, Department of Industrial and Operations Engineering, The
University of Michigan, Ann Arbor, MI, 1993.

[BB91]   R. K. Belew and L. B. Booker, editors. *Proceedings of the 4th International
Conference on Genetic Algorithms.* Morgan Kaufmann Publishers, San Mateo,
CA, 1991.

[BL80]   M. V. Berry and Z. V. Lewis. On the Weierstrass-Mandelbrot fractal function.
Proceedings Royal Society of London, A(370):459–484, 1980.

[Bet81]   A. D. Bethke. *Genetic algorithms as function optimizers.* PhD thesis, University of Michigan, 1981. Diss. Abstr. Int. 41(9), 3503B, University Microfilms
No. 8106101.

[BEHW89]   A. Blumer, A. Ehrenfeucht, D. Haussler, and M. K. Warmuth. Learnability and the Vapnik-Chervonenkis dimension. *Journal of the Association for
Computing Machinery,* 36(4):929–965, October 1989.

[BJS86]   I. O. Bohachevsky, M. E. Johnson, and M. L. Stein. Generalized simulated annealing for function optimization. *Technometrics,* 28(3):209–217, August 1986.

[BGH89]   L. B. Booker, D. E. Goldberg, and J. H. Holland. Classifier systems and
genetic algorithms. In J. G. Carbonell, editor, *Machine Learning: Paradigms
and Methods,* pages 235–282. The MIT Press / Elsevier, 1989.

[Bor78]   J. Born. *Evolutionsstrategien zur numerischen Lösung von Adaptation-
saufgaben.* Dissertation A, Humboldt-Universität, Berlin, 1978.

[BE91]   T. Boseniuk and W. Ebeling. Boltzmann-, Darwin-, and Haeckel-strategies in
optimization problems. In Schwefel and Männer [SM91a], pages 430–444.

[Box57]   G. E. P. Box. Evolutionary operation: A method for increasing industrial
productivity. *Applied Statistics,* VI(2):81–101, 1957.

[BD69]   G. E. P. Box and N. P. Draper. *Evolutionary Operation. A Method for Increasing Industrial Productivity.* Wiley, New York, 1969.

[Bre62]   H. J. Bremermann. Optimization through evolution and recombination. In
M. C. Yovits et al., editor, *Self-Organizing Systems.* Spartan Books, Washington,
D.C., 1962.

[BRS65]   H. J. Bremermann, M. Rogson, and S. Salaff. Search by evolution. In
M. Maxfield, A. Callahan, and L. J. Fogel, editors, *Biophysics and Cybernetic
Systems — Proceedings of the 2nd Cybernetic Sciences Symposium,* pages 157–
167. Spartan Books, Washington, D.C., 1965.

[BG91]   C. L. Bridges and D. E. Goldberg. The nonuniform Walsh-schema transform.
In Rawlins [Raw91], pages 13–22.

[BBM92]   F. Z. Brill, D. E. Brown, and W. N. Martin. Fast genetic selection of
features for neural network classifiers. *IEEE Transactions on Neural Networks,*
3(2):324–328, March 1992.

[Bro58]   S. H. Brooks. A discussion of random methods for seeking maxima. *Operations Research*, 6:244–251, 1958.

[CMM84]   J. G. Carbonell, R. S. Michalski, and T. M. Mitchell. An overview of machine learning. In R. S. Michalski, J. G. Carbonell, and T. M. Mitchell, editors, *Machine Learning. An Artificial Intelligence Approach*, chapter 1, pages 3–23. Springer, Berlin, 1984.

[CES89]   R. A. Caruna, L. J. Eshelman, and J. D. Schaffer. Representation and hidden bias II: Eliminating defining length bias in genetic search via shuffle crossover. In N. S. Sridharan, editor, *Proceedings of the 11th International Joint Conference on Artificial Intelligence*, pages 750–755. Morgan Kaufmann Publishers, San Mateo, CA, 1989.

[CS88]   R. A. Caruna and J. D. Schaffer. Representation and hidden bias: Gray vs. binary coding for genetic algorithms. In J. Laird, editor, *Proceedings of the 5th International Conference on Machine Learning*, pages 153–161. Morgan Kaufmann Publishers, San Mateo, CA, 1988.

[CHMR87]   J. P. Cohoon, S. U. Hedge, W. N. Martin, and D. S. Richards. Punctuated equilibria: A parallel genetic algorithm. In Grefenstette [Gre87a], pages 148–154.

[CMR91a]   J. P. Cohoon, W. N. Martin, and D. S. Richards. Genetic algorithms and punctuated equilibria in VLSI. In Schwefel and Männer [SM91a], pages 134–144.

[CMR91b]   J. P. Cohoon, W. N. Martin, and D. S. Richards. A multi-population genetic algorithm for solving the K-partition problem on hyper-cubes. In Belew and Booker [BB91], pages 244–248.

[CJ91]   R. J. Collins and D. R. Jefferson. Selection in massively parallel genetic algorithms. In Belew and Booker [BB91], pages 249–256.

[Cra85]   M. L. Cramer. A representation for the adaptive generation of simple sequential programs. In Grefenstette [Gre85], pages 183–187.

[Dav90]   Y. Davidor. Epistasis variance: Suitability of a representation to genetic algorithms. *Complex Systems*, 4:369–383, 1990.

[Dav91a]   Y. Davidor. Epistasis variance: A viewpoint on GA-hardness. In Rawlins [Raw91], pages 23–35.

[Dav89]   L. Davis. Adapting operator probabilities in genetic algorithms. In Schaffer [Sch89], pages 61–69.

[Dav91b]   L. Davis. Bit-climbing, representational bias, and test suite design. In Belew and Booker [BB91], pages 18–23.

[Dav91c]   L. Davis, editor. *Handbook of Genetic Algorithms*. Van Nostrand Reinhold, New York, 1991.

[Day90]   J. E. Dayhoff. *Neural Network Architectures: An Introduction*. Van Nostrand Reinhold, New York, 1990.

[DG91]   K. Deb and D. E. Goldberg. Analyzing deception in trap functions. IlliGAL Report 91009, University of Illinois at Urbana-Champaign, IL, 1991.

[DeJ75]   K. A. De Jong. *An analysis of the behaviour of a class of genetic adaptive systems*. PhD thesis, University of Michigan, 1975. Diss. Abstr. Int. 36(10), 5140B, University Microfilms No. 76–9381.

[DeJ85]   K. A. De Jong. Genetic algorithms: A 10 year perspective. In Grefenstette [Gre85], pages 169–177.

[DeJ87]   K. A. De Jong. On using genetic algorithms to search program spaces. In Grefenstette [Gre87a], pages 210–216.

[DeJ92]   K. A. De Jong. Are genetic algorithms function optimizers? In Männer and Manderick [MM92], pages 3–13.

[DeJ93]   K. A. De Jong. Genetic algorithms are NOT function optimizers. In Whitley [Whi93], pages 5–17.

[DS93]   K. A. De Jong and J. Sarma. Generation gaps revisited. In Whitley [Whi93], pages 19–28.

[Dör77]   W. Dörfler. *Mathematik für Informatiker*, volume 1. Carl Hanser, München, 1 edition, 1977.

[Dör78]   W. Dörfler. *Mathematik für Informatiker*, volume 2. Carl Hanser, München, 1 edition, 1978.

[EAH91]   A. E. Eiben, E. H. L. Aarts, and K. M. Van Hee. Global convergence of genetic algorithms: An infinite Markov chain analysis. In Schwefel and Männer [SM91a], pages 4–12.

[Eig71]   M. Eigen. Selforganization of matter and the evolution of biological macro-molecules. *Die Naturwissenschaften*, 58(10):465–523, 1971.

[Eig76]   M. Eigen. Wie entsteht Information? Prinzipien der Selbstorganisation in der Biologie. *Berichte der Bunsen-Gesellschaft*, 11:1059–1081, 1976.

[EG72]   N. Eldredge and S. J. Gould. Punctuated equilibria: An alternative to phyletic gradualism. In T. J. M. Schopf, editor, *Models in Paleobiology*, chapter 5, pages 82–115. Freeman, 1972.

[ECS89]   L. J. Eshelman, R. A. Caruna, and J. D. Schaffer. Biases in the crossover landscape. In Schaffer [Sch89], pages 10–19.

[ES93]   L. J. Eshelman and J. D. Schaffer. Crossover's niche. In Forrest [For93], pages 9–14.

[Fed88]   J. Feder. *Fractals*. Plenum Press, New York, 1988.

[FP63]   R. Fletcher and M. J. D. Powell. A rapidly convergent descent method for minimization. *Computer Journal*, 6:163–168, 1963.

[Fog89]   T. C. Fogarty. Varying the probability of mutation in the genetic algorithm. In Schaffer [Sch89], pages 104–109.

[Fog88]   D. B. Fogel. An evolutionary approach to the traveling salesman problem. *Biological Cybernetics*, 60:139–144, 1988.

[Fog91]   D. B. Fogel. *System Identification through Simulated Evolution: A Machine Learning Approach to Modeling*. Ginn Press, Needham Heights, 1991.

[Fog92a]   D. B. Fogel. An analysis of evolutionary programming. In Fogel and Atmar [FA92], pages 43–51.

[Fog92b]   D. B. Fogel. *Evolving Artificial Intelligence*. PhD thesis, University of California, San Diego, CA, 1992.

[Fog92c]   D. B. Fogel. Personal communication, August 1992.

[FA90]   D. B. Fogel and W. Atmar. Comparing genetic operators with Gaussian mutations in simulated evolutionary processes using linear systems. *Biological Cybernetics*, 63:111–114, 1990.

[FA92]   D. B. Fogel and W. Atmar, editors. *Proceedings of the 1st Annual Conference on Evolutionary Programming*. Evolutionary Programming Society, San Diego, CA, 1992.

[FFA91]   D. B. Fogel, L. J. Fogel, and W. Atmar. Meta-evolutionary programming. In R. R. Chen, editor, *Proc. 25th Asilomar Conference on Signals, Systems and Computers*, pages 540–545. Pacific Grove, CA, 1991.

[FFAF92]   D. B. Fogel, L. J. Fogel, W. Atmar, and G. B. Fogel. Hierarchic methods in evolutionary programming. In Fogel and Atmar [FA92], pages 175–182.

[Fog62]   L. J. Fogel. Autonomous automata. *Industrial Research*, 4:14–19, 1962.

[Fog64]   L. J. Fogel. *On the Organization of Intellect*. PhD thesis, University of California, Los Angeles, CA, 1964.

[FOW66]   L. J. Fogel, A. J. Owens, and M. J. Walsh. *Artificial Intelligence through Simulated Evolution*. Wiley, New York, 1966.

[For85]   S. Forrest. *Documentation for Prisoner's Dilemma and Norms Programs that use the Genetic Algorithm*. The University of New Mexico, Albuquerque, NM, 1985.

[For93]   S. Forrest, editor. *Proceedings of the 5th International Conference on Genetic Algorithms*. Morgan Kaufmann Publishers, San Mateo, CA, 1993.

[Fra92]   P. Frankhauser. *Beschreibung der Evolution urbaner Systeme mit der Mastergleichung*. Dissertation, Universität Stuttgart, 1992.

[Fra57a]   A. S. Fraser. Simulation of genetic systems by automatic digital computers, I. Introduction. *Australian Journal of Biological Science*, 10:484–491, 1957.

[Fra57b]   A. S. Fraser. Simulation of genetic systems by automatic digital computers, II. Effects of linkage on rates of advance under selection. *Australian Journal of Biological Science*, 10:492–499, 1957.

[Fra60]   A. S. Fraser. Simulation of genetic systems by automatic digital computers, VI. Epistasis. *Australian Journal of Biological Science*, 13:150–162, 1960.

[Fra62]   A. S. Fraser. Simulation of genetic systems. *Journal of Theoretical Biology*, 2:329–346, 1962.

[Fri58]   R. M. Friedberg. A learning machine: Part I. *IBM Journal*, 2(1):2–13, January 1958.

[FDN59]   R. M. Friedberg, B. Dunham, and J. H. North. A learning machine: Part II. *IBM Journal*, 3(7):282–287, July 1959.

[FD87]   C. Fujiko and J. Dickinson. Using the genetic algorithm to generate LISP source code to solve the prisoner's dilemma. In Grefenstette [Gre87a], pages 236–240.

[Fut86]   D. J. Futuyma. *Evolutionary Biology*. Sinauer Associates, Sunderland, MA, 1986.

[Fut90]   D. J. Futuyma. *Evolutionsbiologie*. Birkhäuser Verlag, Basel, 1990.

[Gal85]   R. Galar. Handicapped individua in evolutionary processes. *Biological Cybernetics*, 53:1–9, 1985.

[Gal89]   R. Galar. Evolutionary search with soft selection. *Biological Cybernetics*, 60:357–364, 1989.

[Gal91]   R. Galar. Simulation of local evolutionary dynamics of small populations. *Biological Cybernetics*, 65:37–45, 1991.

[GJ79]   M. R. Garey and D. S. Johnson. *Computers and Intractability — A Guide to the Theory of NP–Completeness*. Freemann & Co., San Francisco, CA, 1979.

[GMSW89]   P. E. Gill, W. Murray, M. A. Saunders, and M. H. Wright. *Constrained Nonlinear Programming*, volume 1 of *Handbooks in Operations Research and Management Science*, chapter III. Elsevier, Amsterdam, 1989.

[Gol77]   M. J. E. Golay. Sieves for low autocorrelation binary sequences. *IEEE Transactions on Information Theory*, IT–23(1):43–51, 1977.

[Gol82]   M. J. E. Golay. The merit factor of long autocorrelation binary sequences. *IEEE Transactions on Information Theory*, IT–28(3):543–549, 1982.

[Gol87]   D. E. Goldberg. Simple genetic algorithms and the minimal, deceptive problem. In L. Davis, editor, *Genetic algorithms and simulated annealing*, pages 74–88. Pitman, London, 1987.

[Gol89a]   D. E. Goldberg. *Genetic algorithms in search, optimization and machine learning*. Addison Wesley, Reading, MA, 1989.

[Gol89b]   D. E. Goldberg. Sizing populations for serial and parallel genetic algorithms. In Schaffer [Sch89], pages 70–79.

[Gol90]   D. E. Goldberg. A note on Boltzmann tournament selection for genetic algorithms and population–oriented simulated annealing. *Complex Systems*, 4:445–460, 1990.

[GD91]   D. E. Goldberg and K. Deb. A comparative analysis of selection schemes used in genetic algorithms. In Rawlins [Raw91], pages 69–93.

[Goo88]   R. Goodman. *Introduction to Stochastic Models*. The Benjamin/Cummings Publishing Company, Menlo Park, CA, 1988.

[GS89]   M. Gorges-Schleuter. ASPARAGOS: an asynchronous parallel genetic optimization strategy. In Schaffer [Sch89], pages 422–427.

[GS90]   M. Gorges-Schleuter. *Genetic Algorithms and Population Structures — A Massively Parallel Algorithm*. Dissertation, Universität Dortmund, 1990.

[GS92]   M. Gorges-Schleuter. Comparison of local mating strategies in massively parallel genetic algorithms. In Männer and Manderick [MM92], pages 553–562.

[Got89]   W. Gottschalk. *Allgemeine Genetik*. Georg Thieme Verlag, Stuttgart, 3 edition, 1989.

[Gou82]   S. J. Gould. Darwinism and the expansion of evolutionary theory. *Science*, 216:380–387, April 1982.

[GKP89]   R. L. Graham, D. E. Knuth, and O. Patashnik. *Concrete Mathematics*. Addison Wesley, Reading, MA, 1989.

[Gre85]   J. J. Grefenstette, editor. *Proceedings of the 1st International Conference on Genetic Algorithms and Their Applications*. Lawrence Erlbaum Associates, Hillsdale, NJ, 1985.

[Gre86]   J. J. Grefenstette. Optimization of control parameters for genetic algorithms. *IEEE Transactions on Systems, Man and Cybernetics*, SMC–16(1):122–128, 1986.

[Gre87a]   J. J. Grefenstette, editor. *Proceedings of the 2nd International Conference on Genetic Algorithms and Their Applications.* Lawrence Erlbaum Associates, Hillsdale, NJ, 1987.

[Gre87b]   J. J. Grefenstette. *A User's Guide to GENESIS.* Navy Center for Applied Research in Artificial Intelligence, Washington, D. C., 1987.

[GB89]   J. J. Grefenstette and J. E. Baker. How genetic algorithms work: A critical look at implicit parallelism. In Schaffer [Sch89], pages 20–27.

[dGWH89]   C. de Groot, D. Würtz, and K. H. Hoffman. Low autocorrelation binary sequences: Exact enumeration and optimization by evolution strategies. Technical Report 89–09, Eidgenössische Technische Hochschule Zürich, November 1989.

[Hah93]   S. Hahn. Optimierung von Monte-Carlo-Generator-Parametern mit Genetischen Algorithmen. Diplomarbeit, Bergische Universität, Gesamthochschule Wuppertal, Fachbereich Physik, 1993.

[HBH92]   S. Hahn, K. H. Becks, and A. Hemker. Optimizing monte carlo generator parameters using genetic algorithms. In D. Perret-Gallix, editor, *New Computing Techniques in Physics Research II — Proceedings 2nd International Workshop on Software Engineering, Artificial Intelligence and Expert Systems for High Energy and Nuclear Physics,* pages 255–265. World Scientific, Singapore, 1992.

[HB91]   W. E. Hart and R. K. Belew. Optimizing an arbitrary function is hard for the genetic algorithm. In Belew and Booker [BB91], pages 190–195.

[Har90]   R. F. Hartl. A global convergence proof for a class of genetic algorithms. Technische Universität Wien, 1990.

[HEK82]   J. Hartung, B. Elpelt, and K.-H. Klösener. *Statistik — Lehr- und Handbuch der angewandten Statistik.* R. Oldenbourg Verlag, München, 1982.

[Her92]   M. Herdy. Reproductive isolation as strategy parameter in hierarchically organized evolution strategies. In Männer and Manderick [MM92], pages 207–217.

[HM91]   J. Hesser and R. Männer. Towards an optimal mutation probability in genetic algorithms. In Schwefel and Männer [SM91a], pages 23–32.

[HM92]   J. Hesser and R. Männer. Investigation of the M-heuristic for optimal mutation probabilities. In Männer and Manderick [MM92], pages 115–124.

[Hof91]   F. Hoffmeister. Scalable parallelism by evolutionary algorithms. In M. Grauer and D. B. Pressmar, editors, *Parallel Computing and Mathematical Optimization,* volume 367 of *Lecture Notes in Economics and Mathematical Systems,* pages 177–198. Springer, Berlin, 1991.

[HB92]   F. Hoffmeister and Th. Bäck. Genetic self-learning. In F. J. Varela and P. Bourgine, editors, *Proceedings of the First European Conference on Artificial Life,* pages 227–235. The MIT Press, Cambridge, MA, 1992.

[HS90a]   F. Hoffmeister and H.-P. Schwefel. KORR 2.1 — An Implementation of a $(\mu \overset{+}{,} \lambda)$ – Evolution Strategy. Report of the Systems Analysis Research Group, Universität Dortmund, Fachbereich Informatik, November 1990.

[HS90b]   F. Hoffmeister and H.-P. Schwefel. A taxonomy of parallel evolutionary algorithms. In G. Legendi, T. Schendel, and U. Wolf, editors, *ParCella 90,* volume 2 of *Research in Informatics,* pages 97–107. Akademie–Verlag, Berlin, 1990.

[Hol62]   J. H. Holland. Outline for a logical theory of adaptive systems. *Journal of the Association for Computing Machinery,* 3:297–314, 1962.

[Hol75]   J. H. Holland. *Adaptation in natural and artificial systems.* The University of Michigan Press, Ann Arbor, MI, 1975.

[HJ58]   R. Hooke and T. A. Jeeves. Comments on Brooks' discussion of random methods. *Operations Research,* 6:881–882, 1958.

[INM88]   INMOS Limited. *The Transputer Databook,* Bath Press, 1988.

[JMRS89]   A. Jankowski, Z. Michalewicz, Z. W. Ras, and D. Shoff. Issues on evolution programming. In R. Janicki and W. W. Koczkodaj, editors, *Computing and Information,* pages 459–463. Elsevier, Amsterdam, 1989.

[Jan84]   E. Jantsch. *Die Selbstorganisation des Universums — Vom Urknall zum menschlichen Geist.* Deutscher Taschenbuch Verlag, München, 2 edition, 1984.

[Jet89]   G. Jetschke. *Mathematik der Selbstorganisation: Qualitative Theorie deterministischer und stochastischer dynamischer Systeme.* Vieweg, Wiesbaden, 1989.

[JH91]   T. Johnson and P. Husbands. System identification using genetic algorithms. In Schwefel and Männer [SM91a], pages 85–89.

[Kni92]   F. Knickmeier. Auslegung eines Rechnernetzwerkes mit minimalem Kommunikationsaufwand mittels evolutionärer Algorithmen. Diplomarbeit, Universität Dortmund, Fachbereich Informatik, 1992.

[Koz89]   J. R. Koza. Hierarchical genetic algorithms operating on populations of computer programs. In N. S. Sridharan, editor, *Proceedings of the 11th International Joint Conference on Artificial Intelligence,* pages 768–774. Morgan Kaufmann Publishers, San Mateo, CA, 1989.

[Koz90]   J. R. Koza. Genetic programming: A paradigm for genetically breeding populations of computer programs to solve problems. Technical Report STAN–CS–90–1314, Department of Computer Science, Stanford University, Stanford, CA, 1990.

[Koz91]   J. R. Koza. A hierarchical approach to learning the boolean multiplexer function. In Rawlins [Raw91], pages 171–192.

[Koz92]   J. R. Koza. *Genetic Programming: On the Programming of Computers by Means of Natural Selection.* Complex Adaptive Systems. The MIT Press, Cambridge, MA, 1992.

[Kre65]   E. Kreyszig. *Statistische Methoden und ihre Anwendungen.* Vandenhoeck & Ruprecht, Göttingen, 1965.

[KFM71]   P. Krolak, W. Felts, and G. Marble. A man-machine approach towards solving the traveling salesman problem. *Communications of the ACM,* 14(5):327–334, 1971.

[Küp90]   B.-O. Küppers. *Der Ursprung biologischer Information.* Piper, München, 2 edition, 1990.

[Kur91]   F. Kursawe. A variant of Evolution Strategies for vector optimization. In Schwefel and Männer [SM91a], pages 193–197.

[Kur92]   F. Kursawe. Evolution strategies for vector optimization. In G.-H. Tzeng and P. L. Yu, editors, *Preliminary Proceedings of the Tenth International Conference on Multiple Criteria Decision Making,* pages 187–193. National Chiao Tung University, Taipei, 1992.

[vLA87]   P. J. M. van Laarhoven and E. H. L. Aarts. *Simulated Annealing: Theory and Applications.* Mathematics and its Applications. Kluwer, Dordrecht, 1987.

[Lan89]   C. G. Langton. Artificial life. In C. G. Langton, editor, *Artificial Life*, volume VI of *Studies in the Science of Complexity*, pages 1–48. Santa Fe Institute, Los Alamos, NM, Addison-Wesley, 1989.

[Lic65]   H. J. Lichtfuss. Evolution eines Rohrkrümmers. Diplomarbeit, Technische Universität Berlin, 1965.

[LV90]   G. E. Liepins and M. D. Vose. Representational issues in genetic optimization. *Journal of Experimental and Theoretical Artificial Intellgence*, 2:101–115, 1990.

[Liu68]   C. L. Liu. *Introduction to Combinatorial Mathematics*. Computer Science Series. McGraw-Hill, New York, 1968.

[Loh91]   R. Lohmann. *Bionische Verfahren zur Entwicklung visueller Systeme*. Dissertation, Technische Universität Berlin, 1991.

[Loh92a]   R. Lohmann. Structure evolution and incomplete induction. In Männer and Manderick [MM92], pages 175–185.

[Loh92b]   R. Lohmann. Structure evolution in neural systems. In B. Soucek and the IRIS Group, editors, *Dynamic, Genetic, and Chaotic Programming*, pages 395–411. Wiley, New York, 1992.

[MM92]   R. Männer and B. Manderick, editors. *Parallel Problem Solving from Nature 2*. Elsevier, Amsterdam, 1992.

[Mah91]   S. Mahfoud. An analysis of Boltzmann tournament selection. IlliGAL Report 91007, University of Illinois at Urbana-Champaign, IL, 1991.

[Man83]   B. B. Mandelbrot. *The fractal geometry of nature*. Freeman, New York, 1983.

[May88]   E. Mayr. *Toward a new Philosophy of Biology: Observations of an Evolutionist*. The Belknap Press of Harvard University Press, Cambridge, MA, and London, GB, 1988.

[Mic92]   Z. Michalewicz. *Genetic Algorithms + Data Structures = Evolution Programs*. Artificial Intelligence. Springer, Berlin, 1992.

[Mic93]   Z. Michalewicz. A hierarchy of evolution programs: An experimental study. *Evolutionary Computation*, 1(1):51–76, 1993.

[MJ91]   Z. Michalewicz and C. Z. Janikow. Handling constraints in genetic algorithms. In Belew and Booker [BB91], pages 151–157.

[Mic86]   R. S. Michalski. Understanding the nature of learning: Issues and research directions. In R. S. Michalski, J. G. Carbonell, and T. M. Mitchell, editors, *Machine Learning Vol. II*, chapter 1, pages 3–25. Morgan Kaufmann Publishers, San Mateo, CA, 1986.

[MP69]   M. Minsky and S. Papert. *Perceptrons*. The MIT Press, Cambridge, MA, 1969.

[Müh92]   H. Mühlenbein. How genetic algorithms really work: I. Mutation and hillclimbing. In Männer and Manderick [MM92], pages 15–25.

[MSV93]   H. Mühlenbein and D. Schlierkamp-Voosen. Predictive models for the breeder genetic algorithm. *Evolutionary Computation*, 1(1):25–49, 1993.

[MSB91]   H. Mühlenbein, M. Schomisch, and J. Born. The parallel genetic algorithm as function optimizer. In Belew and Booker [BB91], pages 271–278.

[MK87]   K. G. Murty and S. N. Kabadi. Some NP-complete problems in quadratic and nonlinear programming. *Mathematical Programming*, 1987.

[NS89]   M. Nowak and P. Schuster. Error thresholds of replication in finite populations: Mutation frequencies and the onset of Muller's ratchet. *Journal of theoretical Biology*, 137:375–395, 1989.

[OSH87]   I. M. Oliver, D. J. Smith, and J. R. C. Holland. A study of permutation crossover operators on the traveling salesman problem. In Grefenstette [Gre87a], pages 224–230.

[PR92]   S. E. Page and D. W. Richardson. Walsh functions, schema variance, and deception. *Complex Systems*, 6:125–135, 1992.

[PS82]   Ch. H. Papadimitriou and K. Steiglitz. *Combinatorial Optimization*. Prentice Hall, 1982.

[Per91]   Perihelion Software. *The Helios Parallel Operating System*, 1991.

[Pet91]   E. Peters. *Ein Beitrag zur wissensbasierten Auswahl und Steuerung von Optimierverfahren*. Dissertation, Universität Dortmund, 1991.

[PL89]   Ch. C. Pettey and M. R. Leuze. A theoretical investigation of a parallel genetic algorithm. In Schaffer [Sch89], pages 398–405.

[PLG87]   Ch. C. Pettey, M. R. Leuze, and J. J. Grefenstette. A parallel genetic algorithm. In Grefenstette [Gre87a], pages 155–161.

[Pin84]   J. Pintér. Convergence properties of stochastic optimization procedures. *Math. Operationsforschung und Statist., Ser. optimization*, 15(3):405–427, 1984.

[Rad90]   N. J. Radcliffe. *Genetic Neural Networks on MIMD Computers*. PhD thesis, University of Edinburgh, Scotland, 1990.

[Raw91]   G. J. E. Rawlins, editor. *Foundations of Genetic Algorithms*. Morgan Kaufmann Publishers, San Mateo, CA, 1991.

[Ray91]   Th. S. Ray. Is it alive or is it GA? In Belew and Booker [BB91], pages 527–534.

[Rec65]   I. Rechenberg. Cybernetic solution path of an experimental problem. Royal Aircraft Establishment, Library translation No. 1122, Farnborough, Hants., UK, August 1965.

[Rec73]   I. Rechenberg. *Evolutionsstrategie: Optimierung technischer Systeme nach Prinzipien der biologischen Evolution*. Frommann–Holzboog, Stuttgart, 1973.

[Rec94]   I. Rechenberg. *Evolutionsstrategie '94*, volume 1 of *Werkstatt Bionik und Evolutionstechnik*. frommann–holzboog, Stuttgart, 1994.

[Rén77]   A. Rényi. *Wahrscheinlichkeitsrechnung*. VEB Deutscher Verlag der Wissenschaften, Leipzig, 1977.

[Ric88]   E. Rich. *Artificial Intelligence*. Computer Science Series. McGraw-Hill, 8 edition, 1988.

[Ros58]   F. Rosenblatt. The perceptron: A probabilistic model for information storage and organization in the brain. *Psychological Review*, 65(6):386–408, 1958.

[Ros60]   H. H. Rosenbrock. An automatic method for finding the greatest or least value of a function. *The Computer Journal*, 3(3):175–184, 1960.

[Rud90]   G. Rudolph. Globale Optimierung mit parallelen Evolutionsstrategien. Diplomarbeit, Universität Dortmund, Fachbereich Informatik, 1990.

[Rud91]   G. Rudolph. Global optimization by means of distributed evolution strategies.
In Schwefel and Männer [SM91a], pages 209–213.

[Rud92a]   G. Rudolph. On correlated mutations in evolution strategies. In Männer
and Manderick [MM92], pages 105–114.

[Rud92b]   G. Rudolph. Parallel approaches to stochastic global optimization. In
W. Joosen and E. Milgrom, editors, *Parallel Computing: From Theory to Sound
Practice, Proceedings of the European Workshop on Parallel Computing*, pages
256–267. IOS Press, Amsterdam, 1992.

[Rud94]   G. Rudolph. Convergence analysis of canonical genetic algorithms. *IEEE
Transactions on Neural Networks, Special Issue on Evolutionary Programming*,
1994. (In print).

[Sam59]   A. L. Samuel. Some studies in machine learning using the game of checkers.
IBM Journal, 3:211–229, 1959.

[Sam67]   A. L. Samuel. Some studies in machine learning using the game of checkers.
II — Recent progress. *IBM Journal*, 11(6):601–617, 1967.

[Sch89]   J. D. Schaffer, editor. *Proceedings of the 3rd International Conference on
Genetic Algorithms and Their Applications*. Morgan Kaufmann Publishers, San
Mateo, CA, 1989.

[SCED89]   J. D. Schaffer, R. A. Caruna, L. J. Eshelman, and R. Das. A study of control parameters affecting online performance of genetic algorithms for function
optimization. In Schaffer [Sch89], pages 51–60.

[SE91]   J. D. Schaffer and L. J. Eshelman. On crossover as an evolutionary viable
strategy. In Belew and Booker [BB91], pages 61–68.

[SM87]   J. D. Schaffer and A. Morishima. An adaptive crossover distribution mechanism for genetic algorithms. In Grefenstette [Gre87a], pages 36–40.

[SB93]   M. Schütz and Th. Bäck. A User's Guide to Evos 1.0. Report of the Systems
Analysis Research Group, Universität Dortmund, Fachbereich Informatik, 1993.

[Sch91]   J. Schull. The view from the adaptive landscape. In Schwefel and Männer
[SM91a], pages 415–427.

[Sch65]   H.-P. Schwefel. *Kybernetische Evolution als Strategie der experimentellen For-
schung in der Strömungstechnik*. Diplomarbeit, Technische Universität Berlin,
1965.

[Sch68]   H.-P. Schwefel. Projekt MHD-Staustrahlrohr: Experimentelle Optimierung einer Zweiphasendüse, Teil I. Technischer Bericht 11.034/68, 35, AEG
Forschungsinstitut, Berlin, October 1968.

[Sch75a]   H.-P. Schwefel. Binäre Optimierung durch somatische Mutation. Technischer
Bericht, Technische Universität Berlin und Medizinische Hochschule Hannover,
May 1975.

[Sch75b]   H.-P. Schwefel. *Evolutionsstrategie und numerische Optimierung*. Dissertation, Technische Universität Berlin, May 1975.

[Sch77]   H.-P. Schwefel. *Numerische Optimierung von Computer-Modellen mittels der Evolutionsstrategie*, volume 26 of *Interdisciplinary Systems Research*.
Birkhäuser, Basel, 1977.

[Sch80]   H.-P. Schwefel. Subroutines EVOL, GRUP, KORR, listings and user's guide. Interner Bericht KFA-STE-IB-2/80, Kernforschungsanlage Jülich, Programmgruppe Systemforschung und Technologische Entwicklung, April 1980.

[Sch81a]   H.-P. Schwefel. *Numerical Optimization of Computer Models.* Wiley, Chichester, 1981.

[Sch81b]   H.-P. Schwefel. Optimum seeking methods: Subroutines for the minimization of non–linear functions of several variables by means of direct (derivative–free) methods. Interner Bericht KFA-STE-IB-7/81, Kernforschungsanlage Jülich, October 1981.

[Sch87]   H.-P. Schwefel. Collective phenomena in evolutionary systems. In *Preprints of the 31st Annual Meeting of the International Society for General System Research, Budapest*, volume 2, pages 1025–1033, June 1987.

[Sch88]   H.-P. Schwefel. Evolutionary learning optimum–seeking on parallel computer architectures. In A. Sydow, S. G. Tzafestas, and R. Vichnevetsky, editors, *Proceedings of the International Symposium on Systems Analysis and Simulation 1988, I: Theory and Foundations*, pages 217–225. Akademie-Verlag, Berlin, September 1988.

[Sch95]   H.-P. Schwefel. *Evolution and Optimum Seeking.* Sixth-Generation Computer Technoloy Series. Wiley, New York, 1995.

[SB92]   H.-P. Schwefel and Th. Bäck. Künstliche Evolution — eine intelligente Problemlösungsstrategie ? *KI*, 6(2):20–27, June 1992.

[SM91a]   H.-P. Schwefel and R. Männer, editors. *Parallel Problem Solving from Nature — Proceedings 1st Workshop PPSN I*, volume 496 of *Lecture Notes in Computer Science*. Springer, Berlin, 1991.

[Sel59]   O. G. Selfridge. *Pandemonium: A paradigm for learning*, pages 511–527. H.S.M.O., 1959.

[SZ90]   R. Serra and G. Zanarini. *Complex systems and cognitive processes.* Springer, Berlin, 1990.

[She71]   J. Shekel. Test functions for multimodal search techniques. In *Fifth Annual Princeton Conference on Information Science and Systems*, 1971.

[SW81]   F. J. Solis and R. J.-B. Wets. Minimization by random search techniques. *Mathematics of Operations Research*, 6(1):19–30, 1981.

[Spe93]   W. M. Spears. Crossover or mutation ? In Whitley [Whi93], pages 221–237.

[SD91a]   W. M. Spears and K. A. De Jong. An analysis of multi-point crossover. In Rawlins [Raw91], pages 301–315.

[SD91b]   W. M. Spears and K. A. De Jong. On the virtues of parameterized uniform crossover. In Belew and Booker [BB91], pages 230–236.

[SM90]   P. Spiessens and B. Manderick. A genetic algorithm for massively parallel computers. In R. Eckmiller, G. Hartmann, and G. Hauske, editors, *Parallel Processing in Neural Systems and Computers*, pages 31–36. North–Holland, 1990.

[SM91b]   P. Spiessens and B. Manderick. A massively parallel genetic algorithm: Implementation and first analysis. In Belew and Booker [BB91], pages 279–286.

[Spr93]   J. Sprave. Zelluläre evolutionäre Algorithmen zur Parameteroptimierung. In R. Hofestädt, F. Krückeberg, and T. Lengauer, editors, *Informatik in den Biowissenschaften*, Informatik aktuell, pages 111–120. Springer, Berlin, 1993.

[SWM91]   T. Starkweather, D. Whitley, and K. Mathias. Optimization using distributed genetic algorithms. In Schwefel and Männer [SM91a], pages 176–186.

[Sum92]   B. H. Sumida. Genetics for genetic algorithms. *ACM SIGBIO Newsletter*,
12(2):44–46, June 1992.

[SHMH90]   B. H. Sumida, A. I. Houston, J. M. McNamara, and W. D. Hamilton.
Genetic algorithms and evolution. *Journal of Theoretical Biology*, 147:59–84,
1990.

[Sys89]   G. Syswerda. Uniform crossover in genetic algorithms. In Schaffer [Sch89],
pages 2–9.

[Tan87]   R. Tanese. Parallel genetic algorithm for a hypercube. In Grefenstette
[Gre87a], pages 177–183.

[Tan89]   R. Tanese. Distributed genetic algorithms. In Schaffer [Sch89], pages 434–439.

[TŽ89]   A. Törn and A. Žilinskas. *Global Optimization*, volume 350 of *Lecture Notes
in Computer Science*. Springer, Berlin, 1989.

[TW91]   A. Trew and G. Wilson. *Past, Present, Parallel — A Survey of Available
Parallel Computing Systems*. Springer, Berlin, 1991.

[Val84]   L. G. Valiant. A theory of the learnable. *Communications of the ACM*,
27(11):1134–1142, November 1984.

[Vee90]   B. Veer. *The CDL Guide*. Perihelion Software Ltd., Somerset, UK, 1 edition,
January 1990.

[VL91]   M. D. Vose and G. E. Liepins. Punctuated equilibria in genetic algorithms.
Complex Systems, pages 31–44, 1991.

[Whi89]   D. Whitley. The GENITOR algorithm and selection pressure: Why rank–
based allocation of reproductive trials is best. In Schaffer [Sch89], pages 116–121.

[Whi93]   D. Whitley, editor. *Foundations of Genetic Algorithms 2*. Morgan Kaufmann
Publishers, San Mateo, CA, 1993.

[WS90]   D. Whitley and T. Starkweather. GENITOR II: A distributed genetic algorithm. *Journal of Experimental and Theoretical Artificial Intelligence*, 2:189–
214, 1990.

[Wid62]   B. Widrow. Generalization and information storage in networks of adelaine
'neurons'. In M. C. Yovits, G. T. Jacobi, and G. D. Goldstein, editors, *Self-
Organizing Systems*, pages 435–461. Spartan Books, Washington, D.C., 1962.

[WK93]   Th. Williams and C. Kelley. GNUPLOT – An interactive Plotting Program. C source code Version 3.4, Pixar Corporation, 1993. Available via
anon. ftp from host ftp.germany.eu.net as file gnuplot-3.4.tar.Z in directory /pub/packages/gnu.

[Wri91]   A. H. Wright. Genetic algorithms for real parameter optimization. In Rawlins
[Raw91], pages 205–218.

[Zhi92]   A. A. Zhigljavsky. *Theory of Global Random Search*. Mathematics and Its
Applications. Kluwer, Dordrecht, 1992.

[ZŽ91]   A. A. Zhigljavsky and A. Žilinskas. *Metody Poiska Globalnowo Ekstremuma*.
Nauka, Moscow, 1991. (In Russian).

Index